Democratizing Inequalities

Democratizing Inequalities

Dilemmas of the New Public Participation

EDITED BY
*Caroline W. Lee, Michael McQuarrie,
and Edward T. Walker*

New York University Press
NEW YORK AND LONDON

NEW YORK UNIVERSITY PRESS
New York and London
www.nyupress.org

© 2015 by New York University
All rights reserved

References to Internet websites (URLs) were accurate at the time of writing.
Neither the authors nor New York University Press are responsible for URLs
that may have expired or changed since the manuscript was prepared.

Library of Congress Cataloging-in-Publication Data

Democratizing inequalities : dilemmas of the new public participation / edited by
Caroline W. Lee, Michael McQuarrie, and Edward T. Walker.
pages cm
Includes bibliographical references and index.
ISBN 978-1-4798-4727-3 (hbk.) -- ISBN 978-1-4798-8336-3 (pbk.)
1. Political participation. 2. Social participation. 3. Democracy. 4. Elite (Social sciences) 5. Equality. I. Lee, Caroline W., editor.
JF799.D457 2015
323'.042--dc23
2014027537

New York University Press books are printed on acid-free paper,
and their binding materials are chosen for strength and durability.
We strive to use environmentally responsible suppliers and materials
to the greatest extent possible in publishing our books.

Manufactured in the United States of America

10 9 8 7 6 5 4 3 2 1

Also available as an ebook

Contents

Acknowledgments   vii
Foreword   ix
   CRAIG CALHOUN

PART I   Introduction

1. Rising Participation and Declining Democracy   3
   EDWARD T. WALKER, MICHAEL MCQUARRIE, AND CAROLINE W. LEE

PART II   Participation and the Reproduction of Inequality

2. Civic-izing Markets: Selling Social Profits in Public Deliberation   27
   CAROLINE W. LEE, KELLY MCNULTY, AND SARAH SHAFFER

3. Workers' Rights as Human Rights? Solidarity Campaigns and the Anti-Sweatshop Movement   46
   STEVEN VALLAS, J. MATTHEW JUDGE, AND EMILY R. CUMMINS

4. Legitimating the Corporation through Public Participation   66
   EDWARD T. WALKER

PART III   The Production of Authority and Legitimacy

5. No Contest: Participatory Technologies and the Transformation of Urban Authority   83
   MICHAEL MCQUARRIE

6. The Fiscal Sociology of Public Consultation   102
   ISAAC WILLIAM MARTIN

7. Structuring Electoral Participation: The Formalization of Democratic New Media Campaigning, 2000–2008   125
   DANIEL KREISS

8. Patient, Parent, Advocate, Investor: Entrepreneurial Health Activism from Research to Reimbursement   143
   DAVID SCHLEIFER AND AARON PANOFSKY

PART IV Unintended Consequences and New Opportunities

9 Spirals of Perpetual Potential: How Empowerment Projects'
   Noble Missions Tangle in Everyday Interaction   165
   NINA ELIASOPH

10 Becoming a Best Practice: Neoliberalism and the Curious Case of
   Participatory Budgeting   187
   GIANPAOLO BAIOCCHI AND ERNESTO GANUZA

11 The Social Movement Society, the Tea Party, and the
   Democratic Deficit   204
   DAVID S. MEYER AND AMANDA PULLUM

12 Public Deliberation and Political Contention   222
   FRANCESCA POLLETTA

PART V Conclusion

13 Realizing the Promise of Public Participation in an Age of Inequality   247
   CAROLINE W. LEE, MICHAEL MCQUARRIE,
   AND EDWARD T. WALKER

References   251
About the Contributors   281
Index   285

Acknowledgments

We would like, first and foremost, to thank the institutional supporters of this project when it began as a conference at New York University in 2010: the American Sociological Association's Fund for the Advancement of the Discipline (made possible through the support of the National Science Foundation) and NYU's Institute for Public Knowledge (IPK). We are also indebted to the scholars who supported this conference, volume, and the broader intellectual project of *Democratizing Inequalities*, including Tim Bartley, Debbie Becher, Kelly Brown, Neil Brenner, Charles Heckscher, John Krinsky, John McCarthy, Jeff Manza, Nicole Marwell, Debra Minkoff, Ann Mische, John Mollenkopf, Stephanie Mudge, Marc Schneiberg, Michael Schudson, and Carmen Sirianni. We offer our particular thanks to Craig Calhoun and Elisabeth Clemens, both of whom offered excellent and provocative keynote addresses at the conference and have helped us to build a community around these ideas in the time since. We also thank Samuel Carter and Jessica Coffey at IPK for their assistance with the conference. Lastly, we thank Ilene Kalish and the team at NYU Press for their sustained interest in this project and considerable support for our efforts.

Foreword

CRAIG CALHOUN

Since the 1970s, the United States has seen oddly contradictory trends. On the one hand we have been "bowling alone," as Robert Putnam put it when he described the decline of a variety of long-standing forms of shared, collectively organized social activity. On the other hand we have seen an explosion of new forms of participation, from the online mobilizations for elections to small-scale venture philanthropy to a host of peer evaluations of consumer products and professional services. We are arguably more "linked in" on larger scales than ever before and yet we still lack more effective institutions for democracy.

This stimulating book is among the first to put squarely on the social science agenda the questions of how public participation can fail to amount to democratization—and how extremes of inequality play into this. The authors are not fatalist or determinist; they think a different outcome might be possible. Nor are they pessimists who refuse to acknowledge gains where they have occurred. They point to the reality and the benefits of participation in several spheres from workers' rights to community development. But they are realists who see—and analyze—some of the limits built into the new kinds of participation that have become prominent since the 1970s.

More than thirty years ago, Harry Boyte described the small-scale, often local activism that followed the big movements of the 1960s and early '70s as a "backyard revolution." The implication was that many small mobilizations would change attitudes and eventually, somehow, scale up to major social change. This did happen on some fronts. The human rights movement grew into a global force. Consumer rights activists secured a variety of victories from disclosure of the contents of processed foods to banning several unsafe products. Environmentalists got environmental impact assessments written into law. But these movements have largely been ethical and legal projects at the margin of democratic politics, not organizing efforts at the center.

Likewise, an ideology of participation and consultation has spread through capitalist corporations and government agencies. There are more hearings than ever before. There are not just suggestion boxes but frequent surveys seeking the opinions of employees, customers, suppliers, and the public. Indeed, workplaces have changed in significant ways. More companies offer employees stock options and a chance to participate in profits. More have informal office spaces, even campuses, complete with gyms and organized with a minimum of manifest hierarchy. But then sometimes those perks are for only elite workers, engineers, scientists, and top management—while production workers toil for contractors in China or Malaysia. As the authors of this book rightly recognize, inequality lies at the heart of the paradox of growing participation and declining democracy.

Throughout the long postwar boom, inequality fell in the United States and most industrial countries. Since the 1970s, however, inequality has intensified. It has grown not just a little, but dramatically, and the United States is extreme, even in this global picture of escalating gini coefficients. The U.N. Development Program ranked the gap between the richest and poorest in the United States, and this gap is the third highest level of inequality around the world. The census shows the top one-tenth of 1 percent of the population taking 10 percent of all income, the top 1 percent owning more than 20 percent of all wealth; the top 10 percent owning more than two-thirds of all wealth; the share of the bottom 80 percent in the country's wealth dwindling to just above a tenth. Both income and wealth inequality are up, and so is poverty.

This growing inequality came with surprisingly little protest or organized resistance. Indeed, egalitarian arguments have faced a cool reception since the 1970s, tainted by association with a seemingly discredited socialism and opposed to the widespread identification of freedom with the removal of fetters from private property. This was an era when finance capital was ascendant, transforming wealth and workplaces. In the forty years after the 1974–1975 recession, the total proportion of wealth held in the form of financial assets grew from one-fourth to three-fourths. There was a long bubble in asset prices (marked by three distinct waves of especially dramatic increases). Rising home prices helped to shield those who at least owned their homes from the erosion of earnings and purchasing power experienced by most of those in the bottom 80 percent of the population. A significant increase in the proportion of women working raised the family income of two-earner households, though this was partly offset by an increase in single parents, mostly women. But, crucially, the inequality came packaged together with financialization, globalization, and neoliberalism.

This combination was already evident in the deindustrialization that gathered speed from the later 1970s. Even profitable businesses were starved for capital when markets determined that higher returns could be found elsewhere. Efforts were made to describe deindustrialization in attractive terms: the end of smelly, polluting factories; the coming of a knowledge society in which everyone would be a middle-class, white-collar worker. Of course this picture left out the extent to which industrial work would be replaced by service employment—in which a small minority made fortunes and most made closer to the minimum wage.

In this context, participation was a mixed blessing. On the one hand, it had the potential to reduce workplace alienation, strengthen community, and involve citizens in large-scale electoral politics that otherwise struggled to interest most voters. On the other hand, it also had the potential to disguise the reproduction of inequality and to reinforce rather than challenge structures of authority. Sorting out the relationship between these two sets of potentials is a central task of this book. The news is not entirely encouraging: To a very large extent, the new forms of participation have obscured inequality or made it more palatable, not limited it or even challenged its sources.

The chapters of this book present perhaps the most sustained analysis available of the complicated relationship among the growth of inequality, the rise of a more participatory social *style*, and the challenges faced by contemporary democracy. They address dimensions of this from elections to corporate social responsibility, philanthropy, and social movements. Some key themes stand out.

Nonprofit organizations have been widely touted as a key component of civil society. Some have seen them as crucial alternatives to the government provision of public goods. This was a key theme in George Bush's famous description of them as a "thousand points of light." More generally, enthusiasm for civil society has been rendered problematic and sometimes ideological by a tendency to celebrate what it offers and not think critically about the limits on the offering and the extent to which they depend on inequality. Philanthropy is a good use of wealth, for example, but is not in itself a justification of high levels of social inequality conducive to the acquisition of massive fortunes. Similarly, responsible corporate use of profits to support local community institutions like symphony orchestras is not in itself an adequate justification of corporate capitalism—let alone the rapacious financial capitalism of recent decades.

Behind some of the failure to see the complexity of this issue is liberal ideology with its insistence on political equality and tendency to ignore economic inequality or even celebrate private property as a primary instance of freedom, not differentiating between the very small-scale property of most individuals and the large-scale property of the very wealthy and of corporations. Calls to make economic equality a more primary aspiration have been denigrated as socialist—and an important feature of the era considered here is the extent to which the collapse of the Soviet Union all but eliminated socialism from respectable political discourse.

The issues at stake are not just the extent of inequality but the relationship between elites and others in society. Philanthropy and charity are modalities for such relationships but not the only ones. When organized on a large scale and through formal organizations, they reflect not only generosity and need but also the extent to which the rich and poor no longer live in the same communities, linked by reciprocal personal relationships. There are new forms of participation, often formally organized, but old informal models of participation by diverse citizens in shared communities have not commonly thrived.

* * *

The first section does an excellent job bringing out some of the issues. There is philanthropic support for some issues, including even some issues on rapacious capitalism. As Vallas, Judge, and Cummins point out, there are significant gains from treating workers' rights as human rights, as well as some tendencies for such campaigns to reinforce the market position of corporations in advanced societies. Markets generally have been shaped by calls for more participation—and there are even markets in public-interest participatory organizations and their capacity to mobilize deliberative publics as Lee, McNulty, and Shaffer show. Perhaps most important, for-profit business corporations have entered the arena of civic participation directly and through a host of surrogate organizations. Edward Walker's valuable account of the proliferation of branded corporate efforts to secure legitimacy through participation in public affairs also makes clear that this is not only self-interested but also obfuscating for real attention to those public issues.

All of this is shaped not just by corporate interests, or the interests of the wealthy, but also by the professionals who find employment in the nonprofit and philanthropic sectors. These try to turn available funding into resources for good causes, but they also wittingly or unwittingly sustain ideological compromises and the legitimacy of extreme social inequality. All the chapters in this section (and that by Kreiss) reveal the complexities and ambiguities of the professionalization of philanthropy and, more generally, expertise. The tension between expertise and democracy is old, and the best resolution uncertain. But it is clear that tilting the balance very far in favor of expertise is sharply depoliticizing.

This issue is joined well in the next section where the production of authority becomes an explicit theme. One of the most striking features of the rise of new elite-dominated participatory institutions has been a domestication of social movements. Participation has become a good in itself, often substituting for egalitarian economic reform. But, of course, participation also compensates for perceived weaknesses and exclusions of previous egalitarian projects. Too many of these resulted in frustrating, impersonal, and often inefficient bureaucracies delivering useful services in costly and unpleasant ways.

There are different modalities for the relationships among elites, institutions, and ordinary citizens in modern, ostensibly democratic societies. Consultation is one (see Lee, McNulty, and Shaffer). Negotiation is another, sometimes marked by concessions (Martin). And deliberation is a third—addressed here by Francesca Polletta with nuance and an appropriate sense of ambivalence. But mobilization is particularly challenging. Should the poor actually take to the streets? Should workers actually challenge capitalist production? Or should there be only participation?

Michael McQuarrie's account of different ideologies and strategies of popular participation in urban renewal is challenging and important. He shows the co-optation of once-radical activists struggling to deliver some tangible results, not just an ideological dream, to their followers but in the process finding it necessary to make common cause with real estate developers and political elites. Isaac Martin shows how public consultation is shaped by fiscal, not just substantive concerns. David Schleifer and Aaron Panofsky examine the ways in which these processes play out not just with regard to the old institutions of local government and development, or the national state, but in the new arena of health activism. There, entrepreneurs and exciting new technology interface with the effort to produce informed citizens through new media and blurred boundaries between advocacy and investment.

Even though so much action shifted into participatory domains distant from conventional political parties, electoral politics did not remain untouched and was not irrelevant. As Daniel Kreiss shows, the mobilization of new media for electoral campaigns produced a version of citizen participation but one importantly limited and implicitly but not explicitly structured. This is an example of the top-down character of many institutions and practices in the new participatory society. Yes, ordinary people can participate, perhaps more than in most of history, but only in elite managed institutions.

This naturally recalls the recurrently forgotten and distorted history of populism. Partly because elites write history and generally are not central to populist mobilizations, these are often portrayed as simply eruptions of irrationality, backward-oriented mobilizations of people who can't find their place in the progress. But, of course, as the chapters here help us to understand, progress is not always as obvious or one-dimensional as elites suggest. Ostensible progress involves losses as well as gains, losers as well as winners, and we need always to ask for whom is this particular path of change progress—as opposed to a disastrous loss of employment, home, or community? Populism is often described as right-wing but in fact is inherently hard to fit into a left-right continuum. In the United States there is a proud and important history of genuinely democratic populist activism. Contemporary movements like the Tea Party and Occupy Wall Street (OWS) may offer only distorted mirrors for this. David Meyer and Amanda Pullum bring out why, despite the seeming paradox, it is possible to have a social movement society and still a democratic deficit. And certainly populism is subject to channeling, sponsorship, steering, and demagogues, but it is also a challenge to the depoliticizing character of many conventional forms of allegedly political participation.

Nina Eliasoph nicely characterizes one aspect of the depoliticization of new forms of participation. They involve an infinitely receding horizon for genuinely serious political change. As she shows, promoting participation may not be an effective way of serving the interests of the needy and may be a goal pursued for other reasons. There is a larger history here that is not brought out in chapters mainly focused on current events. And of course there are global comparisons to be made. But this is precisely because the issues brought to the fore in this collection are not idiosyncratic and are not mere accidents but are deeply implicated in the forms capitalism and democracy are taking—and not just in the United States.

* * *

The chapters here are overwhelmingly about cities, and that is also no accident. More than half the world lives in cities, and the dynamics of urbanization and its complex production of new forms of wealth creation, politics, and community are key to our whole era. But attending to this also reveals that cities are not just one scale of governance; in a sense the word "city" is a stand-in for a complex set of challenges to the scale and cohesion of governance and governmentality. The period from the 1960s and 1970s to the present is distinctive in this as in so much else. With the postwar expansion of the welfare state as background, it has brought neoliberalism, "new social movements," legitimation crises, globalization, financialization, and indeed the financial crisis (a package evoked here most substantially by Baiocchi and Ganuza). Until very recently in the United States, radically growing inequality was surprisingly little remarked on. But it is basic, not a minor side effect. It is connected to deep insecurity, that also has other sources, and to anxiety over the future.

The new populism is a struggle over belonging as well as over privilege. It is shaped, especially on the right, by anxieties about demographic diversity. A sense of the erosion of attractive features of community, a living wage, and a meaningful patriotism merge with xenophobia, masculine anxiety about new roles for women, and a politics of resentment. The previous peak in large-scale political mobilization, 1968, was in fact part of an era of white people's movements. It came at a low point in the foreign-born population and it evoked the frustrations and aspirations mainly of home-grown youth wishing America would better live up to its own ideals and best possibilities.

The politics of the 1960s had an impact on all ensuing mobilization. Even the Tea Party, which sometimes declares its contempt for most of what '60s activists stood for, also shows its shaping influence. It is insistent on multiculturalism or at least deference to diversity. It exuberantly claims a unity of sincerity, emotion, and political conviction. Both the Tea Party and, even more, OWS echo the devotion to deliberation that was important to both the civil rights movement and 1960s activism (described well by Francesca Polletta in her book *Freedom Is an Endless Meeting*). This is taken over as well into parts of the culture of the new media and even the renewal of public religion—often denigrated by the left but in fact an arena of both participation and serious deliberation.

* * *

Where does this leave us? We struggle with inequality, we seek solidarity, and we hope to participate in shaping the social institutions that order our lives. Top-down structures of participation offer some paths to engagement but little change to really transform basic social conditions. Above all, they inhibit confronting the deep and deepening inequalities of contemporary social life. We do need to address questions of public interest and public goods through discourse. But we confront this not in an ideal speech situation where equals communicate openly, but in an institutional structure where even participation is shaped and distorted by inequality. We confront an updated version of Habermas's fear of an administered society, the collapsed boundaries between politics, economy, and society, in a period when state politics is discredited and both wealth and "the private" are celebrated. We also face a long-running problem about expanding "the public" beyond a notion of "people like us" to include others often seen as threats or less deserving. And we have trouble producing—at once—new forms of participatory knowledge and practice and also new processes to reverse the forces bringing ever more social inequality.

* * *

This book does not have all the answers, but it forces us to ask better questions.

PART I

Introduction

CHAPTER 1

Rising Participation and Declining Democracy

EDWARD T. WALKER, MICHAEL MCQUARRIE,
AND CAROLINE W. LEE

Introduction: A New Context for Participation

Deliberation in Michigan

In November 2009, three hundred Michigan residents from all walks of life converged on the state capital in Lansing to take part in a high-level public debate about what should be done to improve their state's beleaguered economy. In an atmosphere of brewing unrest about the nation's direction—most clearly marked by raucous congressional town hall meetings over proposed reforms to the health care system—the absence of party activists yelling at one another was notable. This was a sober, state-of-the-art affair paid for by the W. K. Kellogg Foundation, in which technocratic expertise, philanthropic resources, and political capital were brought together. Consistent with a general turn to civil and deliberative practices in diverse institutional contexts, the goal was to facilitate rational deliberation among citizens from across the political spectrum.[1] Governor Jennifer Granholm and the president of the University of Michigan, Mary Sue Coleman, both gave keynote addresses thanking the participants for their service to the state. Business leaders and community groups presented information to the participants over the three-day process. Kwame Holman of *NewsHour* moderated the discussion, and coverage of the events was broadcast on public television stations throughout Michigan. Not pulling any punches, the event was called "Hard Times, Hard Choices."

The intrepid group of Michiganders had been randomly selected by Stanford professor James Fishkin's Center for Deliberative Democracy in order to gather a representative slice of the state's citizens for his "Deliberative Polling" method of assessing public opinion. Such processes are intended to ensure that the collective voice of the people is not drowned out by the most vocal, the most partisan, or those with the strongest preexisting ties to well-heeled interest groups.

Although a principle of deliberative practice is the presumed equality among participants in the dialogue,[2] the outcome of deliberation may not always reflect preferences for a broader social egalitarianism. Indeed, after participants were polled a final time on a number of policy options for facing the state's fiscal crisis, James Fishkin reported the event to be an unqualified success when they voted to increase taxes on themselves but to decrease taxes on business:

Support for increasing the sales tax went up by fourteen points from 37% to 51%. Similarly, support for increasing the income tax went up by 18 points from 27% to 45%.... People were willing to shoulder new burdens they could feel. By contrast, support for cutting the business tax rose by a gigantic 27 points from 40% to 67%.[3]

In Michigan, a state widely recognized as the poster child for capital flight and a bellwether of the crumbling national economy, ordinary citizens engaged in far deeper discussions about their civic responsibilities than even the most faithful voters may do in their lifetimes. The result of such intensive participation was a demonstrated willingness to assume greater burdens in their day-to-day lives and more stress on their families' pocketbooks in order to entice fickle employers to remain in their state. Today, as business health is increasingly dependent on Wall Street investments, and states and localities struggle to balance their budgets and meet their pension obligations, similar deliberations reveal a populace willing to engage deeply in revitalized forms of public deliberation. But in a context of heightened inequality and social precariousness, the capacity of participation to transform that very context may be limited. Indeed, what such a case illustrates is that certain new forms of apparently "empowering" public participation may be doing more to reinforce authority than to challenge it.

Defending For-Profit Education

At the start of 2010, Dawn Connor was just a regular college student, taking night courses to become a veterinary technician at Globe University in Eau Claire, Wisconsin, while working during the day at a local shelter spaying and neutering dogs and cats.[4] She had been active in a variety of leadership roles around the university, including by serving as a student ambassador for the veterinary technology program, being the president of the veterinary technology club, and playing a role in meeting and welcoming new students on campus. She had graduated from high school early, then drifted from one traditional college to another, ultimately changing majors a few times and making progress without earning a degree. Globe University, a for-profit university with eight branches throughout Wisconsin, Minnesota, and South Dakota, turned out to be a great fit for Connor. Despite the substantial tuition for a vocational degree—the two-year associate's degree in veterinary technology runs over $44,000 plus lab fees and book expenses—the school had the advantage of being located in Connor's hometown. She especially liked that she was able to maintain a conventional job during the day while working toward her degree by taking classes at night.

Connor's experience at Globe University was so good, in fact, that when she heard that the Career College Association (CCA)—a trade group for for-profit colleges that has since been renamed the Association of Private Sector Colleges and Universities—was seeking students to represent the school at a Washington lobbying day that March, she jumped at the opportunity. But the lobbying day was just the beginning.

Only a few short months later, Connor would find herself the newly elected president of Students for Academic Choice (SAC), which describes itself as an association of "proud students and graduates of private, post-secondary career-oriented institutions." The association focuses on ensuring "access to a quality education," recognizing both the value that "non-traditional learners" bring to the workplace and the value of career-oriented education for society as a whole. As of September that year, the organization had an estimated 150 members and was working with a lawyer to gain official nonprofit status. More significantly, SAC became active in organizing college students across the entire for-profit university system, ultimately assembling some thirty-two thousand signatures on a petition asking that the Department of Education avoid enacting a proposed new "gainful employment" rule, which would cut off federal aid to colleges whose graduates have high debt-to-income ratios and low loan-repayment rates.[5] The petition was framed to suggest that the rules change would harm disadvantaged groups, including the "single mothers, veterans, and adult students who work full time while attending school."[6]

But despite its efforts to be seen as an independent, grassroots uprising of concerned students at for-profit colleges, the industry's backing was not far behind. Indeed, as Connor herself acknowledged, the idea to form the organization originated not with the students, but with representatives of for-profit schools.[7] Further, the group was formed at the CCA's lobbying day in Washington, and the SAC website and its initial resources were provided by the CCA.[8] As Connor put it, the CCA served as SAC's "grandfather," which gave the group its start and guidance. She says, "They kind of got us going. But now they're taking the training wheels off and saying, 'Go for it and let's see what you guys can do.'"[9]

SAC, then, became a primary support in a full-throated response to what was seen as a life-or-death fight by the $30-billion industry of for-profit colleges against the gainful employment rule. Cass Sunstein, the Harvard Law School professor formerly in charge of rulemaking at the White House Office of Information and Regulatory Affairs, called the industry's lobbying effort nothing short of "extreme."[10] And the lobbying efforts seem to have made a difference, as the rules will only affect a small proportion of for-profit universities at the start, and those penalties won't even go into effect until years down the road.

From Contention to Consensus in Cleveland

Today, the city of Cleveland, Ohio, is a hotbed of civic participation. Yet expanded participation has not necessarily meant a democratic revival, although every day in the city dozens of community organizations, churches, ward clubs, and street clubs meet to discuss issues of concern.

In the city's predominantly African American neighborhood of Hough, residents meet frequently around a host of civic and political projects. Well-attended ward club meetings discuss policing, garbage pickup, and funding for schools. A meeting at a local community center takes up the need to secure the funding necessary to provide children's services. A meeting in a nightclub discusses regulatory approval for a Negro Baseball Hall of Fame. In the name of economic development, a group of men meet at a local community development corporation to develop strategies for locating "mentors" who can nurture aspiring entrepreneurs.

In another of Cleveland's neighborhoods—the increasingly African American but still heavily Eastern European Slavic Village—discussions have a similar flavor. A street club discusses policing and traffic mitigation. A local organization familiarizes residents with a program to paint window sashes on abandoned houses. Community organizers meet with neighborhood residents in order to take action against illegal scrap dealers. One group is discussing outreach to victims of predatory lending, and yet another is attempting to defuse racial tensions through a series of face-to-face relationship-building meetings reminiscent of the encounter groups of the civil rights era.[11] Members of a local church gather to discuss plans for a townhouse development to preserve the viability and cultural flavor of the neighborhood surrounding the church itself.

Comparing these settings, the ostensible topics present an interesting variety but are not radically different. The manner in which they are conducted is also surprisingly similar. They have agendas, they tend to loosely follow Roberts' Rules of Order, and diverse citizens come together to hash out issues of local concern. Within the meetings themselves there are subtle distinctions in the discourse and practice of deliberation: who gets to speak, when they get to speak, and the sorts of authority they invoke when doing so.

However, just as important are the various *purposes* that participation and deliberation are serving. This concern is evident in both cases. To a local blogger and former director of a community development corporation, Hough is not an example of a Tocquevillian associational democracy, but of a "Maoist" personality cult, led by the indomitable city councilor Fannie Lewis, until her recent death. Her allies, on the other hand, celebrated her familiarity with the people of the ward and her willingness to secure resources on their behalf by hook or by crook. Regardless of which characterization is more accurate, one of Lewis's main tools was the facilitation of broad-based participation. Indeed, each of the meetings in Hough referred to above were in some way related to Lewis. Participation was how Lewis maintained connections to constituents. For some, this produced deliberation that was less about democratic decision making than it was about performing loyalty to the councilor. If true, deliberation in Hough is unlikely to produce effective citizens, much less democracy.

In Slavic Village, citizen participation flows across a civic landscape that was largely formed in the neighborhood-based social movements of the 1970s. Perhaps the most visible figure in Slavic Village is Barbara Anderson. When Anderson first moved into the neighborhood, her garage was firebombed by racists. Shortly thereafter, she received a leaflet for a meeting to discuss neighborhood issues. When she arrived she realized "the meeting was about me." Today, the friendly and soft-spoken Anderson leads a street club, Bringing Back the Seventies, which has won awards for civic involvement from the city. She considers the mayor an ally and works with the local community development corporation on residential issues. She is not paid for this work and in street club meetings she keeps a low profile. Anderson has been the victim of predatory lending, an experience that has made her far more willing to be confrontational than she once was. It has also thrust her into the forefront of discussions on the foreclosure crisis. She has testified before committees of the U.S. Senate on the issue, is regularly interviewed by journalists from around the world, and has been the subject of a French documentary. Anderson the political and civic actor has been both created by the civic life of her neighborhood and a creator of it. Participation in Slavic Village does not just accommodate people like Anderson; it celebrates them. Yet the meetings in Slavic Village are not radically different from those in Hough. So what makes some deliberative participation good and some bad?

Participation in an Unequal Context

What do these stories tell us about contemporary public participation? The goal of broadening and deepening public participation has served as a valued mechanism for societal revitalization among democratic theorists, social reformers, and popular commentators.[12] Participation is held up as a means of placing power in the hands of everyday citizens,[13] a device for creating new forms of self-governance intended to put citizens in the role of collaborators in making major institutional decisions,[14] and, importantly, for breaking down rigid hierarchies and entrenched inequalities within state, corporate, educational, health care, and other institutions in society.[15] Many have come to see participation as a remedy for a variety of the organizational and political problems that have emerged in complex, differentiated modern societies. Flexible organizational cultures, a decentralized media environment, and network-based collaboration all seem to augur a more promising environment for new forms of empowered democratic participation.

Modern societies appear to be undergoing a participatory revolution, a development that has been accompanied by an exuberant scholarly and popular celebration of the transformative potential of participation. Across the political spectrum, increasing citizen voice is viewed as a necessary counterweight to elite power and bureaucratic rationality.[16] Stakeholder dialogue sessions, crowdsourcing, town hall meetings, web-based open government initiatives, and deliberative democracy are championed as revolutionary antidotes to the decline of civic engagement and the thinning of the contemporary public sphere.

We call these elite-facilitated civic innovations the "new public participation," which we define as (a) the facilitation of lay participation by elite actors in order to manage or channel the former's voice in support of narrow interests, (b) the creation of collaborative relationships between lay actors and organizational decision makers to reground the authority of the organization, or (c) efforts to arrive at better-informed organizational decisions by relying on the collective wisdom of assembled publics rather than experts.

Much contemporary participation, even when carried out with the best of intentions, is shaped by socioeconomic inequality. In the Michigan case, we see that deliberative goals were working *against* the goal of economic redistribution and egalitarianism, as ideas about the risks of business taxation have permeated popular understandings. In the case of Students for Academic Choice, we see a participatory program that provides backing to a contested industry despite the concern that this industry is seen as exploiting socially disadvantaged groups. In the case of Cleveland community-based organizations, we can see how in some settings participation can expand citizen voice while in others it works to underpin the authority of an elected official.

Cases like these make sense when understood in light of the structural problems of modern societies that limit the potential for true democratization. Vast inequalities of wealth, income, and organization exist both within and across nations, and in the United States these inequalities have expanded dramatically since the 1970s. Rising political partisanship has accompanied this transformation, with ideological divisions becoming sharper and more deeply entrenched.[17] Corporate power has been transformed through the decline of managerialism and the expansion of (often highly participatory) network forms of business organization.[18] Not least, companies have expanded their reach into civil society through new methods of mobilizing the public as a lobbying force.[19] In the public sector, bureaucratic expertise is regularly contested through participatory forums, community consultations, and other dialogues with local citizens. Political representatives are held accountable by constituents in town halls, at primary challenges, and by watchdog groups. Over the last forty years there has been a broad institutionalization of participatory practices, a flattening of hierarchies, and an expansion of the role of stakeholder voices in organizational decision making. We once associated an expansion in participation with an expansion in both broader socioeconomic equality and greater egalitarianism within organizations. Yet over the same period there has been a rapid expansion in socioeconomic inequality and political polarization.[20]

These developments suggest a need to revisit the question of participation. Is participation reinforcing the unequal, undemocratic context of society at large? Once a tool for protesters contesting the authority of hierarchical organizations, is participation now a tool for the creation of authority? Is participation a practice that helps realize broadly inclusive social and political aspirations, or is it a tool for realizing particularistic interests? If the latter, is it because some interests are irreconcilable? Or is it because the practice of participation is conducted poorly? Finally, is reasoned deliberation the best process for locating the welfare of the citizenry as a whole, or is deliberation most productive alongside other modes of participation such as protest and contestation?

Our interest in this volume is to explore implications of new participatory innovations for the exercise of authority and governance. Compared to those involved in promoting empowerment projects, our work in this project may seem simply cynical, but that would be the wrong conclusion. Our goal is to understand what has happened to participation over the last forty years in order to gain a deeper theoretical and empirical understanding of it as a political practice. The goal is not simple critique. It is to enrich our understanding of democracy and the practices that sustain and undermine it.

While in the 1960s participation was offered up as a solution to hierarchy and alienation, participation today is widespread and complicated enough that any equation of participation with democratization cannot be sustained without some ambiguity. This does not mean we should give up on participation. Instead, it presents a challenge to activists, citizens, and scholars to think through what kinds of participation yield the positive outcomes we seek and what prevents their realization. Before we can do this, we need better analyses and an improved conceptual apparatus to understand the complexities of participation today. Celebratory accounts are uplifting, but they do not meet the needs of this moment when expanding participation has occurred alongside the greatest expansion in socioeconomic inequality since the Gilded Age.

For this reason, we set our goals in contrast to those who study participatory projects mainly by evaluating successful cases of stakeholder empowerment. In particular, our volume offers an alternative perspective to the explosion of recent work by proponents of "empowered participatory governance"—defined as efforts to redesign institutions in a participatory democratic fashion in order to facilitate deliberation and civic engagement, while transcending the "familiar configuration of political representation and bureaucratic administration."[21] The intention of this volume is to move beyond the selection of positive cases in order to examine instead (1) the institutional interests in public legitimation through participation and (2) the link between new participatory forms and the highly unequal context in which they have taken root. In addition, (3) we are also interested in exploring how participatory democratic practices (or those that invoke this tradition) have migrated from their origins in civil society organizations to a diverse set of institutional homes and (4) how this migration shapes participatory dynamics. But, first, it is worth considering the sources of this new participatory revival.

Participation in Historical Context

Today we generally accept the idea that participation produces healthier communities, better politics, and more innovative institutions. Government programs and bureaucracies mandate or encourage participation in the name of both democratic governance and more effective policies. Civic engagement and civic participation programs are now widely diffused as programmatic goals among philanthropies, nonprofits, government, and increasingly among for-profit firms as well. Indeed, an entire industry of specialist organizations sells participation services to meet this growing demand.[22] For these actors the question is not whether and how participation matters, but how to encourage it. Given the more or less unquestioned positive associations we have with the idea of participation, it is useful to recall that it was not always so. The idea of participation as a practice with promising democratizing potential has not had a linear trajectory in modern thinking. In historical context, positive associations with participation are relatively new; recalling this enables us to scrutinize theorists' and practitioners' contemporary celebration of it.

Enlightenment thought used the premise that all of us have the capacity to reason as a tool to undermine the authority of monarchical governments and state religions. The Age of Revolution saw the creation of numerous experiments that attempted to institutionalize this premise in democratic and representative constitutions. Political practices changed alongside ideas of legitimate authority. In Britain and the United States, rioting and machine breaking began to cede ground to mass demonstrations and unionization.[23] Debates emerged over the role of organization in politics. Are organizations to be understood as expressions of power rather than reason? What is the relationship between organization and individual reason? Do they fragment people into parochial interests rather than bringing people together in reasoned dialogue? Other debates emerged over the conditions that support the use of reason in politics. Some thought material deprivation turned reason to the question of personal acquisition rather than the general good.[24] Renaissance-era ideas of civic virtue persisted because of the perceived need to ground reason in normative values.[25] Women began to be excluded from the promising universalism of Enlightenment thinking.[26] People of color, manual laborers, and Jews suffered the same fate on the grounds of material circumstance and assumed proximity to nature rather than civilization.[27]

Even as democratization proceeded apace in the 19th century, the belief in broad, reasoned participation in government did not advance with it. Popular conservatism invoked tradition at the expense of reason, nationalism invoked commitments to abstract ideas about cultural essences beyond the scope of reason, and communitarianism and religious revivalism invoked shared values that were not to be subjected to reason's skeptical eye.[28] Ideologies and political practices served to disconnect reason and participation despite the efforts of some to maintain the connection (Max Weber notable among them).[29] These trends reached their apogee in the First World War, understood by many to be a manifestation of collective insanity, a sentiment that was easily extended to related events like the Russian Revolution and the Nazi Revolution.[30] In this context, Freud wrote about the "death instinct," our human drive to destruction.[31] Emotion had exploded out of the private sphere and overwhelmed the reasoning public. Horkheimer and Adorno, looking at the rise of state capitalism, national socialism, and the "culture industry," argued that the Enlightenment's promise of emancipation through reason had merely circled back on itself to reestablish the authority of superstition and myth.[32] Mass participation in politics led, ultimately, to mass delusion.

In the United States the issues were similar, though they took a somewhat different form. American politics in the 19th century could not be considered "inclusive," despite the invocation of self-government in the Declaration of Independence and the Constitution. Women, African Americans, and immigrants were all denied citizenship by various constitutional and legal mechanisms.[33] Even native-born workers and farmers were often excluded from full political citizenship. At the same time, urban politics traded on nativist prejudices and ethnic solidarity. This exclusion produced numerous efforts to reestablish the authority of the "people" in American politics, culminating in the late 19th century with the Farmer's Alliance and the Populist Party.[34]

Populism's high point was checked by an emerging Progressive movement that invoked expertise as the necessary tool of reform in the face of a representative politics that was hopelessly corrupted by parochial interests.[35] The tensions between these strains in politics were integrated in the administration of Franklin Delano Roosevelt during the Great Depression. Electoral politics in the era continued to be governed by sectional interests and the need to respond to emerging movements. At the same time, Roosevelt's administration created new bureaucratic agencies to be managed by experts disconnected from the pressures of popular participation in politics.[36] "Technocratic" movements emerged alongside popular ones. Walter Lippmann summarized the dilemma and proposed a solution in *Public Opinion*, where he questioned the "omnicompetence" of the public.[37] The world is complicated and the reach of reason is limited by a lack of expertise. Public officials should consider the views of experts as well as the voting masses, particularly in day-to-day decision making.

The 1930s were characterized by massive economic and social upheavals and, just as important, by a very ideological brand of politics. Of course, one outcome was another world war, but there was also the sense that mass movements were in a struggle to define the future. However, in the wake of the Second World War, the idea of mass participation as a tool of democratization and emancipation was somewhat battered. Government bureaucracies, staffed by experts, were capable of solving most problems and securing the general well-being. While there were voices that resisted this— Saul Alinsky argued that exclusion would produce more extremism, and the civil rights movement began questioning the justice of any government that could exclude its citizens from self-determination— the faith in experts and bureaucracy was at its height.[38]

In response to the emerging dominance of bureaucratic experts in American society, C. Wright Mills wrote *The Power Elite* in 1956.[39] Mills questioned whether bureaucrats and experts were oriented to the general good or, in fact, were attempting to expand their own power and authority. For Mills, military, corporate, and political leaders composed a distinct social interest that rendered ordinary citizens powerless in an ostensibly democratic society. Mass participation was not to be feared, and decisions by the Power Elite, relatively unchecked by citizen participation, were the real danger. At roughly the same time, concern began growing about general social alienation even amid the rising tide of postwar economic affluence. *The Lonely Crowd* was published in 1950 and in it Riesman, Glazer, and Denney argued that suburban affluence was producing a middle class that was primarily concerned with social validation rather than achievement, a tendency that was easy for bureaucracies to manipulate.[40] In *One-Dimensional Man*, Marcuse similarly argued that advanced industrial society produced "false needs" which ultimately manipulated desires and aspirations away from critique or a drive for excellence.[41]

The thinking that was encapsulated in this work amounted to a collective rejection of the idea that bureaucracies and their experts could be reconciled with broadly participatory democracy and, at the same time, could realize general social improvement and progress. This view was not just important in leftist intellectual circles. Theorists of cybernetics, for example, began imagining a world in which technical mastery would lie with individuals, rather than large organizations, empowering them to know more, do more, and make better decisions— a line of thinking that would take computing out of large organizations and place it on individual desktops.[42] The New Left and the student movement incorporated elements of this thinking. Students, faced with the prospect of working as middle managers in faceless and oppressive bureaucracies, resisted. In the South, the Student Non-violent Coordinating Committee took the view that self-generated movements of regular people were more promising tools of social transformation than experts and charismatic leaders.[43] In Berkeley, the thing to be feared was understood to be bureaucracies and the power elite, including university presidents, not simply capitalists or conservatives. These were merely the opening salvos of a wave of movements that invoked participation and democracy in opposition to bureaucrats, expertise, and traditional authority. Women questioned the authority of men, union members struck in opposition to their own unions as well as their employers, the LGBT community developed a more militant politics and demanded social acceptance, and neighborhoods revolted against the highway building and slum-clearance projects of centralized municipal bureaucracies.[44] Among many in these movements, participation was not simply understood as a check on the authority and power of experts, it was also understood as a tool for creating community and overcoming social alienation and the meaninglessness of consumer society.[45]

These movements also informed the next generations of political theory and intellectual research. Theorists' understanding of mass participation and civic participation was no longer framed as an emotional and easily manipulated crowd, but as a body of empowered "stakeholders" who should be the authors of key decisions concerning their own lives.[46] This participation did not merely enact a democratic right to self-determination; it developed the political sophistication of the participants, ultimately producing a healthier and more sophisticated polity.[47] A general capacity for reason was not invoked with the same insistence that it had been, though it clearly made a revival, most notably in the thought of Jürgen Habermas.[48] A general capacity to solve problems through participation and collective decision making was increasingly invoked. Liberals and communitarians would debate the nature of the best polity, but both accepted the idea that participation was a good, not something to be feared.[49] Bureaucrats and experts, on the other hand, were understood to be distantly interested and somewhat blinded by the abstractions of their training and expertise.[50] These views pervade contemporary intellectual thinking on the polity and society.

Of course, there are intellectual positions that contest this rosy view. Foucauldians associate participation with the disciplining effects of civil society.[51] Participation, from this perspective, does not enable individuals constituted prior to participation to express their essential aspirations and values. It constitutes and disciplines the individual. Sheldon Wolin, at the time very much a supporter of the 1960s movements against the power of unconstrained bureaucracies, now argues that today's fragmented and diffuse modes of participation help enable an "inverted totalitarianism" in which elites can have democratic authority while pursuing antidemocratic goals.[52] But these views are in the minority and it may be that invoking these ideas today is considered mildly impolite or unreasonably contrarian.

The movements of the 1960s sparked a culture war between traditionalists and social liberals. *What is less commented on is that it produced a general social consensus that participation was a good worth pursuing and institutionalizing.* The very bureaucracies that were understood in the 1960s to produce alienation and arrogant experts now routinely make use of participatory practices. Corporations, government, and the military, each part of Mills's power elite, all make use of New Participatory practices today. Of course, when the movements of the 1960s invoked participation, they were not simply saying any old participation will suffice. Indeed, it is clear from research on these movements that the nature and dynamics of participation were constantly debated.[53]

Nonetheless, the ideas developed in these movement settings have often been incorporated into the organizations that sell participatory services to large bureaucracies.[54]

The valorization of participation in the 1960s was not simply pushed by movements. By the late 1970s, it was also widely adopted by government and private-sector organizations. Citizens gained access to policymaking, the management of agencies, the direction of scientific research, and even the capital allocation decisions of corporations. Indeed, in many settings participation was actively pushed as a management tool, not as a method of democratization. American manufacturers adopted "total quality management" techniques wholesale from Japan, disrupting labor relations on the shop floor but potentially transforming work-management techniques to give workers a greater voice. Political theorists on both the left and the right turned to civil society as a realm of authentic social relations that could provide a necessary corrective to the power of bureaucracies, a sentiment that has helped justify the devolution of government and the incorporation of nonprofit organizations and for-profit corporations into governance functions.

Given this history, it is necessary to develop a better theoretical and conceptual language to understand participation in contemporary society. We turn now to a framework for carrying out that task.

The Response: A Participatory Renaissance?

Democratic deficits appear to be prevalent in modern societies,[55] and responses to such concerns have become a prominent aspect of contemporary states and organizations. Government agencies, businesses, and nonprofits are all making efforts to become more open, transparent, accountable, and welcoming of public input than their rigid, bureaucratic, and more hierarchical predecessors of generations past. Organizations are doing what they can not only to *respond* to public concerns, but also to *facilitate the expression* of public concerns by hosting deliberative democratic forums, making political and organizational leaders available to members of the public for dialogue, and even helping to build advocacy organizations so that members of the public can have their say in politics and organizational governance. These new efforts transcend the well-established and routinized mechanisms of agencies' "public comment" periods, the writing of environmental impact statements, and basic efforts to promote the "maximum feasible participation" of disadvantaged members of society in public programs.

What many see as today's participatory renaissance appears to be richer and deeper than the programmatic efforts of earlier generations. Yet it also coincides with a dramatic expansion in socioeconomic inequalities over the past forty years, which have entailed a growing polarization between institutional elites and everyone else. The new participatory revival also coincides with the neoliberal turn in policymaking.[56] The role of markets in determining life chances is being valorized at the same time that state interventions to mitigate inequality are being dismantled. In this context, when material well-being no longer underpins legitimacy, some, like the geographer Mark

Purcell and Michael McQuarrie in this volume, argue that participation is now a necessary component of authority.

Regardless of how we feel about these changes, it seems clear that "participation" is a practice that is increasingly valued not just in government but also in diverse institutional settings beyond the state. Moreover, it is valued not simply because it enables citizens to express their aspirations and priorities. It is valued as a management tool and a socialization tool as well. With the help of new technologies and new fields of expertise, participation has metastasized across the organizational and institutional landscape in dramatic fashion—and in ways that are likely to alter its significance and purpose. This breathtaking expansion raises questions about the relationship between the legal-institutional "home" of participation and its effects, and about how the meaning of the practice shifts when it operates in multiple settings other than the public sphere and formal politics.

Tensions in Participatory Projects

In this context, and given this history, we think any consideration of participation revolves around three primary tensions.

1. *Democratization versus tyranny.* Of course, participation has long been associated with democratization. However, the postwar period is an example of a time when it was widely associated with totalitarianism. This pessimistic view persists in Foucauldian conceptions of the disciplining effects of civil society and collective participation, and more recently, in arguments like Sheldon Wolin's suggestion that we now live in an "inverted totalitarianism," premised on fragmenting and diffuse participation (as opposed to the mass, unifying types of participation that were characteristic of the movements of the 1930s and 1940s). One volume abandons nuance and simply asks the question in its title: *Participation: The New Tyranny?*[57] Short of hyperbole, there are essential questions about participation as a component of rule today. We are accustomed to thinking of elite power and authority as being associated with social closure or as blocking the paths to more inclusion and participation. With participation so often celebrated, it is not surprising that participatory practices might be enrolled in support of governance and authority, underpinning the rule and legitimacy of elites rather than simply challenging them. Is our society more open and democratic? Or is elite rule reorganized to accommodate greater openness and participation without disrupting hierarchies and power relations?

2. *Solidarity versus conflict.* The key question here asks whether participation promotes social solidarity or instead exacerbates conflict. Formal politics is usually understood as a realm of "adversarial" politics, but civil society has often been characterized as a realm of social solidarity that potentially acts as a unifying base for healthier formal politics. Moreover, participation is often understood to promote solidarity by transforming identities and interests so that we are better able to recognize and act on the general good. From this perspective,

participation potentially socializes us to be better and more sophisticated citizens. Critics argue that this emphasis on social solidarity obscures questions of justice. Don't solidarity and consensus in an unequal society come at a cost? On the other hand, given an unequal society, if participation is not transformative and people merely act on their self-interest, is conflict inevitable? Are all questions usefully amenable to compromise and deliberation or are there issues that are better decided on the basis of agonistic contests between organized interest groups?[58] Some activists and organizers argue that conflict is an essential prerequisite to consensus because it forces recognition of groups, issues, and interests that might otherwise be marginalized. Is this true? Or is conflict taken up too readily without an appreciation of the potential for deliberative compromise and consensus?

3. *Better governance or worse?* In Philip Selznick's classic examination of the Tennessee Valley Authority, the relationship between management and participation was not particularly positive.[59] Rather, in that story organizational strategies and purposes were disrupted and defused by participation. However, today, participation is increasingly celebrated as a source of local knowledge, "stakeholder" investment, and as a corrective to the rationalizing effects of abstract, expert knowledge.[60] On the other hand, many lament the relativization of expert authority. What, for example, does it mean when lay voices direct scientific research and assess its value?

We argue that these questions are not best addressed through the use of theoretical reason alone and, indeed, all of the chapters collected here base their analyses on rich and detailed empirical research. The picture that emerges is certainly complicated. Participation is put to a variety of uses, but it also evolves in different ways given the needs of different institutional settings, the outcome of historical conflicts, and the application of new technologies. At the same time, the overall expansion in the use of participation and its spread into a variety of new settings are indicators of its changing practice and purpose. With these three tensions in mind—democratization versus discipline, solidarity versus conflict, and empowered governance versus the loss of expert authority—we can consider a number of types of modern participation that bring these tensions into even starker relief.

First, consider *economic development programs*. The World Bank has taken a strong interest in practical application of the concept of "social capital" and has considerable and wide-ranging programs in empowerment. By this, they mean "the process of increasing the capacity of individuals or groups to make choices and to transform those choices into desired actions and outcomes. Central to this process are actions that both build individual and collective assets, and improve the efficiency and fairness of the organizational and institutional contexts which govern the use of these assets." A wide variety of other aid programs have adopted the "empowerment" mantra in a fashion that is surprisingly apolitical in approach. Critics such as Arundhati Roy have pointed to empowerment in development aid as part of a broader turn toward "the NGOization of resistance," in which nongovernmental organizations (NGOs), in her words, "defuse political anger and dole out as aid or benevolence what people ought to have by right. They alter the public psyche, they turn people into dependent victims and they blunt the edges of political resistance. . . . [NGOs] form a sort of buffer between the [state] and the public."[61] Empowerment rhetoric, critics like Roy argue, is being used as a cover to advance neoliberalism and blunt the impact of harsh structural adjustments, especially in that many of these empowerment programs distribute aid directly to NGOs *instead* of channeling funds through states. Even more interestingly, aid agencies do appear at times to truly empower citizens to confront institutions, namely *local* institutions known for human rights violations, unsustainable practices, or cultural avenues seen as hostile to development.

Second, consider *state-mandated participation*. Participation is often mandated as a condition of funding by foundations and grant-making agencies of the U.S. federal government. Of course, in the U.S., the notion of mandated participation is rooted in the requirement of "maximum feasible participation" as outlined in the Economic Opportunity Act of 1964. The act, as part of the War on Poverty, established the Community Action Programs, which were to be "developed, conducted, and administered with the *maximum feasible participation* of residents of the areas and members of the groups served." These practices survive today especially in the resurgence of programs in community-based participatory research (CBPR). Consistent with the turn toward an inclusion-and-difference-based approach to health sciences research, both the National Institutes of Health (NIH) and the Centers for Disease Control (CDC) have adopted CBPR frameworks into their funding solicitations; these stipulate that research is not only collaborative with affected communities but also *mandates their participation* through making available "structures for participation by communities affected by the issue being studied."[62] Biomedical research grants involving formal community action components, for example, have skyrocketed since 1996. A consistent thread throughout these cases, as Nina Eliasoph argues,[63] is that organizations—whether in welfare, health, community development, or other policy areas—often mandate that their grantees encourage participation, and much of that participation may contradict other mandates and may challenge other institutions for change, especially local institutions like city councils, mayors' offices, and existing social service agencies.

A third set of phenomena includes *elite-driven efforts to mobilize the public*. Strategies like the use of empowerment language, grassroots organizing, and mobilizing links with existing community organizations for political advantage are not limited to the world of traditional advocacy organizations and social movements. There has been a resurgence of research on elite-driven public advocacy and elite social movements. Although this was a largely dormant body of investigation over the past thirty years,[64] a vibrant new body of studies has investigated how elites have appropriated social movement strategies, frames, and organizing processes, often to counter the advocacy of citizens' movements. Steven Teles's account of the rise of the conservative legal movement makes clear that elite conservatives, responding to the vast legal victories of liberal causes in the 1960s and '70s, mobilized foundations and legal networks to transform the law schools and, in turn, the very legal profession.[65] Recent research that one of us (Walker) has done shows that as the civic and business environments changed in the 1970s, a new field of consulting firms came about to help businesses mobilize public participation in their favor;[66] similar to what Teles finds, Walker argues that corporate America adopted an "if you can't beat them, join them" approach to the challenges they were facing from protest groups and civic organizers. Campaigns like the ones Walker describes are designed to mobilize only those who are predisposed to agree with the request of the recruiter, and not to encourage independent public dialogue. These cases provide evidence of elite mobilization of public participation without true empowerment of the broader public, in that participation is a mechanism for the reproduction of institutionalized authority; it is a counterpressure to citizen power that seeks to root elite institutions more deeply in public life. Cases like these remind us that participation and inequality can often be quite compatible, despite the expectation of many—indeed, this includes the very architects of the notion of maximum feasible participation—that participation inherently combats inequality and reshapes authority.

A fourth and final phenomenon is the *professional facilitation of public deliberation*. One of us (Lee) has studied the rapid expansion of an industry of participation experts who manage "deep" engagement initiatives for government, nonprofit, and private clients.[67] These professional deliberation consultants take great pains to produce authentically deliberative, customized processes, and this much is not in doubt. But Lee argues that their institutional and political contexts—and the forms of empowerment they enable—deserve greater scrutiny. Complementing increasingly sophisticated stakeholder management technologies, this type of "designer democracy" has a number of potentially regressive outcomes. Deliberation consultants build public legitimacy for the retrenchment of programs, they enhance the reputational capital of the consultants' clients, and they encourage citizen mobilization focused on short-term, individualized action. As Isaac Martin's chapter in this volume describes, the explosion of government-sponsored deliberative forums is in part a response to increasing social conflicts over scarce public resources, and this explosion raises a number of ongoing challenges for social movement actors facing "anticipatory consultation" designed to forestall future movement activity. As deliberative processes themselves become routine, the relationships among deliberation, contention, and routine politics are far from settled. This is particularly clear in Francesca Polletta's contribution to this volume.

In all four of these cases—economic development programs, state-mandated participation, corporate grassroots lobbying, and professionalized deliberation—we see the tensions inherent in modern participation and the ways in which participation may at times be *consistent* with expanded inequalities, rather than a challenge to them. It would seem, then, that the concept of participation is overdue for a serious rethinking.

Overall, we believe that addressing these questions requires social scientists to examine these institutional changes with a more critical and objectifying take on the basic categories we use to understand democracy, though that does not necessarily mean that we take a critical stance on the practices themselves. We believe that the relationship between participation, political subjectivity, authority, and justice has been reconfigured. It is not entirely clear *how* that has happened, nor are we clear on the exact shape of that reconfiguration. Nonetheless, it is time for scholarship to reground its consideration of the meaning of participation in empirical research on its practice, its settings, and its institutional frameworks. The chapters in this volume all seek to address this issue by challenging settled theoretical assumptions without throwing them out altogether, and by basing their challenges not on theoretical reasoning alone, but on empirical research.

Participation and Inequality

Very little of the discussion of participation is interested in how it might produce and sustain inequality by silencing dissent or relativizing political critique. To the extent that equity has been a concern of studies of contemporary participation, most research has focused on the structuring of power within particular processes, not across the wide array of settings for participation or between participation's institutional sponsors and its subjects. Since the 1960s, very little attention has been paid to the relationship between participation and equity because the assumption has been that the two are conjoined and that participation is an incontrovertible democratic good.[68] As the preceding sections show, the meanings and uses of participation vary strikingly across contexts and time periods, such that the assumed association between participation and equity, or even participation and democratization, must be related to historically specific dimensions of contemporary capitalist societies.

The relationship between participation and equity has always been tenuous and contingent, involving contradictions, trade-offs, and unintended consequences. But the rise of participatory solutions in the current era of increasing inequalities demands even greater scrutiny. To understand the challenges of democratic life today, we need a broader picture of how participation works now, the settings in which it operates, and what it is used for. In so doing, the contributions in this volume seek to avoid both the valorization of participation and an (equally problematic) argument that participatory practices are merely ideological cover for inequality. Strong normative arguments of either kind do not allow for an accurate understanding of how participation may reinforce or transform authority while also promising new opportunities for its contestation. At the same time, because we tend to associate participation with democratization, the contributors to this volume tend to emphasize the role of participation in underpinning contemporary forms of rule and authority. This is not because participation no longer offers democratizing promise. Rather, it is a necessary intellectual maneuver to force a reassessment of the way we understand and analyze participation and, hopefully, move beyond simplistic associations and assumptions. Most generally, a more nuanced analysis of how different kinds of equality are related to different kinds of participation in diverse settings will help us to evaluate what is really at stake in today's participation revolution.

The assembled contributions that follow frame a wholly new research agenda for the study of participation and inequality. We hope to excite those who find that democratic reforms and existing power structures are interrelated in complex ways and may lead to unintended consequences. More important, we hope to demonstrate that there is a larger picture emerging from these empirical studies. From the Tea Party to Obama's online engagement strategies, from health policy to budgeting and taxation, from international development to human rights activism, and from workplace engagement and corporate culture to the civic realms of volunteers and low-income communities, we believe such questions could not be more timely or relevant for understanding extraordinary and everyday forms of political action in a contemporary context that continually demands that its citizens, shoppers, and workers "have their say" and "join the discussion."

What Is to Follow

p. 20-21 methodology

As scholars who discovered common themes across our own studies of elite-driven mass participation, public deliberation, and community organizing, we set about to assemble this volume in a manner that focuses tightly on participation and inequality while at the same time demonstrating the range of questions such investigations can raise. We found junior and senior scholars doing fascinating research on common themes despite their very different subjects. Thus, we grouped chapters according to the questions they share in common.

Beyond this introductory section, the second section addresses the following question: How do new participatory forms help to produce and reinforce inequality? The question is addressed in three chapters that provide unique insights into how inequality is reproduced through participatory practices and that also present the outlines of the contemporary political economy of participation. Lee and colleagues investigate the field of professional public deliberation consultants and how their practices working on behalf of public- and private-sector clients help to provide a democratic veneer for the interests of consultants' clients. As one of Lee's subjects suggests, participation allows organizations to "pluck more feathers with less squawking." Vallas, Judge, and Cummins's chapter examines how discourse in the public debate surrounding sweatshops has come to emphasize a "human rights" frame at the cost of one focused on how to distribute wealth. They contend that one of the consequences of this frame is to divert attention away from issues of inequality and power in global workplaces. Walker's contribution analyzes a new set of "participation consultants"; actors in this field work mainly for corporations seeking to mobilize short-term public support around issues of company- or industrywide concern. He shows that companies are most likely to hire such consultants when they are facing concerns about the legitimacy of their community relations or environmental practices. These corporate campaigns reinforce inequality by mobilizing participation almost exclusively in line with company interests.

Part III asks this question: How does the new public participation produce new forms of authority and legitimacy for elites? McQuarrie's chapter takes as its subject changing "technologies of participation" and finds that while such technologies were once used to challenge the authority of urban elites, they are now a central component of that authority. In the process the role and practices of community-based organizations have been transformed to secure civic consensus rather than express neighborhood interests. Martin's contribution tells a complementary story. He studies what he calls "new deliberative assemblies" carried out by state-level government agencies, and he links their proliferation to the fiscal troubles they face. The major implication is that democratization is conditional: increased participation is granted in return for increased taxation. In electoral politics, Daniel Kreiss asks how new technologies (facilitated by the growth of a new industry of political professionals) are reshaping public participation in a new era of "digital" campaigns promising individual empowerment. Building on interviews with the consultants who harnessed participatory technologies in the 2008 campaign to elect Barack Obama, Kreiss's chapter shows that although these new modes of engagement promise truly open and democratic forms of participation, in reality they increase voter surveillance capabilities and restrict engagement to fundraising, promotion, and political data gathering on behalf of the candidate. Rounding out the third section, David Schleifer and Aaron Panofsky's chapter explores the emerging world of entrepreneurial patient advocates who lobby and raise public awareness about diseases and their treatment. A key part of their account describes how such groups manage apparent conflicts of interest when lobbying for government support for specific drugs in which they also have a financial investment. Often, patient advocacy groups do little to contribute to the broader democratization of society and instead promote greater inequality in medical treatment and drug availability.

The emphasis of part IV is on this question: What unintended consequences and new opportunities emerge from new participatory projects in unequal contexts? Although their manifest purposes are often to facilitate thick public engagement and grassroots empowerment of those at the margins, many new participatory projects hold unintended consequences with respect to both participatory cultures and broader institutional practices. Nina Eliasoph's chapter explores previously hidden consequences of the transformation of volunteering and civic life in the empowerment projects of the last two decades. In opposition to hierarchical social relations, many civic associations, nonprofits, and foundations aim "to empower grassroots, local, multicultural, optional, voluntary communities, to help people break out of their boxes and express their gut feelings." This organizationally sponsored "empowerment talk" is rife with tensions between helping the needy, documenting accountability and transparency, and being "soul-changing" for those involved. Building on findings in her recent book, Eliasoph shows that those who are supposed to become "empowered" are forced to manage unintended contradictions between rhetoric and reality. Gianpaolo Baiocchi and Ernesto Ganuza's chapter also investigates the global reach of the new participation in a genealogy of the concept of "participatory budgeting." Although designed to be a tool of grassroots democracy in Brazil, the practice migrated from local communities into a routinized practice for intergovernmental organizations like the World Bank and USAID. Baiocchi and Ganuza resist the notion that political and economic elites colonized "pure" participation in order to legitimate the expansion of capitalist markets. Instead, the chapter makes the case that regulation and governance questions are always a part of public participation and that participatory practices are never exactly utopian.

The fourth section closes with two contributions that explore how unintended consequences and unequal contexts may actually enable new opportunities for participation and empowerment. David Meyer and Amanda Pullum's contribution examines the Tea Party mobilization since 2009, considering how populist mobilization builds from public sentiments of inequality and democratic deficits in the political system. In so doing, they "explore the tension between grassroots mobilizations animated by democratic rhetoric and their potentially less democratic claims on policy." In the Tea Party case, inequality allowed for new mobilization opportunities, even if these were largely undemocratic in nature. Francesca Polletta's chapter concludes on a hopeful note by investigating participatory opportunities in the boundary between "deliberation" and "public contention." Theorists hold out deliberation as a space in which reasoned dialogue could change minds, reveal shared concerns, and lead to new processes of collective decision making. Protest groups, by contrast, are thought to be committed to winning their case through disruptive action and are unwilling to set aside ideological commitments; activists are thought to be worried that engaging in deliberation will entail co-optation or capitulation. This piece makes clear that these and related assumptions are undercut by empirical evidence on both types of action. Thus, the explicit linking of deliberation and contention may open up new avenues for participation.

We conclude with a capstone chapter that reexamines the pitfalls and unrealized promises of participation in a context of severe structural inequalities. Building on remedies suggested in the prior chapters, we argue that critical perspectives on participation are necessary in order to leverage the opportunities for challenging inequalities created by unfolding fiscal and political crises. In order to meet this challenge, it is necessary to constantly place our categories in dialogue with actual institutional practices.

In the case of participation, this dialogue is long overdue.

NOTES

1. See, for example, Gutmann and Thompson (2004); Lee (2011).
2. For example, Habermas (1984); Knight and Johnson (1997).
3. Center for Deliberative Democracy (2010: 6).
4. The following builds largely from Gorski (2010).
5. Field (2010).
6. SAC (2011).
7. Gorski (2010).
8. Field (2010).
9. Gorski (2010).
10. Lichtblau (2011).
11. Davidson (2007).
12. See, for example, Pateman (1970); Dryzek (2000); Putnam (2001); Barber (1998); Fung and Wright (2003b).

13. Boyte and Boyte (1980).
14. Ostrom (1990); Bingham, Nabatchi, and O'Leary (2005).
15. Fung and Wright (2003a); Ansell and Gash (2006); Fung (2006); Gaventa (2006).
16. For a conservative take on participation and civil society, see Berger and Neuhaus (2000).
17. Abramowitz and Saunders (2008).
18. Davis and Thompson (1994); Podolny and Page (1998); Fligstein and Shin (2007).
19. Walker (2009, 2014).
20. For example, Hacker and Pierson (2011).
21. Fung and Wright (2003a: 15).
22. Walker (2009, 2014); Lee (2011).
23. Thompson (1963); Tilly (1995).
24. Epstein (1994); Calhoun and McQuarrie (2007).
25. Pocock (1975); Vernon (1993).
26. Fraser (1992); Ryan (1992); Clark (1995).
27. Eley (1992); Todorov (1993); Horkheimer and Adorno (2002).
28. Johnson (1978); Eley (1980); Coetzee (1990); Calhoun (1997); Roberts (2007).
29. Radkau (2009).
30. Eksteins (2000).
31. Freud (2010).
32. Horkheimer and Adorno (2002).
33. Keyssar (2000).
34. Foner (1970); Goodwyn (1976).
35. Rodgers (1998).
36. Block (1977); Amenta (1998).
37. Lippmann (1997).
38. Alinsky (1989a).
39. Mills (2000).
40. Riesman, Glazer, and Denney (1963); Kornhauser (2008).
41. Marcuse (1964).
42. Turner (2006).
43. Payne (1995).
44. Evans (1979); Clavel (1986); Aronowitz (1992); Armstrong (2002).
45. Evans and Boyte (1992); Jasper (1999); Polletta (2002).
46. McAdam (1982).
47. Alinsky (1989b); Arendt (1998).
48. Habermas (1989).
49. Rawls (1971); MacIntyre (1981).
50. Handler (1996).
51. Barry, Osborne, and Rose (1996); Cruikshank (1999).
52. Wolin (2010).
53. Polletta (2002).
54. Lee (2011).
55. Pharr and Putnam (2000); Dalton (2008). For a contrasting perspective, see Norris (2002).
56. See Mudge (2008).
57. Cruikshank (1999); Cooke and Kothari (2001); Wolin (2010).
58. The most visible debates around this question have centered on Habermas's

communicative ethics and, prior to that, his historical analysis of the bourgeois public sphere. For example, see Habermas (1989) and the essays in Calhoun (1992). These issues were also central to later debates on multiculturalism. See the essays in Gutmann (1994).
59. Selznick (1949).
60. Lippmann (1997); Callon, Lascoumes, and Barthe (2009).
61. Roy (2004).
62. Wolfson and Parries (2010: 120).
63. Eliasoph (2011).
64. See Useem and Zald (1982).
65. Teles (2010).
66. Walker (2009).
67. Lee (2007).
68. Some notable exceptions include Mansbridge (1980), Sanders (1997), Young (2000), and Verba (2003).

PART II

Participation and the Reproduction of Inequality

CHAPTER 2

Civic-izing Markets
Selling Social Profits in Public Deliberation

CAROLINE W. LEE, KELLY MCNULTY, AND SARAH SHAFFER

> The principles of economics and of participation do not sit easily together.
> —Involve[1]

> Some people say, "Talk is cheap." We say, "Conversation is cost-effective."
> —Practitioner, dialogue and deliberation listserv

Political scholars and reformers envision public deliberation as a restorative, "real utopian" remedy for a public sphere dominated by professional talking heads and well-funded special interest groups.[2] Public dialogue and deliberation processes, which convene lay citizens to engage with each other on the major questions of our time, invoke nostalgia for a less commercial and more public-spirited civic life—"free spaces" light years from the partisan venom and professional punditocracy that have proved so lucrative to international media conglomerates and influence-seekers.[3] Despite these perceptions, today's public deliberation projects do not occur in a space free of commerce. For far too long, scholars have ignored the economic dimensions of the contemporary "participation revolution."[4]

Nonprofit and private consulting organizations produce public deliberation processes for a growing market of public, private, and nonprofit clients who seek to engage their stakeholders in productive dialogue.[5] Professional facilitation consultants are now regular players in formal stakeholder engagement processes for decision making and planning by governments, nonprofit organizations, and private companies. The "organizational infrastructure for public deliberation" offers clients a diverse selection of trademarked processes, including "21st Century Town Meetings®," "Choice-Dialogues™," "Fast Forum Opinionnaires®," "Citizen Choicework," "Deliberative Polling®," "Consensus Conferences," and "Issues Forums."[6] Sample client lists offered by public deliberation consultants reveal a wide variety of household names, from Fortune 500 companies to industry trade groups to federal agencies to transnational organizations.[7] Such processes are becoming so common that 18 percent of Americans in a 2007 survey had participated in face-to-face or online deliberative problem solving with diverse others over the course of the previous year.[8] A conservative estimate based on the 2009 Dialogue and Deliberation Practitioners Survey puts the cost of such processes at least in the low hundred millions per year.[9] But scholars tend to assume that deliberative reforms are the direct result of a progressive movement to reform politics.

Given the scale of demand for deliberation in organizations of all types, this chapter takes a closer look at the deliberation consulting industry and finds that deliberative reforms are actually marketed to sponsors as civic, socially productive interventions protected from "conventional" business logics, even as they draw on new managerialist discourses long enshrined in the "cultural circuit of capitalism."[10] Public deliberation consultants have been extremely attentive to managing the commercial dimensions of their work. But researchers have generally either dismissed the "business" of deliberation as inconsequential or have feared deliberation's contamination by market forces. The analysis conducted here takes a different approach. Using a multimethod field study of the public deliberation industry, we investigate moral claims about the public deliberation market and its impact on citizens and the public sphere, and we find that both perspectives on markets as destructive and as civilizing play a role in justifying the unique virtues of privately facilitated deliberation as a collective good. This multilayered moralization of the deliberation market reveals the impossibility of distinguishing a pure civic space protected from market incursions in an era in which the boundaries of public, private, and nonprofit sectors are continually blurred in practice.[11]

Moral discourses around public deliberation also reveal the stakes involved in producing ostensibly pure civic spaces, inasmuch as these are the products sought after by paying clients. As top-down civic projects and participatory opportunities become more common, and their production by the deliberation industry becomes more sophisticated, the territory being contested is increasingly that ground in which markets are made civic, and markets in turn create civic space. The production and promotion of these civic spaces by private actors, and those actors' understanding of the imperative to protect such spaces from the market, represent a domain of political life that is not so much new because it is privatized, but new because it represents the private pursuit of political authenticity. Such findings have broad implications for those critics who would write off privately sponsored civic space as "astroturfing" or "democracy, inc."[12] While there is a burgeoning market for "real" utopias, the civic empowerment they produce for different stakeholders must be investigated not just in terms of the extent to which political and economic outcomes are interpenetrated in practice, but also the ways in which they are moralized as distinct. This chapter argues that the particular manner in which public deliberation is civic-ized contributes to its utility as one form of quiet regulation for sponsors.[13]

Moralizing the Market for Deliberation

Deliberative democracy scholars have elaborated three different types of responses to the rise of markets for deliberation and the resulting commercialization of democratic processes, which can be categorized according to Hirschman's typology of perspectives on markets as feeble, civilizing, or destructive.[14] In general, deliberative democracy scholars tend to focus on the political rather than commercial aspects of deliberation, and those scholars who have recognized markets for deliberation in most cases have minimized the potential impact of economic logics on political processes, arguing that professional process production only affects a minor corner of the field and does not represent a significant portion of deliberative practice. The area of disagreement here is in the extent to which deliberation is impervious to the market; as such, these perspectives reflect the conception of markets as feeble.[15] As we will argue, this assumption that markets are irrelevant to politics neglects the ways in which (a) the economic dimensions of deliberative processes are pervasive topics of field discourse and negotiation and (b) understanding the economic and civic outcomes of deliberation in fact requires investigating how those outcomes are negotiated alongside each other in the deliberation market.

In contrast, scholar-practitioners Hendriks and Carson lay out the two civilizing and destructive poles of the debate for those scholars who do raise concerns about market colonization, presenting two scenarios for the rise of deliberative facilitation as an industry, one entailing the "prolific spread of deliberative democracy through market forces" and the other producing "competition resulting in non-deliberative and undemocratic outcomes."[16] While Hendriks and Carson assert that the former, civilizing scenario is more likely, in which deliberation sustains a professional "community of practice" "richer than just a 'marketplace,'" some critics have been far more concerned about the negative implications of a market for deliberative processes, particularly in regard to the commodification of participatory products and services.[17]

David Mosse, both an academic and a practitioner on development projects, critiques the marketing of participatory development agendas and the commodification of participation in a project with which he was involved: "Through skilful public relations the project management succeeded in establishing 'participation' as a technique/commodity and itself as the primary local source and supplier, and reaped the rewards of high-profile visibility, and reputation. . . . What it meant was that participation (ultimately a matter of shifting relations of power) could be formatted, printed, wrapped (sometimes quite literally in coloured tissue paper) and delivered as a gift."[18] Action researchers Kashefi and Mort criticize "the extractive, incidental outputs of the consultation industry":

> This network of academics, market researchers, consultants, trainers, advisors, and public relations workers has an ever-increasing supply of new conferences, training workshops, toolkits, Do-It-Yourself Guides and How-To manuals to promote and sell; it has a plethora of fixed models of consultation that are formulaic and can be learned, packaged, and replicated without being contextualized or situated. The guaranteed output of this process is "the public view" in an unproblematic format, easily digestible by the policy process.[19]

Ryfe similarly describes market-oriented practitioners, who "brandish a dizzying array of tools, guides, handbooks, and methods."[20] Swyngedouw argues that, "while enabling new forms of participation," democratic governance reforms produce a "substantial democratic deficit" because "the democratic character of the political sphere is increasingly eroded by the encroaching imposition of market forces that set the 'rules of the game.'"[21]

Like those who believe that deliberation is inherently resistant to the market, those who believe the market is destructive claim that deliberative and market values are antithetical. A deliberation "industry" is either impossibly ironic or oxymoronic, and it can't produce the civic benefits (such as community building and empowerment) that deliberative democrats seek. As Somers argues, "Pairing social together with capital actually threatens the very social relations upon which social capital depends."[22] Feeble, civilizing, and destructive approaches have been extensively critiqued in the economic sociology literature, but the key point for this analysis is that the researchers and scholar-practitioners cited above apply moral judgments to the deliberation market without attending to how such moral arguments are deployed by industry actors themselves to justify or market their services.

Economic sociologists provide a useful theoretical perspective on understanding and contextualizing the ways in which moral perspectives on markets are deployed in practice. These scholars argue that markets are explicitly "moralized"—an approach that allows researchers to investigate how this is accomplished, and how such processes are entangled with the creation and ongoing development of markets themselves.[23] While much of this research has focused on the extent to which seemingly rationalized markets are actually permeated with struggles over social and moral values, others have investigated those markets for products that are acutely invested with "moral ambivalence," such as life insurance, organ donation, and adoption markets.[24]

This study investigates a market for the idealized political "good" of deliberative democracy, in order to understand the ways in which moral values associated with politics, and particularly ambivalence about the relationship of politics to markets, affect the practical production of political processes.[25] In doing so, we describe an understudied dimension of moralized markets—a "civic-ized" market that is increasingly typical in economic markets for the production of structured events designed to reinvigorate civil society. This politically valenced moralization of markets works through nuanced mechanisms, which involve both the rejection of "conventional" market values and an embrace of "authentic," "responsible" citizenship as critical to profitability. In attempting to understand the "civic-ization" of the deliberation market, the analysis below reveals that industry actors themselves use *both* destructive and civilizing perspectives, often simultaneously, to advance their interests in the field—asserting not a blanket condemnation or uncritical celebration of market interests, but carving out an idealized middle landscape of civic purpose, in which the wild nature of the market and the corrupted humanity of urban politics are tamed by seasoned pastoralists with a calling for deliberation.

Defining the Public Deliberation Industry

In order to contextualize the economic dimensions of public deliberation, it is first necessary to understand the development of a professional industry that is dedicated to public deliberation consulting. The field of professional public deliberation facilitation developed in the United States in the 1990s and 2000s, and it is supported organizationally by two major professional associations; national and community-based foundations; specialized training, certificate, and degree programs; and many smaller methods organizations and academic institutes. The International Association of Public Participation Practitioners, or IAP3, was founded in 1990 with the goal of promoting "the values and best practices associated with involving the public in government and industry decisions which affect their lives."[26] The association changed its name to the International Association of Public Participation, or IAP2, in 1996, to reflect its expanded mission: "an organization which looks beyond the formal practitioner to include all people involved in public participation."[27] With 300 members at its first conference in 1992, the association grew by 2009 to include 921 members in the United States and Canada and another 609 in other countries. The U.S.-based National Coalition for Dialogue and Deliberation, or NCDD, was formed after foundation-sponsored conferences in 2001 and 2002 on engaging communities through D&D (dialogue and deliberation) techniques. Founder Sandy Heierbacher and other conference organizers formed an association of fifty individual and organizational members, which has grown to two thousand members and has inspired similar professional associations in Canada and other countries.[28] NCDD's mission, according to Heierbacher, draws a disparate group of consultants, funders, academics, software developers, and enthusiasts together: "All of us in this field would like to see a future in which every individual has the chance to participate in their communities, in politics, in organizations, and make a difference when it comes to making decisions about things that they care about."[29]

Before describing the methods used to study the public deliberation industry, it is critical to describe briefly the object of analysis and further define key terms. The term "public deliberation" is shorthand for "public dialogue and deliberation," and it is used here to refer to facilitated processes aimed at engaging the public and relevant stakeholders with organizations in more intensive ways than traditional, one-way public outreach and information. Public deliberation processes can range from two-way dialogue meetings to more properly "deliberative" processes, which give lay participants an opportunity to learn about, discuss, and change their preferences regarding policy options. The aggregated input resulting from deliberative processes provides rich information to administrators on participant preferences and, in cases in which decision-making power is turned over to participants, may determine the course of organizational action. The terms "public engagement," "public participation," and "public deliberation" are typically used interchangeably by practitioners in the field to refer to the broad spectrum of reforms aimed at broadening and deepening lay roles in governance.[30] We use the terms "practitioner," "professional," "consultant," and "facilitator" to refer to those actors, whether self-employed or working in a nonprofit or private organization, who are paid to provide facilitation services and products (kits and materials, software and websites, and preference aggregation systems like polling keypads) to client organizations. The term "sponsor" refers to client organizations, but also to third-party organizations, such as foundations, media and real estate development companies, and banks, that may subsidize process facilitation services on behalf of client organizations like public agencies or community-based nonprofits. Sponsors may also underwrite process costs intended to subsidize participant engagement (through stipends, translation and childcare services, or transportation).

Typically, the responsibilities of the public deliberation consulting firm involve the full range of services required for process design and implementation, including production of informational materials, stakeholder outreach and process marketing, selection of process methods, design of topical scope and coverage, recruitment of participants, recruitment and training of volunteer small-group facilitators, overall facilitation and "master of ceremonies" duties, event logistics, continued communication and follow-up with participants, presentation to the client of process outcomes, and evaluation of process efficacy. Some tasks may be outsourced to subcontractors for large projects, but most contractors provide the complete range of process design and facilitation services from inception to evaluation, which may last from a few months, in the case of engagement on pandemic flu–planning priorities, to ten years or more in the case of stakeholder collaborations on long-term processes like contaminated-site remediation. As consultants, public deliberation facilitators move among multiple institutional contexts, communities, and regions. Because of their mobility, this group of organizations and professionals comprises a "portable community" that comes together primarily through online outlets such as listservs, over the phone in teleconferences and online meetings called "webinars," and in face-to-face conferences in business hotel chains and on college campuses.[31]

Methods

This project has employed techniques appropriate for a "deterritorialized ethnography" of an emergent industry characterized by the extensive use of online communities and networks.[32] The first author conducted participant observation between 2006 and 2012 at field sites in major cities across the United States and Canada, in a wide variety of forums for peer-to-peer discussions regarding public engagement practice. To complement this research, informal interviews, analysis of archival documents and images, and a nonrandom online survey of deliberation practitioners were also conducted.[33] As a multimethod field study, analysis involved cross-referencing the many different forms of data collected in different sites and organizational settings in order to confirm that inductive findings from one site or source also surfaced in other sites and among different kinds of actors.[34] Ethnographic research of this kind is ideal for identifying "the logics of particular contexts" and "the strategies through which governance is attempted, experienced, resisted and revised, taken in historical depth and cultural context."[35]

The intent of this methodology is to explore practitioner discourse with each other and with clients and stakeholders regarding the business of deliberative facilitation and the economic, political, and social interests pursued within. As such, it resembles the research focus of Healy and Zelizer in their own analyses of moral rhetoric as articulated by organizations and actors in different industries.[36] Because we have focused our data collection on the industry, the research described here is by no means a comprehensive assessment of changes in economic supply and demand for deliberation facilitation services or a fiscal sociology of deliberation.[37] It does, however, allow for an appreciation of the substantial effort that practitioners invest in framing the civic spaces of deliberation as morally worthwhile and protected from both profit-seeking and politicized interests.

A Community, Not an Industry

Contrary to the assertions of those deliberation scholars who adopt the "feeble markets" perspective, deliberation practitioners are highly interested in the role of the market in their work and regularly discuss with each other and with their clients the relationship between civic logics and business interests. These discourses draw on both civilizing and destructive perspectives on markets, allowing for a closer look at the way practitioners "civic-ize" a market for political process.

Practitioners overwhelmingly describe the deliberation industry as a "community of practice" that rejects commercialism and "slick" "peddling."[38] This perspective mirrors the claims of the scholars described above that market values are destructive of deliberative social relations. In a separate article, we explain how practitioners argue that economic perspectives are inadequate for understanding the complex, long-term benefits of deliberation.[39] Quotes from industry documents like the one that begins this chapter routinely state the incompatibility of participation and economics. Facilitators actively work to prevent the "commodified nightmare" feared by deliberation industry critics, in part through an emphasis on their practice as an evangelical, selfless mission.[40] Intellectual property is shared extensively on listservs, and downloadable books are "all free for the taking."[41] At conferences for dialogue and deliberation professionals, the "free marketplace" ethic borrows extensively from the open source and "free culture" movements, with which there is some crossover among attendees.[42] Consultants volunteer their services extensively, and they self-publish guides and newsletters to promote the larger aims of the "community of practice."[43]

Nevertheless, the sense that greed is incompatible with the community mission of deliberation does not mean that practitioners reject the private sector as a venue for their services. One listserv member who conducts work with private clients says, "It's about engagement . . . the venue is irrelevant."[44] Indeed, deliberation in private settings scrupulously maintains its "civic" framing of citizen-centered discussions around common purpose, providing ammunition to "feeble" markets perspectives that deliberation is not contaminated by market logics even while it has spread to private venues. Graphic facilitation from processes conducted within corporate settings reveals discussions permeated with critiques of "old" ways of doing business in favor of more contemporary, sustainable collaborations among people with "shared" values. One such illustration describes "Fossil Values" in business and government, including the phrases "Free markets are always right" and "Legislation 'He will fix it.'"[45] The "hierarchical," "individual-centric" sense that "someone must lose for someone else to win" is replaced in deliberation by a collaborative spirit, depicted for employees of one oil company by a sketch of men and women holding hands in a circle, around a banner titled "doing whatever it takes . . . together."[46]

For the purposes of this chapter, however, the question is not the extent to which processes actually enhance social capital, creatively challenge convention, or empower stakeholder critiques that deliberation scholars would judge authentic.[47] Instead, this project investigates the ways in which the discourses invoked by practitioners as protecting the civic spirit of deliberation are in fact critical to the marketing of deliberation.[48] As such, the "social value" of privately sponsored deliberation is a readily identifiable product with economic and political value for sponsors, even as practitioners take pride in scrupulously rejecting conventional political and economic logics as "fossil values." A better question regards how the melding of civic rejuvenation and organizational problem solving is negotiated in practice—particularly with respect to how readily "civic" discourses and critiques of "business as usual" familiar in the private sector are adopted in the public sector. The following sections describe the ways in which consultants celebrate the uniqueness and irreducibility of their art, while at the same time embracing business practices and tools that gauge the authenticity of deliberative transformations.

From Consumers to Citizens: Deliberation as a Means of Invoking Civic Transformation

Much of the literature on deliberative democracy has focused on improving process design, and enhanced process design is a major selling point for the added value that deliberation consultants provide to sponsors.[49] In promoting these contributions, practitioners are at pains to assert the civic value of professionally managed democratic interventions, and they do so by balancing claims about the artfulness of their custom designs and the ways in which they revamp a civic space that is currently polluted by a "consumer" orientation on the part of demanding and disengaged publics.

Practitioners emphasize that "good" public deliberation, as opposed to "fake public participation," is distinguished by high-touch, long-term, artfully designed facilitation substantially customized to the needs of individual clients and particular communities.[50] One leading independent facilitator describes his projects in this way: "Every single one of them has its own complexity to it, and every single one— none of them are cookie cutters and none of them are pre-designed. They're all sort of unique in one way or another."[51] One practitioner's website emphasizes the "art" of meeting client needs through good process design: "The organization is our canvas."[52] Another website announces, "We do not offer the same prepackaged solutions to everyone. Our services are tailored to address the unique challenges facing each and every organization."[53]

The demanding settings of "designer democracy" should reflect the "localized democratic vernacular," in contrast to the hollow "public rituals" represented by standard hearings and contentious politics, wherein citizens are treated as passive "customers."[54] In one primer describing "Authentic Public Engagement vs. Business as Usual," a leading organization lays out the connection between inauthentic forms of politics and business:

> To the extent that citizens are considered at all, it is usually as consumers or clients of government.... At worst, cynical, empty public relations gestures prevail, as in the rigged "town meetings" that are so common these days. With participants screened and questions carefully controlled, such counterfeit engagement contributes mightily to the cynicism that is so prevalent among citizens today.[55]

Here, the civic spaces of ordinary politics are framed as contaminated by virtue of being mass produced for passive consumption, with "cynical, empty" PR on government's side mirrored by "cynicism" on the part of citizen-consumers.

"Designer democracy," by contrast, is led by "a host of organizations that are assisting communities with cutting edge processes which are custom-made to fit local contexts," such that "communities are actually branding their unique civic processes as a special feature of community life" with names like "the Hampton Approach" or "the Arlington Way."[56] While by no means the norm in facilitation practice, designer processes produced by boutique consultancies are the state of the art, command the highest premiums in the field, and are highlighted repeatedly as models of good practice in conferences, trainings, and scholarship.[57] The National Research Council's definitive report on public participation in environmental decision making devotes two out of nine chapters to the importance of understanding the contexts of the decision-making and community setting prior to designing a public engagement process.[58] Practically, this takes the form of extensive individual conversations with community members and stakeholders prior to deliberative design, a subject covered intensively in IAP2 public participation certification training.[59]

It also takes the form of integrating the visual and performing arts into processes as a way of introducing a noninstrumental, one-of-a-kind, and creative culture of deliberation, whether through graphic recording of dialogue of the sort described above, musical performances, drumming, collaborative poetry performances, individually painted "peace tiles," or "playback theater." Creative process design should engender the creativity of participants as well; a facilitator dedicated to advancing the use of the "expressive arts" in facilitation describes how "people from all over the world participate in these transformative programs, awakening their creative juices and discovering the authentic self."[60] Participants are encouraged to "move into a left-brain/creative mode" and "leave judgement behind"—both of their own artistic skills and of others, including process organizers.[61]

Group art projects where every participant contributes (a 3×5 index card to a wall mosaic, for example) are a way of reflecting the group back to itself: "Seeing everyone's together creates a sense of community as well, and each person can see themselves in that community."[62] Anyone has the potential to contribute to this kind of community-oriented creativity, including elite and nonelite participants from all kinds of organizations: "with CEOs and high school students, academics and nonprofit boards of directors."[63] In the Open Space process, "People really have the experience of open power. They are in charge—which is the reason the level of spirit and creativity are so high."[64] The transformation of passive consumers into creatively empowered citizens in authentic deliberative processes produces changes in feelings and attitudes. A sense of common interests can inspire deliberators to abandon fixed positions in favor of learning about and acting to implement collaborative solutions for the common good.

These changes are routinely described as intangible or incommensurable and not just because they are "unique" to each individual and each process. How does one measure the value of empowerment, sense of community, changes of heart, lessons learned, soul nourishment, or a feeling of belonging or inspiration to act? Practitioners and scholars go so far as to say that the influence of particular processes on decision making matters less than whether deliberation yields higher-order outcomes: giving participants "equal voice," engendering civic attitudes, and "restoring community and therefore hope."[65] In the words of one foundation-sponsored study, "substance was almost irrelevant" when an intensive, ambitious deliberative process for Katrina survivors delivered what one mayor's aide called "motherhood and apple pie."[66]

Even those who do endorse commensuration emphasize that social outcomes should be central. Gastil argues that, in evaluating deliberative processes, "Exclusive focus on problem-solution analysis, per se, would make our conception of deliberation overly *rationalistic* and overlook the social aspect of deliberation." Instead, evaluators should consider "the wide range of additional benefits for public life that deliberative engagement processes hope to realize . . . from beneficial effects on individual citizen participants to broader impacts on the community or even the larger political culture . . . nearly every deliberative enterprise carries ambitions that extend outward in this way."[67]

Civic Change as a Business Imperative, Accountability as a Civic Imperative

While critiquing business values and the failings of a consumption-oriented model of current politics, practitioners nevertheless invoke contemporary corporate models of accountability and devolved responsibility as providing resources on which to reframe citizen expectations and produce "authentic" attitudinal and behavioral change. To this point, scholars have seen the civic outcomes of deliberation as valuable to sponsors because of their interest in social responsibility, with the side benefit of "reputational capital" gained by sponsoring processes that develop civic capacity. For example, Jacobs and colleagues argue that sponsors are "committed to the public-interest contributions of these forums and to reducing the costs to individuals of engaging in public talking."[68] New research points to the economic rather than social value of the "intangible" civic outcomes of deliberation, certainly not a surprise given that Molotch has long argued that urban-growth proponents reap substantial economic benefits from a "community 'we feeling.'"[69]

The fact that interest in the civic outcomes of deliberation has waxed in two decades marked by severe financial strain is no accident. According to Martin, "Democratic states are likely to grant citizens rights of binding consultation at times of fiscal stress, when intensive state extraction of resources provokes citizen resistance that results in procedural concessions."[70] Lee and Romano argue that not just governments, but also corporations and nonprofit organizations use deliberation when they face "existing or potential resistance to austerity policies" in "corporate reorganization, state retrenchment, and urban redevelopment."[71] Deliberation is economically useful in these settings because it allows sponsors to "pluck more feathers with less squawking,"[72] whether because it provides therapeutic benefits or because it channels citizen action away from costly collective challenges and toward individual commitments to tighten belts and pitch in. On one listserv, a facilitator asking for help with a process in a company facing downsizing is advised to include "the whole organization and see who cares to show up": "If people understand the issues and challenges well, and participate in the grieving process of restructuring, they can deal with the pain of downsizing better."[73] A deliberative guidebook advises those who "want to start creating change right away" or "may feel discouraged by the fact that the kinds of changes you're hoping for may be realized too far into the future": "Have no fear! Here are some things you could do right now, which will soothe your anxieties because you will be doing something to address the issue you deeply care about. But also because the pressure isn't on your shoulders (yet) to organize a large effort or produce systemic community changes."[74] Such hopeful "prospectancy" about change yet to come is a typical attitudinal outcome not just of deliberation but also of the many other forms of "empowerment projects" described by Eliasoph in this volume.

Contention and litigation are expensive; deliberation consultants offer to manage potential mobilization through "quieting of angry publics, small-scale actions in support of administrative goals, and greater tax morale."[75] Deliberative proponents argue that the plague of economic self-interest and political special interests is exactly the reason to undertake a proactive deliberative process:

> Officials fear that the demands of the public, both for spending and for information, will be insatiable. They worry that pressure from special interest groups or self-interested voters will warp the messages coming through. . . . Officials . . . often assume that more democratic engagement will lead to more demands for greater spending, with citizens not considering the trade-offs. In fact, practical experience suggests that consultations where citizens are given opportunities to discuss issues and wider scope to make trade-offs produce much richer and more thoughtful results.[76]

As such, creative participation produces civic changes that are both civically productive *and* profitable. In a British report called "Democracy Pays: How Democratic Engagement Can Cut the Cost of Government," the author argues that "deeper democratic engagement can increase productivity, both in pure economic terms, and in terms of 'civic productivity'—where neighbourhood and social civic action replaces higher-cost state intervention."[77] Saving money is a virtue, not just for its own sake but because it invites citizens to take responsibility for themselves. Despite the fact that slick commercialism and "fake" participation are contrasted with the authenticity of participatory, artistic, customized processes, neoliberal logics of contemporary governance—emphasizing devolved accountability and performance measurement—are key to framing the self-actualizing, expressive performances enacted in deliberation as morally rigorous and worthy of serious consideration.

Stakeholder demands on organizations and governments for rights and services are uncivic, in this framing, because they increase costs for sponsors and encourage "consumer" attitudes. The moral virtues of deliberation are directly linked to this new form of citizen "accountability"—as opposed to a "customer satisfaction" model. A workshop for public officials facing budget challenges teaches that from 1970 to 1999, the model of government that prevailed was a "vending machine" model in which "customer satisfaction" dominated; 2010 to the future is the age of "community as partner" and "citizen accountability."[78] Discourses of citizen accountability, with the associated expectation of measurement to quality standards, may seem odd when participants themselves are being asked to turn off their right, rational brains and suspend judgment. In empowering deliberation attendees to be creative and active participants, sponsors can enact performance measurement routines that commensurate ostensibly just social outcomes; they also invoke a reciprocal accountability from those being engaged for participating as requested.[79] The founder of Open Space argues that "Open Space seems to create an incredible sense of community. The key is, it's a safe space within which people can take authority and responsibility for themselves."[80] In this way, the soft value of "sense of community" is linked not to the virtues of collective action or doing for others, but to creative self-actualization and responsibility for self, individual-level outcomes that can be measured in terms of attitudes toward taxation and volunteering, for example. Creativity is efficient, in the words of one consultancy, which argues that their services are

> an engine for creativity. From beginning to end, our work is infused with the use of multiple intelligences, principles of emergence and the power of play. An exciting environment with engaged participants is created when all of these elements "fire" at the same time leading to unimagined creative *results in record time*.[81]

As the harmonizing of "play" with "results in record time" indicates, business logics are not hostile to creative civic transformations but are framed as civilizing forces that rationalize authentic engagement. As Fleming argues, businesses have embraced personal authenticity and play as informal social control, yielding more effective ways of accomplishing traditional capitalist goals such as labor discipline.[82]

Hendriks and Carson similarly celebrate the development of public engagement accountability standards imported from business as a civilizing potential outcome of a market for deliberation: "A diverse deliberative profession emerges resulting in the development of international standards. Pressure to maintain quality standards rises, leading to a growth in training, accreditation, and independent evaluations of deliberative processes."[83] Independent evaluations ensure that deliberative interventions are "real" and of high quality, systematically yielding to the citizen the empowerment and individual action that deliberation promises. A report on deliberative training offered to public administrators highlights the transformational nature of authenticity on the part of government bureaucrats: "Civic engagement involves 'culture change' and 'authenticity.' . . . There are inherent tensions in the idea of government sponsoring citizens to do what citizens need to do for themselves. When this tension is handled well, public administrators are acting . . . 'authentically.'"[84]

Not surprisingly, given the affective discourses of worker self-actualization in the "cultural circuit of capitalism," business administrators are typically understood to be ahead of the curve in abandoning a passive, consumption-oriented culture in favor of crafting reliably authentic engagement experiences for "citizen" stakeholders.[85] One consultant recommends borrowing from the field of corporate social responsibility (CSR) in terms of commensurating soft outcomes like culture change: "The CSR field while relatively new, has a lot more experience when it comes to reporting and measuring things that are largely intangible. It made me realise that we should look at the lessons from the CSR industry's experience with reporting when we look at how we can implement some evaluation and reporting in our industry."[86] Deliberative methods guidebooks draw on corporate change management models, including Six Sigma, General Electric's WorkOut method, and Ford's Whole-Scale Change method, as models for deliberative process. Similarly, survey respondents report Covey, IBM Jam, Scenario Planning, and other corporate trainings alongside public deliberation trainings like National Issues Forums.[87] Businesses are regularly recruited as partners in supporting efforts to disseminate best practices and to reward accountability; the IAP2 provides event-naming rights and a number of other sponsorship opportunities to businesses for the Association's "Core Values Awards," a celebration of outstanding engagement projects.[88]

The emerging market for online deliberation software is also negotiated in terms of moral discourses that blend civic transformation and economic virtues such as profitability. Such software provides front-end functions that guide participants through participatory budgeting and other deliberative methods online; its back-end functions allow for "fully integrated reporting functions." Here the marketing of commensuration of deliberative outcomes and, in most cases, ranking and surveillance of stakeholders' relative power, resistance-level, and participatory behaviors, is repeatedly highlighted. Even for explicitly disciplinary goals, however, social and economic outcomes are blended, with technologies providing participatory experiences that are both fiscally responsible and civically accountable. For participatory budgeting, a deliberative technique whose diffusion is explored by Baiocchi and Ganuza in this volume, and which is typically studied in terms of its effectiveness in producing indigenous civic capacity, a deliberation software firm advertises that "participatory budgeting is sweeping the globe as the latest best-practice for governance transparency and community engagement."[89] Its proprietary budget allocator is "the most *efficient and risk free* way to get your community participating in planning your budget."[90] A website for "stakeholder engagement evaluation software" asserts that "the software has been designed around the United Nations Brisbane Declaration on Community

Engagement.... This software program is an attempt to make evaluation and the Brisbane Declaration more accessible and easier for practitioners to use in a very practical way." Promised results include the following:

- Improved Outcomes
- Reduced risk
- Greater efficiency
- Lower cost
- Improved decision making
- Clear accountability[91]

An analysis of the use of deliberative engagement software as a market device, and the way in which it may force changes in the marketing and practice of deliberation, is beyond the scope of this chapter.[92] But the fact that the marketing of deliberative software is explicitly grounded in discourses of civic best practices and international public engagement standards is interesting precisely because deliberative software commensurates the outcomes of deliberation in starkly revealing ways.

The use of management software in deliberative projects is advertised as enhancing "stakeholder radar," with proprietary techniques aimed at gauging stakeholders' potential for transformation.[93] Stakeholder management software is advertised as supporting "the assessment of each stakeholder's support for the project (either positive or negative) as well as their receptiveness to messages about the project," which facilitates "a tailored communication plan" that "keep[s] the project and its key stakeholders aligned."[94] New tools integrating deliberative events with communications and research strategies have significantly enhanced the scope of custom-tailored deliberative process management and the scale of ongoing engagement monitoring. But the use of the term "alignment" is not unusual in online discussions among deliberation practitioners, with some version of "align" occurring in 11 percent of all files in the listserv database.[95]

The civic transformations that "real" deliberation produces may be authentically felt and personally empowering for participants even if they are in support of administrators' aims, including saving money and reducing costly forms of contention. However, the fact that deliberative projects produce civic authenticity as an intentional outcome should not be uncritically celebrated before realizing that the "social profits" of deliberation have economic and political value for sponsors. Discourses of moral virtue in deliberation look very similar to ideological trends occurring in contemporary business, regardless of how much "old" ways are criticized. The collective good in such processes is redefined in terms of whether civic discourse and citizen actions reflect administrator priorities and economic efficiency, which may shift the direction of civic capacity away from critical forms of social change, even as it enhances civic capacity and cultures that reward citizen action. Simply determining which processes are "real" or "good" deliberation versus which are "bad" will not suffice, inasmuch as the value of processes to clients stems from the social and civic productivity and demonstrable accountability they are able to claim.

When Good Citizenship Means Financial Sacrifice: Deliberative Anticommercialism and the Selling of Political Authenticity

> What is clear is that we have reached a point in which the kind of divides that kept capitalists and anti-capitalists apart are not easily separated linguistically and, in some cases, even practically.... In other words, capitalist firms are increasingly utilizing the weapons of the weak—contextual fleeting practices—to make themselves strong.
>
> —Nigel Thrift[96]

Deliberation facilitators with a personal commitment to the production of transformative, authentic experiences on the part of citizen stakeholders pursue such outcomes despite the professional risks involved in alienating clients, and they often perform volunteer facilitation at personal cost to their own livelihoods. Such actions indicate that the pursuit of profit is not the sole, or even the primary, motivation for deliberation practitioners—and deliberation scholars who focus on practitioners' self-sacrifice and passionate evangelism can be excused for understanding deliberative innovation as a progressive reform movement. But unpacking the multiple ways in which deliberation consultants construct their activities as morally meaningful provides traction on the complex nature of specifically civic moral markets. The construction of a civic-ized market for facilitated deliberation in particular may have consequences not only for conventional economic aims such as profitability but also for political, social, and economic equality.

This chapter takes up such a challenge in two ways. First, we articulate that practitioners' moral discourses of "destructive" and "civilizing" practices—their simultaneous embrace of anticommercialism and accountability—both have their roots in the contemporary "cultural circuit of capitalism" defined by Boltanski and Chiapello, Thrift, and others. Second, scholars of deliberation should avoid distinguishing "bad"/commercialized or "good"/civic-ized deliberation in favor of paying attention to the ways in which the moral framing of the deliberation market as civic is itself a mechanism for greater market attachment and enhanced, if "quiet," management of publics—and not just on behalf of capitalist firms, as Thrift suggests in the above quote.[97] Authentic civic action and enhanced technologies of management are by no means mutually exclusive, nor is their creative combination restricted to civic-ized settings in the private sector. This finding corresponds with recent research, including Martin's in this volume, investigating the fiscal and managerial implications of deliberation as it has been employed in particular historical contexts.[98]

The protective halo reserved for deliberation as a "real utopian" political activity has kept deliberation from being considered alongside other forms of stakeholder management and public relations, except as an idealized alternative.[99] Removing that halo to research deliberation's moral claims allows us to make connections with scholarship investigating the normative practices and larger consequences of other forms of subsidized participation, citizen empowerment, and civic partnerships.[100]

This task is even more urgent because scholars outside of this volume have yet to connect these democratizing practices and their potentially regressive outcomes in a systematic way, despite the fact that there is evidence that deliberation is used strategically in tandem with the grassroots lobbying described by Walker, the digital campaigning described by Kreiss, and other top-down "empowerment projects" as described by Eliasoph.[101] Inasmuch as researchers have a moral obligation to engaged publics in their studies of deliberation in action, it is less to make deliberative empowerment ideals "work" better in practice than to imagine more ambitious opportunities for the "systems change" that deliberation repeatedly offers, and rarely delivers—even, and especially, when it works as promised.

NOTES

1. Involve (2005).
2. Fung and Wright (2003a); Wright (2010).
3. Vogel (1989); Evans and Boyte (1992); Crenson and Ginsberg (2002); Wolin (2010).
4. Walker, McQuarrie, and Lee (this volume).
5. Lee and Romano (2013).
6. Jacobs, Cook, and Delli Carpini (2009: 136).
7. These include 3M, Abbott Laboratories, Allstate, Altria Group, American Express, American Red Cross, AstraZeneca, AT&T, Autotrader, Coca Cola, Cisco, the Clinton Global Initiative, the Consumer Electronics Association, Eastman Chemical, the Enterprise Foundation, the Environmental Protection Agency, Exxon, FedEx, the Food and Drug Administration, the Federal Emergency Management Agency, the U.S. Government Accountability Office, Georgia Pacific, Girl Scouts of America, GlaxoSmithKline, the International Monetary Fund, Kraft, Macy's, SAP America, Shell Chemical, Sierra Club, State Farm, Sun Microsystems, Sun Trust Bank, Teradata, the United Nations, United Way, the U.S. Postal Service, World Bank, and the World Economic Forum.
8. National Conference on Citizenship (2007: 17). In a 2003 survey, Jacobs, Cook, and Delli Carpini found that 25 percent of American adults sampled had participated in a "face-to-face deliberation" on a public issue (2009: 37); the percentage in this survey is likely higher due to the fact that this question did not require deliberation to occur at a "meeting" or with others with diverse views.
9. Lee and Romano (2013).
10. Thrift (2005). Thrift describes this cultural circuit as an "extraordinary discursive apparatus" including "business schools, management consultants, management gurus and the media," yielding "continual critique of capitalism, a feedback loop which is intended to keep capitalism surfing along the edge of its own contradictions" (6).
11. de Bakker et al. (2013).
12. Fligstein (1996); Giraudeau and Gond (2008).
13. Earl (2003); Tepper (2009).
14. Hirschman (1982).
15. Hirschman (1982); Fourcade and Healy (2007).
16. Hendriks and Carson (2008: 305).
17. Hendriks and Carson (2008: 304).
18. Mosse (2003: 57).
19. Kashefi and Mort (2004: 300).
20. Ryfe (2007: 3).

21. Swyngedouw (2005: 1991).
22. Somers (2005: 220).
23. Fourcade and Healy (2007).
24. Zelizer (1979); Cetina and Preda (2004); Healy (2006); Quinn (2008: 740).
25. As in the deliberation literature, scholars of politics who address market influences typically assume the "destructive markets" perspective, with arguments fearing the commercialization and commodification of public life through media conglomerates and interest groups. The approach used in this chapter draws on the work of recent institutional scholars such as Walker (2009) and Kreiss (2012) on the extent to which markets and technologies may produce civic opportunities at the same time that they channel them in particular directions.
26. Database files. All database files are stored electronically by the first author.
27. Database files.
28. Database files.
29. Interview with first author, September 24, 2006.
30. Leighninger notes that "in common usage, 'deliberation and democratic governance' = active citizenship = deliberative democracy = citizen involvement = citizen-centered work = public engagement = citizen participation = public dialogue = collaborative governance = public deliberation. Different people define these terms in different ways—and in most cases, the meanings are blurry and overlapping" (2009b: 5). While public "consultation" connotes one-way processes in the United States, in the Commonwealth countries, it generally connotes more deliberative methods.
31. Chayko (2008). A 2009 membership survey by the IAP2 found that 68 percent of respondents preferred to communicate with the association through an online method (N = 169; database files).
32. Merry (2000: 130).
33. See Lee (2011) for more information on data collection, coding, and limitations.
34. Charmaz (2006).
35. Scheppele (2004: 390–391).
36. Zelizer (1979); Healy (2006).
37. For economic supply and demand, see Hendriks and Carson (2008) for a chart of the growth of privately facilitated processes over time; for a related fiscal sociology, see Martin, this volume.
38. Lee, McNulty, and Shaffer (2013). This chapter is adapted from Lee's forthcoming book and from Lee, McNulty, and Shaffer (2013).
39. Lee, McNulty, and Shaffer (2013).
40. Fourcade and Healy (2007: 286).
41. Database files.
42. Kelty (2008).
43. Lee, McNulty, and Shaffer (2013).
44. Database files.
45. Database files.
46. Database files. All quotes are extracted from examples of graphic facilitation.
47. The question of whether deliberation as practiced meets normative ideals as developed in political theory has preoccupied deliberation researchers (Thompson 2008) to the exclusion of an investigation of the ways in which "real" deliberation, practiced with scrupulous attention to remedying inequality and challenging authority, might be useful

in particular historical and institutional settings in managing or marginalizing the challenges it produces. Not incidentally, deliberative democratic theory is a useful validation tool in these efforts (Mutz 2008).
48. Boltanski and Chiapello (2005); Thrift (2005).
49. Baiocchi (2003: 69).
50. Snider (2010).
51. Interview transcript.
52. Database files.
53. Database files.
54. Mills (2007).
55. Center for Advances in Public Engagement (2008).
56. Mills (2007: 12).
57. Lee (2011).
58. Dietz and Stern (2008).
59. For this reason, "high-quality" deliberative processes actually move stakeholder grievances out of public view; most, but by no means all, stakeholders are willing to trade increased decision-making power for less access to public claims making (Lee 2007). Note that this relocation of politicized negotiation is accompanied by an increase in creative expression, as described in the next paragraph.
60. Database files.
61. Database files.
62. Database files.
63. Database files.
64. Database files.
65. Lukensmeyer (2007: 9). Lee and Romano (2013) provides a case study of scholarly and practitioner perspectives on outcomes in a specific process.
66. Williamson (2007: 24).
67. Gastil (2008: 7), emphasis mine.
68. Jacobs et al. (2009: 147).
69. Molotch (1976: 314).
70. Martin, this volume.
71. Lee and Romano (2013: 742).
72. Zacharzewski (2010).
73. Database files.
74. Database files.
75. Lee and Romano (2013: 748).
76. Zacharzewski (2010: 3–4).
77. Zacharzewski (2010: 8).
78. Database files.
79. See Gastil (2008) on evaluation of social outcomes; see Espeland and Stevens (1998) and Lampland and Star (2009) on commensuration.
80. Database files.
81. Database files, emphasis ours.
82. Fleming (2009).
83. Hendriks and Carson (2008: 305).
84. Database files.
85. Thrift (2005).

86. Database files.
87. Lee and Polletta (2009).
88. That business support for accountability and performance measurement has reputational value might provoke cynicism from "hostile markets" critics. Nevertheless, the Core Values Awards are so rigorous that no awardee was selected for Organization of the Year in 2009 because none of the organizations entered met the IAP2 award committee's standards.
89. On participatory budgeting, see Baiocchi (2003; this volume).
90. Database files.
91. Database files.
92. Callon, Millo, and Muniesa (2007).
93. Database files.
94. Database files.
95. N = 8,473.
96. Thrift (2005: 4).
97. McFall (2009).
98. Hajer (2005); Segall (2005); Head (2007); Maginn (2007); Hendriks (2009).
99. Wright (2010).
100. Boyle and Silver (2005); Soule (2009); Walker (2009); Kreiss (2012).
101. Eliasoph (2011).

CHAPTER 3

Workers' Rights as Human Rights?
Solidarity Campaigns and the Anti-Sweatshop Movement

STEVEN VALLAS, J. MATTHEW JUDGE,
AND EMILY R. CUMMINS

Globalization has confronted workers' movements with strategic challenges from many directions at once.[1] The spread of neoliberal economic policies; the advent of powerful logistic, transportation, and information technologies; and the worldwide dominance of export-oriented industrialization strategies have all combined to drain substantial power from workers' movements across the advanced capitalist world.[2] Adding to labor's difficulties have been new organizational models that invite large firms to engage in a surge of out-sourcing and off-shoring, generating global supply chains that cannot easily be regulated by any single nation-state. Under these conditions, it can hardly be surprising that union membership and strike rates have sharply fallen in most of the developed world, that productivity increases often surpass wage gains, and that violations of labor and employment law have apparently grown more common.[3] And although aggregate trends are difficult to capture empirically, evidence has begun to emerge that the growth of export-oriented economic strategies, which tie the fate of developing nations to the global marketplace, have led to a sharp erosion of workers' rights, especially in Latin America, Africa, and the Caribbean.[4]

But globalization has also had a second effect that, on the face of it, is potentially empowering: the growth of public awareness and concern for the conditions of existence and human rights abuses faced by people living in distant corners of the world. Some of the most prominent examples of such concern are the anti-apartheid movement that targeted corporate investment in South Africa; efforts to respond to famine in Biafra and other parts of Africa; solidarity work during the Salvadoran civil war; and movements to stop the genocide and kindred atrocities in Rwanda, Bosnia, and Darfur. These and many other movements supporting human rights have quite clearly resonated with much of the American public, generating a pool of social movement participation (and, more broadly, normative support) that has fueled boycotts, petition drives, the fair trade movement, and countless "name and shame" campaigns that have engaged students, rank-and-file workers, human rights activists, labor leaders, members of religious communities, and other movement participants.

These movements have shed light on the most egregious conditions that face workers and other vulnerable groups throughout much of the developing world. They have also drawn attention to the resurgence of sweatshops in the United States as well.[5] Yet, alongside these gains, there has also emerged an ongoing debate concerning the nature of the movements at hand. At issue are the consequences that flow from the convergence of two social movement traditions—those specific to the workers' and human rights movements—that had previously been distinct. This convergence of social movement frames would, of course, seem to be a mutually beneficial relationship. The global orientation of the human rights movement has enabled activists to draw attention to the spread of forced labor in various regions of the world.[6] And for their part, the workers' movement has often placed training, personnel, political leverage, and legal resources at the service of highly vulnerable populations, deepening transnational ties in ways that would seem unproblematic. At a deeper level, however, can be found sharp differences in the organizing principles that govern the human rights and workers' movements, bringing to light what many commentators have come to view as hidden dangers and constraints that might well take their revenge on the ability of these movements to achieve their goals.[7]

Participants in this debate have sometimes fastened on tactical questions, as when labor activists challenge the wisdom of relying on retail-based strategies that subject designer brands to "name and shame" campaigns.[8] As some have suggested, such tactics may only propound a seemingly radical form of consumerism, while playing into the hands of large corporations with abundant budgets for advertising and brand management. At its heart, however, this debate hinges on a deeper question: whether or not the adoption of human rights discourse, strategies, and tactics might inadvertently collide against the needs and traditions of the workers' movement, whether in the United States or abroad.[9] Indeed, in the view of a widening circle of critics, the human rights frame stands at odds with many of the most fundamental concerns of the workers' movement generally—most notably, its emphasis on collective rights, on class struggles, and on the need to empower workers at the point of production itself.[10] According to its critics, while participation in human rights campaigns may generate the feel-good experience of solidarity for movement participants, features of the human rights movement may, when uncritically embraced, undermine the pursuit of collective bargaining by workers in the developing world (as when factory inspections become a surrogate for union organizing). If so, the danger is that the infusion of human rights orientations into the anti-sweatshop movement may inadvertently reproduce the very inequalities its members claim to reject.

Is this the case? Has the effort to conjoin the workers' and human rights movements had problematic effects? Previous efforts to address the question have been limited by their reliance on small and often highly selective case study methods. Such research strategies, of course, remain indispensable tools. They sensitize us to the meanings, identities, and experiences that develop within local struggles, and they provide a fine-grained analysis of the social and political contexts in which workers live. What has been missing from previous studies, however, is any effort to draw conclusions that might capture the full swath of anti-sweatshop movements and the convergence of human rights and workers' rights movements more generally. In this chapter, we begin to take steps in this broader direction. Using existing ethnographies and archival data from ten anti-sweatshop campaigns that center on apparel workers in Central

America, we aim to weigh the conflicting claims made by adherents in this debate, thereby assessing the consequences that have in fact flowed from the convergence of previously distinct social movement frames. Though our findings are preliminary in important respects, they are instructive—and complex. We do indeed find instances in which tensions have emerged among the forms of leadership, strategies, and goals embraced by human rights and labor movement activists. At times, a naïve embrace of human rights discourse and practices has seemed to peripheralize the concerns held by workers in foreign contexts, even operating at odds with strategies that might empower foreign workers at the point of production itself. At the same time, however, we also find evidence that solidarity movements have often been able to learn from and surmount these tensions. Key, we suggest, is the capacity of privileged groups to develop a reflexive awareness of the challenges that accompany consumer-based movements, forming social alliances and hybrid forms of activism that can overcome (rather than blindly reproduce) the inequalities that solidarity campaigns seek to address.

The Debate

It is difficult to sketch the general logic that underlies human rights and workers' rights movements, given the enormous differences that have historically characterized both traditions over time.[11] Still, without essentializing either movement, it seems possible to delineate four abiding distinctions that have often emerged between human rights and workers' rights movements.[12]

1. Human rights movements are almost by definition universalizing; that is, they apply to *all* human beings, regardless of their social positions or geographic locale. By contrast, workers' movements generally seek to advance rights that are specific to the members of a particular social class. This difference has strategic consequences, for it leads to very different conceptions of movement practices. For human rights campaigns, success rests on the effort to attenuate the boundaries between members of distinct collectivities. For workers' movements, however, success depends precisely on the effort to *delineate* such boundaries, emphasizing the conflicting interests and needs that attach to occupants of different social positions.

2. Human rights movements have generally focused on *the state*, viewing it either as a defender or enforcer of fundamental human rights or as a perpetrator of human rights abuses. Though there are, of course, many exceptions here, the point remains that human rights movements have largely been concerned with establishing legal protections of one kind or another, while only seldom raising questions involving property rights and the distribution of wealth. While workers' movements have never been blind to the state, they have typically fastened on the distribution of power within *civil society* itself. Key to the workers' movement have been the rights to organize, to strike, to establish collective bargaining, and to defend one's economic needs within the sphere of production as such.

3. Relatedly, most human rights theorists operate with a juridical conception of the individual citizen, a reflection perhaps of their intellectual debts to liberal political theory. For their part, workers' movements are almost by definition fastened on the rights of the *collectivity*, in turn an outgrowth of the influence that socialist thinking has exerted in its domain.
4. Human rights movements tend to fasten on the enforcement of rights through the enactment of protective statutes (such as laws banning child labor). Again, although workers' movements have often supported such efforts, they have placed greater priority on mechanisms that enable workers to defend themselves, rather than relying on legal protections emanating from the state. Key to workers' movements, in other words, has been the effort to build organizational arrangements that equip workers to enforce their rights directly and on their own behalf, typically at the level of the workplace, firm, or industry.

It is one thing to delineate abstract theoretical differences. But it is quite another to determine whether these differences have material effects on actually existing struggles. These questions must therefore be asked: Does the coevolution of the two movement frames entail important risks, with human rights thinking diverting workers' movements down paths that weaken such movements' ability to challenge social inequalities? What consequences seem to flow from the commingling of the discourses, strategies, and tactics that are invoked by these previously distinct social movements?

It seems possible to identify three discrete positions on these questions in the scholarly literature. *Advocates* of the convergence of the two social movements perceive unalloyed benefits from the convergence of the two social movement frames. Representative here is the work of Compa, who sees much to be gained when labor groups invoke the human rights frame.[13] Compa is the author of an influential report, written for Human Rights Watch, which used the human rights lens to interpret the myriad shortcomings of workers' rights within the United States. His argument holds that the human rights organizing frame can infuse a newfound moral energy and normative authority into the workers' movement, broadening the latter's focus beyond the instrumentalities that business unionism pursues.

> So long as worker organizing, collective bargaining, and the right to strike are seen only as economic disputes involving the exercise of power in pursuit of higher wages for employees or higher profits for employers, change is unlikely. Reformulating these issues as human rights concerns can begin a process of change.[14]

The notion here is that the human rights frame can redress some of the deficiencies that have engulfed the labor movement, restoring the energy and global vision the workers' movement sorely needs if it is to confront an increasingly global adversary. Put differently, advocates find the appeal of the human rights frame to lie in its ability to provide newfound sources of normative support for a movement that has increasingly been seen as insular and self-serving.[15]

A second, more guarded (or *wary*) perspective sees a partial truth in this position, but it registers important concerns about the long-term implications of the movement convergence. As Kolben put it, "While strategic deployment of human rights discourse might appear to be advantageous in the short run, the fundamental differences between this discourse and that of labor rights may inhibit the long-term effectiveness of this approach."[16] Kennedy goes further, in an essay entitled "The International Human Rights Movement: Part of the Problem?"[17] He characterizes the human rights frame as a potentially corrosive influence that papers over the very structural inequalities that generate vulnerable populations in the first place.

Perhaps the fullest expressions of this wary posture toward the human rights frame can be found in the work of theorists such as Espenshade, Rodriguez-Garavito, and Seidman.[18] Espenshade, for example, fears that the anti-sweatshop movement has inaugurated a "new paternalism in labor relations" in which "workers are 'protected' rather than empowered; consumers are placated; and transnational companies maintain their power and profits."[19] Monitoring alone does not challenge global production systems, she writes; it "neither alters the structural conditions under which sweatshops flourish, nor allows workers to address their own exploitation."[20] And because of their human rights heritage, human rights movements often fail to anticipate the class-based pressures that are brought to bear on monitoring agencies, whose independence is constantly under siege by powerful corporations.

Rodriguez-Garavito develops a parallel argument, drawing a sharp and especially important distinction between the human rights concern for "protective" rights and the concern on the part of the workers' movement for what he terms "enabling" rights. The idea here is that anti-sweatshop movements have borrowed so heavily from the human rights frame that they often fail to advocate reforms that would empower workers, equipping them to express their own voice and defend their own rights in an organizationally durable way.

Seidman's analysis bears special consideration here. She focused particular attention on three relatively successful instances in which "concerns over labor issues were in each case reframed as human rights issues."[21] She found important cause for concern and identified two problems that she believes are inherent in this convergence of social movement frames. First, in their effort to garner public attention, transnational labor activists tend to fasten on the most sensational and egregious cases in which workers' rights have been violated—typically those involving physical harm, violence against workers, or the use of child labor—as a means of gaining public sympathy. This diverts attention away from the most pressing issues that foreign workers confront; also, it casts workers as defenseless "victims who are vulnerable to 'global pillage' and dependent on outside support" (Seidman 2007: 32, 34). This symbolic construction may win public sympathy for solidarity work, but it simultaneously acts to reinforce the vulnerability of the very groups that activists claim to support.

The second conclusion Seidman draws also warrants close scrutiny. In her view, anti-sweatshop campaigns have adopted a reading of global capitalism that is ill-equipped to advance the movement for workers' rights. Because activists have recently grown convinced that globalization has generated a "thinning" of the state, they have adopted a consumer-based emphasis on the *private* regulation of labor regimes, as if monitoring organizations might do the work of the nation-state. In her view, this strategy is inherently self-defeating, for it abandons the democracy-building powers that local states can and do exert. Rather than depending entirely on independent monitoring systems, she counsels a broader strategy that brings the state back into the picture.[22]

A third, still more *critical* view of the convergence of human rights and workers' rights movements adopts the most skeptical posture of all. The notion here is that this convergence represents an infusion of utopian, middle-class biases into the workers' movement in ways that threaten only to reproduce (however subtly) the very inequalities that movement participants bemoan. This perspective is not easily captured, given sharp differences in the intellectual influences on which adherents draw. Thus, this view is held by defenders of traditional trade unionism, who are put off by human rights activists' seeming willingness to allow independent monitoring to substitute for independent trade unionism and collective bargaining arrangements.[23] The critical view is sometimes advanced by Marxists, who reject the liberal-utilitarian lineage of the human rights tradition.[24] It includes moral philosophers such as Alistair McIntyre, who rejects the Realist ontology of much human rights thinking on the grounds that "there are no such rights, and belief in them is one with belief in witches and unicorns."[25] The critical view is also held by poststructuralists like Brooks, who challenge the radical credentials of anti-sweatshop activists by showing the ways in which their campaigns implicitly conform to contours of the global capitalist commodity chains that activists nominally oppose.[26]

Brooks uses as her empirical referents anti-sweatshop campaigns in El Salvador, Bangladesh, and New York City. Three points anchor her argument. First, she speaks of a structural congruence between global supply chains and anti-sweatshop campaigns. In her view, both are heavily consumer-based, both center on brand management, and both place marketing at the center of their respective strategies. Because *buying* is the hinge on which both action systems depend, she argues, the focus of anti-sweatshop campaigns tends to shift away from the shop floor, as "privileged agency is given to consumers of signs and commodities."[27] Second, she argues that transnational solidarity campaigns are typically dominated by activists in the global north. When this is the case, "older imperial and colonial relations are drawn on, reproduced, and often reinforced *even though the explicit goal of the organizers is stated to be otherwise.*"[28] Finally, much like retailers and their contractors, transnational activists "employ" sweated labor as "raw materials" (as when foreign workers are brought to the importing country and asked to give testimonials).[29] Thus "the transnational structure of the campaigns," which emulates the structure of global capitalism, "limits in many ways the extent to which they are able to address labor rights and change conditions on the shop floor."[30] However radical in appearance, then, *anti-sweatshop campaigns ingest such sizeable doses of consumerist logic that they undermine their capacity to effect social structural change*. It seems highly problematic, then, to view anti-sweatshop activism as necessarily advancing the cause of egalitarian social relations.

It is certainly possible to evaluate the theoretical cogency of these three postures quite apart from empirical evidence. For example, the "advocacy" posture seems largely driven by pragmatic considerations, as if the workers' movement might derive enhanced support and improved moral credentials by adopting the language and tactics of the human rights tradition. As such, it seems to pay insufficient heed to the tensions and schisms that often occur when social movements embrace competing frames (as occurred in the collision between the civil rights and feminist movements in the 1960s and 1970s, to take but one example). Without sufficient reflexivity and circumspection, in other words, dangers may be too easily smuggled unnoticed into anti-sweatshop movements, whose outcomes may thereby be put at risk. For their part, "wary" analysts sometimes seem equally vulnerable to theoretical critique. This is especially true of Seidman, who counsels much greater reliance on state regulation than the anti-sweatshop movement has embraced. Yet her position seems to abstract away from cross-national variations in the nature of state institutions. Arguably, a state-centered strategy might make sense in some contexts (e.g., in the hand-woven rug industry, where production is heavily concentrated in India and Bangladesh), but not in others (such as the global apparel industry, where production is far more spatially dispersed and highly mobile).[31] Moreover, to rely on a state-centered strategy as a means of humanizing neoliberalism, as Seidman does, is to neglect the political context of repression that characterizes so many regimes in the developing world. Moreover, in many parts of Latin America, *autonomista* movements have tended to refuse state-centered politics in favor of direct action strategies that seek to expand workers' and peasants' independence *from* the state.[32] Finally, for its part, the critical perspective runs the risk of exaggerating the degree to which solidarity work inadvertently mimics consumer capitalism, mistaking a caricature for an accurate portrait. Ironically, many of the arguments that Brooks develops (e.g., her critique of U.S. legislation that banned the importation of products made with child labor) are *also* cited by Bhagwati, one of the more virulent defenders of global capitalism.[33]

The key question to be addressed, however, is empirical. What *has* been the result of this confluence of social movement frames? To put it baldly: Has participation in the anti-sweatshop movement taken real steps to challenge the most egregious instances of unfree labor that global capitalism has spawned? Or has it instead uncritically embraced movement traditions that have limited the movement's efficacy, fostered internal tensions with it, or even generated a feel-good species of left-wing consumerism that in effect reproduces the very class inequalities that global capitalism has wrought? Answering these questions requires that we move beyond the limitation in the existing literature that we identified above: its reliance on small and often highly selective case studies. What is needed is a more inclusive and comparative, multisited approach that can generate a broader portrait of the patterns and experiences that movement participation has produced. This chapter cannot claim to have achieved that goal, but it does represent an initial step in this much-needed direction.

Grounding the Analysis

In this chapter, we limit our concerns to Latin/Central American and Caribbean *maquilas* in the apparel and footwear industry, in effect holding constant both industry and region. In selecting cases for analysis, we have looked for solidarity campaigns that have generated substantive documentation, whether in the form of published ethnographies, journalistic or judicial accounts, or coverage on the websites or blogs maintained by such solidarity groups as United Students Against Sweatshops (USAS), the Maquila Solidarity Network (MSN), SweatFree Communities (SFC), the Worker Rights Consortium (WRC), and the International Labor Rights Forum. Especially helpful has been access to the archives—mainly, correspondence, flyers, and reports—maintained by SFC, a prominent solidarity group with offices in Massachusetts. In addition, we also conducted in-depth interviews with four key informants who have participated in solidarity campaigns that were led by USAS, MSN, and SFC.

The initial selection of cases for inclusion began with the literature review phase. Beginning with key concepts often used in the literature, we searched for papers and articles using such terms as "transnational advocacy campaigns," "boomerang strategy," "human rights framing," and "workers' rights framing."[34] Our searches on Google Scholar and Ebsco Host included these terms and identified empirical cases in the journalistic or scholarly literature involving transnational advocacy campaigns. Based on the ethnographic accounts that emerged in these searches, we focused on cases centering on apparel production processes within Central America (including Mexico), in order to control for region. We included only cases involving transnational solidarity work that utilized the transnational "boomerang strategy" outlined by Keck and Sikkink's influential work.[35] Based on these search criteria, our initial search identified four fairly well-documented campaigns to protect the rights of apparel workers in Central America. Further analysis of the SweatFree Communities archives and the Maquila Solidarity Network website identified an additional six cases that met our criteria. Tables 3.1 and 3.2 provide an overview of these ten campaigns, broken down by the outcome (favorable/unfavorable) that unfolded at each.

Three of our ten cases involved apparel plants located in Honduras, while two were in Guatemala, another two in Nicaragua, and one each in Mexico, El Salvador, and the Dominican Republic. With two exceptions (Phillips Van Heusen and Russell Athletic), all worked as contractors for such brand-name retailers as Nike, the Gap, Reebok, Liz Claiborne, Wal-Mart, and J.C. Penney. Interestingly, four of these cases (Choishin, Chentex, Kimi, and Kukdong) involved Korean contractors, a common pattern in the Central American apparel industry—and one that often heightens the boundary between local workers and foreign-based employers.[36] Although each case involved a distinctive series of events, there are certain broad commonalities. Workers in the exporting countries encountered material deprivations in one or another form (e.g., extremely low wages, endemic sexual harassment, unhealthy working conditions, forced overtime, or unduly long working days). When they mobilized against such conditions, their efforts were typically blocked—for example, through mass firings (as at Chentex in Nicaragua and Kukdong in Mexico) or through police intimidation or violence (as at NLC-Gap). Their struggles then escalated. In the NLC-Gap case, for example, the workers' struggle first led to a strike and factory occupation that (following police violence) eventually exploded into a solidarity strike that won support from all five thousand workers throughout the entire San Marcos export processing zone.[37]

Table 3.1. Ten Solidarity Campaigns in the Central American Apparel Industry: Favorable Outcomes

Case	Alta Gracia	Calypso	Choishin	Kukdong	NLC-Gap	Russell
Factory and Location	Alta Gracia, Dominican Republic	Calypso Factory, Masaya, Nicaragua	Choishin, located near Guatemala City, Guatemala	Kukdong Factory, Puebla, Mexico	San Marcos EPZ in El Salvador	Russell Factory, Honduras
Plant Owner and Contractor	Now: Knights Apparel. Previous owners (BJ&B) supplied Nike, Reebok.	Argus Group, supplies Dickies, Cintas, and Lan Dau.	Choishin supplies Liz Clairborne.	Kukdong, supplies Nike and Reebok.	Mandarin, supplies The Gap.	Fruit of the Loom (owns Russell Athetic), supplies Jerzees.
Labor Issues	Unfair labor practices, harassment of unionists, severance pay owed to wrongfully terminated workers.	Unfair labor practices, harassment of union leaders.	Forced overtime, low wages, and ongoing physical abuse.	Low wages, illegally withheld earnings, abusive supervision, rancid food, child labor.	Low wages, endemic sexual harassment, and unsanitary conditions.	Harassment of union workers, low wages, unfair production targets.
Initial Mobilization and Response	Union organizes in the D.R.. USAS engaged in long-term organizing to establish living wages and fair labor standards.	Initial unionizing campaign met with firing of union organizers and a 'closed' governmental structure for redress.	Initial unionizing campaign was met by firings, violence, and death threats.	Workers occupied the plant. In response, Mexican authorities raided the factory and used violence and threats against hundreds of workers.	Unionizing blocked by police violence. Workers occupy the plant, and 5,000 workers throughout the EPZ walk out in solidarity.	Unionizing drive undermined by coercive pacts that penalized workers for union support.
"Boomerang" Effort	Unionists appeal to USAS, which leads university based naming and shaming campaign against Nike and Reebok. Organizing effort by former BJ&B unionists. USAS led to reopening of the factory under new ownership.	Local unionists form alliance with WRC, SweatFree Communities, and UNITE, which target Cintas brand for shaming. This wins concessions from Argus.	COVERCO helps union connect with MSN, AFL-CIO, who pressure the US trade representative to pressure Guatemala using trade privileges as lever.	AFL-CIO, USAS, WRC, and human rights groups run naming and shaming campaigns against Nike. Nike pressures Kukdong to recognize union and accept collective bargaining.	NLC runs naming and shaming campaign against Gap who pressured Mandarin Apparel.	CGT (local Honduran union) reaches out to WRC, USAS, Clean Clothes Campaign (CCC), MSN, which pressures retailers and Honduran government.
Outcome	Conditions greatly improved; wages now triple local industry standards. Alta Gracia has become a "brand" in itself.	Workers reinstated and given back pay. Union recognized.	Conditions have materially improved but union remains weak.	Child labor eliminated and Union recognized. Workers reinstated but wages unchanged.	Union recognized. Wages have marginally increased. Working conditions greatly improved.	Russell signs union contract, re-hires workers, increases wages.

More typically, workers sought out help from local activists and nongovernmental organizations (NGOs), who put them in touch with transnational activists in the global north. In some cases, solidarity organizations conducted field trips to establish networks of support. In other cases, the activist organization maintained offices in Central America and used its presence to maintain ties with workers and local unions in the exporting nation. By the late 1990s, activists were able to use email, cell phones, Skype, and (more recently) social media to stay in touch and to share information and strategic discussions. All of these cases found activists invoking the rhetoric and practices of the human rights tradition, mobilizing "name and shame" campaigns (among other tactics) that threatened the reputational capital of the retailer, thereby holding the company accountable for its supplier's behavior.

Our analysis of these ten cases centers on three specific dimensions of these solidarity campaigns. We pose our questions from the standpoint of the "wary" and "critical" accounts, which warn of the dangers the human rights perspective may bring to bear on indigenous workers' struggles as such.

1. *The origins and locus of strategic leadership.* Here we ask: While participating in these solidarity campaigns, did activists in the global north come to play especially central or directive roles, shaping the course of the struggle over the heads of the maquila workers themselves? And did the movement's practices seem engulfed by a consumerist discourse that seemed to marginalize the workers' concerns or portray them as passive victims?
2. *The nature of the strategy employed.* Were these campaigns limited to "naming and shaming" brand-name retailers, in effect using a "stateless" strategy? In other words, did activists implicitly embrace privatized solutions to the workers' conditions of employment?
3. *The goals of the campaign.* Did these campaigns largely aim to establish "protective" rights (i.e., labor standards and outcomes) irrespective of workers' own capacities? Did concern for monitoring receive emphasis at the expense of (or substitute for) collective bargaining and independent unionism?

A rigorous analysis of the effects of these campaigns would need in-depth accounts of the communication patterns and organizational practices found among all participants in these solidarity campaigns. Our data fall far short of such requirements, of course, and should therefore be viewed with some caveats. Yet, this point notwithstanding, the patterns that obtain are highly instructive.

Table 3.2. Ten Solidarity Campaigns in the Central American Apparel Industry: Unfavorable Outcomes

Case	Chentex	Gildan	Kimi	Phillips Van Heusen
Factory and Location	Chentex, Managua, Nicaragua	El Progreso Factory, Honduras	Kimi Factory, Honduras	PVH in Guatemala
Plant Owner and Contractor	Chentex supplies the Pentagon, Wal-Mart, K-Mart, and J.C. Penny.	Gildan owns El Progreso.	Kimi supplies J.C. Penny, the Gap, and Macy's.	Phillips Van Heusen (direct ownership).
Labor Issues	Sweatshop conditions, unfair labor practices.	Unfair labor practices, harassment of pro-union workers.	Low wages, long hours, poor working conditions.	Low wages, intense social control, and piece-rate issues.
Initial Mobilization and Response	Initial unionizing campaign results in mass firings.	CBC broadcasts prompts investigation by EMIH and MSN while local union organizes. Gildan fires thirty-eight union members.	Initial unionizing campaign results in mass firings.	Initial unionizing campaign met with death threats and bribery of public officials and union members.
"Boomerang" Effort	NLC managed boomerang using shaming against retailers, political pressure on Pentagon.	Begins with CBC broadcast. MSN et al. sponsor letter writing campaign as well as effort to block Gildan's FLA application.	Workers run covert unionizing drive and reach out to UNITE and NLC who name and shame J.C. Penny. NLC contacted US trade representative to pressure Honduran state via trade privileges.	An international coalition, including Human Rights Watch, pressured the US trade representative to pressure Guatemalan government to force PVH to relent.
Outcome	Union defeated; conditions unchanged.	El Progreso Factory is closed and Gildan built another in the region.	Union recognized, however, the EPZ pulled Kimi lease, The factory closed and Kimi moved.	Union was recognized and signed a contract; however, the factory was closed sixteen months later.

A first point to note concerns the outcomes or efficacy of these solidarity campaigns. To what extent did they materially improve the conditions under which workers were employed, or otherwise transform the employment relations that existed at the targeted plants? On this score, we find that material improvements did obtain at Calypso, Choishin, Alta Gracia, Russell Athletic, Kukdong, and NLC-Gap, amounting to six of the ten cases in this analysis (see table 3.1). In these cases, the support of transnational solidarity groups did seem to provide significant leverage, helping workers secure both union recognition and (most often) collective bargaining agreements (as at NLC-Gap, Kukdong, Calypso, and Russell). The case of Kukdong is especially significant, inasmuch as this was the first case in which an independent union was able to secure a labor contract anywhere in the Mexican apparel industry.[38] In some cases (as at Choishin), the union established a viable presence but remained relatively weak and isolated. Even at Choishin, however, material conditions did improve, as physical abuse was brought to a halt and wages were increased.[39] On the other hand, in the four remaining cases studied here—Chentex, Gildan, Kimi, and Phillips Van Heusen—workers' efforts seemed to come to naught (see table 3.2).[40] In three of these four failed cases, some beneficial effects occurred but soon unraveled, as the contracting firm used its "exit" option, opting to relocate the plant to more hospitable terrain.[41] Here, workers were left completely abandoned, without recourse of any sort.

Paradigmatic of the relatively successful campaigns is the case of Russell Athletic, whose parent company is Fruit of the Loom. In 2007, plant management sought to cut workers' wages and increase their workloads. It did so by presenting workers with "collective pacts," unilaterally defined by management, with clauses that explicitly penalized workers who pursued union representation. When workers resisted the imposition of these pacts, the parent company sought to close the plant, prompting the WRC to declare the firm's decision as driven by anti-union animus, and thus a violation of ILO Convention 98 (an international agreement to which Honduras was a signatory). The struggle escalated, and Russell Athletic workers were subjected to mass firings, with the company insisting that production targets, salaries, and benefits were all "off limits" for discussion. Faced with a virulent struggle, the company again sought to shutter the plant.

With the Central General de Trabajadores (or CGT, the local Honduran union), several solidarity groups—the WRC, USAS, the Clean Clothes Campaign, and the MSN—mobilized a transnational campaign to challenge the closing of the Russell factory. Key to this campaign was the effort to utilize the consuming power of major universities as an economic lever (in effect, activists threatened to deny the company access to its market). Equally important was the effort to threaten not only the reputational capital of Fruit of the Loom, but also the prestige of the National Basketball Association (which licenses Russell Athletic's goods). Faced with such staunch resistance on several fronts, Russell Athletic finally agreed to reopen its plant, to recognize the CGT, and to negotiate a contract that included wage increases and improved working conditions. Russell also agreed to the addition of 250 new jobs, wage increases of 28 percent, and investments in new equipment to improve overall health within the factory.

A similar and equally favorable dynamic unfolded at the Calypso factory in Masaya, Nicaragua. Calypso, which manufactures mainly for the Dickies, Cintas, and Lan Dau brands, is owned by the Argus Group, which has been the target of the MSN for violations at three separate factories. At the Calypso plant, nineteen workers were fired in July and August of 2006 in response to a unionizing campaign. Workers contacted the Nicaraguan Ministry of Labor, which refused to certify their union and instead blamed the workers for poor productivity. The Calypso workers then reached out to solidarity groups in the north—chiefly, the Worker Rights Consortium, SweatFree Communities, and UNITE—and a name and shame campaign took off that targeted the Cintas brand. Subsequent communication between the workers and the Argus Group proved successful: Argus signed a collective bargaining agreement with the Calypso workers, agreed to reinstate the fired workers, and provided them with back pay.[42]

But it is one thing to suggest that transnational solidarity work can have positive effects, or even that they often do so. It is something else to explore the contours of these movements, thereby disentangling the consequences implied in the confluence of the workers' rights and human rights frames. What organizational and discursive dynamics seem to flow from the confluence or coevolution of these social movement frames? Have there been demonstrable points at which movement participation has operated in ways that stand at odds with its stated goals? Table 3.3 provides a schematic overview of the results that emerge from close scrutiny of these ten cases.

Three points emerge from our analysis. First, there *is* evidence of a gulf or schism between activists in the global north and those in the global south. This tendency seems especially pronounced in the case of the NLC-Gap campaign. Here, NGO leaders in the north assumed a highly central and even directive role, invoking a discourse that seemed to disempower the very workers they sought to support. The major NGO (the National Labor Committee [NLC]) mobilized a nationwide campaign in the U.S. media that publicized the workers' plight—but did so in ways that arbitrarily stressed the issue of child labor while largely neglecting the issues that the workers themselves found most salient in their daily working lives.[43] This point perfectly aligns with Seidman's wary posture, in that this solidarity campaign engaged in a form of media sensationalism that took great liberties with the workers' own struggles. Moreover, during a crucial stage in collective bargaining, the NLC and other U.S.-based NGOs negotiated *on behalf of* the Salvadoran workers, without the presence of the union leaders at the bargaining table. Only *after* agreements had already been negotiated were local union leaders brought in to sign the resulting agreements. Put simply, bargaining was conducted largely over the workers' heads, in a way that seems highly paternalistic. And although indigenous Gap workers were included in media tours in cities around the United States, they were not allowed substantive roles in the consummation of the struggle. Nor were they materially helped after they returned to their home country. In this case, a successful campaign seems to have occurred *in spite of* the tensions and conflicts evident between the two movement frames. What is crucial to note, however, is that such pronounced evidence of such troubling forms of leadership was largely confined to the NLC-Gap campaign. In none of the other cases did such clear evidence emerge regarding this kind of north/south inequality among movement participants.

Table 3.3. Dimensions for the Ten Campaigns: Locus of Decision Making, Strategic Target, and Goals

Case	Alta Gracia	Calypso	Chentex	Choishin	Gildan
Locus of Decision Making	Joint USAS worked with local unionists and the WRC in 2007, when abuses were brought to light.	Joint locally initiated struggle in 2006, union reaches out to WRC who manages boomerang with SweatFree Communities.	Joint U.S. media embolden local struggle in 1996, with TAN providing support.	Joint locally initiated struggle begins in 1999; COVERCO and TAN providing support.	Joint CBC broadcast exposed conditions at factory while union was forming, EMIH (Honduran monitoring group) works with MSN, who manages boomerang strategy.
Strategy/Target	Retail-centered campaign targeted Nike and Reebok and USAS threatened university boycotts of apparel.	Retail-centered pressure campaign along with direct negotiations with sub-contractor.	Hybrid-movement targets retailer, while also pressuring U.S. Congress.	Hybrid-TAN pressures United States to block imports from Guatemala, while NGOs shame Liz Claiborne.	Hybrid. Retail-centered campaign "shaming" Gildan, along with state centered pressure (stalled application to join FLA).
Goals of Campaign	Both protective and enabling rights stressed.	Emphasis on enabling rights alone.	Emphasis on enabling rights alone.	Both protective and enabling rights stressed.	Emphasis on enabling rights alone.
Case	Kimi	Kukdong	NLC-Gap	Phillips Van Heusen	Russell
Locus of Decision Making	Joint locally initiated struggle begins in 1993, with NLC, UNITE providing support.	Joint locally initiated struggle begins in 2001, with WRC, other NGOs providing support.	TAN-directed locally initiated struggle begins in 1993, with TAN assuming leadership by 1995.	Joing locally inated struggle begins in 1989, with TAN providing support through 1990s.	Joint locally initiated, TAN managed boomerang.
Strategy/Target	Hybrid campaign–TAN "shames" J.C. Penny while moving to block Honduran exports.	Retailer-centered campaign "shames" Nike to foster union recognition, monitoring by supplier.	Retail-centered campaign, "shaming" Nike.	Hybrid campaign–TAN "shames" PVH while moving to block exports from Guatemala.	Hybrid campaign–"naming and shaming" threatened Russell's contractors but groups also targeted state actors in Honduras.
Goals of Campaign	Both protective and enabling rights, but conflict arises between the two.	Both protective and enabling rights stressed.	Emphasis on protective rights, which gradually dominate enabling rights.	Emphasis on enabling rights alone.	Emphasis on enabling rights.

Nor did the discourses adopted by the solidarity campaigns seem to reflect such conflicting organizational needs.

Second, in contrast with analysts who warn of the dangers of "stateless" or privatized approaches (as with Seidman and Espenshade), the evidence at hand provides a number of interesting points. For one thing, relatively few of these campaigns adopted a purely retail-centered form. Indeed, six of the ten campaigns utilized a "hybrid" strategy—one that invoked naming and shaming tactics *in combination with* tactics that targeted state institutions as well. In the two Guatemalan cases (Choishin and Phillips Van Heusen), for example, U.S.-based NGOs not only sought to "shame" name-brand retailers (Liz Claiborne and PVH itself); in addition, they also used the Generalized System of Preferences (GSP), a provision of the World Trade Organization, in ways that threatened to deny Guatemalan firms access to the U.S. market unless its factory regimes improved. In two of the Honduran cases (Kimi and Gildan), a very similar hybrid strategy emerged. In the Kimi campaign, UNITE not only publicly "shamed" J.C. Penney, but also pressured the U.S. trade representative, again using the GSP, to gain material leverage over the exporting nation. And in the Gildan campaign, MSN not only sought to hold the firm open to public rebuke—Gildan is the largest T-shirt manufacturer in the world—but *also* acted to block the firm's effort to join the Fair Labor Association (a monitoring group sponsored by the U.S. State Department that certifies factory codes of conduct). These campaigns demonstrate the ability of solidarity groups to fashion complex strategies that fasten on *both* private and public levers of influence. Equally interesting, where solidarity work *did* adopt a retail-centered strategy, the results generated the most successful movements in our analysis. Indeed, *all four* of the retail-centered campaigns (Alta Gracia, Calypso, Kukdong, and NLC-Gap) had favorable outcomes. By contrast, only two of the six campaigns using "hybrid" strategies—Choishin and Russell Athletic— achieved a modicum of success. It would seem that the retail-centered strategy is less pervasive—and entails fewer pitfalls—than its critics have alleged.

The third point to be made here concerns the goals of these campaigns—a point best approached by returning to Rodriguez-Garavito's distinction between "protective" and "enabling" rights. Recall that analysts who adopted the wary or the critical posture expect that the human rights approach tends to favor the establishment of protective standards (e.g., the establishment of factory codes of conduct and independent monitoring to ensure compliance). The notion here is not only that such "protective" arrangements do little or nothing to empower workers; in addition (and far worse), they may actually come to substitute for mechanisms (such as strong union representation at the point of production) that would equip workers to defend their rights for themselves. Is there evidence of such tendencies? The answers are complex. Although there is partial support for the critical posture, the bulk of the evidence stands at odds with this view. Table 3.3 outlines the locus of decision making, the strategy (or strategies), and the goals of each of the ten campaigns.

The results suggest that the outcome depends on the ways in which the two social movement frames combine. The most prevalent pattern in these campaigns is one in which the workers' rights frame predominated, with the campaigns simply defining workers' rights (e.g., to self-representation and collective bargaining) *as* human rights. In effect, these campaigns utilized the trappings of the human rights frame while consistently emphasizing "enabling" rights at work. This pattern obtained in five of the campaigns studied here: Phillips Van Heusen, Russell Athletic, Gildan, Chentex, and Calypso. In each of these struggles, the key goal emphasized by both local workers and their allies in the global north was that of improving workers' conditions of existence through union recognition and collective bargaining. Most notably, *there was little or no mention of factory codes or independent monitoring in these cases*, even though human rights organizations figured prominently in these struggles. Paradigmatic are the campaigns at Phillips Van Heusen and at Calypso. At the former, the issues that provoked worker mobilization—long hours, no breaks, arbitrary cuts in piece-rate wages, physical abuse—led to prolonged labor struggle for union recognition, aided by Human Rights Watch and other solidarity groups. As noted, the victory this struggle earned proved to be Pyrrhic, a victim of capital mobility. Although the outcome at Calypso was ultimately far more favorable—the union was recognized and conditions improved in a sustainable way—the character of the Calypso campaign was largely similar. Endemic problems (underpayment, forced overtime, and safety problems) generated a union movement that met with repression; only when transnational alliances were formed (here, with WRC and SFC) did the workers succeed in establishing independent union representation. In these cases, human rights organizations played vital and constructive roles in furthering more egalitarian relations, but with the workers' movement frame serving as the dominant logic that governed these campaigns.

A second pattern was one in which the two movement frames combined in complementary ways, drawing impetus from each. Here, human rights organizations did not so much subordinate their discourse and tactics to workers' rights organizations so much as adapt them to mesh with or reinforce the pursuit of workers' rights at the point of production. Here, factory codes of conduct and monitoring were embraced but were defined in ways that required a contractor to respect the workers' right to organize on their own behalf. Thus, monitoring was defined as a means of ensuring that union recognition would be an attainable goal. This interwoven or integrated pattern conforms to Rodriguez-Garavito's call for an "empowered-participatory" approach toward codes of conduct and monitoring, representing a tense yet fruitful synthesis of the human rights and workers' rights frames. This pattern emerged with particular clarity at three cases in our study: Kukdong, Choishin, and Alta Gracia. At Kukdong, the WRC consciously defined factory codes and monitoring regimes in such a way to protect workers' rights of association and collective bargaining. At Choishin, COVERCO and the Fair Labor Association acted in much the same way, using codes and monitoring campaigns to *complement* workers' rights of combination. In both these cases, workers struggled to establish independent unions at the same time that human rights groups used monitoring associations to expose the abuse that workers confronted, and the groups invoked the corporate codes of conduct that Nike and Liz Claiborne had publicly embraced, all to support the workers' unionization campaigns. A similar pattern unfolded at Alta Gracia. In all three of these cases, then, human rights organizations achieved a high level of cooperation and coordination *with* traditional labor organizations (the AFL-CIO, Labor Education in the Americas Project, UNITE), successfully integrating the effort to "protect" and to "enable" workers at one and the same time.

There was, however, a third, "conflicted" pattern that did conform to the caveats that the wary or critical posture predicts. Again, at NLC-Gap and at Kimi, clear evidence emerged of tension between the organizing principles that informed the two movement genres. As noted, at NLC-Gap, human rights activists implicitly usurped the role of the local labor leaders, excluding the latter from the most critical instances of labor negotiation. Underlying this pattern was an overriding commitment on the part of human rights activists (as embodied in NLC) to establish powerful codes of conduct and an independent monitoring regime, *in lieu of* labor organization. The monitoring group (GMIES, or Independent Monitoring Group of El Salvador) eventually came to operate as a surrogate for collective bargaining, implicitly transferring power *away* from the shop floor into the hands of the nominally independent monitors. At Kimi, the campaign adopted a hybrid strategy that targeted the brands that the factory supplied (the Gap, J.C. Penney, Macy's) while also fastening on trade provisions and access to the U.S. market. Still, here again, sharp contention arose between human rights advocates (who emphasized the need for monitoring) and workers' rights activists (who invested heavily in the struggle to gain union recognition). In both cases, participants in the campaigns repeatedly expressed their belief that these divisions greatly weakened the workers' cause.[44]

Discussion

What inferences can be drawn with respect to the ongoing debate over the consequences that flow from the convergence of once-distinct social movement frames? Given the preliminary nature of our analysis, we must invoke more than the customary admonitions and qualifications. Still, a few suggestive points do begin to come into view. First, within the Latin American apparel industry, we find only scattered evidence of a tendency for NGOs and unions in the global north to play directive roles within these solidarity campaigns. Certainly, the great bulk of the campaigns we have studied did not manifest the postcolonial paternalism predicted by critics such as Brooks. Nor is there evidence that the initiation or direction of these campaigns reflected the power or prestige of northern activists. And although there is evidence of media sensationalism (as in the arbitrary stress on child labor at NLC-Gap), this, too, is more the exception than the rule. It seems vital to point out that the NLC-Gap and Kimi campaigns were among the earliest of the movements in our sample: Both originated in the early 1990s, culminating in the latter part of that decade. Although much more data would be needed to explore the point, this point suggests that there may have been a "learning" effect within the solidarity movement, with more recent campaigns (such as Kukdong, Choishin, Russell Athletic, and Alta Gracia) managing to transcend the tensions and pitfalls evident at an earlier point in the movement's evolution.[45]

Further, we find little to indicate that the strategies evident in these campaigns singlemindedly fastened on a "privatized" or retail-centered approach that neglected the significance of state institutions. For one thing, the majority of these cases adopted hybrid strategies that fused an emphasis on naming and shaming—what Keck and Sikkink have called "accountability politics"—with a politically sophisticated ability to use the international trade agreements and diplomatic apparatus on the workers' behalf.[46] For another, the data suggest that the retail-centered strategy does indeed have the potential to lend support to the workers' cause. Put simply, movements that mounted a plausible threat against prominent brands did indeed compel corporations to adopt meaningful reforms, with results that made a significant difference in the conditions of existence that workers encountered at the point of production. If, as theorists of global commodity chains contend, supply chains have adopted a "buyer-driven" structure that vests power in the hands of brand-name retailers at the point of consumption, this very structure (formidable though it may be) may in fact create a point of vulnerability, leaving companies open to strategies that target their reputational capital. The point is well put by Klein, who writes that "the brand, Brand Image, the source of so much corporate wealth, is also, it turns out, the corporate Achilles's heel."[47]

A final point here concerns the goals of these solidarity campaigns. These movements do at times veer into the terrain that critics have forewarned: a space in which the human rights frame begins to operate in ways that conflict with the pursuit of workers' rights, as when human rights activists embrace the notion of "protective" standards that neglect or even undermine efforts to foster direct empowerment of workers on the shop floor. Our analysis reveals that this terrain does indeed exist, but that it lies at the edges of a much larger space in which the human rights and workers' rights frames manage to combine in fruitful ways, redressing the severe imbalance of power that Central American apparel workers have had to confront. Under certain conditions, it seems, the result adds much more to workers' empowerment than it seems to subtract.

Conclusion

This chapter has merely begun what is a necessarily larger task: that of reading the nature and effects of activists' participation in transnational solidarity campaigns, doing so in the light of the rival interpretations of such participation that have recently emerged. The questions we have addressed are complex. Can the human rights tradition easily commingle with the discourse, strategies, and tactics of the workers' rights movement? Are there not dangers that lie down this path: a new paternalism, or new forms of radical consumerism that conform to (or even reproduce) the very circuits of power they aim to confront? Perhaps. Yet what we are led to conclude is that these solidarity campaigns bear only a partial resemblance to the representations their critics have conveyed. The critics' accounts may in the end be valuable mainly for the reflexivity they provoke on the part of movement participants, instilling in them a deeper, more self-aware understanding of the inequalities out of which the campaigns have grown. A hopeful sign, evident in the above analysis, is that the more recent campaigns we have studied—especially those with Russell Athletic and Alta Gracia plants—seem to manifest an increasing sign of such reflexivity. Perhaps, in other words, transnational activism has evolved beyond its critics' accounts, in ways their criticisms have helped bring about.

These are speculative observations, which begin to draw attention to the limited knowledge that currently exists with respect to the contours of transnational solidarity work, the tensions and contradictions that it manifests, and the conditions that impinge on its chances of success. This chapter will hopefully prompt more systematic and rigorous forms of multisited work that can in turn overcome the limitations of our own research. One obvious need is for research that can overcome the "left-censored" nature of our data. That is, we have focused only on cases that survived long enough to provoke attention. Arguably, some of the very tensions and contradictions that critics forewarn may have taken their toll at an earlier point in the emergence of the campaigns, limiting our ability to detect their full effects. Relevant here is the research strategy recently invoked by Bartley and Child, who compiled a more inclusive sample (really, a population) of anti-sweatshop campaigns by scrutinizing industry periodicals, thereby compiling a more comprehensive dataset than would otherwise be possible.[48] Needed, too, is research that can transcend the regional limitations of our own analysis, which has been confined to cases in the Central American region. Arguably, extension of our analysis beyond the Central American apparel industry will identify a different pattern, not least because movements in support of Asian workers do not enjoy the historically close ties that have characterized the U.S. and Latin American solidarity movements.[49]

Equally important, however, will be research that extends not only the breadth but also the depth of our knowledge of solidarity campaigns. Although the literature on globalization has fostered an increasing emphasis on multisited ethnography, and we do have a growing literature on anti-sweatshop struggles, we lack the kind of multisited ethnography that is needed to understand the nature and development of solidarity campaigns across the north/south divide.[50] In this way, a fuller understanding may begin to develop both of the social relations that shape solidarity campaigns and of the ways in which power and discourse are experienced at different points in the social movement network. Research strategies that can fill this void will hopefully provide a firmer empirical basis on which to grasp the nature and potential of solidarity campaigns, the tensions they generate, and the challenges they increasingly confront.

A final point concerns the capacity of *corporations* to learn from the struggles that solidarity movements have waged. As noted, anti-sweatshop campaigns have usefully engaged in what Keck and Sikkink have termed "accountability politics," using name and shame tactics to threaten the reputational capital that widely recognized brands have accumulated.[51] Not discussed here, but vital to the future of these movements, is the fact that many large retailers have moved to pre-empt these solidarity campaigns, often adopting factory codes of conduct and monitoring regimes that appear to institutionalize basic rights for workers—but in ways that do little to empower or protect workers' interests in any authentic way. In a sense, such tactics constitute a corporate effort to adopt a reputational shield (an exoskeleton) that can insulate the firm against efforts to target its public image, and they even seem to operate in respect of the norms that social movements have fostered. This is more than a matter of public relations and advertising, because firms have begun to underwrite the operation of NGOs and to hire committed professionals and activists to establish practices that can symbolize the firm's commitment to corporate social responsibility (see Lee, McNulty and Shaffer, this volume; Walker 2009, this volume). Although this development is relatively new, the danger here is one in which solidarity campaigns will have new lessons they must learn, as well as new realities to confront. Any gains that have flowed from the confluence of human rights and workers' rights frames may prove contingent, then, as the organizational context develops down new and uncharted paths. Whether the lessons learned from the convergence or social movement traditions will prove equal to the growing potency and sophistication of corporate-led forms of activism remains to be seen.

NOTES

1. Versions of this chapter were presented at the annual meeting of the American Sociological Association in 2010 and at the 2011 meeting of the Society for the Advancement of Socio-Economics in Madrid. Thanks are due to Kate Bronfenbrenner, Daniel Faber, Randy Hodson, Robert Ross, and Liana Foxvog for the varying forms of support they provided during the course of this project, though, of course, none are responsible for its contents.
2. Bronfenbrenner (1997, 2000); Bronfenbrenner and Luce (2004).
3. Bernhardt, Boushey, Dresser, and Tilly (2008).
4. Rudra (2005); Mosley and Uno (2007).
5. Bonacich and Appelbaum (2000); Collins (2003).
6. Keck and Sikkink (1998); Espenshade (2004); Seidman (2007).
7. Robinson (2008); Seidman (2007, 2008). A terminological point: Throughout this analysis, we use the term "social movement frame" to capture the organizing logic or paradigm that informs the discourse, strategies, and tactics adopted by movement participants. Our use is distinct from, though partly indebted to, the literature on frame alignment and Goffmanian frame analysis.
8. Brooks (2007).
9. Kolben (2010); Hilgert (2009).
10. Lukes (1982); Hilgert (2009); Savage (2009); Dembour (2010).
11. Dembour (2010).
12. See Kennedy (2002); Kolben (2010).
13. Compa (2000, 2008).
14. Compa (2000: 17).
15. See also Lichtenstein (2003); Macklem (2004).
16. Kolben (2010: 452); see also Brody (2001).
17. Kennedy (2002).
18. Espenshade (2004); Rodriguez-Garavito (2005); Seidman (2007).
19. Espenshade (2004: 11).
20. Espenshade (2004: 10).
21. Seidman (2007: 120).
22. It seems odd to lay this emphasis on private regulation at the door of the human rights movement, given the latter's traditional stress on the need for state intervention to enforce citizens' rights. See Kennedy (2002); Kolben (2010).
23. Brody (2001).
24. Lukes (1982).
25. Cited in Dembour (2010: 17).
26. Brooks (2007).
27. Brooks (2007: xx).
28. Brooks (2007: xvii), emphasis added.
29. She cites several cases in which workers were returned to their home countries with little regard for their fate thereafter.
30. Brooks (2007: 165).
31. See Robinson (2008: 362).
32. Graeber (2002); Starr and Adams (2003); Kennedy and Tilly (2008). Kennedy and Tilly refer to the "third left" within Latin America, distinct from either insurrectionary movements or populist movements for reform through electoral politics. For a

sophisticated discussion of these and other political movements in Latin America, see Escobar (2010).
33. Bhagwati (2004).
34. Keck and Sikkink (1998); Seidman (2007).
35. Keck and Sikkink (1998). The "boomerang strategy" involves the effort by local producers to form transnational alliances, with their foreign allies putting pressure on multinational companies and governmental institutions in ways that secure the rights that local producers had been denied.
36. Seidman (2007: 122–123).
37. See accounts in Kaufman and Gonzalez (2001); Frundt (2002, 2004); Espenshade (2004: 138–176); Armbruster-Sandoval (2005a, 2005b); Brooks (2007: chap. 2).
38. See accounts in Thompson (2001); Carty (2004); Rodriguez-Garavito (2005); Ross (2006); Knight and Wells (2007).
39. See Frundt (2000); Connolly (2004); Rodriguez-Garavito (2005); Pipkin (2004).
40. On Chentex, see Raphaelidis (1997); Ross and Kernaghan (2000); Ricker and Wimberley (2003); Armbruster-Sandoval (2005a, 2005b). Data on Gildan are drawn from SweatFree Communities archives, Northampton, Mass.
41. See especially Armbruster-Sandoval (2005a). See the accounts of the Phillips Van Heusen plant in Frundt (2000); Traub-Werner and Cravey (2002); Anner and Evans (2004); Armbruster-Sandoval (2005a, 2005b). See also Plankey Videla (2012).
42. "Calypso Update," August 2006, accessed May 2011 through the SweatFree Communities internal database; "Letter to the CEO of Landau Uniforms," August 2006, by Jeremy Blasi at the Worker's Rights Consortium, accessed May 2011 through the SweatFree Communities internal database.
43. The media were partially responsible for the results, but the NLC has acknowledged consciously choosing to focus on child labor as a means of gaining public sympathy. This effort worked only too well: Newspaper articles of this struggle highlighted the child labor issue, and they barely mentioned such key issues as wages and the workers' right to organize (Anner, cited in Espenshade 2004: 242, fn. 18).
44. See especially Armbruster-Sandoval (2005a, 2005b). At least some of the tension between the NLC and U.S. labor unions stems from the latter's history of support for anticommunist policies throughout the Americas (though this history seems to have had little purchase on the other campaigns in this study).
45. One of our key informants (the labor scholar-activist Mark Anner) observed that a learning process has indeed been key to the maturation of the anti-sweatshop movement. Workers in the exporting nation have learned to test the sincerity and commitment of their partners in the global north, who in turn have had reason to grow more aware of the hierarchical tendencies they exhibited in the past.
46. Keck and Sikkink (1998). In the Kukdong campaign, activists went so far as to approach NGOs and diplomatic officials in Korea, successfully using such outreach to pressure the Korean-based contractor who operated the Kukdong plant in central Mexico.
47. Klein (2000: 343; cited in Rodriguez-Garavito 2005: 224).
48. Bartley and Child (2011).
49. Seidman (2007: 121–122).
50. For multisited ethnography, see Marcus (1998); Collins (2003). For literature on anti-sweatshop struggles, see Plankey Videla (2012).
51. Keck and Sikkink (1998).

CHAPTER 4

Legitimating the Corporation through Public Participation

EDWARD T. WALKER

In *Between Facts and Norms*, Jürgen Habermas makes clear that the public sphere is not a mere organization, institution, or even a social system; it is an emergent phenomenon that refers "neither to the *functions* nor to the *contents* of everyday communication but to the *social space* generated in communicative action."[1] This space requires a critical-rational public. But how best to understand the very notion of such a public in a context in which the pressures of bureaucratic administration and market accumulation increasingly infringe upon its territory? Here, Habermas goes beyond his argument in *The Structural Transformation of the Public Sphere* and proposes a distinction in the interest of preserving the autonomy of the public sphere as a social space: We must, he argues, differentiate between those, on the one hand, who emerge from the public sphere and promote its independent reproduction as such, and those who "occupy an already constituted public domain in order to use it [strategically]."[2] This distinction, consistent with the notion of the idealized public sphere as a noncoercive, noncontentious space for public dialogue, makes possible a boundary between authentic engagement in the public sphere and inauthentic interventions made on behalf of a strategic, preconstituted interest. This distinction reveals a positive role for civil society in the public sphere, in that nongovernmental, nonmarket (i.e., third-sector) associations can help to "anchor the communication structures of the public sphere in the society component of the lifeworld."[3] However, it also makes the strong assumption that less civically rooted forms of participation—"fronts" and those seeking to manipulate the public sphere in defense of undeclared market or state interests—will lose credibility in the public domain once their sponsor becomes apparent.

Habermas was correct that strategic interventions in the public sphere by privileged interests would become a mainstay of modern life. Indeed, modern corporations, industry groups, and wealthy advocacy organizations regularly seek to mobilize participation in public life as a strategy to enhance their sociopolitical legitimacy, and a multi-million-dollar industry has emerged to help facilitate public engagement on behalf of these interests.[4] The expansion and institutionalization of this field of organizations suggest that attempts to mobilize participation on behalf of strategic institutional interests in the state and market have become routinized, although it is not entirely clear that such efforts are necessarily crowding out third-sector organizations in the process.[5]

How exactly do such elite efforts to mobilize the public take place today? Although it is plain that state actors in pluralist democratic systems make routinized interventions into the public sphere during election cycles, the confirmation processes of administrative and judicial candidates and in the media, private businesses have become a dominant presence in public life beyond simply advertising, philanthropy, and traditional forms of "corporate citizenship." Corporations today are an overlooked but highly significant sponsor of public participation, especially as large companies have rooted themselves more deeply in the social fabric of citizens' everyday lives and have become a major topic of critical public discussion and protest.[6] Further, expanding corporate power has raised major public questions about the legitimacy of corporate actions in the areas of environment, community relations, and employment practices.

This chapter asks how major corporations are mobilizing public participation today.[7] In particular, the study investigates how corporate interventions in the public sphere are related to companies' interests in maintaining their sociopolitical legitimacy when faced with societal controversies and protest. As critical publics challenge corporations in the public domain, then, corporations have responded with their own forms of public engagement. And, as I show more extensively in the larger project of which this chapter is a part,[8] companies tend to recruit activists who are most likely to say "yes" to their requests, who tend to be among the most privileged social actors. Thus, consistent with the broader theme of this volume, these corporate-driven advocacy campaigns tend to further exacerbate problems of inequality in American democracy.

I begin by providing background on corporate grassroots mobilization programs, which are well established among segments of the *Fortune* 500. I then review research on the sources of social legitimacy among firms and what the political implications of such societal relations are. I continue by examining how firms respond to protest. Next, I review the measures and data sources, and this is followed by a series of negative binomial regression models of the count of grassroots lobbying consultants retained by each company; in major grassroots campaigns, corporations often retain multiple consulting firms, and, indeed, nearly 20 percent of the *Fortune* 500 appeared on two or more consulting firms' client lists. I conclude by considering the implications of these findings for changing forms of engagement in the public sphere in a context of heightened inequalities and expanding corporate interventions in public life.

Corporate Mobilization of Public Participation

What strategies do companies take to maintain their legitimacy when challenged by societal controversies about their practices? Recent literatures have made clear that challenges brought by civil society groups can have significant negative effects on firms' resources and reputations.[9] Protests highlighting unsound investment practices in low-income communities, threatened boycotts over poor labor and human rights conditions for subcontracted employees in the developing world, and evidence of a poor environmental record would all appear to threaten the firm's legitimacy. On the other hand, extra-institutional challenges often encourage firms to engage in certain pro-social activities, such as disclosure, accountability measures, augmented reporting, and voluntary self-regulation.[10] Thus, many management and organizational scholars have called attention to the ways that firms can actually *enhance* their legitimacy through being responsive to the claims of NGOs and social movement groups, turning what would appear to be threatening circumstances into opportunities to showcase the firm's unique social commitments.[11]

While contributing much to our understanding of how social movements and nongovernmental actors destabilize established practices, create new institutions,[12] and encourage firms to engage in a higher degree of pro-social activity, existing research has done less to examine the civic and political strategies that firms often take in order to ward off the threat of consumer, labor, and environmental contention. And, while there have been a number of innovative and insightful studies on corporate-community ties[13] and broader public and issue management strategies,[14] we know very little about how such ties affect firms' political strategies. Although some have recognized that firms often respond to institutional pressures by co-opting sources of pressure, building coalitions among supportive citizens, or even engaging in full-throated efforts to shame and marginalize threatening actors,[15] scholarship on firms' responses to public pressures has paid considerably less attention to grassroots mobilization on behalf of the firm.[16]

However, it is clear that the past forty years have involved a significant change in the public face of business, with a considerable expansion in the public affairs function of the firm.[17] As the Public Affairs Council (PAC), the leading association for corporate public affairs officers, puts it, the practice of public affairs "combines government relations, communications, issues management and corporate citizenship strategies to influence public policy, build a strong reputation, and find common ground with stakeholders,"[18] but the predominant focus of the practice involves corporate grassroots mobilization of the public; managing federal, state, and local government affairs; and managing public issues.[19] The practice of public affairs got off the ground in response to the threat of organized labor and the policies of the Eisenhower administration in the 1950s, with considerable expansion following the enactment of major federal regulatory initiatives and public protest in the 1960s and early 1970s. As corporate public affairs expanded, so, too, did the market for grassroots mobilization services, which increasingly came to be provided by public affairs consultants that could assist in public mobilization and the management of issues on behalf of the firm.

A wide variety of large and prominent firms engage in regular and ongoing campaigns to make their constituents aware of the political priorities of the organization, as well as to mobilize them as a force in shaping firms' legislative, regulatory, and civic environments.[20] They do this not only when firms face challenging political environments, but also because new communications technologies have enhanced firms' capacities for facilitating low-cost forms of engagement.[21]

Consider, for instance, how Wal-Mart has engaged the public in participatory campaigns. Seemingly borrowing a phrase from the War on Poverty, Wal-Mart has developed a Community Action Network (www.walmartcommunity.com) that won the 2010 Grassroots Innovation Award from the Public Affairs Council. As the PAC puts it, Wal-Mart won the award because the site "educates customers and others about news, legislation, and other developments that might affect the company, customers or their local stores. In one public place, the website offers information on political advocacy, corporate citizenship, and communications."[22] Thus, there is evidence that Wal-Mart sees its grassroots mobilization efforts as intricately tied to its other corporate citizenship strategies.[23]

Other major retailers also have considerable grassroots public affairs operations. Best Buy, for instance, operates the Blue Grassroots Network, which encourages the involvement predominantly of employees.[24] The firm explains, "As a leading global retailer and corporate citizen, Best Buy believes that it's important to work with policymakers on issues impacting our customers, employees, businesses, shareholders and communities.... Our public policy work directly aligns with our aspiration to be environmentally and socially accountable."[25] Thus, in the case of Best Buy, corporate political mobilization is a direct extension of the company's corporate citizenship strategies. Best Buy has also used its public affairs program for purposes of protest against taxes on computer services. In order to express this message, the firm carried out a Lobby Day in which uniformed members of its "Geek Squad" team of technical employees made a dramatic appearance before the Maryland legislature. The PAC credits this visit with the governor's repeal of a major technology tax.[26]

Of course, other large firms outside the retail sector also have strong grassroots public affairs programs. For instance, Harrah's Entertainment has sought to challenge negative public and political sentiments about gambling through its Harrah's Winning Together program, which encourages the civic and electoral engagement of gaming employees. Firms with a poor reputation (as well as whole industries that have poor reputations), then, appear to rely on the mobilization of primary stakeholders like employees to counteract negative public sentiments. As stated in a 2006 issue of Harrah's *Winning Together Insider*, the program's newsletter,

> While we offer our customers a fun and enjoyable experience like many other businesses, we are often treated differently just because we are in the gaming industry. It is important for us to be treated like other businesses in America so we have the same chance to grow our business, our employee base and our contributions to the community. Political involvement can help our company grow and prosper. Unfortunately, there are times when politics, public impressions, and media attention do not treat gaming fairly. Our industry is often targeted for large tax increases and is under constant threat from lawmakers attempting to change the way that we are allowed to do business. Through Winning Together, our fellow employees have made contact with lawmakers, community leaders, and media to let them know how they feel on common issues affecting us and our company.... The power of our vote makes us all Winning Together Superheroes.[27]

Pharmaceutical manufacturers like Pfizer (whose program is called Pfizer Advocates) and Merck (Merck Action Network) also have major grassroots operations, as do large banks like Wachovia (SpeakOut Wachovia!) and Wells Fargo. Although many pharmaceutical firms rely on the political power of the industry group PhRMA in place of lobbying by individual firms, the Merck Action Network is quite well developed, and it integrates PAC activity, employee voting, and issue-based grassroots campaigns. As in the case of other firms, grassroots campaigns seek to leverage the social capital of the firm as a means of political management. The Merck Action Network, for instance, is a key sponsor of a program called We Work for Health, which "unites health consumers, biopharmaceutical company employees, vendors, suppliers and other business, academic and community partners to demonstrate how these diverse groups contribute to the socioeconomic climate and provide shared benefits and a better quality of life to all. The program includes local chambers of commerce, universities and research centers, labor, businesses, patient advocacy organizations, provider groups and biopharmaceutical research companies that work together to improve America's health care system and strengthen our economy."[28]

All of these examples illustrate the ways in which these new forms of engagement make civic and political participation less autonomous from the interests of the marketplace. These forms of participation are built from the top down, and they either create new structures for participation that are beholden to their institutional sponsor or co-opt existing voluntary associations for short-term strategic alliances.[29] As corporations became more concerned with their legitimacy in civil society since the financial and regulatory changes starting in the 1960s and '70s, they sought to encourage public participation in a fashion similar to many traditional advocacy organizations. Thus, these corporate strategies fit into the broader set of cases in which new forms of participation have developed that reinforce civic inequalities.[30]

Linking Corporate Reputation to Grassroots Activities

Corporate grassroots and constituency-building programs are a key part of firms' tactical repertoire in managing their external political environment, as one aspect of the broader set of types of corporate political activity (CPA).[31] However, unlike PAC contributions or direct lobbying activity, corporate grassroots activities are targeted both at political officials and at the general public; they represent an effort to legitimate the firm both in civil society and in the political sphere.[32]

Following from the above examples, then, we should expect that firms that have a poor public reputation might seek to mobilize public participation as a means of challenging that negative image. Wal-Mart, for instance, may struggle with concerns that its operations are harming local businesses in the communities in which it operates, but the company is also known for inspiring strong positive sentiments among moderate-income consumers and many of their employees. These key stakeholder groups, it would appear, help the firm to combat negative public images about the firm's broader economic impacts. Further, high-reputation firms are, by comparison, relatively secure in their standing and should not require these additional displays of the firm's public legitimacy.

I therefore expect the following:

Hypothesis 1: Reputation is negatively associated with corporate grassroots activities.

Stakeholder Relations and Corporate Legitimacy

The concept of legitimacy refers to the public endorsement or support for an organization or its activities.[33] More specifically, it can best be understood as "a generalized perception or assumption that the actions of an entity are desirable, proper, or appropriate within some socially constructed system of norms, values, beliefs, and definitions."[34] Firms' sources of legitimacy are rooted in self-interested evaluations by the organization's audiences (pragmatic legitimacy), on the basis of normative judgments (moral legitimacy), and also on whether its form is taken for granted (cognitive legitimacy). Considering a firm's ties to external communities, pragmatic legitimacy appears to be paramount, as community members are often concerned with the practical goods the organization can deliver.[35] Most important for present purposes, organizations often seek to legitimate themselves in sociopolitical terms by garnering the approval of key authorities in the state, professions, and civil society, and controversial events that challenge that legitimacy should encourage firms to enhance their standing in other ways.[36]

In most discussions of firms' legitimacy, institutionalists have presented an image of organizations as primarily passive subjects of the coercive, normative, and mimetic forces in their environment.[37] Professional associations, industry groups, community organizations, and local community members, for example, help to make clear the standards for permissible organizational conduct,[38] thus locating the sources of firms' legitimacy among multiple relevant publics. Although, indeed, business organizations' market activities are embedded within institutional contexts and the rules, norms, and standard practices they require, firms do have strategic capacities not only for selective nonconformity to institutional rules, but also for shaping their sociopolitical environments.[39]

There is a common image among political activists and the general public that corporations have, in the age of neoliberalism and deregulation, lost touch with the communities on which they rely for employees, resources, and physical space.[40] Urban sociologists like Harvey Molotch, for example, called attention long ago to the notion of the city as a "growth machine" in which firms that are unhappy with local conditions in a given community can simply relocate elsewhere.[41] Especially as technological and service-sector markets have expanded, firms in these industries are no longer forced to root their operations in one place, and communities are in a position to compete over firms to locate there.[42] Instead of becoming closer to local communities, then, large firms have become seen as less organic members of their communities and many worry that firms are beyond the reach of local residents.

But the massive growth of multinational companies has not severed the tie between private industry and communities, as recent decades have also witnessed the considerable growth of corporate philanthropy, employee volunteering programs, environmental self-regulation, and other efforts to enhance the social legitimacy of the firm.[43] It is increasingly coercive upon firms to become more responsive to stakeholder groups, as legal regimes have given more power to firms' constituents.[44] Thus, while poor community relations associated with negative economic impacts (plants closing, the replacement of local businesses with chain stores, etc.) remain common, firms in this era have increased their social and environmental commitments.[45] Corporate social responsibility (CSR) has become a mantra not only for management gurus and scholars of organizational behavior, but also for many firms; these firms find justification for such action in studies, arguing, for example, that social activities make sense in terms of the creation of value, and, more significantly, can have indirect public relations benefits.[46]

Managing Legitimacy: The Moderating Effects of Reputation

While there are benefits to having the support of influential constituents, many firms lack social legitimacy and, as a result, struggle to attract talented employees, face negative media coverage, and should be more likely to be targeted for protest by social movement organizations. However, firms that are household names and have major recognition among consumers are often targeted by social movements and community groups in part because of their prominent position in their industry,[47] and these firms have developed major public affairs programs to manage these circumstances.[48] Further, firms that have strong reputations, as field leaders, should be in a better position to manage contention—such as challenges and controversies related to the firm's community relations, treatment of employees, diversity policies, or environmental practices—because their reputations help to protect them from negative information.[49] By comparison, firms with poor reputations do not have this protection, which makes challenges to the firm's activities much more threatening, thus calling for a strategic response on the part of the firm.

Hypothesis 2a. Among high-reputation firms, having poor relations with constituents should have no association with grassroots activities.

Hypothesis 2b. Among low-reputation firms, the presence of poor constituent relations should be associated with a significantly greater engagement in grassroots activities.

Buttressing Legitimacy: Responses to Anticorporate Protest

Beyond public controversies about a firm's practices, public protest events also convey negative information about a firm to shareholders and other key publics on which the firm depends. As multinational corporations have expanded their power and reach since the 1970s, companies have become a frequent target of contention by protest groups.[50] Protests against corporations can tarnish their image in the media, while also reducing firms' value by, for example, causing significant dips in stock prices.[51] Protests tend to be targeted against prominent industry leaders, in the interest of encouraging other, less prominent organizations to take notice as well, as social movements seek to capitalize on firms' attention to industry leaders and key authorities in the field.

The role of protest in shaping firms' public legitimacy is complex and multifaceted, as protest challenges firms' legitimacy in the short run by making clear that the firm lacks the support of certain secondary stakeholders (e.g., environmental groups, animal rights organizations) or primary stakeholders (e.g., employees during a labor dispute), but in the long run protest may galvanize corporate responses that allow the firm to showcase its commitment to sustainable and/or socially responsible practices.[52]

What has been overlooked to this point, however, has been the means by which corporations respond to outside challenges by encouraging constituents to help defend the firm's reputation against such negative information. Scholars of social movements have long recognized that the targets of popular contention regularly adapt their strategic repertoires in response to protest, in something akin to a tactical game of chess between movement and an institutional target in which targets seek to neutralize the challenge they face.[53] There is evidence that firms may seek to organize stakeholder opposition when faced with protest. For example, as health advocates began to mobilize heavily against the tobacco industry in the 1990s, Philip Morris (now Altria) contracted with the public affairs consulting giant Burson-Marsteller, which helped the firm to develop the faux-grassroots National Smokers' Alliance (NSA).[54] The political plan behind its development is telling:

> When it comes to individual officeholders and policy-makers, the current political environment is one-sided. Up to now the politicians and the anti-smoking activists have free shot at their political goals. . . . The lawsuits, studies, public education, etc. are even further removed from the basic touch point as to the reason for the anti-smoking crowd's string of successes. The reason politicians have joined or rolled over on this issue: They have felt no political pain.[55]

The NSA sought to add political legitimacy for smoking by creating an organization that smokers could join, thus rooting the firm's interests in civil society. They stirred up the grassroots activism of smokers by holding press conferences, issuing press releases, holding special events, encouraging the submission of op-eds, sending action alerts to members, publishing advertisements, and more.[56] Similar pro-industry grassroots campaigns in response to public activism have been documented in domains including energy, pharmaceuticals, and other health industries.[57] As a growing body of sociological work illustrates, elites often mobilize their own social movements to pressure for social and political change,[58] although the degree of influence such elite-driven movements can have may be contingent on the field in which change is sought.[59] Thus, even *Fortune* 500 firms may benefit from generating pressure from below.

Thus, I expect the following:

Hypothesis 3a. Among high-reputation firms, being the subject of consumer or labor protest should not be associated with grassroots activities.

Hypothesis 3b. Among low-reputation firms, consumer or labor protest should be associated with greater engagement in grassroots activities.

Data Sources and Measures

The Dependent Measure: Appearances as the Client of a Grassroots Lobbying Firm

Data on corporate grassroots mobilization practices come from a broader project on the role of public affairs professionals in reshaping public participation and policymaking.[60] In that larger project, data were collected on all organizations listed under the "grassroots lobbying" and related subheadings in the directory listings of *Campaigns & Elections* magazine's annual "Political Pages" directories for all years 1990–2004, as well as in a series of pullout "Grassroots Lobbying Buyer's Guides" in 1995, 1996, 1999, 2001, and 2003. Coders then aggregated the cases from both sources into a data file of the unique firms, using a data-reduction protocol I provided, yielding $N = 712$ unique firms.

These 712 consulting firms were then tracked to see which survived and were still active in providing broad-based public mobilization services as of 2010 ($N = 171$ met this criterion). Then, once the survivors were determined, the project continued by collecting data on the clients of these grassroots lobbying firms. Thorough searches of the websites of the surviving firms indicated that fifty-six organizations provided a full client list, thirty-three provided a list they described as "partial" or "representative," and thirty-two provided a set of case studies of recent successes that identified their clients; the remaining fifty (29.2 percent) organizations declined to identify any clients, illustrating their degree of experience by describing work impersonally on behalf of "health interests" or "a *Fortune* 500 corporation." Thus, more than 70 percent of active firms identified at least some of their clients, with a large plurality offering their full or representative client list.

Once all the 2010 client lists of the grassroots lobbying consultants were collected, these were aggregated into a file of the full client base of all 121 firms that identified any clients. All of the publicly traded firms listed in the 2007 *Fortune* 500 were then searched to see if they appeared as the client of at least one public affairs consulting firm, using searches for alternative spellings and abbreviated versions of the firm's name, as well as major subsidiaries of the firm in question (e.g., both "AMR Corp." and "American Airlines").

Thus, the dependent measure is a count of the number of times a *Fortune* 500 firm appeared as the client of a professional grassroots lobbying/public affairs consulting firm; 60.6 percent of firms did not appear on any client list, while 19.8 percent of firms appeared on one list, 7.7 percent appeared on two, and the remaining 12 percent appeared on more than two lists. The firms that appeared on the greatest number of client lists include Wal-Mart, IBM, AT&T, Comcast, Ford, PG&E, Pfizer, Procter & Gamble, Verizon, and Waste Management, all of which are *Fortune* 200 firms with major interests in managing their public image. As public affairs consultants often make clear, any corporation in the middle of a major grassroots campaign almost always requires certain services from an outside consultant, as such campaigns regularly overwhelm the capacities of firms' in-house public or government affairs offices.[61]

Therefore, this measure is a better indication of firms' grassroots activities than any alternative measure that might be available, such as firms' membership in the PAC.[62] I find that out of the 444 publicly traded firms in the 2007 *Fortune* 500 list, some 39 percent (174 corporations) were clients of a grassroots lobbyist in 2010. Thus, it would appear that grassroots activities are quite well institutionalized among a subset of *Fortune* 500 firms.

Independent Variables

Given the analytic questions outlined above, a goal of this investigation is to evaluate the relationships among reputation, protest, and controversies in a firm's stakeholder relations, and hiring a public affairs consultant to mobilize participation. Consistent with other studies of corporate reputation,[63] I use *Fortune*'s "Most Admired Companies" score for the year 2007 as my measure of a company's standing among its peers. Data on consumer and labor protest come from searches of the ABI-Inform database of newspaper and trade publications.[64] Data on external controversies come from KLD Analytics for the year 2007. The models also control for a number of other measures, not shown. These measures include the following: (1) KLD measures of a firm's internal and external strengths in its stakeholder relations (community, environmental, diversity, employee); (2) measures of internal controversies from KLD (diversity, employee); (3) the measure of the political context comes from the VoteView project[65] and reflects the conservatism of members of the House of Representatives in the firm's headquarters state; (4) the measures of lobbying and PAC contributions come from and reflect, respectively, lobbying expenditures for the year 2007 and PAC contributions for the 2008 election cycle; (5) industry-sector information comes from firms' NAICS classification; (6) all firm financial data for 2007—including employee size, cash flow, and market-to-book ratio. Full results are available by request from the author.

Analysis

Using the dependent measure described above, I estimate negative binomial models of the count of public affairs consultants hired by *Fortune* 500 firms as of 2010. Results appear in table 4.1. The leftmost model displays coefficients for all firms unconditional on reputation, whereas the center and right columns are conditional on reputation (with low-reputation firms in the center and high-reputation firms on the right). Comparing the results of the latter two models offers the opportunity to consider how reputation may moderate the link between corporate controversies and protest, on the one hand, and grassroots activities on the other.

The first model, importantly, makes clear that firms in a stronger reputational position are no more or less likely to hire a public affairs consultant. On its own, then, reputation is not a significant predictor of corporate grassroots activities. But comparing between the center and right models, it becomes clearer that reputation does in fact moderate the relationship between a firm's poor external relations and its likelihood of

Table 4.1 Negative Binomial Regression Models of Corporate Grassroots Mobilization on Protests, Community Relations, and Organizational Characteristics

Variable	All Firms	Low-Reputation Firms	High-Reputation Firms
Reputation			
Fortune Score, 2007	−0.029	—	—
Protest			
Consumer Protest	0.295	0.560*	0.021
Labor Protest	0.210	0.298	0.061
External Controversies			
Community Controversies	0.324**	0.676***	0.917
Environmental Controversies	0.171**	0.310***	0.129
Constant	−0.327	−0.752	−0.376
N	344	165	179
Pseudo R-Square	0.215	0.320	0.181
Log Likelihood	−361.8	−124.9	−220.5

Significance levels: * $p < .10$, ** $p < .05$, *** $p < .01$
All models include controls (not shown) described in the text.

hiring grassroots consultants.[66] The models illustrate relatively strong support, then, for the moderating effects of reputation (hypotheses 2–3) but do not support hypothesis 1. Combined, these results suggest that major corporations are engaging in grassroots mobilization practices at relatively high rates but that such organizational behaviors may be conditioned upon the challenges a firm faces in its external environment, and these challenges are moderated by a firm's position among its organizational peers. Firms held in high standing face controversy and protest quite often, but their reputational standing appears to serve as a buffer against such negative information. The less privileged position of low-reputation firms provides no such buffer, making them much more likely to hire consultants when faced with problems in their stakeholder relations. For protest in particular, the models also show that it is only consumer protest that is consequential for low-reputation firms, as labor protest does not appear to be associated with the response of pro-corporate grassroots mobilization.

Discussion and Conclusion

This study sought to examine the role that corporations play in the public sphere through mobilizing popular activism as a legitimating strategy. In particular, the study sought to examine how businesses attempt to root themselves in civil society through the mobilization of constituent groups like employees, consumers, distributors, shareholders, and sympathetic members of the general public, using the services of professional consultants that help corporations to adopt the tactics of advocacy organizations. The study asked how this type of legitimacy-seeking organizational behavior is related to firms' relationships with their external communities (in particular, community and environmental stakeholders), as well as the protest they face from consumer and labor groups. I found that firms' engagement in grassroots practices is associated with controversy and/or protest but that this relationship is moderated by a firm's reputation.

More broadly, these results indicate that public claims-making against business is linked not only with an expansion of CSR programs, but also with efforts by corporations to mobilize the public on its behalf. My research has shown that the founding of new grassroots consulting firms was shaped most significantly by the political mobilization of business and also the expansion of the interest group field.[67] As one consultant described to me in an interview about the founding of the field of public affairs consulting firms, the field took off because of the combination of (a) consultants reaching out to corporations and (b) corporations reaching out for consultants' help.

My interviews with these consultants were also informative about the model of the public accepted by those involved in mobilizing corporate participation from the top down. In this model, it is assumed that participation need not be truly empowering or encouraging of critical public dialogue (although, in fact, the term "empowerment" is often used in campaign materials and on consultants' websites). The boundary between authentic and inauthentic participation is seen as having little to do with the sponsorship or strategic interests behind the request for participation, but it is instead simply a matter of whether the corporate sponsor has a legitimate reason to be concerned about the issue in question. As one consultant put it in a media report, "The difference between grass-roots and Astroturf is whether the [consultant working for a corporate sponsor to mobilize the public] knows what he's talking about and has a legitimate reason to be involved. . . . Have we come to a point in our democracy where it's legitimate for environmentalists to take their message to the people but not for industry to do the same?"[68]

These industry-driven campaigns, then, inherently involve the decoupling of participation from challenges to institutionalized power in society, and they are most often seen as an extension of other forms of corporate lobbying.[69] Scholars have most often conceptualized citizen participation as an antidote to bureaucratic rigidity and formalism,[70] a mechanism for challenging authority,[71] and a means for establishing public opinion beyond the inherent misrepresentations of opinion polls (as described by Habermas and Bourdieu).[72] Today, we see an outpouring of work celebrating citizen participation for many of these same reasons, while also celebrating the potential of participation to transform governance in response to the increasing complexity of modern institutional systems.[73] But in a context in which many forms of low-cost participation have been unlocked by new communications technologies and in which business has become increasingly concerned about its stakeholder relations and image in civil society, we can no longer simply equate participation with empowerment and shared governance; the very notion of the public has been transformed in such a fashion that participation is often a means of defending established practices by states and market actors.

What these bodies of work have overlooked is not only the expansion of corporate efforts to mobilize participation (as documented here), but also the appearance of an entire *industry* devoted to such activities, with an accompanying shift in the constitution of the "public."[74] The major implication of industry-driven grassroots campaigns, then, is that the modern public has been redefined such that it becomes exceedingly difficult to distinguish between types of participation that have true empowering potential from those that reinforce institutionalized practices in state and market organizations. In a context of heightened inequalities, low-cost communications technologies, and thinner forms of civic engagement, participation may just as easily be associated with progressive change in institutions as with its opposite. This is not, of course, to deny the transformative power of civic engagement, only to recognize its conditional nature in the contemporary context.

NOTES

1. Habermas (1996: 360).
2. Habermas (1989: 364).
3. Habermas (1989: 366–367).
4. Walker (2009, 2014).
5. Indeed, many organizations in this participation-facilitation industry have, as their primary purpose, the creation of coalitions between, for example, major corporations and preexisting local community organizations (Walker 2010, 2014).
6. See Vogel (1989); Soule (2009); Ingram et al. (2010).
7. This chapter is adapted from the broader research reported in Walker (2014). I thank Graeme Boushey, Forrest Briscoe, Jerry Davis, Matt Desmond, Marc Dixon, Brayden King, Caroline Lee, Trevon Logan, Michael Lord, John McCarthy, Michael McQuarrie, Brendan Nyhan, Kiyo Tsutsui, and Mayer Zald for comments on earlier versions of this chapter. My research was supported in part by the Robert Wood Johnson Foundation and also builds on research funded by the National Science Foundation (#SES-0527344; #SES-0851153). Neither the RWJF nor the NSF bears any responsibility for the analysis presented.
8. Walker (2014).
9. Eesley and Lenox (2006); King and Soule (2007); King (2008).
10. Respectively, Potoski and Prakash (2009); Bartley (2007); Vogel (2008).
11. For example, see Schepers (2006); Lyon and Maxwell (2008).
12. Rao (2008).
13. Burt (1983); Galaskiewicz (1985, 1997); Galaskiewicz and Burt (1991); Marquis, Glynn, and Davis (2007); Guthrie and McQuarrie (2008); Guthrie et al. (2008).
14. McWilliams, Siegel, and Wright (2006).
15. Oliver (1991); see also Oliver and Holzinger (2008).
16. But see Rowley and Moldoveanu (2003).
17. Marcus and Irion (1987); Meznar and Nigh (1995).
18. Public Affairs Council (2010). See also Meznar and Nigh (1995); Griffin and Dunn (2004).
19. Public Affairs Council (1998).
20. Baysinger et al. (1985); Heath et al. (1995); Meznar and Nigh (1995); Hillman and Hitt (1999); Lord (2000a, 2000b, 2003).
21. Walker (2009); Lord (2000a, 2000b).
22. http://pac.org/content/2010-grassroots-innovation-award-winners-0.

23. See especially Walker (2014: chap. 5).
24. http://www.bluegrassrootsnetwork.com.
25. http://www.bluegrassrootsnetwork.com.
26. http://pac.org/content/2009-grassroots-innovation-award-winners.
27. Harrah's Entertainment (2006).
28. http://merckvotes.com/page.asp?g=merck&content=wework.
29. Walker (2010).
30. However, although the decline of federated organizations over the course of the 20th century may be implicated in this change, a wide variety of professionalized civic organizations since the 1960s continue to be active in mobilizing independent citizen participation (Minkoff et al., 2008; Walker et al., 2011).
31. Lord (2000a, 2000b, 2003); Hillman, Keim, and Schuler (2004).
32. Walker (2009).
33. Perrow (1961).
34. Suchman (1995: 574).
35. Walker and McCarthy (2010).
36. While institutionalists have often emphasized constitutive legitimacy or an entity's capacity to become recognized as part of a known category to the point that it becomes taken for granted as a social fact (Meyer and Rowan 1977; Baum and Powell 1995; Hannan and Carroll 1992), organizational scholars writing in the tradition of Stinchcombe (1965) have highlighted instead sociopolitical legitimacy, in which organizations are recognized by authorities for their compliance with laws and institutional norms (see also DiMaggio 1988).
37. For example, see Zucker (1987). See also Frooman (1999).
38. DiMaggio and Powell (1983).
39. Oliver (1991); Hillman, Keim, and Schuler (2004).
40. For example, see Perrucci et al. (1988).
41. Molotch (1976).
42. Galaskiewicz (1991: 296).
43. See Vogel (2005) for a review.
44. See Donaldson and Preston (1995).
45. Hoffman (2001); Vogel (2005).
46. McWilliams and Siegel (2001); Porter and Kramer (2002).
47. Bartley and Child (2011).
48. Lerbinger (2006).
49. Fombrun et al. (2000).
50. Soule (2009).
51. King and Soule (2007).
52. See, respectively, Raeburn (2004); Briscoe and Safford (2008); Rao, Morrill, and Zald (2000); Lounsbury, Ventresca, and Hirsch (2003); and Martin (2008).
53. McAdam (1983). This dynamic should occur at heightened levels during periods in which the state does not step in to adjudicate the dispute (Meyer and Staggenborg 1996), as is often the case in contention between protest groups and corporations.
54. See Magzamen et al. (2001); Givel (2007).
55. Givel (2007: 343), quoting from an internal Philip Morris legal document.
56. Givel (2007: 344).
57. See, respectively, Rowell (1996); Castellblanch (2003); and Walker (2010).

58. Useem and Zald (1982); Vogus and Davis (2005); Walker (2009); Dixon (2010).
59. Duffy, Binder, and Skrentny (2010).
60. See Walker (2009, 2014) for a more detailed description of this methodology.
61. Jalonick (2003); see also Public Affairs Council (2008).
62. Indeed, fewer firms appear in the public directory of corporate members of the Public Affairs Council (29.2 percent) than are listed as the client of a grassroots lobbying consultant (39.4 percent).
63. For example, see King (2008).
64. The measures of consumer and labor protest rely on searches of three databases available through ProQuest: ABI/INFORM Dateline (local and regional business publications), ABI/INFORM Global (including company profiles, the *Wall Street Journal*, and *Financial Times*), and ABI/INFORM Trade and Industry (more than 1,200 trade publications such as *Airline Industry Information*, *Candy Industry*, *Hospital Business Week*, and *R&D*). Further details are available in Walker (2014).
65. Poole and Rosenthal (2001).
66. Additional models (not shown), for example, show that the interaction between reputation and community controversies is significant when this interaction term is added to the left model.
67. Walker (2009, 2014).
68. Stone (1993).
69. Although this type of lobbying is mediated rather than direct; see Goldstein (1999).
70. Kweit and Kweit (1981); Alford (1969).
71. For example, see Pateman (1970).
72. Bourdieu (1979); Habermas (1989).
73. For example, see Fung and Wright (2003a); Lovan et al. (2004); Fischer (2006).
74. Walker (2009); see also Barley (2010).

PART III

The Production of Authority and Legitimacy

CHAPTER 5

No Contest

Participatory Technologies and the Transformation of Urban Authority

MICHAEL MCQUARRIE

The meaning of participation has been transformed in urban civil society.[1] Once used as a tool for empowering urban citizens against politicians and growth-oriented elites, participation is now a tool for grounding political authority in the context of urban decline. Many sectors of urban civil society have become less independent even though they are well funded and participatory. Large numbers of community-based organizations no longer empower neighborhoods, but instead weigh on them.

Yet we have trouble grappling with this transformation. Participation is still automatically associated with democratization, and community with authenticity and solidarity. Using a case study of the trajectory of participatory practices in community-based organizations (CBOs) in Cleveland, Ohio, I will show how participatory practices have been transformed from tools of democratization into tools of elite authority.

Cleveland is a revealing site from which to examine this transformation and it presents a puzzle. Cleveland is a large manufacturing city that has been in decline since the late 1960s. This decline has posed a distinct challenge to the authority of the city's elites. Through much of the postwar period their authority had been premised on the promise of economic and population growth.[2] The decline made it impossible to deliver on that promise and the result was a general political crisis, capital strike, and municipal bankruptcy. In Cleveland, more than in other cities, the tensions and conflicts that emerged from the crisis of elite authority were highly visible and highly contentious; indeed, Cleveland has become the prototypical case of the "crisis of growth politics."[3] That crisis opened the door to populist and neighborhood-based critiques of urban authority that undermined popular consent to the rule of growth-oriented elites. In response, governance was rescaled to the neighborhood and reorganized to be more participatory. In some cases this was done through changes to the formal apparatus of political representation, in others through the devolution of governance functions to civil society organizations and nonprofits.

Despite leading the way in many of these transformations—and in spite of many premature celebrations of Cleveland's renaissance—in 2004 Cleveland became the poorest big city in America. The city's neighborhoods were again in crisis due to ongoing economic decline, outmigration, and predatory lending. Cuyahoga County, which contains Cleveland, had fifteen thousand foreclosures in 2007 alone. Along with foreclosures came a cycle of abandonment, demolition, and crime. Many of the city's neighborhoods were visibly collapsing. The scale of the destruction and the absence of effective response evoke images of an "organizational desert," an absence of "social capital," and a dead civil society.

Yet on paper, Cleveland seemed well situated to cope with the current crisis. Unlike in the 1970s crisis, the city is now armed with dozens of CBOs that are broadly supported by the city's wealthy philanthropic community and the municipal government. Most of them exist to deal with neighborhood and housing issues. Many of them are self-consciously "participatory." The problem, then, is not an absence of organizations designed to work on behalf of the city's neighborhoods or even an absence of participation by community residents in governance. The city's civil society is thriving in organizational terms, but it is programmatically paralyzed. In fact, many of these organizations are only being kept alive through public subsidies.

This very fact is indicative. In a moment of declining revenues, why would a municipal government use taxpayer money to subsidize the housing production of community-based nonprofits when there is already excess housing and collapsing prices? The answer given by an official in the municipal Department of Community Development was simple: They want to keep the infrastructure of nonprofit CBOs alive, even if it puts a dent in the municipal budget and even though the houses produced will have no measurable positive effect on surrounding communities. What this demonstrates is that the city's CBOs are *legitimate* in the eyes of funders and community development professionals even though they are not programmatically *effective*. The contrast with the 1970s, when many CBOs were illegitimate to funders even though they were effective, is notable.

This shift poses a natural question: What is the legitimacy of CBOs based on if not programmatic effectiveness? The answer, in brief, is that CBOs underpin the authority of urban elites when promises of growth are understood to be empty. In this context, CBOs facilitate elite authority, not based on their programmatic effectiveness but on their claim to effectively represent the city's neighborhoods. From this perspective, what matters is that the organizations are *participatory* and that they are organized at the scale of the *community* or neighborhood.

Unfortunately, most scholars of urban governance and civil society have not so much rejected the idea that these organizations underpin elite authority; they simply have not asked the question. The biggest obstacle to thinking about participation as a component of authority is that participation is usually discussed as a practice that has some essence that produces determinate effects. Instead, I want to emphasize that "participation" is a flexible signifier, the content of which is fought over for political gain. Advocates of participation claim that it results in more authentic deliberation, gives access to forms of knowledge that are marginalized among academic and policy elites, produces citizens that have greater concern for the general good, and furthers the democratization of society. On the other hand, critics argue that participation opens the door to extremism, enables the imposition of norms that can be exclusionary or repressive, corrupts the efficient operation of rational governance, produces political docility, and facilitates the management of the citizenry.[4]

This chapter analyzes the changing role of participation in the constitution of urban political authority. I do this by tracing its institutional articulation in CBOs in Cleveland, Ohio, over the last forty years. Broadly, I address the following question: What makes participation worth fighting about in the context of urban governance? The short answer is that the collapse of the politics of growth and the emergence of populist and neighborhood-based critiques in the 1970s made it clear that expanded participation had become a necessary component of legitimate authority. Authority here is understood as beliefs that secure consent to the rule of another even when such consent is not self-serving. In other words, when consent cannot be justified rationally it rests on beliefs that legitimate rule.[5]

The promise of growth was central to urban authority in postwar America, but urban decline undermined the viability of growth as a legitimating belief. This vacuum was filled by the promise of neighborhood self-determination. Once this was understood, resistance to broad-based participation in governance diminished and was replaced by a competitive struggle to define *technologies of participation* that would make participation safe for use as a component of the authority of elites.

Treating participatory practices as *technologies* is a necessary step to break with tacit assumptions about the essential qualities of participation. By "technology" I mean a bundle of practices, metrics, discourses, and actors, which is useful but only has moral value based on how it is linked up to different actors, institutions, and goals. "Technologies of participation" refers to arrangements of practices, metrics, discourses, and actors that perform community self-determination in ways that are designed to realize specific goals. For example, deliberation can be sold as a commodity or it can help create group solidarity and identity. It can enable democratization or elite rule. From this perspective, participation should be thought of not as a practice with essential characteristics but as a practice that derives its significance from how it is situated relative to other practices, actors, and meanings.[6] Treating participation this way enables a break with the assumption, prominent since the 1960s, that participation yields democratization and the expression of the unmediated voice of the citizenry.

The analysis reveals three stages in the transformation of participatory technologies between 1970 and 2010, each characterized by a type of CBO. The first stage was characterized by community organizing groups that engaged in contentious politics and used participatory deliberation to make decisions. The community organizing groups were eliminated from the field in the course of competition with emergent community developers. The second stage was characterized by a competition between clientelist and technocratic community development corporations (CDCs). This resulted in the ascendancy of expert authority in the field. Finally, since 2000 consensus organizing has been deployed as a participatory practice that valorizes collaboration and partnership. Rather than serving as a challenge to elite and expert authority, participation is now deployed as a tool of that authority.

Why Participation Matters: The Crisis of Growth Politics in Cleveland

In the 1960s and 1970s Cleveland's politics were exceptionally turbulent. Notable events included civil rights protest followed by neighborhood-based populist protest, two riots, election of the country's first African American mayor, election of a self-described "populist" mayor, a recall election, a capital strike, and municipal bankruptcy. These dramatic events were the product of a general crisis of growth politics. The politics of growth had secured the authority of urban elites when the city was thriving. However, economic and political crises in the 1970s made the promise of growth appear to be empty. The city became embroiled in a three-way struggle between mobilized neighborhoods, elected politicians and corporate elites over the right to define the content of legitimate political authority in the city.

The precipitating factor in this change was the economic crisis of 1973, which made it clear that American manufacturing was no longer competitive. For manufacturing cities like Cleveland, the implications were dire and the city descended into a cycle of unemployment, declining revenue, declining neighborhoods, rising crime, and out-migration. This shifted the political dynamic from one focused on securing growth and dealing with its consequences to a zero-sum competition for state investment to minimize the consequences of decline. For example, to preserve the value of downtown real estate, Cleveland's governors scandalously spent tens of millions of dollars in Community Development Block Grant and Urban Development Action Grant money on white elephant projects, all while the city's neighborhoods collapsed. When added to the ledger of violence perpetrated against the city's neighborhoods by extensive highway building and urban renewal, these projects undermined the claim of elite private interests to be acting civically rather than out of self-interest. The city's neighborhoods, black and white, revolted.

The revolt took two forms. The most obvious one was the emergence of a new urban populist political coalition centered on the "boy mayor," as he was known: Dennis Kucinich (1977–1979). His victory signaled the effectiveness of a platform that empowered neighborhoods against centralized bureaucracies and growth-oriented elites. His claim to be the "people's mayor" signaled a new deference to the authority of neighborhood residents at the expense of experts and self-proclaimed civic leaders.

Unfortunately for Kucinich, mayors need the support of pro-growth fractions, like the bankers who provide the liquidity necessary to do things like pay police officers and firemen. Unimpressed with Kucinich's pro-neighborhood platform and his valorization of "the people" as a voice in urban politics, the city's bankers staged a capital strike and launched a recall election (the precipitating issue was the privatization of a public utility). Perhaps to his credit, Kucinich refused to be disciplined by these maneuvers, but the cost to the city was high. A crisis of governance was laid on top of the economic crisis, a combination that resulted in municipal bankruptcy a few years later. Kucinich defeated the recall but lost the next election to the pro-growth Republican George Voinovich (1980–1989).

Kucinich's mayoralty has been described as the institutionalization of Alinskyite organizing in formal politics.[7] While this view can be sustained by a common valorization of "the people" and a privileging of neighborhoods at the expense of growth-oriented elites, it is incorrect. Community organizing in Cleveland was just as hostile to elected politicians like Kucinich as it was to the city's growth-oriented elites. A new breed of community organization disrupted the simple opposition, proposed by Kucinich, between neighborhoods and downtown.

In addition to being a hotbed of civil rights organizing, Cleveland had also been home to early experiments in community organizing. By the mid-1970s, the city had several contentious organizations known as "community congresses." Like Kucinich, they claimed to represent "the people" and they wanted neighborhoods to have priority both in terms of policy and private investment. They were happy to use protest to realize their goals.[8] While the organizations had a similar policy agenda to Kucinich's, it quickly became clear that the new mayor and the congresses were going to be enemies, not allies. Shortly after Kucinich was elected he agreed, after weeks of pressure, to attend a "neighborhood summit" to work out a policy program with the congresses. Kucinich failed to show and sent members of his administration instead. When they chose to lecture the audience rather than engage in a dialogue about policy, a neighborhood leader seized the microphone and hit Kucinich's representative on the head with it. The amplified whack sparked a brawl that spilled out onto the grounds of the church that hosted the event. Relations between the two self-proclaimed representatives of the people never recovered and Kucinich was a target of protests by the congresses for the remainder of his term.

The crux of the issue was the question of who had the authority to represent the people. It is not surprising that politicians claim that they do. What changed was the emergence of community organizations that also claimed to represent the people and that were intent on deploying their power to ensure that they were recognized. These organizations traded on New Left critiques of bureaucracy and civil rights critiques of political representation. Formal politics and government were not venues for the people to be heard, community organizations in civil society were. The breakdown of authority was complete. None of the competing mobilized interests—neighborhoods, politicians and their allies, and growth-oriented elites—were able to secure consent from the others.

While Kucinich disagreed with the congresses' understanding of neighborhood representation, his successor, George Voinovich, did not. Unlike Kucinich, Voinovich was happy to devolve authority and governance functions onto new community-based organizations. Voinovich traded this recognition for political space to recommit to the politics of growth. Some funds would be allocated to CBOs for neighborhood stabilization, but the bulk would go for economic development. City councilors supported this devolution of governance in exchange for greater control over federal Community Development Block Grants and the prospect of having a CBO in their wards that would be reliant on them for funds.

The demise of the congresses paved the way for this emerging accommodation. As the congresses won victories they became involved in neighborhood redevelopment programs and, in the process, they began creating CDCs to implement the agenda of the people. At the same time, the congresses became heavily involved in national and local campaigns to secure private investment in urban neighborhoods. One Cleveland campaign targeted the SOHIO Corporation, a large oil company (since purchased by BP). They protested shareholder meetings and pursued the company's CEO. Their demand: $1 billion to reinvest in neighborhoods. The campaign culminated in 1982 at an elite suburban country club, the Hunt Club. With polo ponies as a backdrop, video footage of the event portrays amused Cleveland residents yelling slogans at the city's nonplussed and nattily attired social elite. But the protest divided the movement over the necessity of the "hit." The consequences of the protest became dire when outraged philanthropists rescinded their funding while reserving future funding for organizations engaged in "bricks-and-mortar" development, not organizing. The congresses died as a result of internal conflict and a loss of funding, but the civic leadership of the city was committed to funding neighborhood redevelopment through CDCs.

Growth was not restarted as an outcome of Cleveland's crisis of growth politics. Despite many and frequent announcements of recovery, the city has continued to lose jobs, corporate operations, and population (from nearly a million in 1970 down to four hundred thousand today). However, authority had been reestablished and since the early 1980s decline has not been associated with political polarization. Through community foundations and strategic investments, growth-oriented elites have acknowledged that neighborhood stabilization is important for economic development. Politicians have learned to coexist with organizations that claim to be more authentic representatives of community. Bureaucrats are happy to fund CBOs to perform governance functions that were once performed by government agencies. The population of CBOs rode this wave of legitimacy and funding to a peak of fifty-five in 1996, even as the community organizing groups died.

The question, then, is why were these organizations funded? Programmatic effectiveness has always been, at best, ambiguous. At the same time, community foundations and intermediary organizations have repeatedly demonstrated a commitment to the idea of participation in CBOs and the idea that neighborhoods should have organizations that represent them. There are two reasons for this. First, the dual challenge of Kucinich's populist coalition and the community congresses made it clear that the authority of urban institutions would have to rely on some expansion of popular participation and a decentralization of responsibility. Effectively, the neighborhood revolt of the 1970s was not defeated so much as it was institutionalized, not in the way preferred by many movement activists, but institutionalized nonetheless. Second, collaborating with CBOs, funding them, training them, and recognizing their legitimacy enabled growth-oriented elites and political leaders to reestablish their own authority. Politicians had been criticized for being a distinct class that acted to realize its own particular concerns. Likewise, the capital strike against Kucinich undermined the civic credentials of growth-oriented elites. By supporting CBOs (organizations that presumably represent the authentic voice of neighborhoods), growth-oriented elites and political representatives establish their claim to be civic actors rather than self-interested ones. In Cleveland, funding and recognition for CBOs are being exchanged for the symbolic capital that enables civic leadership.

The question of whether or not participatory institutions were good or necessary in urban governance was eclipsed by this question: Which sort of participation is best? This question was decided, not in public debate, but in inter-organizational struggles for recognition, funding, and legitimacy. Participatory *technologies* were being developed to meet a variety of ends within the basic constraint that participatory practices were necessary. It is to these technologies that I now turn.

Participation and Contention: The Rise and Fall of Broad-Based Organizing

The community congresses were innovative and insistent experiments in citizen development. They challenged the way urban governance worked, forcefully arguing that neighborhoods should be heard and accounted for in policy. They privileged the power of people working together on issues of common concern and the power of confrontation and tension to alter the balance of power between urban communities and their governors. Participation by diverse neighborhood residents and stakeholders was essential to both of these aspects of the congresses. Together, their internal deliberative practices, their effort to address the people of the city as a whole, and their contentious rejection of both formal representative practices and the authority of growth politics meant that the congresses constituted a neighborhood-based counterpublic.[9]

Participation in the congresses played two distinct roles. First, broad-based participation was utilized as a tool to constitute the community through internal dialogue, deliberation, and strategic work on issues. Street club meetings represented geographic aspects of the neighborhood. At the level of the congresses there were "issue committees" responsible for research on issues of concern. Some worked on community issues; others worked on citywide or even national issues. Finally, there were committees that dealt with internal governance. These deliberative forums were supported by professional organizers who were paid with dues collections, foundation grants, or government grants.[10] Internal authority in the organizations was channeled through "leaders," unpaid neighborhood residents who had a broad following in the neighborhood or who became skilled practitioners of community organizing. They led internal deliberations and negotiations with targets. Nationally, the congresses operated under the umbrella of National People's Action (NPA), a Chicago-based community organizing network led by Gail Cincotta and Shel Trapp. NPA annual meetings were, like those of the member congresses, representative, deliberative, multi-issue, and strategic. Whatever else they were, the congresses were organized to ensure that the priorities of neighborhood residents would correspond with the goals of the congresses, undiluted by experts or professionals.

Second, participation enabled the congresses to perform the basis of their authority in confrontation with their opponents. This was intended to be pedagogical for people on both sides of the issue. Politicians were to be disciplined into respect for their constituents by the constant pressure applied by the congresses. They were disciplined through protest actions, civil disobedience, and disruption. The congresses shut down shareholder meetings and City Hall. They ran pickets against recalcitrant corporations and unresponsive city officials. For the members of the congresses, these actions were classrooms of effective citizenship. One leader, Marlene Weslian, argues that "over time, organizing ... did empower you." "The more I gained in self-confidence and self-esteem the ... more assertive I was in all areas of my life ... [and] the more open to issues like the environment and war."[11]

By constructing skilled and knowledgeable citizens, the congresses hoped to reconstitute the polity and the economy, both of which had become enemies of neighborhoods and the people. Rather than running candidates for city council or negotiating new union contracts, this reform was to be accomplished from without by subordinating economic and political actors to the authority of neighborhood-based civil society organizations. In its newsletter *Disclosure*, NPA claimed that in its member organizations the people were forged into a democratic instrument that could confront and be victorious against "bankers and bureaucrats." The newsletter promised that the callow and self-interested would ultimately submit to the will of the people now that NPA had "jammed open" the "revolving door" to "decision-making offices," thus allowing "the People to pass through" and reclaim their authority.[12]

The congresses developed a variety of internal metrics that were used as indicators of organizational health and effectiveness. Some of them are entirely standard organizational practice: turnouts for events and actions, the use of agendas, and the presence of a broad bench of neighborhood leaders making strategic decisions for the congresses. Others were less formal. One important indicator of organizational health was the willingness of neighborhood leaders to engage in confrontational protest. The congresses claimed to be more authentic representatives of the people than politicians were, but that could only be performed if leaders could overcome their deference to their targets. Mobilizing African Americans was also central, in part because they were understood by organizers to be easier to mobilize than whites. Building cross-race organizations also enabled the congresses to claim to be better and more authoritative representatives than racially and ethnically fractious politicians. However, just as important was the fact that the congresses had difficulty recruiting African American organizers. For white organizers the ability to mobilize African Americans was a key marker of professional skill as was the ability to get whites to focus on their common opponents. Recalling this aspect of the congresses, a Buckeye-Woodland community congress leader's thoughts are telling: "I'm not saying people weren't prejudiced, but they managed to put it in their back pockets long enough to deal with the issues that assaulted all of us."[13] One of the symbols of the congresses in the 1970s was a white hand shaking a black hand.

Discursively and dramaturgically, the congresses made the case that they were more authentic representatives of communities than elected politicians, and, therefore, they were the true source of political authority. It was the participatory and organizational construction of the people in the congresses that gave them the right to hold politicians, bureaucrats, and corporate leaders accountable. A neighborhood leader, Kathy Jaksic, notes that the main issue was not policing, housing, energy prices, or anything else. Instead, "it was a question of authority. Who was going to decide for this neighborhood?"[14] For this reason, actions against these targets were never simply about resolving the issue in question; it was also about disciplining and reorienting the city's rulers to be responsive to the true source of their authority.

The people did not exist naturally as an actor on the public stage. It was constituted through these internal and external modes of participation. But to leave it there would fall into the trap of assuming that participation produces determinate effects such as democratization. In the case of the congresses this assumption would be valid. In their hands it was a technology that enabled the creation of the people in opposition to "interests." However, this capacity is not inherent to participation or deliberation. Participation in the congresses derived its meaning and its purpose from the particular context and from a wide variety of connections to other places, people, institutions, and organizations.

The Reagan era was generally not friendly to community organizing. This became clear in the wake of a protest at the Hunt Club in suburban Cleveland. The protest brought together people from throughout Cleveland and the Midwest as a demonstration of neighborhood power that targeted the CEO of the SOHIO Corporation. The event disrupted a gala of the city's elite, including the philanthropists who funded many of the congresses. They reacted by withdrawing funding for organizing in favor of "bricks and mortar" development. The action also managed to fracture the people along two of the core fault lines of the movement: more versus less confrontational congresses (which partially mapped onto more and less African American), and organizers versus leaders. Many in the less-experienced and less-radical congresses felt the action served no strategic purpose and that they were manipulated into it by the professional organizers. The action also cost the congresses the support of the archdiocese. Perhaps more important than these problematic tensions was that the participatory technology deployed by the congresses was already losing some of its effectiveness. Most of the congresses were already turning to physical redevelopment because it was a core part of their agenda and because their victories had made available necessary resources. Also, a new generation of politicians, led by George Voinovich, was happy to acknowledge the authority of community organizations over neighborhood governance. In doing so Voinovich eliminated the contentious issue of recognition and begged that CBOs and municipal government should work together. Many responded to this question by becoming essential contributors to the institutionalization of a system for the large-scale redevelopment of the city's neighborhoods. This came to be known as the "community development industry system."[15]

The organizing style of the congresses would persist at a couple of the new CDCs and many initially viewed organizing and development as complementary. But with staff turnover, little funding support for organizing, and the growing professional requirements of community development, the participatory practices of the congresses fell by the wayside.[16] Instead, a very large population of CDCs emerged. With the elimination of the congresses, CDCs became the authorized representatives of the city's neighborhoods, and they were expected to take on a broad range of governance functions as well as responsibility for neighborhood well-being and physical redevelopment. Despite the demise of the neighborhood counterpublic, the struggle over what participation was to mean was not over. Instead, the conflict shifted to the field of community development itself.

Community Development and the Rise and Fall of Professional Closure

In 1980 there were three types of organizations that claimed to represent Cleveland's communities; CDCs, the congresses, and the ward operations of city councilors. The trajectory of these organizations makes clear that the organizational form of the CDC came to be broadly useful, a utility that is evident in the very rapid increase in the number of CDCs from ten to fifty-five between 1975 and 1996. CDCs were useful to community residents because they served as brokers of resources coming from government and private philanthropy to rebuild the city's neighborhoods—a central goal of the congresses. They were useful to city councilors because they could serve as vehicles for spending funds in ways that tied neighborhood residents to their electoral operations. Finally, they were useful to growth-oriented elites because physical redevelopment served the purpose of maximizing the exchange value of the city's real estate in an apparently civic rather than self-interested manner.

Community development is frequently presented as a unified movement that works to rebuild urban neighborhoods.[17] There is indeed much that unifies CDCs, characteristics that were defined in the struggle with community organizing over the authoritative organizational form for the representation of neighborhood interests. CDCs in Cleveland represent a defined geographical area at the sub-urban scale, such as a ward, a neighborhood, or a statistical planning area. They realize their goals through the use of collaborative public-private partnerships rather than confrontational protest. Finally, they measure community well-being using real estate values and engage in physical development to increase those values. These organizations were producing several hundred houses per year before the foreclosure crisis, though this volume did not come close to outstripping the foreclosure rate in Cleveland even before the crisis that began in 2007. Nonetheless, many neighborhoods did experience a visible improvement in their well-being and, according to some, benefited in other ways as well.[18]

These ideas about development were part of a philanthropic project to develop tools and metrics of successful community development. The Ford Foundation in particular was instrumental in developing program-related investments to facilitate philanthropic support of development projects. Alongside this interest in development was a new emphasis on the importance of real estate values as the primary measurement of community well-being. CDCs deal with the particular problems of different parcels using a variety of development tools, such as Low-Income Housing Tax Credit (LIHTC)–funded housing or market-rate developments. The strategic deployment of development tools is enabled by an objectifying gaze that is manifested in land-use maps and strategic plans. Often, CDCs have design-review powers that enable them to block development that cannot be integrated into the plan. Housing development is the most powerful tool that CDCs have available for reviving local markets because of the combination of its desirability from the point of view of the CDC, the availability of a well-funded and diverse set of tools, and the availability of relevant skills among CDC staff.

The differences between the development corporations that emerged from the neighborhood movement and the congresses themselves are stark. Contemporary CDCs have generally empowered technocrats, expert in physical redevelopment and urban planning, as the representatives of community interests. It has also empowered funders and lenders as the arbiters of appropriate interventions in the city's neighborhoods.

The empowerment of expert managers at the community scale had serious consequences for participation in CBOs. The authority of CDCs within the city's neighborhoods hinged upon the ability of community development experts to define needs and apply appropriate solutions. However, community developers—trained to see the world through the prism of real estate values—naturally define problems and solutions in ways that do not necessarily correspond with the priorities of community residents. Indeed, once real estate values become the measure of community well-being, physical redevelopment in poorer neighborhoods began to target suburban professionals rather than existing residents, transforming the representative logic of community organizations. As for existing residents, they become a nuisance "indigenous population" standing in the way of development.[19] CBOs were disconnected from the communities they represented and were creating a setting to attract an "imagined community" of affluent future residents.

Because of its emphasis on the revalorization of real estate, this technocratic approach to community development has been broadly supported by the municipal bureaucracy, private philanthropies, and local growth-oriented elites. Nonetheless, even though community organizing was marginalized, the consensus that emerged around the technocratic model of community development by 2000 was not unchallenged. CDCs were also a useful organizational form for ward-based politicians. Clientelistic politicians, in particular, use CDCs to engage in what Marwell calls "triadic exchange."[20] Effectively, CDCs enable politicians to link the programmatic activities of CDCs to electoral politics. Programs are used to create "organizational adherents" that are then assumed to be loyal to the councilor on Election Day. For many in the field of community development, this sort of relationship is a modern-day form of "legitimate graft." It siphons resources from appropriate community development activities and, moreover, it enables corrupt councilors to maintain their grip on their wards. Community development, in the case of these CDCs, is subordinated to the needs of electoral politics.[21]

However, the view from these clientelist CDCs is quite different and the participatory practices of these organizations are worth considering. One CDC executive director presented her organization not as "interests" or "corporations," but as representatives of the people of the ward. She claimed they are distinguished by a desire to build amenities for existing residents rather than "golf clubs" for suburbanites. Their authority as representatives of the community is not derived from a broad base of leadership or the demonstration of community solidarity through mobilization and protest. There is little in the way of democratic deliberation. She claimed it, naturally enough, based on electoral authority—the councilor was elected by the residents of the ward. But alone this is not enough. Clientelist ward politicians have dense networks of relations with people throughout their wards. Ward clubs are often participatory venues, though participants tend to be highly deferential to the status and authority of the councilor. Despite how they are presented by their technocratic opponents in the field, these politicians are not simply venal. Indeed, many of them live in nondescript houses and use their relative poverty as a marker of authenticity, something that is often augmented by invocations of religious faith. They pursue equity in the distribution of resources and sometimes pursue redistributive policies as well.

Nonetheless, the mode of participation in these organizations does little to develop the political sophistication of anyone other than the councilor. Nor is the point to constitute an autonomous neighborhood voice or the civil society organizations that might underpin one. The effective clientelist councilor is the central node in a dense network of relations that ensures accountability to neighborhood residents. In contrast with technocratic community developers, clientelist CDCs rely on the charisma of the councilor and his or her ability to use the position to secure goods and services for constituents, even by shaking down technocratic CDCs for a share of developers' fees. This is justified in the name of acting on behalf of "the people" against the needs of other CDCs that are obsessed with development.

Clientelist CDCs have difficulty reproducing themselves due to their dependence on individual politicians. Status in the field of community organizations as a whole has increasingly privileged professional community development and urban planning skills. Clientelist organizations have trouble securing funds without their patrons. Consequently, the death rate of these organizations is far higher than other types of CDCs, and the clientelist position is slowly being eliminated from the field. In terms of the ability of CBOs to effectively represent neighborhood residents, the elimination of the clientelist position has the effect of eliminating an organizational type that relies on neighborhood participation, however undemocratic, for its ability to represent the community. This, alongside the increasing dominance of more technocratic practices, largely eliminated participation from the city's CBOs.

However, rather than securing the uncontested authority of community development experts over the field of urban CBOs, the eventual dominance of technocratic CDCs threatened the very purpose of community organizations. Professionalizing CDCs made sense in the context of the struggle with clientelist CDCs and their political patrons, but this also undermined their utility as a foundation for elite authority. Once we recognize this function it is not surprising that renewed calls for neighborhood participation in CBOs did not come from politicians or the residents themselves, it came from private-sector funders of CDCs. By 2000 it had become apparent to funders that the meaning of community had been reduced to a synonym for organizational territory. The term was being drained of its association with authentic and unmediated social relations, self-governance, and democratic deliberation. An intermediary organization vice president explained the dilemma simply: "Funders were coming to annual meetings [of CDCs] and there was nobody there." Technocratic

CBOs were unable to effectively consecrate the legitimacy of urban elites because they no longer plausibly represented the city's neighborhoods.

Making Participation Safe for Use: Consensus Organizing

The return to community organizing among Cleveland's CBOs began in 2002 with a new round of philanthropic funding and a commitment by support organizations to train new organizers. Organizing has since come to be considered a core component of professional community development practice and many CDCs have hired full-time staff organizers. These organizers mostly organize and service street clubs in CDC service areas. This effort would solve a problem that had emerged with the rationalization of technocratic CDCs around the goal of physical redevelopment: how to support the claim that CDCs were legitimate representatives of the city's neighborhoods? Because resources were being given in exchange for the symbolic capital necessary to legitimate the rule of political and growth-oriented elites, it became necessary to recreate participatory practices in the city's CBOs. But while organizing street clubs can help solve that problem, it creates a new one: What is to prevent newly organized community residents from recreating the contentious congresses that helped precipitate the crisis of growth politics?

The key puzzle that CDCs had to resolve was how to be legitimate representatives of the community when they were organized to respond to the imagined community of future residents. Why would people participate? What would happen when they pursued their interests? New technologies of participation made this possible; the most important of these for CDCs is *consensus organizing*. Consensus organizing enables CDCs to offer neighborhood stakeholders voice and venues to construct community solidarity. But this comes with costs. As with all extra-governmental participatory forums, one cost is the marginalization of formal mechanisms of representation that can hold decision makers accountable. Moreover, the privileging of markets as the primary metric of well-being and the determinant of appropriate organizational action eliminated the organization as a buffer between community residents and the effects of markets. Finally, this mode of participation requires accepting normative standards of civility that trump the use of power or contention to secure goals. This type of citizen participation leaves no room for the recreation of a neighborhood counterpublic.

Consensus organizing was developed by Michael Eichler as a direct competitor of community organizing groups influenced by Saul Alinsky.[22] Despite being eliminated in Cleveland, community organizing groups have grown nationally. In many cities Alinskyite community organizations are often recognized as legitimate community voices. Without having to demand recognition, the need to protest outdoors has declined, but contention over issues has often simply moved indoors. Nonetheless, Eichler argues that "conflict organizing" worked in an era when there was a single, politically unsophisticated enemy that was easy to identify. Of course, many community organizers would argue that conflict is often still necessary because of power inequalities. For Eichler inequalities do not prevent finding the common ground necessary for consensus. The implication is that there are no Bull Connors or Richard Daleys anymore. Authority rests on different practices that are not as exclusive. Because of this, technologies designed to disrupt older forms of authority are rendered impotent. Community organizing has not adapted to new modes of authority built on participation and, therefore, it is "tired" and "ineffective."

None of this is really true in the details. Community organizing has changed quite a bit since Alinsky and it is often criticized by scholars for being devoid of ideology, not overly ideological as Eichler portrays it. Nonetheless, while missing the target, Eichler is on to something. Namely, the nature of urban authority has indeed changed. Alinsky's community organizing was a technology that was designed to deal with the authority of growth politics, premised as it was on political closure and economic mobility. In the neoliberal era this mode of authority is inverted. Access and participation are expansive and relativized in a context of downward mobility and increasing socioeconomic inequality, short-circuiting institutional critiques that emphasized inadequate democracy rather than socioeconomic inequality.

Eichler's technology has been attractive to community developers since the mid-1990s. The reason is clear: Consensus organizing enables community developers to effectively challenge the claims of community organizers to be the authorized representatives of neighborhoods. While this was unnecessary in Cleveland where community organizing had been marginalized before consensus organizing emerged, it was an issue elsewhere. The Ford Foundation initially funded consensus organizing demonstration projects in support of community development efforts in Little Rock and Baton Rouge, strongholds of ACORN.[23] LISC, the Ford-funded community development financing organization, also funded Eichler's consensus organizing center in San Diego and disseminated the technology around the country. In cities with a significant community organizing presence, consensus organizing serves as an alternative technology of participation that competes with Alinskyite organizing.

This is not to say that consensus organizing is only about competition between participatory practices. It is entirely appropriate for a field of CBOs that relies heavily on connections with banks, developers, and City Hall to be effective. Technocratic community development in Cleveland has always distinguished itself from organizing by emphasizing the efficacy of partnerships rather than conflict. However, for a decade technocratic CDCs had ignored community residents; now they energetically organize them into street clubs. Organizing is now considered an essential component of CDC activity and an essential component of physical redevelopment.

Nonetheless, this new mode of participation is radically different from the practices in clientelist CDCs and the congresses. Contemporary street clubs have little to do with land-use decisions, the allocation of capital, or developing neighborhood plans. These essential questions continue to be the realm of the professional community developer. In fact, when CDC directors are asked about street clubs and what they do, they generally cite their effectiveness on quality-of-life issues (policing) and their input on design. When architectural plans are developed, street clubs are often asked for comment. Of course, community residents are not architects, so they are unlikely to produce an alternative. However, examples of residents making decisions about the height of yard fences, parking arrangements, and the depth of porch overhangs are not uncommon. The most widely celebrated success of consensus organizing is a case where organizing reduced racial tensions prompted by a large housing development designed to attract suburban buyers. In this case, the organizing paved the way for physical redevelopment that was not popular among existing residents by subordinating the interests and aspirations of neighborhood stakeholders to the normative expectation of civility.

These characteristics are reflected in the self-understanding of contemporary community organizers in Cleveland. They claim to be "consensus builders" who establish "positive relationships" even though this means "not encouraging residents" who are more combative. When issues are difficult, norms of civility are deployed to avoid contention. One organizer encourages residents to "be mindful of who you're addressing and how you address them because there are ways to get what you want without causing a fight." After all, "we're all partners." It is now possible for residents to "be more inclusive" and have "residents sit down with businesses." Among the accomplishments of consensus organizing celebrated in one CDC are "community building walks," a "welcome wagon" program (that welcomes new residents to the neighborhood), and ideas for neighborhood improvements such as the installation of yard lights.

When asked why CDCs should be doing organizing at all, a CDC organizer says stakeholders are essential "for legitimacy." "If you just plop a development in the middle of a neighborhood and nobody knows about it, it may be accepted, but it might not be." This goes to the heart of the purpose of consensus organizing in Cleveland. If interests were grounded in social position and aligned with the CDC, the issue of "acceptance" would not come up. The question arises when physical redevelopment is disconnected from community needs. How then can CDCs claim to be authoritative representatives of neighborhoods? "Welcome wagons" and street clubs serve that purpose admirably.

Consensus organizing is a technology of participation that enables CDCs to claim popular authority for the actions of expert developers even when developers fail to act in the interest of existing residents. As such, they are also able to consecrate the activities of their funders, politicians and growth-oriented elites, as legitimately civic. In the absence of this participatory technology CDCs would be able to engage in physical redevelopment, but they would not be able to serve their primary role, which is to underpin the legitimacy of the city's governors.

In other words, consensus organizing relies on the expert management of participation itself. This is a significant shift. While once participation was opposed to technocracy, in consensus organizing and other new technologies of participation they have been fused. This does not mean that all organizing is a mere charade. CDCs pay very close attention to street clubs and not merely for the purpose of keeping a lid on them. Instead, they are useful forums for venting concerns and gleaning insights that can enhance the management of development. In other words, this type of participation is not merely about securing authority, but also about capturing the benefits of local knowledge and further socializing citizens into collaborative practices—even when the issues are not being addressed in ways that benefit the participants.

Not surprisingly, the positive effects of participation are among the most widely celebrated in contemporary policy, though some urban scholars have observed similar technologies and recognize that the effect is to render a politics of community interest normatively out of bounds. When situated against the overall history and trajectory of conflict over the meaning and practice of participation in Cleveland, this arrangement is less an achievement to be celebrated than the product of the imperatives of contemporary urban governance and the narrowing of organizational diversity among CBOs. Participation is now an input in technocratic decision making and a foundation for the authority of elites that are unresponsive to pressing issues like unemployment and foreclosure.

Conclusion

Cleveland's crisis of political authority in the 1970s changed the way the city's political and economic leaders viewed participation. Once something to be limited as much as possible, the community congresses and Dennis Kucinich altered the way political closure was understood in the city. The costs of limiting public participation had become too high. The issue was no longer to figure out whether or not it should be tolerated, it was what type of participation would be most useful. The congresses had a very sophisticated technology of neighborhood participation, but it underpinned a neighborhood counterpublic and undermined elite authority. Nonetheless, the experimentation with participatory technologies began migrating out of protest movements and into elite foundations, bureaucratic agencies, strategic business organizations, and the ward operations of local politicians until these technologies were reworked as a basis for legitimate rule.

Events in Cleveland were merely one manifestation of a much broader institutional revalorization of participation and experimentation with participatory technologies. Nonetheless, it is not simply a representative case. Cleveland's crisis of political authority throws the issue into sharp relief. In Cleveland, growth—the basis of urban authority through much of the postwar period—could no longer legitimate the rule of political and economic elites. Of course, growth, or at least preventing decline, remained a broadly valued policy goal, but it no longer functioned as a justification for exclusionary decision making. Likewise with political authority. Simply being elected was no longer an adequate basis for legitimate rule, as Kucinich learned. The people would have to be heard before decisions could be made. The question was how should they be heard? The potential of a counterpublic to disrupt governance was on display for everyone to see in Cleveland. Unlike institutional leaders in most American cities, governors and philanthropists in Cleveland made the choice to crush rather than tolerate a neighborhood counterpublic. But this merely put the question in stark terms: What sort of participatory technology can elites use to ground their authority? Part of the answer was to rescale governance functions to the neighborhood, but this was inadequate when there was no actual community participation. Instead, consensus organizing solves many of the dilemmas that arise from using participation as a tool for authority. Not surprisingly, it was philanthropic funders, not communities, that renewed the push for participatory venues in CBOs in the early 2000s.

Our understanding of participation does not come from the observation of its practical uses or the battles to define its meaning. We lament the decline of civic participation and assume that expanding participation can be a source of democratic renewal, social solidarity, and better decisions. Of course, some kinds of participation can do this, but other types do not do anything of the sort and, in fact, participation can simply reinforce hierarchies, discipline public behavior into noncontroversial dialogue, and undermine social solidarity. Simply put, participation has no inherent content. What matters is how participatory practices are linked up with institutions, actors, and goals. Different participatory technologies produce different effects and our conceptual and analytical efforts should be directed at the question of what types of participation are desirable and what effects do we value? Of course, this point is not original. However, it becomes much more significant when we appreciate that the meaning and practice of participation are objects of active intervention not simply by movement activists and radical democrats but by corporate managers, growth-oriented elites, bureaucrats, and politicians. Participation is no longer a threat to elites; it is a resource. To talk intelligently about participation today requires confronting this fact.

Institutions are no longer based on limiting the public role in decision making in exchange for the promise of affluence and economic mobility. This was the principle of growth politics in cities and it was also the exchange entailed in the creation of a bureaucratic welfare state: economic openness and political closure. It is increasingly apparent that one of the most important changes in this neoliberal era is an inversion of this dynamic. The popular voice is now broadly accepted as legitimate and valuable. At the same time, we have increasingly abandoned socioeconomic equity as a goal. Labor unions have been crushed, the social safety net has been dismantled, and the logic of the remuneration of labor is no longer based on income security. How is this possible alongside increased participation? In Cleveland it is apparent that part of the gambit is that people will accept economic sacrifices when they are heard in the process of decision making. But this is too simple. The other component is that participation is not organized to produce a collective position. Today's participatory technologies do not enable the creation of a collective actor—"the people," or neighborhoods, or African Americans—to act as a political subject in the public sphere. Rather, participation today often works to fragment discussions into a plethora of distinct institutional settings and topically focused forums. In those settings, responses are heard, they are often measured, and the variety of opinions demonstrates, above all else, that there is variety. This diffusion and proliferation of participatory practice relativizes its significance for decision making because no single perspective has the authority of a collective actor behind it. The authority of "the people" has been acknowledged in institutional practice, but when combined with contemporary participatory technologies, the effect is to relativize and reduce the significance of that authority such that participation is little more than a step in the successful management of an issue, a mere box to check on the "to do" list of campaign managers and institutional leaders.

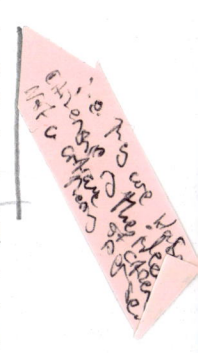

My goal has been to make this process visible in order to advance our understanding beyond semiotic associations between participation and democracy. By treating participatory practices as technologies designed to produce particular effects rather than as a "thing" with predictable effects, it is possible to see how participation has been transformed. Once essential for challenging urban political authority and constructing vibrant counterpublics, participation is now a foundation for that authority and a tool for fragmenting and relativizing oppositional views. This is made visible, not by studying participatory practices themselves, but by situating participation in its institutional and organizational settings. The process I describe is not automatic. It is the outcome of decades of struggle over the meaning, content, and practice of participation. The practical fate of participation reveals the danger of treating it as a stable and transparent signifier. Instead, we must treat it as an object and stake of political struggles before we can hope to stabilize its content for theoretical discussion.

NOTES

1. A previous version of this chapter appeared in *Public Culture* (McQuarrie 2013b). I benefited greatly from the discussions that took place at the Democratizing Inequalities conference. For this reason, I should also acknowledge the funders of that conference, the American Sociological Association Fund for the Advancement of the Discipline and New York University's Institute for Public Knowledge. This chapter was inspired by many generative discussions with my always delightful collaborators, Caroline Lee and Edward Walker.
2. Logan and Molotch (1987).
3. Swanstrom (1985).
4. See the introduction of this volume for a discussion of the relevant literature.
5. Weber (1978: 941–955); Sennett (1980).
6. The following demonstrate the analytical utility of a relational approach to political practices and participation: Gregory (1998); Polletta (2002); Baiocchi (2005); Mische (2009); Eliasoph (2011).
7. Swanstrom (1985).
8. Cunningham (2007).
9. Fraser (1992); Warner (2002).
10. Cleveland's community foundations were intermittently supportive, but the Gund Foundation was more consistent than the Cleveland Foundation, which preferred to fund the local development corporations. The Catholic Campaign for Human Development was an early and consistent funder. Finally, the federal VISTA program funneled young volunteers into the congresses. VISTA was imagined as a domestic version of the Peace Corps that was initially funded as part of Johnson's War on Poverty. During the Clinton administration it was rolled into the Americorps program.
11. Cunningham interview with Marlene Weslian, Western Reserve Historical Society, Cunningham Collection.
12. *Disclosure*, June 1976.
13. Cunningham interviews with Diane Yambor, Tom Gannon, John Calkins, Kathy Jaksic, and Mike O'Brien, Cunningham Collection.
14. Cunningham interview with Kathy Jaksic, Cunningham Collection.

15. Yin (1998).
16. For a discussion of this dynamic, see Stoecker (1997).
17. Rubin (2000); Von Hoffman (2004).
18. Krumholz et al. (2006); Cunningham (2007).
19. For more on the consequences of this development, see McQuarrie (2013a).
20. Marwell (2004, 2007).
21. Looking at maps in the city's Department of Community Development does not suggest any difference in the ability of technocratic or clientelist CDCs to affect real estate values.
22. Eichler (1998).
23. Gittell and Vidal (1998).

CHAPTER 6

The Fiscal Sociology of Public Consultation

ISAAC WILLIAM MARTIN

On Wednesday, February 18, 2009, the Los Angeles Chamber of Commerce and a nonprofit organization called California Forward jointly convened a meeting of about forty local businesspeople to discuss possible reforms to the state's tax structure. Through "small group dialogue, electronic keypad voting and written comments," the participants weighed in on policy options that included new sales taxes, changes to property tax rules, and simplification of the income tax code.[1] The meeting was only one of dozens of hearings, stakeholder convenings, public workshops, focus groups, Choice-Dialogues™, visioning sessions, "community conversations," and town hall forums convened in 2008 and 2009 to discuss options for fundamental reform of the state's governance structure.[2] The interest groups convening these meetings took names—such as California Forward, Repair California, Common Sense California, and Saving California Communities—that evoked progress, civic healing, and even salvation. It was as if the state of California was convulsed by a civic revival: Call it the Great Consultation. The immediate purpose of this revival, however, was not spiritual but mundane. Conveners sought to elicit public participation in setting a policy agenda. "Certainly this forum is about informing people," said the organizer of one such town hall meeting in suburban Thousand Oaks, "but more importantly it's about collecting feedback from the public."[3]

The Great Consultation exemplifies the recent transformation in governance described by Walker, McQuarrie, and Lee in the introduction to this volume as the "new public participation." Governments and interest groups have long sought to elicit the participation of the public by means of such techniques as public opinion polls and voter registration drives. What sets apart the new techniques for "collecting feedback" considered in this chapter is their collective and deliberative character. At their most basic, all of these techniques, whether they be called community conversations or visioning sessions or Deliberative Polls®, consist of getting people in the same room and prompting them to discuss what should be done.[4] Scholars have begun to document and describe a new industry focused on facilitating public consultation through the convening of these new, occasional deliberative assemblies.[5]

Explaining the rise of the new deliberative assemblies is of considerable scholarly interest because of their problematic status in democratic theory. In contrast to the anonymous, mass-mediated election campaigns of the 21st century, the new assemblies involve face-to-face discussion and deliberation of the kind that we may associate with idealized images of the classical polis or the New England town meeting. It can be tempting to see in them a revival of the ideal of participatory democracy.[6] On the other hand, the new deliberative assemblies are typically small, temporary, privately facilitated, irregularly scheduled, and open by invitation only to people who meet sometimes informal and only vaguely defined criteria for participation. All of these characteristics may limit access to these occasional assemblies in ways that seem inconsistent with democratic ideals of equal participation. For example, there is some evidence that those who participate tend to be highly educated, high-income people who already have a disproportionate voice in the American political order, much like the Los Angeles businesspeople convened by California Forward.[7] We might worry whether the rise of the new deliberative assemblies is symptomatic of a broader retreat from democracy.

In this chapter, my purpose is not normative evaluation, but sociological explanation; I conceptualize the new deliberative assemblies as a form of consultation between states and citizens, and I attempt to explain their rise in late 20th-century California by drawing on a general theory of where such innovations come from. State officials and citizens invent new forms of consultation in order to manage the potentially conflictual process of bargaining over the allocation of shared burdens and benefits. Explaining the emergence of any particular innovation in forms of consultation thus requires attention to the historical sequence of forms that preceded it, because such innovations are likely to be introduced only when previous modes of consultation have failed. In particular, as the example of the Great Consultation illustrates, the emergence of the new deliberative assemblies—like the emergence of other techniques of public consultation from elections to public opinion polling—resulted from social conflicts over the appropriation and distribution of public resources. To understand the rise of the new deliberative assemblies we need to turn to fiscal sociology.

The Paradox of Participation, Illustrated with the Case of Late 20th-Century California

To explain the rise of the new deliberative assemblies we must first describe it. Social scientists in the 1960s observed increasing demands for political participation on the part of formerly excluded people around the world, and they anticipated a coming "participation explosion" that would transform governance across the globe.[8] But the following decades brought something different in the United States. Instead of a rise in mass civic activity, the next decade saw a decline. Voter turnout began to trend downward, as illustrated for the case of California by figure 6.1. Other forms of civic participation fell off even more precipitously. National survey data over the same period show that fewer and fewer people attended political rallies, volunteered for political parties, served on local committees, participated actively in clubs or associations, or showed up for public meetings on local affairs.[9] This decline in routine forms of political participation may have been partly balanced by an increase in irregular, informal, and occasional forms of participation—for example, even as fewer and fewer Americans reported attending political rallies in the previous election cycle in the last decades

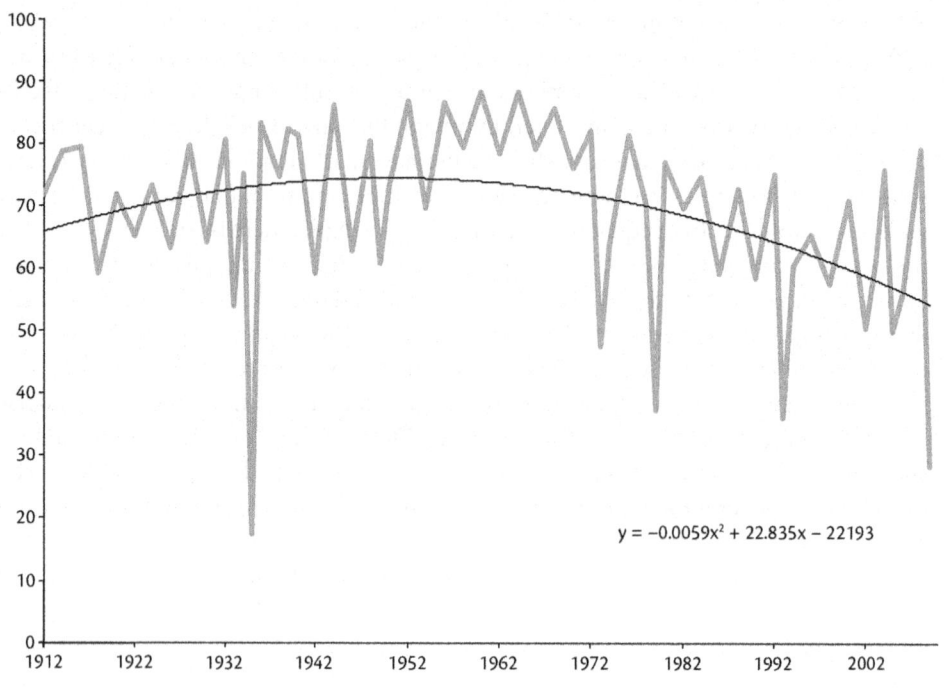

Figure 6.1 The falling demand for participation: Votes cast as a percentage of all registered voters in California elections, 1912–2009. *Source*: California Secretary of State (2010).

of the 20th century, slightly more Americans reported having signed a petition or attended a demonstration at least once in their lives—but at best such data moderate the impression of declining participation.[10] There was no apparent explosion of demands for public participation in the United States.[11]

At the same time, there was an explosion in the supply of *opportunities* for ritualized consultation, as public and private organizations in the United States institutionalized various new forms of consultation with the public. A longer time series can help us put the rise of these forms of public consultation in historical perspective. In the absence of survey data or organizational directories covering a sufficiently long period, I rely on a time series of the number of articles mentioning a "public workshop" or a "town hall forum" in the *Los Angeles Times* (see figure 6.2). Although the data are obviously subject to all of the potential biases of newspaper reporting, the general picture of change over time that this indicator provides is consistent with what scholars have found using other data sources.[12] Sirianni and Friedland, relying on case studies constructed by a combination of interviews and archival research, date the emergence of public consultation to government agencies in the 1970s, with increasing uptake by nongovernmental organizations in the 1980s and 1990s.[13] Lee and Romano rely on various interview and documentary sources to date the birth of the "field of professional public engagement facilitation" roughly to the 1980s.[14] And Jacobs, Cook, and Delli Carpini's survey of 396 organizations "that plan and run public forums" found that two-thirds of the organizations they were able to identify and survey had been founded since 1980.[15] In short, something changed in the 1970s that began to increase the availability of occasions for public deliberation.

This, then, is the paradox of participation: Certain temporary occasions for the public to consult on civic decisions proliferated, even as the share of the public participating in politics appeared to be on the wane. The paradox is resolved if we shift our attention from *average* civic participation to the increasing *dispersion* of civic participation: The trend is toward participatory inequality, as public officials have come to engage in more intensive consultation with a smaller share of the populace. And to explain this trend, we must shift our attention from the demand for participation in general, the sort of thing indexed by figure 6.1, to the supply of opportunities to consult on particular decisions. Under what conditions do organizational elites seek to intensify their consultation with particular segments of the public? In order to answer this question, I offer a fiscal theory of consultation that draws on classic works in the sociology of democratic government. The answer that theory provides, in its briefest form, is that organizational elites may institute new forms of consultation with particular publics when their organizations depend on those publics' willingness to provide material resources.

The Fiscal Sociology of Consultation

The fiscal theory of consultation presented here is a generalization of the fiscal theory of democratization. The latter draws on the classic tradition of "fiscal sociology"

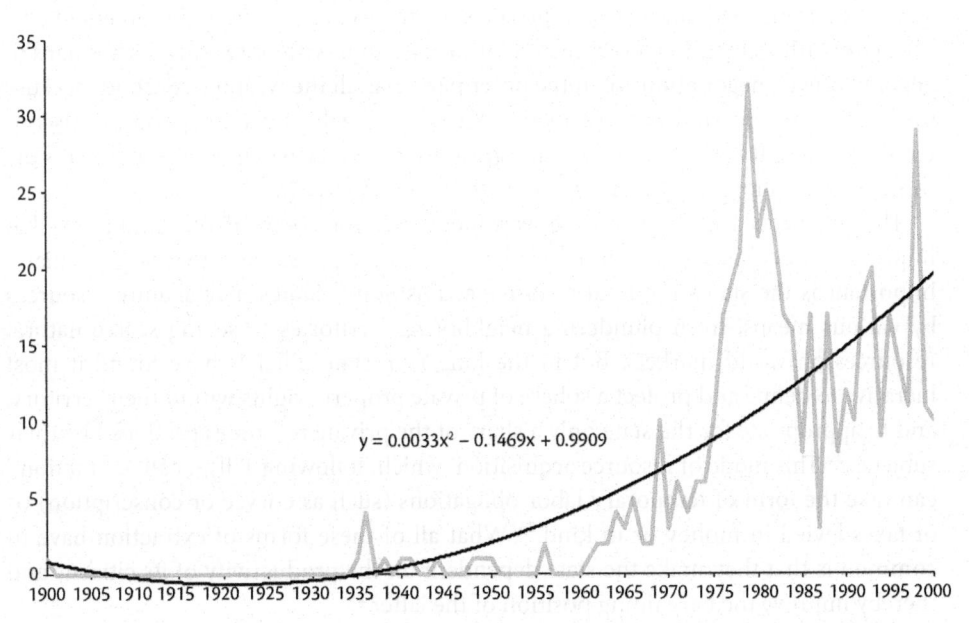

Figure 6.2 The increase in opportunities to be consulted: Number of articles mentioning "public workshop" or "town hall forum" in the *Los Angeles Times*, 1901–2000. *Source*: Author's calculations from ProQuest *Historical Los Angeles Times* database.

$y = 0.0033x^2 - 0.1469x + 0.9909$

associated with the Austrian scholars Rudolf Goldscheid and Joseph Schumpeter.[16] These two scholars sought to explain the rise of constitutional democracy as a byproduct of the need for taxation in the competitive state system of early modern Europe. Later scholars refined their theoretical arguments and tested their ideas with comparative data; noteworthy contributions to the theoretical literature include Bates and Lien, Levi, and Tilly.[17] My exposition of the theory draws particularly on the later work of Charles Tilly, but my generalization of the theory to the case of the new deliberative assemblies is perhaps more in the spirit of Goldscheid and Schumpeter, both of whom went beyond asserting the importance of fiscal policy for understanding the origins of democratic government to hypothesize that the fiscal needs of the state shaped many important features of civil society as well.[18] In this section I explain how and why the fiscal needs of the state might be relevant to the explanation of the consultation explosion in the late 20th-century United States and late 20th-century California in particular.

The fiscal theory of democratization begins with the premise that democracy is best understood as an institutionalized form of consultation between state officials and citizens, where the state is conceptualized in realist terms as a coercion-wielding organization that exists in a field of such organizations.[19] We may define a state more specifically as a compulsory membership organization that successfully claims rule-making priority "over all other users of coercion within a given territory," and we may define a citizen as anyone with compulsory membership in that organization.[20] The problem for a theory of democracy is to explain why officials of any state should bother to consult with its citizens. The answer is not obvious, for at least two reasons. First, because a state is an organization that sets the rules for the use of coercion, discontented citizens have little bargaining leverage in their negotiations with state officials. It is hard to get anything by negotiation when the other party has all the weapons. Second, because membership in the state is compulsory, exit is not usually a viable option for discontented citizens. It is hard to bargain for greater democracy when you cannot plausibly threaten to go shopping for a more democratic state to live in.

The prospects for democratic government therefore depend on conditions that improve the bargaining position of citizens. One such condition that is particularly important is the state's mode of resource acquisition.[21] States may acquire resources by various means, from plundering neighboring territories to selling scarce natural resources on world markets. But in the long run, state officials have found it most lucrative to define and protect a sphere of private property rights within their territory, and to appropriate for the state only a share of the private resources produced by their subjects.[22] This mode of resource acquisition, which, following Tilly, I call "extraction," can take the form of temporary labor obligations (such as corvée or conscription) or of taxes levied in money or in kind.[23] What all of these forms of extraction have in common is that they make the state dependent on the productivity of its citizens and thereby improve the bargaining position of the latter.[24]

All of the ways in which states acquire resources may involve conflict, but extraction gives state officials reasons to resolve that conflict peacefully. Citizens may resist the extractive demands of state officials, and in the face of such resistance officials may be tempted to resort to force. But state officials will ordinarily restrain their use of coercion because they need their citizens to remain alive and productive—and perhaps even, to some degree, positively willing—if those citizens are to continue supplying the state with taxes or labor services.[25] Dead or jailed citizens are not much use as taxpayers, and a surly, foot-dragging taxpayer is not as productive as a happy one. Conflicts over extraction therefore tend to end in bargained settlements between state officials and citizens, rather than in total victory for either side.[26]

Although the classic treatments of the fiscal theory of democratization emphasized conflicts over resource extraction, nothing in the fiscal theory of democratization assumes that extraction is the only source of conflict between states and citizens. Indeed, the history of contentious interactions between citizens and states is filled with conflicts over language rights, religious freedom, the conditions of labor, and countless other questions. But even when the conflict concerns other issues, as with religious civil wars, the fact that state officials are extracting resources from citizens is often what leads rebellious citizens to direct their ire against the state, rather than against other citizens; also, the fact that state officials depend on citizens for resources is what gives state officials an incentive to resolve such conflicts by bargaining a settlement.

The bargain typically goes beyond agreement on a particular division of resources to encompass agreement on rights and duties of consultation over the extraction of additional resources in the future.[27] Citizens demand a binding commitment to consult with them in the future because they are interested in security against unpredictable or arbitrary demands. State officials, for their part, often find it advantageous to commit themselves to a future process of consultation because such consultation can reduce the cost of acquiring information about how much extraction citizens will tolerate.[28] Early constitutions that formalized the creation of parliaments and competitive elections are classic examples of such bargains.[29] But fiscal bargains may also go beyond parchment institutions to include informal institutions whose rules are not codified in any document. "In relatively democratic regimes, competitive elections certainly give citizens a voice," Tilly wrote, "but so do lobbying, petitioning, referenda, social movements, and opinion polling."[30] All of these are examples of routine forms of consultation that might be invented, tolerated, or institutionalized as part of a fiscal bargain.

The fiscal theory of democratization was invented to explain the origins of democratic government, but in the remainder of this section I will argue that the basic logic of the theory suggests that even regimes that are already democratic will continually invent new institutions and procedures for public consultation. There are at least three mechanisms that will tend to generate such continual invention.

The first mechanism is the tendency for citizens' demands to escalate. When state officials strike a fiscal bargain that includes procedural concessions to their citizens, they change the process by which future fiscal bargains will be negotiated. A state may grant voting rights to the majority of its citizens (e.g., as the price of extracting resources from them). But even after state officials have struck this bargain, the need may arise for more resources, and with it the risk of a new round of resistance and bargaining. The resistance of already-enfranchised citizens cannot be calmed by promising them the right to vote: They have it already. Moreover, they may use it to demand

and win additional rights of consultation. In short, each new mode of consultation confers additional leverage on citizens. They may use that leverage to extract procedural concessions that include new modes of consultation.

The mechanism of escalating demands is most likely to apply when state officials confront new demands for spending and when they elect to meet those demands with a strategy of *intensive* extraction. By intensive extraction, I refer to an increase in the rate at which state officials appropriate resources that are already subject to some state claims—for example, an increase in the rate of an existing tax. The alternative is extensive extraction, which refers to the appropriation of new categories of resources to which the state previously laid no claim—for example, a broadening of the tax base to encompass a new category of property or the conscription of a previously exempt category of person. Both strategies may provoke resistance. But intensive extraction is especially likely to affect citizens who have been taxed before and who have already won procedural concessions in prior rounds of resistance and bargaining. Intensive extraction is therefore particularly likely to result in escalating demands for consultation.

Note that the mechanism of escalating demands may exacerbate political inequality. Because canny state officials often target the citizens with the most resources for intensive extraction, any procedural concessions they offer in exchange are likely to be offered first to those citizens who are comparatively economically advantaged. And because the citizens targeted for intensive extraction are precisely those who are most likely to have been granted procedural concessions already in prior rounds of bargaining, their escalating demands for consultation may result in the accretion of political rights by those who are already *politically* advantaged, too. In the long run, the mechanism of escalating demands contributes to the process of democratization. But in the short run, it may actually exacerbate inequalities of political voice—much as the earliest parliaments increased the political rights of the nobility relative to the rights of peasants.

The second mechanism is what I call anticipatory consultation. The interests of state officials in securing a predictable revenue stream may motivate them to invent new forms of consultation. State officials in democratic regimes know that they will need to consult with their citizens over resources in the future. They will often attempt to acquire intelligence in advance about the bargain they can hope to obtain. In order to get that information, they may be forced to invent or adopt new forms of consultation that allow them to anticipate future bargains. For this purpose they will usually prefer nonbinding forms of consultation—hearings, listening sessions, and the like—that provide them with information without limiting their freedom of action.

The third mechanism is information arbitrage. Democratic regimes will continue to incubate new forms of consultation as long as there are opportunities for nongovernmental actors to profit by brokering the exchange of information. State officials and citizens have a shared interest in replacing the costly and unpredictable dialectic of extraction and rebellion with routinized and predictable forms of consultation. But no form of consultation is perfect. Intermediaries who promise new ways to make consultation easier, more informative, and more predictable therefore may be able to insert themselves as brokers between state officials and citizens. Examples of such intermediaries include political parties, interest group lobbies, and public opinion polling firms. By solving a common problem, such intermediaries can make themselves indispensable to state officials and citizens alike. They may thereby reap prestige, material rewards, and power in the form of subtle influence over the public agenda. Often such organizations seek to position themselves as information brokers in order to advance a particular substantive agenda: An interest group lobby, for example, may advance its constituents' interests most effectively by developing a reputation as a credible broker that can supply officials with reliable information about what constituents will tolerate, and constituents with reliable information about what officials will do. Other intermediaries, such as some nonpartisan polling and campaign consulting firms, may have no particular substantive agenda beyond seeking for their own sake the profits, prestige, or power that accrue to information arbitrageurs. The crucial point is simply that those who invent new processes of consultation—and insert themselves into those processes as expert brokers of consultation—may enjoy advantages, and such advantages create an incentive for innovation.

The three mechanisms of escalation, anticipatory consultation, and information arbitrage may help to explain why the institutions of democratic consultation have generally evolved in a particular sequence. Consider a stylized history of the sequence in which practices of consultation emerged in modern European democracies. The history of such practices in Europe began in the middle ages with sporadic rebellions, and then proceeded to parliaments, followed by the right to petition, then competitive elections, then referenda, then opinion polls, and finally focus groups and the other forms of consultation that I have called the new deliberative assemblies. This sequence does not follow from any technological necessity—in principle, the focus group was as feasible in the time of Charlemagne as it is today—but the sequence has an immanent logic that might be expected from the three mechanisms of escalation, anticipatory consultation, and information arbitrage. Citizens escalated their demands, using one form of consultation to demand the next form of consultation on the list—as when European rebels demanded a parliament, or parliaments demanded that citizens be granted the right to petition, or petitioners asked for the suffrage (see Tilly 2004, 2009). State officials embraced new forms of anticipatory consultation—as when elected officials examined results of a referendum to anticipate how a candidate would do, or read opinion polls to anticipate the results of a referendum, or convened a focus group to help them predict the most favorable wording on an opinion poll. Finally, parties, interest groups, and consulting firms have invented and marketed new forms of consultation in order to secure positions as mediators between state officials and citizens.

Can this theory account for the consultation explosion in California since the 1970s? The theory does offer reasons to think that any given conflict over state extraction may result in new forms of consultation, but that is not the same as predicting that any given boom in new forms of consultation results from a conflict over extraction. Nothing in the theory suggests that conflicts over state extraction of resources are the only or the most important source of innovation in modes of consultation. If this theory helps to explain the consultation explosion at all, then we should expect to observe a few things about the rise of new deliberative assemblies.

First, if the theory sheds light on this case, then we should expect to find that state officials were central innovators in the new deliberative assemblies and that conflicts over state resources were the original sites of the recent institutional innovation. This hypothesis need not imply that states are the only organizations to use the new deliberative assemblies. Consider the secret-ballot election: Although this mode of consultation is commonly used in the governance of private organizations, for example, the central claim of the fiscal theory of consultation is that this form of consultation originated and diffused globally in the course of conflicts between states and citizens over the public purse. By analogy, we might expect to observe that the new deliberative assemblies received their early impetus from conflicts over extraction of resources. And this prediction is, indeed, consistent with what some scholars have reported about the rise of new deliberative assemblies. Sirianni and Friedland, for example, describe cases in which renaissance of civic participation began with federal mandates for government agencies to solicit public participation and only later spread to nongovernmental organizations.[31] Jacobs, Cook, and Delli Carpini report survey evidence that the state remains a disproportionately influential organization in the field of deliberation.[32] Federal, state, and local governments make up 22 percent of their sample of organizations that "plan and run public forums," indicating substantial overrepresentation relative to the share of governments among all organizations.[33]

Second, we should expect to observe that new forms of consultation emerge and spread particularly rapidly in times of fiscal stress. State officials concede new procedural rights of consultation—and create new opportunities for nongovernmental brokers of consultation—when their extractive demands provoke resistance. We should expect to observe these sequences of resistance and new bargaining when states facing fiscal strains attempt to extract resources in excess of whatever customary settlement currently governs their relationship to their citizens.

Third, we should expect such bursts of innovation to be associated particularly with intensive extraction. State officials who intensify their reliance on an existing levy are particularly likely to provoke the resistance of citizens who have resisted before—and who have been empowered by previous forms of consultation. The bargain struck with these citizens is likely to require new kinds of procedural concessions.

Fourth, we should expect to observe path dependence. Initial bargains will be conditional on the content of earlier bargains over rights of consultation. Different states that make similar fiscal demands may therefore yield different forms of consultation, depending on the prior rights of consultation enjoyed by their citizens.

The following section will show that these expectations are met with a comparative analysis of extraction and consultation in two similar polities, California and New York, over the 20th century. These are big-spending states with a similar pattern of public expenditure growth over much of the century.[34] As subnational governments, they have neither the territorial control nor the coercive power of a national state, so their citizens possess substantially more bargaining leverage than in the democratizing contexts emphasized by Tilly.[35] But, as we shall see, these states experienced substantially different patterns of public consultation in the late 20th century, for reasons that are related to the differing fiscal bargains they struck with their citizens.

Extraction and Consultation in California and New York

In the mid-1960s, both California and New York appeared poised for an explosion of consultation. The proliferation of state and local government agencies, and increasing federal mandates to solicit public participation as a condition of receiving federal monies, encouraged officials in both states to seek out new ways of consulting with the public. But then the two polities began to diverge, as illustrated in figure 6.3. This graph describes the annual count of town hall forums noticed in the *Los Angeles Times*, and it compares them to the number of notices of the same kinds of deliberative assemblies in the *New York Times* over the same period. Figure 6.4 repeats this exercise for the annual count of public workshops. These two figures disaggregate the two kinds of deliberative assemblies that were shown in figure 6.2. What they show is that the California consultation explosion simply was not evident in New York.[36]

The distinctive path of California at the end of the 20th century reflects a different sequence of fiscal bargains that began almost a century earlier. In the middle years of the 19th century, California and New York had depended on general property taxes to finance their public expenditures. In the late 19th century, both states confronted demands for rising public expenditures to finance the infrastructure needed for growing and increasingly urban economies.[37] But public officials chose different strategies

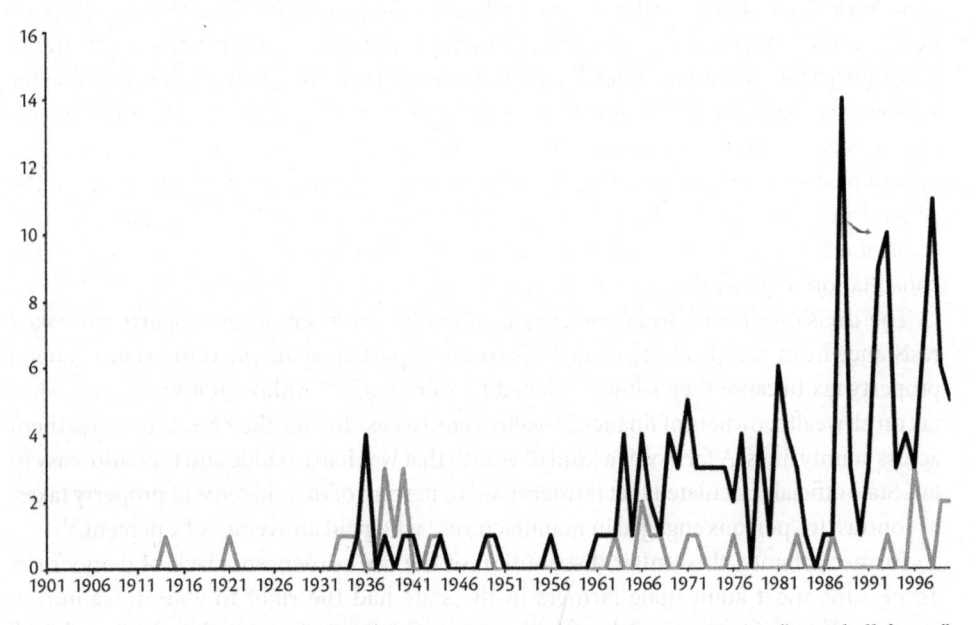

Figure 6.3 Town hall forums in California and New York: Articles mentioning "town hall forum" in the *Los Angeles Times* (black) and the *New York Times* (gray). *Source*: Author's calculations from ProQuest *Historical New York Times* and *Historical Los Angeles Times* databases.

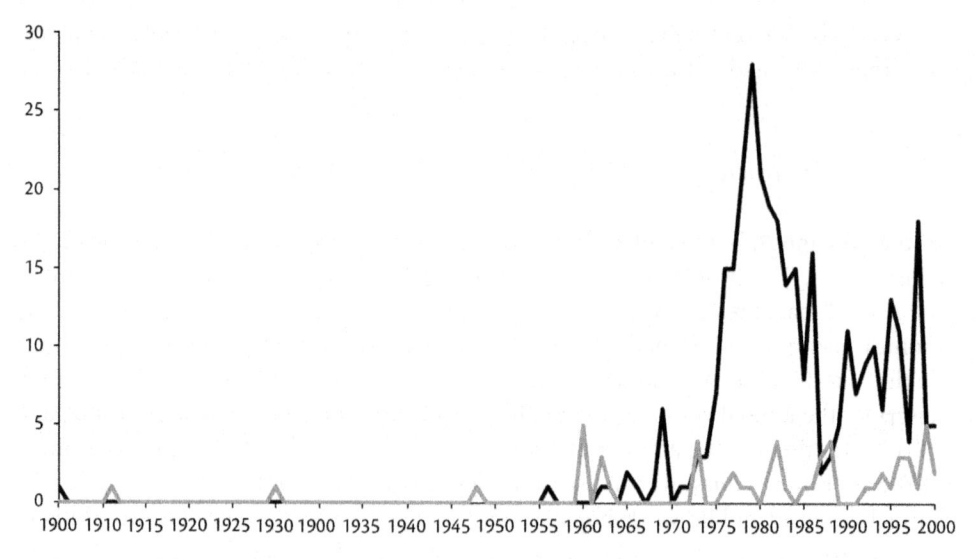

Figure 6.4 Public workshops in California and New York: Articles mentioning "public workshop" in the *Los Angeles Times* (black) and the *New York Times* (gray). *Source*: Author's calculations from ProQuest *Historical New York Times* and *Historical Los Angeles Times* databases.

for financing those expenditures. Officials in California initially chose the intensive path, increasing the state's prior dependence on the taxation of property. Officials in New York chose an extensive strategy, relieving the property tax burden by enacting new taxes on inheritances, foreign corporations, domestic corporations, stock transfers, mortgages, and liquor sales.[38] By the dawn of the 20th century, it was possible for an observer to note that "California depends almost entirely upon the general property tax for state, county, and municipal revenues," whereas New York "has developed a system of state taxes which makes the state government practically independent of the general property tax."[39] These divergent strategies of extraction led to different patterns of resistance and bargaining and thereby ultimately to different patterns of public consultation in general.

The decision of California's officials to intensify the taxation of property provoked resistance from real property owners. Farmers in particular resented the state's general property tax because they felt it burdened them unfairly.[40] Although it was nominally a tax on all wealth, owners of financial wealth found it easy to hide their assets or move them across county lines. A farm was a kind of wealth that was hard to hide and therefore easy to tax. State officials calculated that farmers paid 10 percent of their income in property taxes, in contrast to "persons engaged in manufactures," who paid an average of 2 percent.[41]

Farmers blamed this unfair distribution of the tax burden on a lack of democracy. To be sure, most adult male farmers in the state had the right to vote in California elections.[42] But it was an article of faith among California farmers that the "machine," a cabal of legislators in the pocket of the Southern Pacific Railroad Company, really controlled the state government.[43] The railroad company was notorious for bribing or coercing local assessors to win favorable tax treatment and even, when a state agency took over assessment of railroad property in the 1880s, for simply refusing to pay.[44] The Southern Pacific also used its influence in the legislature to block or change regulation and tax bills it opposed. Machine legislators used a combination of deception and procedural legerdemain to get their way even when they were in the minority. They would take advantage of their strategic committee positions to keep a bill bottled up until the last days of the session, then amend it surreptitiously, and attempt to sneak the changes by their colleagues unnoticed in the last-minute rush of legislation.[45]

Farmers therefore demanded both tax relief and procedural reforms. The link between extraction and consultation was illustrated vividly for the state's property tax payers in 1909. Years of grassroots agitation by farm organizations "'whereasing' and 'resolving' on tax reform" had finally persuaded the governor to appoint a tax commission that would recommend a new revenue strategy for the state.[46] The commission's first proposal failed at the ballot in 1908 because urban voters feared that it would simply increase their property taxes further, but a revised proposal, put forward by a reconstituted tax commission, appeared poised to pass in 1909.[47] The commission's proposed constitutional amendment would relieve real estate owners of state taxes, and it would impose new taxes on railroad receipts and on the stock issued by banks. The machine was unable to block the bill. But somewhere between the first introduction of the bill and the final vote, an unknown legislator quietly cut three words from the legislative text, turning the proposed tax on railroads' annual receipts ("gross receipts . . . for *the year ending* the thirty-first day of December") into a tax on their daily sales for only one day out of the year ("gross receipts . . . for the thirty-first day of December"). The change went undetected in the flurry of bills at the end of the legislative session.[48] When it was finally discovered, few doubted that the omission was deliberate. San Francisco property owners had to pressure the governor into calling the legislature back into special session in 1910 to undo the damage.[49]

Tax resistance led to new demands for consultation. The finance professor Carl Plehn described an "army of tax reform . . . manned by over-taxed farmers and real estate owners" that fanned out through the state.[50] The state's real estate dealers formed "active campaign societies" that joined forces with the State Grange to support the constitutional amendment (see figure 6.5).[51] In the fall of 1910, voters approved the amendment (with the railroad tax restored) and elected a slate of progressive Republican reformers, led by the gubernatorial candidate Hiram Johnson, who pledged to grant the people new rights of binding consultation in the form of the initiative and referendum. The progressives deliberately courted farmers with talk of tax reform and direct democracy, and farm votes were critical to putting the Johnson candidacy over the top.[52]

The election resulted in a new fiscal bargain that included new rights of consultation. The Johnson administration received the support of property tax payers.

Figure 6.5 Button from the grassroots campaign for tax reform, 1910. *Source*: Plehn (1911: 82).

In exchange, it agreed to tax reforms that would slow future property tax increases, and it established new institutions for consulting voters over future tax increases.

In New York, there was no such bargain struck because state officials did not intensify their extraction of property taxes. Instead they followed an extensive revenue strategy that provoked only scattered and piecemeal resistance. State legislators gradually reduced the burden on property tax payers by enacting various new taxes. They began with a franchise tax on corporations in 1880; a long list of selective taxes followed, most notably an inheritance tax in 1885 and a particularly lucrative liquor tax in 1896.[53] Each of these taxes provoked resistance and bargaining by the affected constituency— the corporation tax in particular provoked "a great deal of litigation"—but the gradual division of the tax burden among multiple constituencies over an extended period limited the size of the coalition that formed to protest any given tax.[54]

As long as New York State did not intensify its extraction of property taxes, demands for intensive consultation did not arouse much enthusiasm at the grassroots. New York farmers were slow to take up the cause of the initiative and referendum.[55] Advocates complained in 1909 that the New York State legislature treated their proposal for direct legislation as "a joke."[56] Comparative evidence suggests that the weakness of agrarian populism and the strength of traditional patronage party organizations kept initiative and referendum off of the legislative agenda in New York and many other eastern states.[57] New Yorkers might have had a brief window of opportunity to circumvent the legislature and introduce these forms of intensive consultation at the state constitutional convention of 1915, but the rural delegations were dominated by conservative Republicans who "prevented any serious discussion of direct democracy."[58]

In short, because New York did not pursue intensive extraction, it provoked few demands to intensify consultation with existing landowners. State officials addressed resistance to corporation taxes by adopting new forms of occasional and nonbinding consultation with corporate interests, including a variety of temporary state commissions and unofficial consultation with pro-corporate "research bureaus."[59] But there was no grand cycle of mass resistance and bargaining, and state officials did not institute broad forms of binding consultation such as the initiative or referendum.

Extraction and Consultation in the 1970s

These different fiscal bargains struck in the Progressive Era had important consequences for the subsequent evolution of consultation in California and New York. In the 1960s, growing public expenses for education, welfare, and local infrastructure again required state and especially local officials to find new strategies for appropriating resources. This time, officials in both California and New York chose intensive strategies of extraction that relied heavily on the property tax, and both states thereby triggered cycles of resistance and bargaining. But the outcome was different because of prior bargains they had struck in the Progressive Era.

In both states, judicial pressure forced legislators to modernize the assessment and collection of property taxes. In California, a major corruption scandal involving many of the state's local assessors prompted the legislature to impose new standards for the assessment of property in 1966. The result was improved measurement of rising property values—and a sudden increase in the pace of tax increases. Homeowners across the state resisted with direct action. Los Angeles homeowners and landlords organized a property tax strike.[60] Homeowners in the San Francisco Bay Area burned tax assessment notices. And property owners in communities across California demonstrated in tax assessors' offices and demanded that their tax burden be reduced.[61]

California property owners also used the rights of consultation that voters had won in the Progressive Era to secure a new bargain that further increased their rights of consultation. A coalition of Southern California homeowners' associations began circulating a ballot initiative petition to abolish the property tax in 1968. When that petition failed, several competing groups of activists began circulating alternative ballot initiative policies to cut or limit the tax on homes.[62] In 1978, voters had their choice of two initiatives that would severely cut or limit property taxes. The one that passed—an initiative listed on the ballot as "Proposition 13"—combined a strict limit on property taxation with reforms that further increased voters' rights of consultation. Local governments could increase certain local taxes only after submitting them to the voters for approval. A statutory initiative in 1986 extended this requirement to all local tax increases, and a constitutional initiative in 1996 sealed the bargain.[63] The result was a settlement that gave citizens new rights to veto state extraction.

In New York, the decision to intensify property taxes also provoked resistance. A 1975 decision of the state's highest court forced the state legislature to impose new rules that standardized property assessment. As in California, local officials in New York chose to treat the improved measurement of rising property values as a revenue windfall. As in California, rising property taxes provoked resistance. Farmers and homeowners across New York State organized tax strikes, heckled local assessors, and picketed public agencies demanding property tax relief. They also petitioned for an end to rising property taxes, and they organized protest candidacies in local and state elections.[64]

But the New York tax resisters were constrained by their own Progressive Era bargain. Unlike their California counterparts, they did not have the right to consult in the form of referendum or initiative. New York State legislators attempted to appease angry taxpayers by increasing the intensity of consultation, but they relied characteristically on the nonbinding and explicitly temporary forms of quasi-corporatist consultation that had their roots in the Progressive Era fight over corporation taxes. The governor and the state legislators appointed several temporary state commissions to deal with different dimensions of the property tax crisis, and the commissioners included representatives from affected interest groups ranging from public schools to real estate lawyers. The Temporary State Commission on the Real Property Tax, for example, was led by representatives of major New York real estate firms.[65]

If New Yorkers had the institution of the statewide ballot initiative in 1978, they probably would have voted for a constitutional bargain like that the Californians had struck. The National Election Study from 1978 showed that 55 percent of U.S. adults in the Northeast said they were willing to vote for "a measure similar to Proposition 13."[66] When the Temporary State Commission on the Real Property Tax took taxpayer testimony throughout the summer of 1978, the hearing record quickly filled up with New Yorkers clamoring for their own version of the California bargain. On July 23, a realtor named Philip Pagliarulo submitted testimony calling for "Our Own 'Proposition 13.'"[67] A conservative candidate for the state senate appeared before the commission in order to announce his support for "a Proposition 13 type of Constitutional Amendment and a temporary freeze and then reduction of real property tax rates."[68] The Senior Homeowners' Association of Spring Valley called for a "1% Maximum Property Tax Amendment to the State Constitution (Proposition 13)."[69] But New Yorkers did not have access to the initiative, and they did not get a Proposition 13 of their own.

Instead, the fiscal bargain took a different form in New York. In 1980, the legislature relieved the property tax on homes by shifting some of it onto commercial property. The new law included no new institutional arrangements for consulting with the voters on tax increases. Nor did it substantially impair the ability of state officials to raise property taxes in the future.[70] In the absence of the threat that taxpayers would veto their actions at the ballot box, public officials and interest groups in New York devoted less effort than their California colleagues to the task of figuring out what exactly the taxpayers would tolerate. Property taxes continued to increase much as before.

In California, meanwhile, the new fiscal bargain triggered processes of anticipatory consultation and information arbitrage—a flurry of invention that culminated in the new deliberative assemblies. State officials, constrained by the new rules of consultation with voters, responded by resorting to additional, anticipatory forms of consultation, chartering frequent opinion polls and other forms of nonbinding consultation to figure out what level and kind of taxation voters would tolerate. The rise of the new deliberative assemblies was part of this increase in anticipatory consultation.

It was not just public officials who began to convene deliberative assemblies. The demand for anticipatory consultation created new opportunities for information arbitrage, and a flood of new consulting firms seized the opportunity to insert themselves as brokers between state officials and the citizens of California. Observers of California politics described this as the rise of a grassroots initiative campaign consulting industry, sometimes colorfully called an "initiative-industrial complex," that took inspiration directly from the campaign for Proposition 13.[71] To be sure, such firms had existed in California since the first days of the initiative process,[72] but they began to proliferate in the late 1970s,[73] at least in part because the intense conflicts between California officials and California citizens over resource extraction created an intensive stimulus to the market for their services. The clients of such firms were not only state officials, but also client groups dependent on state largess, trade associations concerned about public regulation, and interest groups of all kinds. The portfolio of issues that such firms consulted on, too, went well beyond questions of extraction. But extraction, and taxation in particular, has remained the single most common subject of ballot initiatives since 1978,[74] and conflicts over this issue have been critical to the development of a new set of interest arbitrageurs in California.

These new intermediaries in turn have contributed to the invention and diffusion of new deliberative assemblies as one technique among many for facilitating consultation between state officials and citizens. One interview study of California political campaign consultants, for example, found that leading firms in the late 1990s offered their clients an elaborate sequence of increasingly costly modes of anticipatory consultation, beginning with deliberative assemblies in the form of focus groups, in order to inform the crafting of an opinion poll that would inspire the drafting of an initiative, which only then would be submitted to voters at the ballot box[75]—a sequence that dramatically illustrates the historical evolution of forms of consultation in reverse. By the 1990s, the consultation explosion depicted in figure 6.2 clearly had begun.

The Initiative and the Consultation Explosion: Quantitative Evidence

If this historical account is correct, then the increasing use of the ballot initiative in California following the property tax revolt should make a measurable contribution to explaining the quantitative divergence of indicators of public consultation in these two states. To test this implication, I regressed the annual change in the number of *Los Angeles Times* articles mentioning deliberative assemblies on the annual change in the number of initiative measures appearing on the state ballot, as reported by the Initiative and Referendum Institute. I repeated the analysis separately for the count of public workshops and the count of town hall forums. I controlled for the annual change in the total number of articles in the *Los Angeles Times*, to allow for the possibility that any trend in reporting might simply reflect the variable availability of space in the newspaper. I also controlled for annual change in the number of articles mentioning deliberative assemblies of the same kind in the *New York Times*, in order to focus on the divergence between the two states that I depicted in figures 6.3 and 6.4. I report coefficient estimates from a linear regression with a Prais-Winsten transformation to correct for serially autocorrelated errors.[76] The regression results, reported in table 6.1, confirm that increasing use of the ballot initiative went hand-in-hand with increasing use of consultation via deliberative assemblies.

The results are consistent with the historical argument presented here that the property tax revolt—or something that coincided in time with the property tax revolt—really was critical in setting California on a different path from New York. Models 2 and 4 test whether the association between direct democracy and consultation was greater after 1978, when state officials in California increasingly worried about securing public approval for any new expenses of government. These models estimated an interaction between ballot initiatives and time by estimating separate slope coefficients for the annual change in the number of ballot initiatives in the years 1901–1978 and in the years 1979–2000. Splitting the time period in this way improved the fit of the regression models. The difference across periods was dramatic. The annual change in the number of initiatives until 1978 was virtually uncorrelated with the annual change in the number of deliberative assemblies. After 1978, it was strongly correlated with the annual change in the number of deliberative assemblies. The results reported in table 6.1 imply that in the post-1978 period, we might expect one additional town hall forum and one and a half additional public workshops a year to be noticed in the *Los Angeles Times* for every six new ballot initiatives.

Table 6.1. The Consultation Explosion and the Ballot Initiative in California, 1901–2000: Results from Time-Series Regression Models

	Public workshop		Town hall forum	
Intercept	−3.4 (2.6)	−1.1 (2.5)	−1.7 (.52)	−1.05 (.56)
Years since 1900	.10 (.045)	.026 (.049)	.042 (.012)	.024 (.014)
LAT articles, in 1,000s	.015 (.011)	.020 (.011)	.011 (.0072)	.011 (.0070)
Mentions in NYT	−.58 (.25)	−.64 (.23)	−.046 (.29)	.025 (.29)
Initiatives on the ballot				
all years	.16 (.051)	—	.10 (.042)	—
1901 through 1978	—	−.013 (.068)	—	.018 (.060)
1978 trhough 2000	—	.30 (.06)	—	.15 (.058)
After 1978 (=1 if yes)	—	6.2 (2.6)	—	1.2 (.84)
P	.78	.78	.22	.20
R^2	0.19	0.32	0.36	0.42

The dependent variables are annual counts of articles in the *Los Angeles Times* mentioning the phrases "public workshop" and "town hall forum." The reported coefficients are from linear regression models with Prais-Winsten corrections for serially autocorrelated residuals. Standard errors are in parentheses.

In short, the rise in new deliberative assemblies was part of a general increase in intensive consultation between state officials and citizens, and this general increase was associated with a period of fiscal conflict.

The Great Consultation and the Fiscal Theory of Democratization

The Great Consultation, then, had its origins in the sequence of fiscal bargains struck over the course of the 20th century. Organizations such as California Forward, many of them organized with the participation of current or former state officials, hired grassroots consulting firms to convene deliberative assemblies because they wanted to gather information about public preferences that would allow them to craft legislative proposals that would stand a chance of winning enough votes to pass at the ballot box. The new deliberative assemblies took their place alongside a profusion of older forms of consultation, including opinion polls and referendums—indeed, the Great Consultation took the form it did precisely because state officials and interest groups hoped that consultation with new deliberative assemblies would help them anticipate the outcomes of these older forms of consultation. It is not surprising that officials and interest groups should wish to test out their messaging in a series of small dialogue sessions, for example, before they sink resources into an opinion poll for a referendum campaign that might go down to defeat. They had to resort to such anticipatory consultation because of a history of citizens' resistance to state extraction, and in particular, because of property tax revolts in 1910 and 1978 that expanded citizens' rights to binding consultation.

What are the implications of this account for the governance of California in the 21st century? It is too much to hope that the Great Consultation will deliver civic salvation. But the rise of the new deliberative assemblies may indeed smooth the process of fiscal bargaining, by allowing public officials to calibrate their fiscal demands more carefully to the political tolerance of the citizenry. It is striking, for example, that no movement of resistance like the property tax revolt has occurred in California since 1978, despite continued, acute fiscal strain; and the invention of the new deliberative assemblies may help us to explain how the dialectic of extraction and rebellion has been avoided. It would appear that public officials and information arbitrageurs rely on new deliberative assemblies in part because such assemblies do, in fact, help them to resolve conflicts preemptively.

So much for the process of negotiation. But what implications might this change in the form of consultation have for the *substance* of the fiscal bargain? In very general terms, the fiscal theory of consultation suggests that we should expect the content of any fiscal bargain to be driven by fiscal exigencies rather than ideological commitments. Thus, given the substantial increase in economic inequality in California since the 1970s, we should probably expect future rounds of fiscal bargaining in California to take place between public officials and economically privileged groups. Public officials who are strapped for resources will attempt to extract those resources disproportionately from their high-income and high-wealth citizens, not because these officials are ideologically committed to progressive taxation, but instead out of necessity—because that is where the money is. But if the fiscal theory of consultation is correct, we may predict that the state will not get that money without making procedural concessions to high-income and high-wealth citizens. The temporary tax increase approved by California voters in 2012 exemplifies these principles; although it included a sales tax increase, the bulk of the revenues came from income tax increases on personal incomes over $250,000. This tax measure was designed after extensive focus-group consultation and ad hoc negotiation with organizations representing business and high-income professions, along with the state's most influential labor unions; it was supported by many of the state's big business associations.[77] The tax initiative has earned the state a temporary reprieve. Solving California's fiscal crisis on a more permanent basis, however, may require elite negotiations that potentially include increased rights of consultation. The long-term solution to the fiscal crisis, in other words, may exacerbate inequalities of political voice.

To be sure, California is not a representative or typical state. It is probably an influential state, however, in part because it is an innovative state in the practice of consultation, and such innovations have a tendency to spread. It is also an instructive case study because of its implications for the study of consultation and deliberation more generally.

One such implication concerns the promise of a state-centered account of the changing practices of consultation. Many classics of political sociology attempted to explain the rise and fall of democratic governments by generalizing from studies of nongovernmental organizations such as political parties[78] or trade unions,[79] which were treated as governments in miniature. The pioneering scholars of fiscal sociology would reject this analogy. States are sufficiently unlike nongovernmental organizations in relevant respects that it is invalid to generalize from the conditions that make for democratic nongovernmental organizations to the conditions that make for democratic states. Indeed, the distinctive qualities of states make them sufficiently influential that for some purposes it is more useful to reverse the lens, and to inquire about the causes of democracy in nongovernmental organizations by studying the causes of democracy in states. Rudolf Goldscheid, who was one of the founders of the German Sociological Society, went so far as to assert that "sociology that is not oriented towards public finance and fiscal history must remain in an incomplete [lückenhaft] and unsatisfactory condition."[80] His injunction to attend to fiscal history is not good advice for understanding every subject in sociology, but it is probably good advice for understanding this one. Nongovernmental organizations that practice consultation are typically structured by their participation in a political field in which states, and the fiscal needs of states, are central. When nongovernmental organizations take up new forms of consultation—the election, the deliberative assembly, and so on—they are often simply taking up practices (or toolkits or "mutable mobiles," in the terminology employed by Baiocchi and Ganuza in this volume) that were invented for the purpose of fiscal consultation between states and citizens.

Another implication concerns the theory of democracy more generally. Are the new deliberative assemblies a grassroots revival of participatory democratic ideals, or a retreat from formal democratic norms of equality? If we wish to *evaluate* the assemblies, the question is inescapable. But if we wish to *explain* the assemblies, the question presents us with a false opposition, because democratic and undemocratic forms of consultation may arise from similar causes. Every actually existing polity that we call a "democracy" is a congeries of institutionalized practices whose relationship to the ideal of rule by the *demos* is tenuous, approximate, and contested. The history of any such polity is not a one-dimensional tug of war between democratic and antidemocratic ideals. It is a history of conflicts and accommodations between real social groups, in which the disposition of shared resources is at stake, and in the course of which conflicts the very modes of negotiation are continually invented and reinvented. The new deliberative assemblies are one such mode of negotiation. They take their place in this history as a technique of consultation that arose and became institutionalized for some of the same reasons as the other techniques—elections, opinion polls, petitions, and parade permits—that we have come to identify with actually existing democracies. The new deliberative assemblies are not the last such invention we will see.

NOTES

1. California Forward (2009: 3).
2. See, e.g., Rosell, Furth, and Gantwerk (2008); Small and Neyestani (2008); Agee et al. (2009); California Forward (2009). ChoiceDialogue™ is a trademark of Viewpoint Learning, Inc. The genus that I am calling "deliberative assemblies" would also include several other species, including charrettes and Deliberative Polls®; the latter is a registered trademark of the Center for Deliberative Democracy at Stanford University.
3. Herdt (2009).

4. I focus here on the rise of face-to-face deliberation, although there has been a parallel increase in Internet-facilitated remote deliberation; see Jacobs, Cook, and Delli Carpini (2009).
5. See Sirianni and Friedland (2001); Jacobs, Cook, and Delli Carpini (2009); Lee and Romano (2013).
6. Cf. Pateman (1970), Polletta (2002).
7. California Forward (2009); Jacobs, Cook, and Delli Carpini (2009: 48–52); cf. Schlozman et al. (2005).
8. Almond and Verba (1963: 4).
9. Putnam (2001: 45, 60–61).
10. Norris (2002: 200–201); Caren, Ghoshal, and Ribas (2011: 1, 4).
11. The literature provides little reason to think that the share of the public participating in civic affairs has increased since Putnam's work was completed. For example, Norris (2002) presents evidence that Americans over the period from the late 1960s to 2000 have become less likely to vote (42); belong to a political party (110); or report that they have attended a party meeting, worked for a candidate or party, or donated to a party or candidate during the most recent presidential campaign (117). The literature on other forms of participation is also consistent with a picture of stagnation or decline in the share of the public that is civically engaged. For example, Caren, Ghoshal, and Ribas (2010) note that the rise in the percentage of people who report having attended a demonstration at least once in their life is attributable to the rising share of survey respondents who were young adults in the 1960s, rather than to any secular increase in civic participation. Smith et al. (2009) show that those who engage in political activity on the Internet are usually people who already report above average levels of offline civic participation as well—implying that Internet-mediated civic participation, while novel, has not much expanded the percentage of the public that participates in politics.
12. I selected these search terms as appropriate indicators of long-run change because—unlike neologisms such as "ChoiceDialogue™" or "stakeholder convening"—they were in use by the early 20th century to describe assemblies, increasing my confidence that the time series represents changes in the frequency with which such assemblies are mentioned, rather than changes in the words used to describe them. The graph shows the trend in the *number* of articles mentioning public workshops or town hall forums, but the overall picture is the same if we instead examine the *fraction* of *Los Angeles Times* articles mentioning public workshops or town hall forums.
13. Sirianni and Friedland (2001).
14. Lee and Romano (2013: 741).
15. Jacobs, Cook, and Delli Carpini (2009: 142).
16. Goldscheid (1917); Schumpeter (1991).
17. Bates and Lien (1985); Levi (1989); Tilly (1992, 2007, 2009).
18. Goldscheid (1917: 3); Schumpeter (1991: 100); Tilly (2007, 2009).
19. See Tilly (2007).
20. Tilly (1992): 44; see volume 1 of Weber (1978). For convenience, I do not distinguish between the rights-bearing citizens of a state and the subjects of a ruler.
21. Tilly (2007, 2009).
22. Ardant (1965); Tilly (2009).
23. See Tilly (1992, 2009).
24. Tilly's analysis of extraction has some interesting formal similarities to the analysis of

class exploitation by Wright (1994). The general point that the coercive appropriation of resources can empower the person from whom those resources are taken—and can thereby lend a dynamic quality to the relationship—is at least as old as Hegel's discussion of the master-slave dialectic in the *Phenomenology of Spirit*.

25. Levi (1989).
26. Tilly (2007: 142).
27. Tilly (2007: 142).
28. Bates and Lien (1985).
29. See, e.g., Mann (1980); Ross (2004).
30. Tilly (2007: 13).
31. Sirianni and Friedland (2001).
32. Jacobs, Cook, and Delli Carpini (2009).
33. Jacobs, Cook, and Delli Carpini (2009: 147). An exact measure of this overrepresentation is impossible to estimate without more detail about how the authors defined an independent organization for the purposes of their sampling procedure. But as a point of comparison, the Census records 89,527 federal, state, or local governmental units, equivalent to six governmental units for every one hundred private nonprofit organizations in the United States and two governmental units for every one hundred private organizations with employees. If one adds the total number of governmental units to the denominator of these ratios, then it is possible to calculate that independent governmental organizations comprise fewer than 6 percent of all nonprofit or governmental organizations and fewer than 2 percent of all public or private organizations with employees. The numerator in these calculations refers to the total of federal, state, and local "governmental units" current as of the 2007 Census of Governments (see U.S. Census Bureau 2010a), and the denominators, representing 2008 and 2006, come from the Urban Institute (2009) and the U.S. Census Bureau (2010b), respectively.
34. See McCubbins and McCubbins (2010).
35. Tilly (2007).
36. The divergence is just as apparent if we standardize on the number of articles appearing in each paper. The *New York Times* was consistently a far larger publication over this period, and it reported far fewer deliberative assemblies. The relative shift might reflect a California-specific shift in reporters' biases—perhaps the new deliberative assemblies simply became much more culturally salient to California reporters?—but any such cultural shift would be hard to explain without assuming that there was, in fact, a greater quantitative prevalence of actual assemblies in California. The basic comparative picture is validated by other indicators of innovation in forms of political consultation in this period. Walker's (2009) analysis of the national population of grassroots political consulting firms listed in trade directories since the 1970s, for example, includes a dummy variable for California firms, because the state is such a statistical outlier in the number of such firms.
37. Higgens-Evenson (2003).
38. Teaford (2002: 52); see Newcomer (1917).
39. Plehn (1907: 660, 765).
40. Clemens (1997: 178–179).
41. California Commission on Revenue and Taxation (1906: 9).
42. The California Constitution of 1879 granted the suffrage to adult male citizens with the exceptions that "no native of China, no idiot, insane person, or person convicted of any infamous crime, and no person hereafter convicted of the embezzlement or

misappropriation of public money, shall ever exercise the privileges of an elector in this state" (Article 2, Section 1).
43. Hichborn (1909); see also Shefter (1983); Magliari (1989: 466–467).
44. California Commission on Revenue and Taxation (1906: 105–107); Hichborn (1909: 228–232); Magliari (1989: 465).
45. See Hichborn (1909: 37–42).
46. Plehn (1911: 86).
47. Higgens-Evenson (2003: 83).
48. Plehn (1912: 122).
49. Plehn (1912: 122).
50. Plehn (1911: 86).
51. Plehn (1912: 121).
52. Olin (1966); Rogin (1968: 301–302).
53. Newcomer (1917: 59, 63).
54. Newcomer (1917: 59).
55. Goebel (2002: 107).
56. Schmidt (1989: 254).
57. Shefter (1983); Bowler and Donovan (2006).
58. Goebel (2002: 108).
59. Higgens-Evenson (2003: 50–51, 929–993).
60. Lo (1990: 132).
61. Martin (2008: 50–57).
62. See Lo (1990); Martin (2008: 91–95, 100–104).
63. See Rueben and Cerdán (2003: 9).
64. Kuttner (1980: 161–162); Martin (2008: 118–120).
65. See Martin (2008: 119).
66. The 95 percent confidence interval is from 50 percent to 60 percent. Among New York State respondents, support for "a measure similar to Proposition 13" ran even higher (at 59 percent), but the National Election Study sample was not designed to be representative at the state level. These statistics are calculated from Miller and National Election Studies (2000).
67. Letter from Philip Pagliarulo, July 23, 1978; Box 1, Folder: Public Hearing 7/27/78 Nassau/Suffolk, papers of the New York State Temporary State Commission on the Real Property Tax, New York State Archives (NYS TSC, NYSA).
68. Testimony of Jim Lack, July 26, 1978; Box 1, Folder: Public Hearing 7/27/78 Nassau/Suffolk, NYS-TSC, NYSA.
69. Newsletter of the Senior Homeowners Association, Spring Valley, n.d. (November 1978?), Box 7, Binder: Rockland Hearing, NYS-TSC, NYSA.
70. See Martin (2008: 120).
71. McCuan et al. (1998); Schrag (1998).
72. McCuan et al. (1998).
73. Donovan et al. (2001); see Walker (2009).
74. Cf. Initiative and Referendum Institute (2011).
75. Donovan et al. (2001: 107–108).
76. The finding of a positive and significant correlation between initiatives and town hall forums is robust to a variety of other modeling strategies that ignore the time-series properties of the data (including a linear model estimated by ordinary least squares and a

negative binomial model estimated by maximum likelihood). The finding of a positive and significant correlation between initiatives and public workshops, by contrast, is sensitive to the assumptions made about serial autocorrelation. This is to be expected, because the latter time series exhibits more serial autocorrelation. A Durbin-Watson test after ordinary least squares regressions indicated the presence of serially autocorrelated errors, so the Prais-Winsten specifications are preferred. Because Dickey Fuller tests failed to reject the null hypotheses of a unit root at $p<.05$ in both time series, the models are differenced to render the series stationary.

77. Buchanan (2012); Buchanan and Lagos (2012).
78. Michels (1959).
79. Lipset and Trow (1956).
80. Goldscheid (1917: 3).

misappropriation of public money, shall ever exercise the privileges of an elector in this state" (Article 2, Section 1).
43. Hichborn (1909); see also Shefter (1983); Magliari (1989: 466–467).
44. California Commission on Revenue and Taxation (1906: 105–107); Hichborn (1909: 228–232); Magliari (1989: 465).
45. See Hichborn (1909: 37–42).
46. Plehn (1911: 86).
47. Higgens-Evenson (2003: 83).
48. Plehn (1912: 122).
49. Plehn (1912: 122).
50. Plehn (1911: 86).
51. Plehn (1912: 121).
52. Olin (1966); Rogin (1968: 301–302).
53. Newcomer (1917: 59, 63).
54. Newcomer (1917: 59).
55. Goebel (2002: 107).
56. Schmidt (1989: 254).
57. Shefter (1983); Bowler and Donovan (2006).
58. Goebel (2002: 108).
59. Higgens-Evenson (2003: 50–51, 929–993).
60. Lo (1990: 132).
61. Martin (2008: 50–57).
62. See Lo (1990); Martin (2008: 91–95, 100–104).
63. See Rueben and Cerdán (2003: 9).
64. Kuttner (1980: 161–162); Martin (2008: 118–120).
65. See Martin (2008: 119).
66. The 95 percent confidence interval is from 50 percent to 60 percent. Among New York State respondents, support for "a measure similar to Proposition 13" ran even higher (at 59 percent), but the National Election Study sample was not designed to be representative at the state level. These statistics are calculated from Miller and National Election Studies (2000).
67. Letter from Philip Pagliarulo, July 23, 1978; Box 1, Folder: Public Hearing 7/27/78 Nassau/Suffolk, papers of the New York State Temporary State Commission on the Real Property Tax, New York State Archives (NYS TSC, NYSA).
68. Testimony of Jim Lack, July 26, 1978; Box 1, Folder: Public Hearing 7/27/78 Nassau/Suffolk, NYS-TSC, NYSA.
69. Newsletter of the Senior Homeowners Association, Spring Valley, n.d. (November 1978?), Box 7, Binder: Rockland Hearing, NYS-TSC, NYSA.
70. See Martin (2008: 120).
71. McCuan et al. (1998); Schrag (1998).
72. McCuan et al. (1998).
73. Donovan et al. (2001); see Walker (2009).
74. Cf. Initiative and Referendum Institute (2011).
75. Donovan et al. (2001: 107–108).
76. The finding of a positive and significant correlation between initiatives and town hall forums is robust to a variety of other modeling strategies that ignore the time-series properties of the data (including a linear model estimated by ordinary least squares and a

negative binomial model estimated by maximum likelihood). The finding of a positive and significant correlation between initiatives and public workshops, by contrast, is sensitive to the assumptions made about serial autocorrelation. This is to be expected, because the latter time series exhibits more serial autocorrelation. A Durbin-Watson test after ordinary least squares regressions indicated the presence of serially autocorrelated errors, so the Prais-Winsten specifications are preferred. Because Dickey Fuller tests failed to reject the null hypotheses of a unit root at $p<.05$ in both time series, the models are differenced to render the series stationary.

77. Buchanan (2012); Buchanan and Lagos (2012).
78. Michels (1959).
79. Lipset and Trow (1956).
80. Goldscheid (1917: 3).

CHAPTER 7

Structuring Electoral Participation
The Formalization of Democratic New Media Campaigning, 2000–2008

DANIEL KREISS

Barack Obama spoke to the nation for the first time as president-elect at the site where forty years earlier police and activists clashed during the Vietnam War protests at the Democratic National Convention.[1] Obama attributed his historic victory to "the millions of Americans who volunteered, and organized, and proved that more than two centuries later, a government of the people, by the people and for the people has not perished from this Earth." During the course of the long primary and general election season, the president defined himself, his campaign, and his leadership style in terms of empowering citizens to bring about change in Washington. And, in many journalistic and scholarly accounts, the campaign appears more as a bottom-up social movement than a traditional electoral effort.[2] Indeed, at first look Obama's campaign appeared to fulfill the promise of participatory democracy fought for by the activists of the 1960s.[3]

The 2008 Obama campaign mobilized extraordinarily large numbers of citizens to participate in electoral activities. Taken together, the efforts of Obama's supporters rivaled the levels of civic participation common during the era of strong party politics and torchlight parades.[4] Millions knocked on doors and made phone calls from field offices. Millions more made small donations throughout the campaign, remaining well below the legal limits. Legions of supporters organized for Obama on Facebook and posted their own videos for the candidate on YouTube. Over two million supporters set up accounts on the campaign's social networking platform, My.BarackObama.com, where they used tools to independently host tens of thousands of volunteer and fundraising events for Obama and set up over 35,000 geographic and affinity-based supporter groups. Supporters made more than thirty million phone calls to voters using an online calling tool that the campaign launched during the general election.

Analytical work over the last decade seemed to predict much of this electoral participation in identifying shifts in the nature of collective action given a radically new information environment. In these accounts, digital media provide previously disenfranchised social actors such as individual citizens, resource-poor organizations, and social movements with new opportunities to mobilize and challenge elites.[5] This political participation, scholars argue, often takes place through nonhierarchical social relationships, given that formal structures are no longer necessary for organizing.[6] At the same time, political expression is more authentic than one-way, capital-intensive broadcast politics, given that candidates can commune directly with supporters and citizens are newly empowered to forge ties with one another.[7] Conventional wisdom about the 2008 campaign cycle echoes many of these scholarly accounts. Obama triumphed over his establishment rival Hillary Clinton, this story goes, because the Internet enabled millions of citizens to engage in political action and circumvent party elites. Meanwhile, from the campaign manager revealing strategy in webcasts to blog posts that chronicled the activities of supporters in swing states, politics seemed more direct and authentic than the professionalized communication practices of the pre-Internet era.

In contrast to these claims, this chapter argues that mediated citizen participation in Obama's electoral effort was largely the product of new media campaign strategy and organizing practices nearly a decade in the making—not simply the technical characteristics of digital media or "self-organizing" among a mobilized electorate. The Obama campaign was the culmination of a long struggle among political staffers and consultants specializing in new media to realize, convene, and leverage participation for electoral ends. Since the presidential election of 2000, campaigns have sought to both generate and expand online citizen participation for fundraising, messaging, and fieldwork purposes. In 2000 these efforts were halting and erratic, with campaigns on both sides of the aisle vacillating between using the Internet as an extension of broadcast advertising and experimenting with some of the medium's more interactive and social "affordances," or the qualities of technology that provide users with capacities for action.[8] During the 2004 Democratic presidential primaries, new technical applications, changing online social practices, and a charged political environment helped create a highly unsettled period in electoral politics.[9] The independent online organizing of the anti-establishment and antiwar activists backing Howard Dean surprised and challenged not only elites in the Democratic Party, but also the campaign's staffers, who engaged in ad hoc and reactive practices in an attempt to channel it toward electoral ends.

The practices and tools of online campaigning that were deeply unsettled in 2004, however, became more formalized and standardized control technologies by 2008. I use "control" in Beniger's sense of processes that are probabilistic, not deterministic.[10] Political staffers deploy technologies and organizational practices to generate and coordinate the participation of supporters in electoral activities online outside of formal management structures. These technologies and practices were refined on the Democratic side of the aisle during the period between the 2004 and 2008 presidential elections. Soon after the primaries, many of the political neophytes that ran the online campaigns of the 2004 cycle stayed in politics and founded or joined a number of political consultancies, think tanks, and training organizations specializing in digital campaigning.[11] Taken together, these organizations constituted a set of what I call "infrastructural intermediaries" that produced new forms of participatory knowledge and practice to help realize and coordinate online electoral mobilization. These intermediaries also created a stable group of political technologies and trained staffers specializing in digital campaigning to staff electoral and advocacy campaigns, including the 2008 and 2012 Obama campaigns.

These new forms of participatory electoral practice are a hybrid of top-down, professional management and citizen-driven, horizontal forms of electoral collaboration. As such, contemporary new media campaigning resembles mixed modes of professionally facilitated civic participation that scholars have chronicled in other domains. At the field level, for instance, Minkoff, Aisenbrey, and Agnone have revealed a diversity of organizational models and forms of civic participation in the advocacy sector.[12] Walker, McCarthy, and Baumgartner have shown how professional advocacy and membership organizations often complement one another in pursuit of their political goals.[13] Walker has shown how business interests can subsidize grassroots participation to build support for commercial policies.[14]

In the electoral context, this chapter argues that through designed forms of interactivity and cultural appeals, Obama's staffers realized and leveraged participatory networked social and symbolic action for the ends of fundraising, messaging, and fieldwork. These participatory practices are primarily transactional, despite the deeply felt ethos of the Obama campaign as a transformative, empowering movement. There was, for example, little citizen participation in the formal campaign organization outside of the fundraising and canvassing that have long been features of electoral politics. Obama's supporters had little chance to engage in more substantive forms of politics that would live up to participatory ideals, such as contributing to a policy platform. Indeed, even massive supporter mobilization online to challenge Obama on a policy change failed to produce a substantive response from the campaign.

That said, while the Obama campaign, and much of online electoral politics more generally, falls well short of the transformative ideals of theorists and fails to create more robust forms of political representation, this does not mean that participation is without value or consequence. Digital media provide powerful means for citizens to engage in institutional forms of agonistic pluralist politics—when they are already sure of their political desires and interests. As scholars have demonstrated in the context of online social movements, networked technologies offer both amplified and qualitatively new opportunities for collective action.[15] In contemporary online campaigning, mobilized partisans have increased power to affect election outcomes. Engagement in campaigns may serve as a gateway to long-term political involvement, and it can provide an opportunity for young voters to create partisan attachments that last a lifetime—a potentially considerable consequence of Obama's initial victory and subsequent reelection, given his youth support. Even more, the nature of online campaigning, with partisans across the country participating independently of formal managerial structures, requires campaign staffers to be sensitive to the needs and desires of supporters. At the same time, as McQuarrie shows in this volume, participation may also work to reinforce, not subvert, the authority of elites.[16] I return to these ideas in the conclusion of this chapter.

To reveal the evolution of online participation in electoral politics and trace its democratic implications, this chapter proceeds in three parts. I begin by detailing the work of the infrastructural intermediaries that emerged after the 2004 electoral cycle and were instrumental in formalizing practices and tools for online campaigning. Given space constraints, I focus narrowly on political consultancies.[17] I then show how the 2008 Obama campaign benefited from the work of these intermediaries in terms of the staff, practice, and tools that lay behind its new media operations. The 2008 Obama campaign is an appropriate case, given that it marked the coming together of a number of disparate trends in online campaigning, inspired many to see a radical transformation in participatory democratic practice, and provided the foundation on which the president's lauded reelection bid was built. I provide an in-depth look at how the campaign's new media staffers crafted hybrid practices to mobilize supporters and coordinate their participation. This discussion, in turn, reveals both the democratic limits, and potential power, of networked electoral participation.

Crafting Digital Campaigning

The uptake of new media in electoral politics over the last twenty years took shape amid a more general revaluation of citizen participation in campaigning by staffers and consultants. For much of the 20th century, the practice and art of participatory electoral politics was in steep decline. As Michael McGerr has detailed, by the 1920s the passionate and popular party-oriented politics of the 1800s had largely given way to marketing and advertising-driven campaigns conducted through mass media.[18] With the rise of mediated campaigns a democracy of the streets premised on the need for "the visible assent of the governed" largely disappeared.[19] As a consequence of this change in political style, McGerr argues, there was a decline in radical politics and the wealthy elite assumed greater control over political life. Meanwhile, the image makers that blossomed into a consulting class during the middle of the 20th century were later joined by new professional groups with specialized electoral technologies, from focus groups and polls to direct mail and voter databases.[20] In response to these changes, which seemingly paralleled shifts in civil society, a generation of scholarship decried the increasing management of and subsequent decline in American political and civic life.[21] The drastic decline in voting over the last century tells this story well. In the 1880s and 1890s, an average of 80 percent of eligible males turned out, compared to just over 50 percent of citizens in the presidential race in 1996.[22]

During the last decade, however, there has been a significant rise in voter turnout (61.6 percent in 2008 and 58.2 percent in 2012).[23] There are a number of reasons for this, including increasing partisanship and polarization.[24] Another key factor is a major organizational change in the way campaigns are run, which has led to a resurgence in popular participation in electoral politics. Campaign staffers and consultants, as well as their civil society allies, have placed renewed emphasis on what Nielsen calls "personalized political communication," or practices that utilize people as mediums of political messaging.[25] Nielsen analyzes personalized political communication in the context of a revival of field campaigning during the 1990s and 2000s.

Faced with the diminishing effectiveness of mediated forms of voter contact, such as direct mail and broadcast advertising, campaigns began organizing supporters to make personal appeals to and generate data on voters through phone banking and door-to-door canvassing. These field efforts are premised on popular participation, particularly for large-scale presidential campaigns that contest multiple primaries and general election battleground states. For a presidential campaign to conduct voter identification, persuasion, and turnout operations, thousands of volunteers need to be mobilized, often with the assistance of ideologically aligned civil society and social movement organizations, and their labor coordinated through local field offices.[26] This coordination is premised on massive data infrastructures that campaigns use to generate targets among the electorate, capture and archive the results of canvasses, and deploy volunteers.[27]

It was in this context of a revaluation of interpersonal voter contact and citizen participation that campaigns began to use the Internet. It took many years, however, before campaigns fully realized and leveraged the potentials of the medium. Throughout much of the 1990s, campaigns mostly used the Internet as a broadcast medium, creating static HTML versions of campaign literature that scholars referred to as "brochureware."[28] During the 2000 cycle, however, political staffers recognized for the first time that the primary users of candidate websites were supporters, not undecided voters.[29] To take advantage of this, instead of detailed policy positions written for voters seeking information on candidates, campaigns began promoting supporter participation, such as making donations. Campaigns also began using the Internet to involve supporters in visibility and communications efforts, such as providing printable literature and signs for supporters to distribute in their own communities and tips for contacting local media to promote candidates. In 2000, for example, John McCain's primary campaign demonstrated the possibilities of Internet fundraising. Al Gore's campaign, meanwhile, forged new ground in enabling supporters to create their own customized webpages based on policy content.

During the 2004 cycle, with staffers largely new to electoral politics, the Howard Dean campaign developed a host of new tools and practices to mobilize supporters and guide their electoral participation.[30] In the process, the campaign built the prototypes for a new generation of political technologies and helped forge a new area of campaign practice around online electoral organizing. The campaign developed a blog, the first for a presidential campaign, that served as the interlinked interface between the formal campaign organization and independent supporter sites. The blog enabled supporters to easily find and join affinity groups for Dean and make themselves visible to one other, creating bonds of solidarity. At the same time, it enabled staffers to communicate directly with supporters to help them feel invested in Dean's candidacy and keep them working toward the campaign's fundraising goals.

The Dean campaign was also the first electoral effort to deploy what are now widely known as social networking technologies to generate and coordinate supporter participation. Alongside its use of the online event-planning service MeetUp, the campaign developed an extraordinary array of social technologies that lowered the cost of supporter participation in field and fundraising efforts. For example, the campaign created DeanLink, a social networking website modeled after the early commercial site Friendster that supported events organizing, and it implemented TeamRaiser, a fundraising application developed for nonprofits by the firm Convio, which the campaign modified to enable volunteers to set fundraising goals on personalized web pages.[31]

The Dean campaign was also the first electoral effort to begin systematically tracking this supporter participation by using what in the industry is known as a "customer relations management" platform, which enabled staffers to gather and store data about supporter involvement and craft targeted email appeals. Databases were not new to the 2004 electoral cycle, of course. Long before the direct-mail boom of the 1980s, in the 19th century parties developed national voter databases.[32] For example, Kazin chronicles the use of data in what was one of the first independent candidate campaign organizations, detailing how William Jennings Bryan's brother and wife created a detailed file on supporters with information such as party affiliation, job, religion, and income, all gleaned from letters to Bryan.[33] They used this information to communicate with supporters: "The index contained some two hundred thousand names in 1897 and grew to a half a million by 1912. It represented, in embryo, the type of candidate centered machine that would become utterly routine by the last decades of the twentieth century."[34]

There were qualitative differences between these databases and what was first used on the Dean campaign, however. Dean's staffers had access to much more timely data on supporter participation and the outcomes of strategic messaging. For example, the campaign could estimate how much each email fundraising appeal would garner, measure progress toward overall fundraising goals, and narrowly target certain categories of donors to spur them to increase their involvement. After learning the email techniques of the social movement organization MoveOn.org from its principals, the Dean campaign also became the first electoral effort to test messages and monitor response rates to particular emails so staffers could implement changes in messaging and craft more effective appeals.[35]

This data, coupled with many other streams of information such as the number of supporters gathering on Meetup, enabled the campaign to quantify both the amount and worth of supporter participation on the campaign. Former staffers describe how campaign manager Joe Trippi would often jump out of his office to demand status reports on fundraising and email subscribers. There were large charts on the wall at campaign headquarters that staffers kept constantly updated in order to track money raised and numbers of email subscribers. These categories of data, in turn, reflect the electoral priorities of the campaign and ends of supporter participation. Email was a fundraising and one-way communications tool. Staffers designed Get Local, an event-planning tool, to facilitate supporter field efforts in early voting states. There was little supporter participation in the more substantive aspects of the campaign, such as the candidate's policy platform. Indeed, the campaign organized a working group to draft a policy statement regarding the use of open source technologies in a future Dean administration. This working group was made up of technology forecasters and industry luminaries such as Howard Rheingold and Joi Ito with no public or even supporter participation.

The Dean campaign ended up being highly successful in at least one of these participatory domains: fundraising. The campaign broke records for online and primary fundraising, which catapulted the long-shot, insurgent candidate into frontrunner status, for a time. All this supporter participation, however, failed to help Dean win the caucuses in Iowa, which was a vastly underorganized effort. Dean's rivals, John Kerry and John Edwards, had much more effective and well-planned field efforts in place. Even more, ironically given technical innovation at the national level, the campaign's on-the-ground staffers lacked very basic tools for field organizing.

Even though Dean's bid effectively ended on the snowbanks of Iowa, the candidate's former staffers brought about significant shifts in online electoral participation in the years after the primaries. Dean's Internet staffers found a wealth of new employment opportunities with candidates and advocacy organizations looking for help navigating the seemingly bold new world of participatory online politics on display during the cycle. To capitalize on these opportunities, these former political amateurs founded and joined an extraordinary range of political consultancies, training organizations, practitioner forums, and conferences oriented around the theory and practice of online politics. Taken together, these infrastructural intermediaries tied together much of the extant knowledge, tools, and practice of participatory online campaigning and extended them to address the concrete problems of control and capacity campaigns encountered during the 2004 cycle.

Political Consultancies

Political consultancies were chief among the intermediaries that disseminated, standardized, and formalized the innovations in digital tools and participatory online campaign practices honed on the Dean campaign. After Dean's run there was enormous demand for political staffers that understood and could leverage the participatory affordances of the Internet for electoral ends. To help meet this demand, many of Dean's former Internet staffers launched political consultancies. Given that their founders had the unique cultural legitimation as the inventors of a new kind of online politics, a number of these consultancies subsequently became among the most prominent in Democratic campaigning. In addition, many of their principals occupied senior-level positions in the new media divisions of Democratic presidential campaigns during the 2008 election cycle. For example, veterans of the Dean campaign had senior roles in the campaigns of Bill Richardson, Tom Vilsack, and, most notably, John Edwards and Barack Obama. A number stayed on for Obama's reelection bid as well.

Taken together, these political consulting firms and staffers, along with other veterans of the 2004 campaigns, ushered in a major shift in the Internet's *organizational* role in Democratic campaigning. Much as field efforts took on a more important role in electoral campaigning during the late 1990s and early 2000s, in the years after 2004 the Internet and a host of attendant networked technologies, such as databases and customer relations management platforms, became much more fully incorporated within the core operations of campaigns.

The Internet played this organizational role in campaigning through the development of a set of dedicated electoral tools and strategies designed to facilitate networked participation. The technologies provided by these firms include more standardized sets of advocacy and event-planning tools, blogs, email platforms, and databases. These firms expressly designed these tools to meet the needs of campaigns, with their larger traffic and unique fundraising needs as compared with the nonprofit and advocacy sector. These tools enable campaigns to track supporter involvement, responses to campaign appeals, and optimize the content and design of webpages and email appeals. These firms, in turn, offer strategy consulting services around these tools. These services include email messaging, online marketing and fundraising campaigns, and website design.

These consultancies specializing in online campaigning were the key conduits for the transfer of participatory knowledge and practice across campaigns and electoral cycles. One firm, Blue State Digital (BSD), founded by four veterans of Dean's run shortly after the primaries in 2004, illustrates the movement and refinement of these participatory tools and practices across Democratic campaigning in the years in between presidential elections. In the months after the election, BSD acquired the intellectual property in and gradually rebuilt the disparate applications of the Dean campaign into a sophisticated campaign platform and carried it to many prominent sites in Democratic politics. A set of social ties that grew out of the Dean campaign afforded this professional work. For example, soon after the election Democracy for America, a political action committee founded by Howard Dean to serve as a mobilization vehicle for his supporters should he decide to run for president again in 2007–2008, granted BSD the rights to the tools used on the campaign. BSD developed what in the industry is known as a "software as a service" business model, wherein clients lease and commission modifications for this suite of networked tools that all other clients then benefit from. BSD manages its toolset as a partisan "club good," only working with Democratic Party and ideologically aligned clients.[36]

In the fall of 2006, after working with a number of clients in Democratic politics, BSD launched its electoral platform for the Party under the rubric of "PartyBuilder." Developed during Dean's tenure as party chair, PartyBuilder was the most sophisticated political platform developed at that point in its bundling together and extension of many of the applications developed in piecemeal fashion on the Dean campaign. For example, party supporters could set up online profiles, individual fundraising pages, and affinity groups as well as manage offline events, engage in online petition and letter-writing campaigns, and blog. Underlying these applications was a system for aggregating and analyzing the data generated by supporters using these tools.

Soon after the launch of PartyBuilder, Joe Rospars, a former blogger, Dean campaign email writer and cofounder of BSD, joined the Obama campaign as its new media director. The fledgling campaign subsequently hired BSD to provide its online infrastructure, and PartyBuilder became the campaign's online electoral platform hosted at My.BarackObama.com.

The Obama Campaign: Transformative and Transactional Electioneering

Canovan argues that the "redemptive" and the "pragmatic" are the two faces of democracy, each as essential as the other.[37] The ritual of electoral campaigning shows both of these faces. Candidates and their staffers strive to articulate pure civic ideals while gathering the resources necessary to secure electoral victory.[38] It was the transformative promise of Obama's run, embodied in the candidate's charisma, outsider status, and redemptive message, that brought millions of new voters to the polls and mobilized millions more to donate their time and money. For the Obama campaign, the pragmatic lay in the need to establish transactional relationships with supporters so staffers could coordinate this citizen participation and channel it toward strategic electoral ends.

Institutional and technological shifts have transformed these two faces. In the era of strong party politics, elements of which persisted through the first decades of the 20th century, campaigns served as appendages of political parties. Parties provided much of the organizational infrastructure, incentives, and meaning for electoral participation through large-scale patronage systems and the cultivation of cultural and social attachments among members.[39] While party participation declined throughout much of the 20th century, the nominating reforms after the Democratic National Convention in Chicago in 1968 also played a key role in weakening parties. These reforms, especially the direct nomination of presidential candidates, along with the growing ubiquity of broadcast media, gave rise to an increasingly candidate-centric politics.[40] Campaign organizations began to work largely independently from parties to compete in electoral contests. As a consequence, candidates sought to transfer what had formerly been attachment to the parties to their campaigns, motivating and mobilizing individuals for electoral contests.[41] To do so, and to compete in primary and general election contests without the benefit of a strong party infrastructure, campaigns increasingly directed the bulk of their resources to broadcast media advertising, used direct mail to compensate for the lack of the personalized contact that parties formerly provided, and relied on computerized electoral databases to replace the formerly rich knowledge local party organizations had of their memberships. As detailed above, it was only in the last two decades in the face of the diminishing returns from mediated communication that campaigns returned to personalized political communication, although now they are often reliant on civil society actors to compensate for diminished party infrastructures.[42]

New media provide new opportunities for campaigns to couple transformational and transactional styles of politics. The 2008 Obama campaign used design and rhetoric to frame the effort to elect Obama as a participatory social movement and create the collective identity and generate the mobilization necessary to gain electoral resources. On a transactional level, the campaign deployed new media to translate this participation into money, volunteers, and votes. In other words, the transformative discourse of the Obama campaign overlay a sophisticated machinery of electoral politics. Achieving balance between these orientations was a cultural, organizational, and technical achievement. With expectations of transformation high, staffers needed to negotiate the twin perils of under- and overorganizing to coordinate volunteers' efforts.[43] All of which reveals that new media campaigning is not the formally managed enterprise that some scholars have feared, even as it is not the radically liberating domain of participatory political practice others have suggested.

Transformative Cultural Performance

New media staffers framed participation in transformational terms, developing a host of cultural strategies to mobilize supporters around the idea of the candidate and campaign as a social movement. This was clear in the campaign's approach to the design of My.BarackObama.com. Through design the campaign sought to "communicate the excitement that this candidate offered the United States of America and what this election season really offered to the country."[44] Towards this end, in September of 2007 the campaign hired an art director and design director who were responsible for the design of much of the campaign's media, including not only all of the online presence but also electoral materials from lawn signs to the wrapper around the candidate's plane. The breadth of these design responsibilities was an explicit attempt to impose brand consistency on a campaign that, until that point, used a number of different colors and fonts. Through much trial and error, these staffers developed what Design Director Scott Thomas calls an "aesthetic of Obama" that, as much as the candidate's rhetoric, articulated, reinforced, and constructed the larger themes of the campaign.[45] It also helped inspire and mobilize supporters to perform the hard electoral work central to Obama's victories.

Design extended the broader symbolic work of the campaign to the lawns of supporters and, more importantly, the interactive interfaces where citizens literally connected with it.[46] As part of this Obama aesthetic, designers created a number of different "brand groups," or themes intended to convey particular understandings of the campaign and candidate. The general "campaign brand" featured the iconic Obama blue, campaign logo, and standardized typeface. This theme both created consistency and actively worked to suggest certain qualities about the candidate. For example, designers saw consistency as crucial to providing the visual impression that the candidate, the junior senator from Illinois, was both efficient and experienced. To communicate this organizational efficiency, and the candidate's experience, the campaign matched everything from the color blue of the website, placards, podium signs, and even Obama's necktie. Meanwhile, the campaign's Gotham typeface was explicitly chosen for what Thomas described as its "truly American qualities."[47]

Other brand groups sought to convey, through design, the larger themes of the campaign. Designers intended the "instant vintage" theme to evoke the American past and suggest, through imagery and not words, the historic nature of the campaign. To do so, designers looked through archives of historical documents and images and pulled elements into campaign design. For example, designers presented materials in the style of historical documents such as the Declaration of Independence and drew on imagery of the civil rights movement. Meanwhile, designers incorporated the "timeless" theme to help citizens imagine Obama as president. In essence, it was design in the style as if Obama was already president, with official-looking documents and evocations of state imagery, such as the white textured background on the website that was intended to suggest the official government buildings in Washington, D.C. Finally, the campaign deliberately crafted a "supporter" theme that involved customized versions of the campaign's logo for different demographic and affinity groups.

The new media division staffers also worked to symbolically construct the My.BarackObama.com platform as a technology of participation. In turn, the campaign framed this participation in terms of a social movement convened around a candidate and driven by supporters. One of the first goals of the art and design directors, for instance, was to clearly and concisely use "we" rather than "he [Obama]" in all the messaging related to the website. This construction quickly became a central part of all of the campaign's communications with supporters and was actively performed through online actions that stressed this supporter involvement. Email to supporters, for example, explicitly used the language of "ownership" and "social movement" with regard to the campaign. Thomas explains the decision to use "we" rather than "he":

> I think it partly came from the message "Change We Can Believe In," but I think that in the core group of new media those things that we kept finding is that we should not focus on Barack Obama the man but we should definitely be focusing on the people because that is actually what our platform is about. And so for us the community, building our online community doing these things it was all focused around "we." . . . If we were crafting the headlines or e-mail, or if a consultant was trying to write something for the blog, we were definitely always trying to focus it around "we" rather than "he." . . . Whenever we had the moment to deliver something based on "we," we'd do it. For example we did a t-shirt contest style where it was democratic voting kind of process . . . instead of calling it something like "Threadless for Obama" or something along those lines it turned into "Tees bought by people for the people," right so it is about the people it is about "we" not about "he."[48]

Transactional Politics: Balancing Under- and Overorganizing

Design and rhetoric were cultural tools that staffers used to mobilize supporters and shape understandings of participation on the campaign. At the same time, staffers had to be wary of setting the expectations of supporters too high. In this, Obama's staffers faced what Chen describes as the dilemma of "under- and overorganizing" that is a characteristic of voluntaristic organizations. As Chen argues, the challenge of voluntarism lies in the need to craft hybrid organizational forms that mix "collectivist and bureaucratic practices, but avoid exercising coercive control."[49] In voluntaristic relations, individuals can always exit, so they continually need to feel like they have agency and their contributions are meaningful. And yet too little in the way of formal management means that contributions are not coordinated or useful to campaigns, leading to highly dispersed supporters pursuing ill-defined and electorally ineffective tasks.

Meanwhile, too much in the way of formal management, such as explicitly dictating what supporters need to do or using the campaign's email list simply as an ATM, also causes supporter participation to diminish.

This balance between under- and overorganizing is a particularly pressing issue in the context of online electoral politics. In a shifting technological context that supports new forms of independent collective action and collaboration, campaigns sought to develop new techniques to leverage online participation for resources—not just follow the persuasive and targeted online communication tactics of an earlier generation of political consultants that Howard has chronicled.[50] In other words, Obama's staffers needed to structure and coordinate participation, a challenge made especially acute, given the numbers and geographic distribution of supporters. These supporters were outside of formal organizational structures and thus not accountable to the campaign and its electoral goals—most of which revolved around fundraising and field voluntarism. At the same time, the campaign had to make participation meaningful for supporters for the purposes of mobilization.

The explicit design of the campaign's tools helped solve this dilemma of under- and overorganizing electoral participation. When programmers designed the affordances of the electoral platform, they created a management structure that directed supporter participation. It is the general invisibility of these design decisions that allowed the campaign to direct users subtly, avoiding the perception of overorganizing. In this sense, staffers "delegated" much coordination work to their tools, which stood in for a formal managerial relationship between the campaign and its participating supporters.[51] The campaign's new media tools had designed in affordances that made it easy for supporters to raise and donate money to the candidate and call voters to identify their preferences. For example, My.BarackObama.com featured fundraising pages that supporters personalized by setting individual goals and circulating appeals to family and friends to donate, much like the paper-based "walkathon" pledges common in nonprofit fundraising. The platform featured a calling tool that enabled supporters to access targeted scripts for contacting voters and the campaign's voter file online so they could generate and record data on the electorate.

This delegation of coordination tasks to technologies is also apparent in the campaign's field efforts. Through integrating much of the functionality of Dean's original applications, My.BarackObama.com provided an unprecedented set of tools that enabled supporters to become active field agents of the campaign. As a number of staffers on campaigns during the cycle attested, the primary race would likely have been even closer had it not been for the campaign's participatory online platform during the month of February 2008. After four early primaries that resulted in a split decision, the Obama and Hillary Clinton campaigns had a little more than a week to feverishly turn to the twenty-three-state contests that would take place on "Super Tuesday." While the Obama campaign directed much of its field staffers' and volunteers' attention and resources to the four early voting states, new media staffers were helping supporters in Super Tuesday states use My.BarackObama.com to set up independent volunteer operations. These efforts helped provide the basic infrastructure for the formal campaign organization when the primaries drew near.

For example, field staffers marveled at how when they hit the ground in these states, sometimes less than twenty-four hours after seeing the returns from another state's primary, there were hundreds of volunteers already working for the campaign. This is a striking example of how independent, largely autonomous efforts by a distributed network of supporters participating across the country played a key role in the campaign's success. It also reveals the power of designed-in affordances and expectation setting to direct supporters toward the electoral work the campaign needed accomplished. The affordances of the participatory electoral tools themselves structured citizen participation in defined directions, means of "control" where "actions are not predetermined . . . yet the routes are navigated."[52] Through the design and structured interactivity of the My.BarackObama.com applications Obama's new media staffers directed supporter efforts toward organizing, voter identification, and fundraising ends. This was a result of work in between election cycles, as Obama's new media staffers had more powerful tools at their disposal, and they had more developed organizing practices in place than the Dean campaign four years prior. One high-level volunteer for both campaigns contrasts his experiences during the two primary cycles:

> They [Obama's campaign staff] made it very clear that they wanted you to do what you can do to become your own organizer, to use the tools to organize locally in whatever way you wanted to. Things were much more rigidly defined [than on the Dean campaign], so that people could very quickly recognize what role they might bring to the table. . . . They were much clearer about what they wanted out of their community, because they set the parameters for what the community could do as well—more specifically in language and in the actual tools.[53]

The Limits of Participation

The campaign's reliance on this participation did not necessarily make the candidate more responsive to his supporters on a policy level. Indeed, the Get FISA (Foreign Intelligence Surveillance Act) Right campaign orchestrated by supporters illustrates this. During the summer of 2008 supporters created a My.BarackObama.com group called "Get FISA Right" in an attempt to pressure the candidate to return to his position during the primaries of opposing retroactive immunity for the telecommunications companies that may have complied with the Bush administration's program of warrantless wiretapping. Through professional media attention and a supporting network of blogs and Facebook groups, the Get FISA Right group grew to more than fifteen thousand members, making it the most popular group on My.BarackObama.com. The group even raised enough funds to produce a national cable television advertisement.

Yet, even with this extensive mobilization, little suggests that these supporters had any greater means of holding Obama accountable for his policy positions than during the broadcast era. Despite these extensive protest activities, Obama did not change his position with respect to FISA. In a nod to this impressive effort, the campaign did post a message signed by Obama defending his decision and thanking supporters for working to hold him accountable. The campaign also made three members of its foreign policy team available for ninety minutes to take questions about the policy. In interviews, many members of Obama's new media staff cited this moment as an example of how the campaign invited dissent and was responsive to and transparent with supporters. Yet there is another interpretation. As one new media staffer explained, the campaign deployed social media "to give up control below, to increase control above." Some on the campaign viewed allowing supporters to have their say as a safety valve, even as staffers were able to monitor the discussion in these online forums, a practice that scholars have noted in other contexts.[54] At the same time, given that supporters had unchecked ability to organize these protests on My.BarackObama.com, it also created the advantageous perception that the candidate was hearing dissenting voices. This potentially increased the legitimacy of the final decision and the loyalty of supporters, and, as a consequence, it provided the candidate with greater control over policy positions. In this sense, the FISA protests suggest that while citizens have increased agency to make themselves visible to candidates they continue to lack meaningful opportunities for "voice"—particularly in situations when there are few political alternatives.[55] Yet it also shows how the campaign's digital tools effectively provided the *illusion* of voice, openness, and transparency.

This reading of the Get FISA Right protest draws attention to how participation, in providing an illusion of voice, can serve to legitimate and reinforce political authority. The Obama campaign exerted high-level control over all substantive matters and provided scant opportunities for supporters to have meaningful interactions with staffers. In this sense, the deployment of digital tools worked ideologically to create the perception of participatory openness that increased buy-in and legitimacy. The Get FISA Right protests reveal the way that My.BarackObama.com served as a predetermined channel for voice that the campaign could, ultimately, control while increasing loyalty. These predetermined channels were not limited to the protests around FISA. The campaign even set up a largely ceremonial application called MyPolicy for citizens to submit policy ideas. Yet there was no one on the campaign end actually accounting for these submissions.[56]

Conclusion: Evaluating New Media Campaigning

The need for campaigns such as Obama's to strike a balance between under- and overorganizing suggests that many scholarly fears over the management of contemporary political engagement are overstated. For example, scholars argue that technological shifts provide campaign professionals with new opportunities to "manage" citizens by targeting communication, conjuring up issue publics, and providing very thin avenues to engage in politics.[57] The social movement scholar Victoria Carty extends this work in her discussion of the Obama campaign, arguing that staffers used new media to create managed citizens.[58]

And yet, as the case of the Obama campaign demonstrates, the nature of voluntaristic contributions and need to avoid overorganizing set bounds around the explicit management of electoral politics. While the Obama campaign engaged in sophisticated forms of data profiling and targeted its persuasive communications, these scholarly accounts generally overstate the control that campaign staffers and political consultants had over the electorate. Staffers always had to remain responsive, at least to a degree, to the concerns of supporters, given the voluntaristic nature of their participation. Meanwhile, staffers could not formally manage these supporters and even lacked the close, in-person coordination of volunteers that are a characteristic of embodied field campaigns.

Indeed, many scholars concerned with the management of electoral politics have generally overlooked the fact that the interests and goals of campaigns and the publics they mobilize are *aligned* most of the time. While supporters often desire transformative forms of participation and see their engagement in terms of civic renewal, supporters also expect campaigns to do everything they can to win. Supporters want campaigns to maximize their financial and volunteer contributions and extend the candidate's base of support. Supporters want opponents to be defeated, and they are willing to serve in that effort as best they can. Campaigns, for their part, strive to win and use supporters as implements of electoral strategy. Their staffers, however, often frame their work in terms of democratic renewal, valuing participation as a good in and of itself. It is only during extraordinary moments when there is a significant crisis that fissures appear in the way these goals are balanced, such as when Obama supporters feared the candidate they worked for was someone different than they imagined during the Get FISA Right protest. Supporters desired more accountability over policy positions. In this case, after supporters exercised their voice and the campaign or candidate responded to this discontent, the alignment of interest was restored.

In light of these empirical findings, it is clear that certain veins of the literature take an overly deterministic view of campaigns' ability to structure and control political participation. At the same time, the Dean and Obama campaigns were not robust proving grounds of democratic citizenship. A number of scholars have advanced overly optimistic claims about new media campaigns, particularly the Obama campaign. These accounts generally overstate the agency of citizens vis-à-vis campaigns and electoral institutions. Networked media have not necessarily made campaigns more responsive to supporters or their concerns. As the Get FISA Right protest suggests, the Obama campaign set its policy agenda according to its own strategic needs, and supporters could not do much about it. Meanwhile, grand claims for democratic transformation are only sustained if the ends toward which campaigns direct supporter collaboration are left out. The Obama campaign, like the Dean campaign before it, spent much time and effort translating energy and collaboration into the staples of political campaigns: money, message, and votes.

The danger is that there will be long-term consequences to these delimited forms of electoral participation. On one level, participation on the Obama campaign was generally about mobilization among those already most engaged, considering that participation and turnout were still far from that of the era of public spectacle that McGerr chronicles. As Rosenstone and Hansen argue, this has significant consequences: "efforts to move the organized, the employed, the elite and the advantaged into politics exacerbate rather than reduce the class biases in political participation in America."[59]

Network-based forms of political engagement have strengthened the voices of those already most inclined to participate, in turn reinforcing extant inequalities.

Even more, participation can work ideologically to legitimate extant arrangements of power and actively constrain the voices of challengers. McQuarrie notes that particular arrangements of participatory practices, metrics, discourses, and actors can reinforce authority: "Rather than serving as a challenge to elite and expert authority, participation is now deployed as a tool of that authority."[60] The case of the 2008 Obama campaign reveals how participation can work to frame choices and dissuade the exit that could potentially undermine the power of elites. As the consequences of Obama's change in position on FISA as a candidate in 2008 and subsequent expansion of national security surveillance have recently made clear, the danger is that participation divorced from accountability may cause people to act in ways that undermine their power.[61] For example, a poignant post appeared on June 6, 2013, on the Get FISA Right blog in the wake of recent revelations about the expanded national security apparatus of the Obama administration:

> Did the 23,000 of us who originally formed the group that ultimately set up this blog make the wrong call back in July 2008 and after, when we told our candidate, "You made the wrong choice on the FISA warrantless wiretapping act, but we will support you anyway"? Would we have been better to walk away and support a third-party candidate? There is no way to know, of course; the much-desired glimpse into an alternative universe for comparison is not possible except in science fiction. The clear truth is that we are at least disappointed, at most frightened for our democracy. While we can still post here, spied upon or otherwise, welcome back to the conversation![62]

The choice to exit and turn to a third party or support a rival is shaped, if not determined, by the sense of voice that participation provides. Participation shapes the contexts within which activists make choices about their engagement, whom to lend their support to, the strategies and tactics they use, and the goals they pursue. In this sense, challengers need always to ask hard questions about participation and accountability.

NOTES

1. This chapter is adapted from Kreiss (2012).
2. For journalistic accounts, see Exley (2008). For scholarly accounts, see Anstead and Straw (2009).
3. Miller (1987).
4. Schudson (1998).
5. Bimber and Davis (2003); Chadwick (2008).
6. Bimber, Flanagin, and Stohl (2005); Shirky (2008).
7. For the former, see Coleman (2005); for the latter, see Jenkins (2006).
8. Norman and Collyer (2011).
9. This chapter focuses on Democratic online political campaigning. While there was relative parity in Internet campaigning during the general elections of 2000, and much suggests

that the Bush reelection campaign was ahead of its Democratic rival in 2004, in 2008 and 2012 Obama's campaigns proved far more successful at raising money and garnering volunteers online than Republican counterparts.
10. Beniger (1986).
11. Up until 2004 most Internet staffers came from outside of electoral politics, especially from commercial firms, and did not work in politics during off-election years. Many in this new generation of political professionals that got their start during the 2004 cycle, however, stayed in politics and worked on various presidential campaigns in 2008. At the same time, the field has always been open to new entrants, particularly from the commercial technology industry. This drove innovation in 2004 (Kreiss 2009) and, to a lesser extent, in 2008 (Kreiss 2012).
12. Minkoff, Aisenbrey, and Agnone (2008).
13. Walker, McCarthy, and Baumgartner (2011).
14. Walker (2009).
15. Earl and Kimport (2011).
16. McQuarrie (this volume).
17. For more extensive treatment of these intermediaries, see Kreiss (2012).
18. McGerr (1988).
19. McGerr (1988: 6).
20. For focus groups and polls, see Sabato (1981); for direct mail and voter databases, see Howard (2006).
21. Skocpol (2003).
22. Fischer (2010).
23. United States Elections Project, available online at http://elections.gmu.edu/.
24. Abramowitz (2010).
25. Nielsen (2012).
26. Nielsen (2012).
27. Kreiss (2012).
28. Foot and Schneider (2006).
29. Bimber and Davis (2003).
30. Kreiss (2012).
31. Larry Biddle, personal communication, October 20, 2008.
32. McGerr (1988).
33. Kazin (2007).
34. Kazin (2007: 82).
35. Kreiss (2012).
36. A "club good" is a good that many can enjoy but that can be excludable. In this sense, BSD, the private owners, managed their platform in a way that defined the "club" as Democratic-allied organizations and excluded non-ideologically aligned groups (although BSD has commercial clients as well). Investments in the good benefited all members of the club; for an extensive discussion of club goods, see Cornes and Sandler (1996).
37. Canovan (1999).
38. Alexander (2010).
39. Schudson (1998).
40. Polsby (1983).
41. Rosenstone and Hansen (1993).
42. Nielsen (2012).

43. Chen (2010).
44. Scott Thomas, personal communication, August 3, 2010.
45. Scott Thomas, personal communication, August 3, 2010.
46. For a discussion of the campaign's symbolic work, see Alexander (2010).
47. Scott Thomas, personal communication, August 3, 2010.
48. Scott Thomas, personal communication, August 3, 2010.
49. Chen (2010: 21).
50. Howard (2006).
51. Latour (2005).
52. Guins (2009: 7).
53. Neil Jensen, personal communication, November 10, 2008.
54. Lee (2011).
55. Hirschman (1970).
56. Neil Jensen, personal communication, November 10, 2008. The idea of involving supporters in some form of policy discussion is not new, and it was not pursued, at least symbolically, by the Obama campaign.
57. Howard (2006).
58. Carty (2010).
59. Rosenstone and Hansen (1993: 33).
60. McQuarrie (this volume).
61. For a summary, see Kaminski (2003).
62. sallijane (2013).

CHAPTER 8

Patient, Parent, Advocate, Investor
Entrepreneurial Health Activism from Research to Reimbursement

DAVID SCHLEIFER AND AARON PANOFSKY

This chapter discusses a phenomenon we call entrepreneurial health activism, which emerges as a response to what its practitioners perceive as the limitations of traditional health activism. We show how entrepreneurial health activists disrupt some conventional modes of governing business and science, namely intellectual property rights and conflict-of-interest disclosures. Entrepreneurialism expands the range of practices available to health activists, potentially resulting in tangible benefits for certain disease communities. But it risks further exacerbating existing inequalities in the distribution of American health care resources.

Health activists often see their projects in terms of life and death. They are driven by the prospects of death or severe disability and by the perception that these prospects might be delayed or avoided through new research, pharmaceutical breakthroughs, diagnostic or treatment practices, or insurance coverage. They may be sick themselves or may be advocating on behalf of friends, family members, or fellow citizens.[1] But the stakes may be higher when participants are disease sufferers or "survivors" or when they are parents of children who are or may become sick.[2] The universality of health and illness, and the notion that well-being enables all other activities and potentials, gives health activism its broad legitimacy and potent emotional valence. The mortal stakes experienced by the activists discussed in this chapter differ from those discussed elsewhere in this volume, where democracy and inclusion are often viewed as ends in themselves. In health activism, participation as a matter of right is not the fundamental issue at stake. Instead, participation is seen as a means for securing health and avoiding death.

All health activism in the United States takes place in a domain of expensive technologies and services. Health care accounts for roughly 18 percent of the United States' gross domestic product and 20 percent of all federal spending.[3] Biomedical research, health care delivery, and payment are handled by a heterogeneous network of for-profit, nonprofit, and governmental organizations, making health care a domain where distinctions among "civil society," "state," and "market" are already hazy.[4] For health activists, including what we call entrepreneurial health activists, the notion that life itself is at stake sets in motion and is used to justify a further blurring of these already tenuous distinctions among civil society, state, and market.

In entrepreneurial health activism, patients, their families, and their allies pursue economic activities such as property ownership, patenting, or direct financial investment with for-profit pharmaceutical, biotechnology, and medical device companies. They see themselves as pursuing interests created by their or their families' diseases. Responding to what they see as the health system's failure to deliver treatments for their conditions, they blur the roles of consumers and producers of health technologies by trying to find ways to produce or procure treatments themselves. Entrepreneurial health activists turn to the market because of the limits they perceive with traditional advocacy and activism. Yet, rather than abandoning activism entirely, they seek to bolster their advocacy efforts by melding them with entrepreneurialism.

This type of activism differs from other examples described in this book. These are not strategic deployments of public participation in cynical bids to bolster corporate legitimacy and profits. They are not consultants' efforts to build popular legitimacy for institutional clients like Lee, McNulty, and Schaffer describe.[5] They are not efforts by nonmedical corporations to burnish their public images by aligning themselves with diseases like breast cancer.[6] Nor are these instances like Walker describes in which corporations mobilize their employees or consumers as a means to pursue economic interests.[7] Entrepreneurial health activism seems often to start with pressing health problems, and then to pragmatically employ the tools of activism and entrepreneurialism to achieve its substantive goals.

That the activists we consider here see the pursuit of entrepreneurialism in pragmatic terms is not a statement about the legitimacy or authenticity of them or their interests. Critical researchers who believe that activism can or should be a purely civil society activity have sounded alarms about overly cozy relationships between activists and corporations, including pharmaceutical corporations.[8] Such overly cozy relationships arguably damage the kinds of transparency and disclosure that are necessary for consumers, citizens, and politicians to make informed choices. However, we sidestep such normative questions and approach entrepreneurial health activism on its own complicated terms. The bulk of our discussion concerns how activists' entrepreneurial activities redefine the politics of intellectual property and of conflicts of interest. We nonetheless conclude that entrepreneurial health activism has subtle yet potentially serious implications for the democratic or nondemocratic character of the health care system in the United States by amplifying the already unequal distribution of health care resources in the United States.

Entrepreneurial health activism arises within a history of health activism that began roughly in the 1970s. While Brown and colleagues maintain that broad-based health access movements do indeed exist,[9] no major social movement has emerged to advocate for universal health care, not even for the 2010 Patient Protection and Affordable Care Act (ACA).[10] Instead, perhaps the major activity of health activists has been to fight for recognition and resources for new disease categories and previously neglected populations.[11] Some health activists have resisted medical interventions and medicalization, such as women's resistance to radical mastectomy in the 1970s and gay and lesbian activists' efforts to remove homosexuality from among the disorders in the American Psychiatric Association's *Diagnostic and Statistical Manual of Mental Disorders*.[12]

But health advocacy is overwhelmingly expansive, seeking more money, research, and treatment for specific conditions such as breast cancer, multiple sclerosis, HIV/AIDS, autism, or muscular dystrophy.

This proliferation of interest politics in health may be "democratic" in that more voices, often previously marginalized, participate in decision-making processes. But it is oriented less toward representing a general public interest and more toward serving particular disease sufferers' interests. Several scholars have shown how this disease-specific activism distributes resources unfairly in light of broader health concerns.[13] Best also argues that this type of interest-based activism encourages policymakers to think of medical research funds as a benefit given to patients rather than to researchers or to members of the public.[14]

Recent work on health activism has focused on activists' impact on nonstate institutions, particularly biomedical research and health care providers.[15] This is consistent with a broader focus in social movement research on activism targeted at firms and industries in addition to states.[16] Research on health activism targeted at for-profit enterprises has generally followed one of two approaches. One approach, in the contentious politics tradition, has been to see health activists' engagement with markets and corporations as fundamentally oppositional.[17] The other has been to consider health activism in terms of consumer movements.[18] Consumer movements have been tactics in many political struggles, arguably starting with the American Revolution.[19] Consumerism is therefore not necessarily a depoliticizing notion. It recognizes that patients and other types of consumers can drive changes through market exchanges.

However, neither of these approaches is particularly useful in understanding the activists that we investigate. Although they may be health care consumers, they also engage in health care production through ownership and management. Furthermore, they do not take an oppositional approach to markets or corporations. Instead, they purposefully synthesize economic activity with activism, implicitly rejecting the notion of a separation between these spheres. They use property ownership, patenting, or direct financial investments to address interests created by their diseases, to assist communities of those with the same illnesses, and to potentially profit financially. However, they seem less motivated by earnings than by the limits they perceive in traditional models of activism. Entrepreneurial activism appears to be driven by expediency rather than by political motivations to change the health or research system. The value these activists see in entrepreneurialism is that it allows for new partnerships and opens new spaces for maneuvering.

To describe this phenomenon, we draw from examples collected from two related research projects: Panofsky's work on patient activists in the rare disease field and Schleifer's work on health care costs.[20] Panofsky's discussion of property rights and conflict of interest is based on interviews with leaders of organizations that advocate for patients with rare diseases, as well as on secondary research on the wider rare genetic disease field. Schleifer's discussion of reimbursement and conflict of interest is based on a qualitative analysis of transcripts of hearings at the federal Centers for Medicare and Medicaid Services (CMS) about coverage of a prostate cancer treatment called Provenge. He also analyzed conflict-of-interest disclosure statements submitted to CMS, obtained via a Freedom of Information Act request, and related financial media coverage.

Our examples concern those who see themselves as activists and also have financial stakes in the health conditions and health care technologies for which they advocate. It is difficult to know how widespread the kinds of entrepreneurial activism we discuss are, but we know these are not unique or novel arrangements. For example, feminist activists created the Women's Capital Corporation in 1997 to bring the Plan-B emergency contraceptive pill to market.[21] However, we do not claim to offer this as a definition of entrepreneurial activism that covers all its possible variations or distinguish it from "ordinary" activism. We recognize variations among those whom we describe as entrepreneurial health activists—and recognize that they would not necessarily use our term to describe themselves. As will become clear, we also note variations in the types of economic activities and financial relationships that entrepreneurial activists pursue. These include owning and licensing intellectual property, owning shares of stock, and creating health information websites funded by advertising fees. Some individuals also participate in or manage more traditional nonprofit efforts alongside their entrepreneurial activities or work alongside trade associations and 501(c)(4) political organizations.

Our case selection is designed to explore and illustrate thematic areas and not to be comprehensive. We start by discussing how groups manage the economic and intellectual interests of research scientists. Then we discuss the use of property, especially intellectual property. Lastly we consider how activists manage their own conflicts of interest in securing reimbursement for new drugs and, meanwhile, how they attempt to separate the state's multiple roles in health care. We conclude by discussing the implications of this type of activism, particularly the challenges it poses to the concept of conflict of interest and the concerns it raises about distribution of health care resources.

Property Rights

As the social system of research is currently organized, medical innovations—drugs, devices, medical tools—depend on the existence of patents and intellectual property (IP). In this sense, patents and IP help patients. However, simultaneous with this is a general sense among many advocates, activists, and policymakers that intellectual property is no friend of patients. For one, IP monopolies and restrictive licenses keep drug prices high. This, of course, limits access to the poor, burdens medical systems, and leads to de facto rationing of care via cost. This pattern has been evident in the controversy over HIV/AIDS drugs, particularly in developing countries.[22] A more direct example is the case of Moore versus the UC Regents in which the Supreme Court of California ruled that patients have no property rights to their "discarded" body tissues, even when they are used to create lucrative products.[23]

Several examples of the fraught status of property rights come from the rare genetic disease field. Take the case of the rare genetic disorder Canavan disease. Several patient groups worked with researchers at Miami Children's Hospital, donating money and tissue samples in the hopes that a genetic test could be developed and a research program launched. The genetic mutation was successfully identified in 1993, but without the advocates' knowledge the hospital patented the gene and imposed a license restricting access to genetic testing and research uses.[24] In a more recent example, the drug company Genzyme has had difficulty meeting the demand for the drug Fabrazyme, an enzyme replacement therapy for sufferers of Gaucher disease, another rare genetic disorder, because of contamination in the manufacturing plant. Gaucher advocates, frustrated with repeated delays, have petitioned to have Genzyme's patent exclusivity revoked, hoping competition, or the threat of it, will speed production.[25]

These examples dramatize various ways that property can drive wedges among patients, researchers, doctors, and medical institutions. Property illustrates patients' dependence on researchers, companies, and doctors and the ease with which patients' bodies and identities can be objectified and alienated from them. Thus, it is not surprising that patient advocates have often opposed the principle of intellectual property. A vivid example is the 2013 Supreme Court decision in the American Civil Liberties Union (ACLU) and other codefendants versus Myriad Genetics.[26] The case contested Myriad's patent on the BRCA mutations for breast cancer, which they have used to develop an exclusive genetic test. The ACLU contested the very principle of gene patenting, a pillar of the biotech industry for the last several decades. Several disease advocacy groups submitted *amici curae* supporting the ACLU in the argument that genes are natural objects that cannot be patented and that gene patents slow the pace of research.[27] On June 13, 2013, the Supreme Court found in favor of the plaintiffs, agreeing that genes are "products of nature" and therefore cannot be patented.[28]

However, there is no consensus among advocates on the matter of genetic property rights. The Genetic Alliance, an organization representing a coalition of disease advocacy groups and others engaged in the field of genetic diseases, filed an *amicus* brief supporting Myriad. The Genetic Alliance argued that genes are patentable and that eliminating patents would undermine research progress. They argue that other policy means, not the abolition of patents, should be used to avoid the misuse of patents to unreasonably restrict access to research and clinical use. Behind this position is Sharon Terry, a parent of two children with pseudoxanthoma elasticum (PXE) and also the president and CEO of the Genetic Alliance and cofounder of the advocacy group PXE International. PXE International is famous as one of the most entrepreneurial rare disease advocacy groups in the field. Most notably they were the first patient group to secure the patent rights to a gene, ABCC6, the gene responsible for pseudoxanthoma elasticum.

It would be a mistake to view the Genetic Alliance *amicus* brief as a simple attempt to defend PXE International's property rights. Rather it reflects a different orientation toward property advocated by Terry and a small set of entrepreneurial health activists. Terry's position is that property is a tool that advocates can use to mobilize and organize scientists to get research done on diseases that would otherwise attract little attention. In an interview describing her and her husband's advent into the field, Terry said, "We quickly figured out that there was a lot of competition [among scientists] and the way that you reduce competition is you figure out what commodity can you own or control that everybody else wants access to and you can therefore call all the shots and make all the rules."[29] Initially that commodity was the bodies and tissue samples of PXE disease sufferers. So the Terrys set up PXE International and created a registry of disease sufferers and a biobank of tissue samples. By offering researchers access to these resources on particular terms, PXE International was able to reduce researchers' upfront costs but also to enforce cooperation and thus to speed research.

When the PXE mutation was discovered, Terry was able to convince the scientists to assign their patent rights to the organization. She explained her belief that the patent enables the organization to do two things. First, it signals to the research community that the group is well organized and attentive, which she believes makes them more attractive partners. Second, licensing the genetic test based on the patent to a single lab has enabled the aggregation of data on genotype/phenotype correlations that would not have been possible if the test were openly available to all labs. Terry states that "we didn't patent it to own it, we patented it to be stewards of it." Their aim, apparently, has not been to use the patent to profit, but to drive their research agenda.

Other organizations might object that PXE International was fortunate to be at the right place at the right time with the right relationship to scientists and that few others (witness the unfortunate Canavan disease groups) have such opportunities to control patents. But Terry does not believe that the gene patent has been crucial to the group's success. It has automatically put the group at the center of any scientific efforts that use the gene, but Terry says, "We would have figured out some way to be in the game in some kind of benefit sharing arrangement and some kind of stewardship arrangement with the scientists if we weren't able to patent the gene."

Terry's downplaying of the importance of patents and of IP more broadly, despite her group's success, is echoed by Brad Margus. His two children have ataxia-telangiectasia (AT) and he founded a nonprofit patient advocacy organization called the AT Children's Project. He explained in an interview,

> I can't point to any situation where someone having intellectual property rights resulting from the research we've funded, actually ended up impeding anything. From my perspective, if that were the only obstacle we had, that would be a blast. I could blow that away just with the moral level we can come in on—the fact that because the disease is rare, a carve-out for AT would never hurt anybody's business plan. Now, I don't really see that as a big deal.[30]

For patient groups like these, there is nothing special about patents or property in this field. They do not fetishize their property as either symbols of objectifying people or their diseases or as sources of exorbitant costs. Entrepreneurial approaches may constitute a small subset of activism strategies. But these activists' positions on property may be driven in part by the rarity of their children's diseases, which are subjects of only scant clinical knowledge and tend not to attract as many scientists or funds as do other, more common diseases. At a political level, these minority players strengthen the authority of those who tend to support private ownership of intellectual property and reveal the fractures in what might be assumed to constitute the public position on property. Beyond these rare diseases, to see property rights as in themselves impeding research would be to presume that patients have a passive relationship to research. Instead, patients and parents may actively use property as another tool to address their health needs.

Managing "Conflict of Interest"

Patents are only one form of property or ownership that patient groups can take. Patient registries, data sets, and banks of biological materials are also widely believed to be powerful tools for driving research on rare diseases.[31] Hughes reports that patient groups sometimes serve as angel investors or pseudo-venture capitalists in early and long-shot research efforts.[32] This is because their devotion to disease research and the often limited range of opportunities make them willing to make riskier financial bets on science. Some patient groups have established for-profit enterprises to work alongside them in research and product development, such as the Pachyonychia Congenita Project's TransDerm Incorporated and Novazyme Pharmaceuticals, founded by the father of a child with Pompe disease and later acquired by Genzyme.[33]

These relationships raise the issue of conflicts of interest. The notion of a conflict of interest is a problematization of converging financial and organizational relationships.[34] Conflicts of interest are subject to rules disclosures and other forms of governance in a variety of scientific fields. How can patient advocates balance the fact that they control potentially lucrative resources but that the profits to be derived will come from their fellow disease sufferers? Although few rare genetic diseases have any treatments in the pipeline, how can advocates balance the fact that their commercial interests might put them at odds with other companies, researchers, and organizations developing potentially competing but equally effective or even improved therapies? Alan Stockdale's account of the Cystic Fibrosis Foundation suggests that scientists promoting high-risk gene therapy cures essentially captured the organization's agenda, leading it to ignore more prosaic efforts to alleviate sufferers' symptoms.[35] This spurred a conflict wherein organization leaders actually barred the participation of ordinary members and suppressed their protests.

A more directly economic case comes from Anand's journalistic account of the work of John Crowley, a parent of two children with Pompe disease.[36] Crowley began with a fairly ordinary patient organization that raised money and then donated it to researchers. Frustrated by the slow pace of progress, Crowley became the CEO of Novazyme, a company started by a scientist developing an enzyme-replacement medication for Pompe disease. In Anand's account, many of the people surrounding Crowley worried about his conflict of interest: Would he sacrifice sound business decisions for his children's sake? However, apart from his frequent absences from home, the possibility that his professional decisions might not have been best for his children was left unexamined. When the therapy was developed, Crowley navigated the conflict of interest related to getting his children into the clinical trial by resigning from his leadership in Novazyme, though he later went on to positions in other biotech companies. Ultimately "conflict of interest" is a trope in Anand's account. Anxieties about conflicts are attributed to characters of limited imagination; the heroic CEO/activist/father easily navigates any problems.

The very notion of conflict of interest presumes actors have a set of preestablished interests owing to their locations in different spheres of action. In other words, patients have an interest in cures, scientists have an interest in truth, businesses have an interest in profit, and governments have an interest in regulation. But, empirically, how do actual patient advocates understand and manage the conflicts that arise when their disease interests converge with their economic interests? Many nonentrepreneurial health advocacy organizations are concerned about conflicts of interest in fairly traditional ways. As Panofsky has shown, they often strive to keep their research, advocacy, and patient service functions separate from each other.[37] When they support research, for example, many organizations do not trust their own discretion to choose how to disburse grants. They may attribute this partly to a lack of technical expertise to discern quality but partly to worries that their interests as advocates might limit their appreciation of the most fruitful directions of research. They therefore often assemble scientist committees to evaluate and fund grant requests.[38]

The more entrepreneurially oriented organizations, who actively coordinate the actions of scientists, intimately involve themselves in the research process. They work to combine their different goals and functions and often argue that traditional patient organizations are actually much more subject to conflicts of interest than their entrepreneurial forms of action. First, they often complain that in traditional patient activism, the organization itself becomes too much of a focus and distracts from the real goals, with too many resources devoted to organizational perpetuation, bureaucratic rules, and procedures.[39] In other words, patient advocacy organizations become about organizations and not advocacy. One entrepreneurial leader of a patient organization said in an interview,

> If your time and energy is spent on your organization quote unquote, you cannot devote what's needed to finding therapies and treatments.... [At a meeting of another group she went to] they told [a scientist] off for some stupid administrative whatever, I don't know. ... Three different people [important researchers] went to their meeting. They never even realized who was in their midst. They were so busy with their stupid administrative stuff. That's what I mean about I don't want to be an organization.[40]

Second, the traditional organization can become a victim of scientists and can have difficulty managing the conflicted interests of other groups. The advocate Brad Margus said that a common situation is for a scientist to "become the guru in this rare disease and they start to collect samples and they horde them and they use them as a currency for collaborating with people." This can happen especially when advocates are overly deferential about the propriety of their acting in the research field. Sharon Terry suggests that many patient groups give scientists too much control over the organization: "I spend a reasonable amount of my time [as the head of the Genetic Alliance] helping other organizations navigate the conflicts of interest from their Medical and Professional Advisory Board because they do have those people making decisions about the grants and about the research objectives."

Third, some see the disease identity and the practice of advocacy embedded within the organization as producing conflicts as well. Jamie Heywood founded a nonprofit organization for Lou Gehrig's disease called ALS Therapy Development Institute. Here, he described the decision to establish a later venture, PatientsLikeMe.com, as a for-profit business: "In an environment where you don't have income as your primary objective and your primary measure of success is moral righteousness, it tends to put people against each other in ways that are less than constructive."[41]

Notable about the views of this entrepreneurial breed of patient advocates is that they see conflicts of interests as the product of precisely those arrangements designed to avoid them. These arrangements include bureaucratic rules that separate economic from scientific or patient interests and that make sure that parties with categorically different interests (e.g., advocates and scientists) are kept separate. These entrepreneurial health advocates do not believe that their interests are in conflict. That is, they think they can better meet the needs of disease sufferers by stimulating dynamic research and also mobilizing close relationships with researchers and doctors for medical advice to individuals. Their strategy involves building trust and mutual accountability with researchers through close relationships. They understand that different actors have different interests. But rather than papering these over or using artificial boundaries to solve the problem, they use their close relationships and their own goal orientation to negotiate ad hoc arrangements to minimize the conflicts.

Reimbursement, Disclosure of Interests, and the State's Multiple Roles in Health Care

Entrepreneurial health advocates focus considerable attention on research and drug development. By the same token, sociologists of science and technology have focused substantially on research processes and to some extent on the use of technologies, but less on how technologies are bought and sold. However, if biomedical research goes far enough, someone eventually has to pay for any resulting therapies. And because the federal government pays for a significant portion of American health care technologies, advocacy for drug reimbursement has unique implications for public resource distribution. In 2010, Medicaid insured about sixty-eight million Americans and Medicare insured about forty-seven million Americans.[42] Medicare decisions about whether to reimburse for a new drug or treatment often set precedents that private insurers follow. Federal programs also insure military families, veterans, and some disabled people and injured workers. And the ACA includes federal subsidies for individuals buying private health insurance. Various branches of the U.S. government therefore play major roles in health care markets.

As of 2014, Provenge was the only product of a Seattle biotechnology company called Dendreon. Provenge treatments involve removing some of a patient's own cells, combining them with immune system–stimulating proteins, and infusing the altered cells back into the patient. This novel approach, called autologous cellular immunotherapy, straddles regulatory categories because it involves both a custom-made drug and a treatment technique. The Food and Drug Administration (FDA) approved Provenge in 2010. But two patient advocacy groups filed lawsuits seeking internal documents from the FDA. They alleged that scientists on FDA committees intentionally slowed the approval process because they had financial interests in competing drugs. Because Provenge is meant to treat late-stage disease, activists argued that these delays, caused by conflicts of interest, cost lives. The case was eventually decided in favor of the FDA.[43]

CMS then initiated an unusual additional review to decide whether Medicare would reimburse for Provenge. In 2010, a course of Provenge treatment was estimated to cost $93,000, extending life for a median of four additional months.[44] Although $93,000 sounds expensive, some commentators argued that it was comparable to now-standard chemotherapy treatments for other cancers.[45] Currently, the FDA approves drugs and CMS pays for them, but both agencies are barred by law from considering how much a drug costs. CMS only considers whether treatments are "reasonable and necessary." However, efforts to define "reasonable and necessary" have repeatedly been derailed over the verboten subject of cost-effectiveness.[46] The debate over reimbursement for Provenge illustrates how activists and other health care actors envision the differences between the state's multiple roles in health care. When CMS announced its additional review of Provenge, a coalition of patient advocacy organizations and professional medical associations released a statement accusing CMS of considering cost, which it is not permitted to do, and of inappropriately questioning the FDA's determination that Provenge was effective.[47] "It is 'extremely chilling' to innovation in cancer research if new FDA-approved treatments against cancer must now go through a second round of efficacy and safety review from CMS," the coalition stated.[48] The coalition also claimed that the additional review would stifle the commercialization of other innovative therapies, including autologous cellular immunotherapies for other cancers.

As part of its additional review, CMS held a public hearing in November 2010 of its Medicare Evidence Development and Coverage Advisory Committee (MEDCAC) in order to take public input about Medicare coverage of Provenge. Open hearings are among the techniques of democratization that regulators have institutionalized as part of drug approval and reimbursement decisions. Many of those who spoke at the Provenge hearing accused CMS of violating those boundaries by appearing to consider both costs and effectiveness.

The Provenge hearing also demonstrates the varying ways in which activists, including entrepreneurial activists, selectively manage the disclosure of their economic interests. Those who officially serve on expert panels at the CMS must disclose conflicts of interest. It might seem essential for advocates also to disclose financial interests when they speak at hearings, so that regulators can weigh those interests as part of their decisions. The FDA does not require advocates or scientists to make such disclosures at hearings.[49] By contrast, at CMS hearings, scheduled speakers must fill out disclosure forms in advance and are asked to highlight any conflicts at the beginning of their presentation.[50] An entrepreneurial activist at the Provenge hearing framed his investment in the drug's manufacturer as evidence of his commitment to fighting prostate cancer. An ostensibly more traditional activist, however, did not mention his organization's receipt of a charitable donation from the drug's manufacturer, nor did he mention it on the written disclosure he submitted to CMS. As the committee secretary explained at the opening of the meeting,

> We ask in the interest of fairness that all persons making statements or presentations disclose if you or any member of your immediate family owns stock or has another formal financial interest in any company, including Internet or E-commerce organizations that develops, manufactures, distributes and/or markets any autologous cellular immunotherapy treatment for metastatic prostate cancer. This includes direct financial investments, consulting fees and significant institutional support.[51]

Some of those who spoke at the Provenge hearing disclosed their financial relationships with the drug's manufacturer, but others did not. Moreover, activists and industry representatives alike argued that the government's role as an insurer should be kept separate from its role in drug approval and that both approval and insurance should disregard costs. For example, Laurel Todd spoke on behalf of the Biotechnology Industry Organization, a trade association of which Dendreon is a member. Noting that her father had prostate cancer, she argued, "There should be no question that an FDA-approved therapy should be covered by Medicare for patients and conditions indicated on its label."[52] She continued, "We are concerned that CMS opening a national coverage analysis on an FDA-approved therapy so soon after approval could establish a precedent that would reduce Medicare patient access to a wide range of novel drugs and biologics."[53]

An entrepreneurial health activist at the Provenge hearing similarly argued that CMS's additional review was inappropriate because Medicare should automatically reimburse for any FDA-approved drug. Bradley Loncar, who traveled from Kansas to Baltimore for the hearing, described himself as an activist motivated by his grandfather's prostate cancer. But he also owned Dendreon stock and would later use his equity to call for changes in the company's management.[54] While he disclosed his investment, he appeared to vacillate about its significance. Loncar at first said, "I don't represent any specific company or organization, I'm just here as a citizen. . . . In 2006 my grandfather, Michael Loncar, passed away from late stage prostate cancer."[55] But he then described his financial stake in the company as part of his prostate cancer activism. "I'm also an investor in the maker of Provenge, a proud investor I might add, because I believe in the innovative work that they're doing with this disease and I want to support that. However, I have never had any direct relationship with that company or any company and I'm 100 percent here on my own today."[56]

Loncar was displeased that CMS panelists were asked to consider two questions about "evidence gaps" in outcomes research on Provenge (MEDCAC 2010a). Loncar argued that by asking about efficacy, CMS was overstepping the bounds of its role as an insurer. Loncar described himself as "deeply concerned" that CMS would "openly second-guess" the FDA's approval of Provenge.[57]

> I think it's very concerning that this agency today seems willing to consider something that very recently the FDA has already said is unethical. I think that raises a lot of questions, two of which at the top of my list are, how many men will have their lives prolonged [sic] because of potential confusion or delays caused by the CMS and how much future innovation will be stifled by a government that regulates with two voices? When it comes to informing the public about the safety and efficacy of drugs, the United States Government needs to speak with one clear and concise voice and that voice is the FDA.[58]

The Provenge hearing took place not long after the heated debate over passage of the ACA, during which some opponents argued that health care reform was tantamount to rationing.[59] Loncar claimed that CMS's questions about outcomes were in fact a veiled way of considering costs. "I am very concerned that this Agency, seemingly for financial reasons, seems willing to consider [these questions] that another government agency, the FDA, has already publicly said would be neither ethical nor feasible because substantial evidence of efficacy already exists."[60] He continued, "I think one has to wonder if today's meeting is indeed about something other than the science, namely the cost."[61] Clifford Goodman, chair of the CMS panel, responded, "I would also just remind our panel that as we look at our questions, none of them deals with financial matters, cost or the like."[62]

A seemingly more traditional patient advocate who spoke in favor of Medicare covering Provenge did not reveal his organization's financial relationship with the drug's manufacturer in his statement at the hearing or in the disclosure statement he submitted to CMS. James Kiefert, chairman emeritus of the prostate cancer activist group Us TOO International, described himself as having "no financial interest in Provenge or the Dendreon Corporation."[63] Us TOO's 2010 tax return lists a $58,700 contribution from Dendreon and the organization's website listed Dendreon as a "platinum" corporate supporter.[64] He may have interpreted the disclosure requirement as applying only to himself and not to the organization he represented. Kiefert spoke pointedly about the value of life, regardless of the cost of treatment.

> When one of the men in my group who is 67 years old heard that we're going to have this [CMS] meeting, I see tears running down the side of his face. He said I can't, I can't go through this not having an opportunity to extend my life by four months. So what does four months mean? When Steve in my group died at age 42, I can tell you his three kids that were still in school and his daughter who had just gone on to college would have given anything to have four months with their father.[65]

Kiefert also participated in the FDA's Provenge approval process as a patient representative.[66] He told the CMS panel that, having reviewed Provenge's safety and efficacy as part of his service to the FDA, he "felt very comfortable" participating as a research subject in a clinical study of the treatment.[67]

Another advocate at the hearing was Thair Phillips, president of RetireSafe. RetireSafe is a "grassroots" advocacy organization for seniors that describes itself as "a bulwark against encroachment by government and any number of threats that seek to prey upon vulnerable seniors and deprive them of the personal freedom and retirement security."[68] Phillips told the CMS panel that RetireSafe receives 92 percent of its funding in small donations from individuals. According to SourceWatch, RetireSafe is an astroturf project of the Council for Government Reform, formerly the National Center for Privatization, a 501(c)(4) organization that is not required to disclose its donors.[69] Phillips framed CMS's review of Provenge as an "overstep of regulatory oversight" that "makes seniors very nervous."[70] Phillips implied that the CMS hearing was really about cost and was an example of health care rationing.

> When a pharmaceutical industry who spends billions of dollars seeking cures to diseases loses faith that an FDA approval means a drug can be manufactured, distributed, prescribed and sold, then we have severely crippled the very mechanism that has made America the world's leader in the development of lifesaving medicines. . . . Whether the [CMS] admits it or not, the real core of this discussion is price and price is the very thing that should not be a point of discussion. If the government is willing to break its own rule and precedent in reviewing Provenge because of its cost, we have started down the road to rationed healthcare. I see no other word to use in this case but rationing.[71]

The chair of the CMS panel responded to Phillips as he had to Loncar saying, "None of our questions concerns costs or other financial matters."[72]

Two prostate patient groups later sued CMS, seeking information about its additional review.[73] But CMS did ultimately approve reimbursement for Provenge in May 2011. Dendreon's stock price rose accordingly. Investors, including S.A.C. Capital Advisors, Vanguard, BlackRock, and Soros, took bullish positions. However, Dendreon subsequently cut its Provenge sales forecasts. The company blamed physician uncertainty about Medicare reimbursement for the change in its sales forecasts. But several stock analysts attributed the lackluster sales forecasts to Provenge's limited effectiveness in extending life. Dendreon's stock price dropped 67 percent on August 4, 2011, although that happened to be the American financial markets' single worst day since the beginning of the 2008 recession.[74] Bradley Loncar reportedly sold all but one of his Dendreon shares, thus apparently suspending the entrepreneurial aspects of his activism—or the health activist parts of his investing. Although the stock eventually rebounded, its share price has continued to be volatile.[75]

Many regulatory bodies and research agencies now include advocates and other "public voices" in decisions about drug approval and health care resource distribution, as well as in decisions about nonmedical topics like zoning and environmental reviews. The notion of conflicts of interest posits financial stakes as problems and disclosure as the (weak) solution. We know that ostensibly traditional patient activist groups accept corporate donations, without necessarily disclosing those donations.[76] But once they have been disclosed, how are apparent conflicts of interest supposed to be interpreted in decision-making processes? Brad Loncar, the entrepreneurial activist in the

Provenge case, argued that his financial stakes should be interpreted as a measure of his commitment to fighting for treatment—at least until he decided to sell Dendreon's stock. At a more general level, by spanning the supposedly oppositional realms of civil society and the market, entrepreneurial activists fundamentally challenge the assumption that economic interests conflict with and should be separated from social, political, medical, or personal interests. This purposeful convergence of interests may seem marginal. But it is arguably just the other side of consumers boycotting goods manufactured under dangerous working conditions or choosing to buy fair trade products. And it is contiguous with the broader, socially responsible investment sector that includes microfinance, impact investing by philanthropies and socially responsible investment management by companies like Calvert and Domini, or socially responsible funds within more mainstream investment companies. The challenge of appropriately governing convergences of social and economic interests is thus not unique to entrepreneurial health activism.

Conclusion

Health activism has usually been viewed as a democratizing influence in health care and biomedical research. In the broadest strokes, health activists have worked to give voice to patients' interests and have influenced legislators, regulators, research funders, insurers, medical manufacturers, doctors, and researchers. Health activists would seem to fill the role of advocating for the public interest versus other powerful actors in the system who have their own financial interests. But in fact, most health activists operate more narrowly, articulating and advocating for the interests of specific diseases.

The entrepreneurial health activists we have discussed in this chapter are driven by pragmatic urges to solve the problems of patients with specific diseases. Their activism is implicitly driven by a dissatisfaction with the effectiveness of traditional advocacy and with the conventional separation of advocacy from markets. Activist entrepreneurs are skeptical of the notion that merely articulating patients' interests is sufficient to see those interests met. Researchers and regulators alike might be deeply moved by advocates' stories, but, as entrepreneurial activists indicate, this does not necessarily spur them to act. By combining advocacy with ownership of research resources, management of research enterprises, and direct monetary investment—which differs from no-strings-attached grant making—activists seek to solve problems of management, coordination, and interest stimulation. The examples of entrepreneurial health activism described here seem motivated less by profit or ideological commitments to the virtues of free enterprise than by the pragmatics of problem solving and sidestepping problems they associate with more traditional activism. But the possibility that these activists could profit means that they cannot be considered pure civil society actors and indeed reveals the limitations of such categorical thinking.

In our discussion, entrepreneurial activists offered numerous implicit and explicit attacks on traditional patient advocacy as a form of politics. These included charges that advocacy without property is ineffective, that traditional advocates are open to exploitation, that financial stakes in drugs are a measure of commitment (not conflict), and that advocates mistakenly value unproductive organizational, political, and representational authenticity even if it constrains their abilities to meet their goals. The entrepreneurial ethos, the control of property and resources, and, in some cases, the discipline of the bottom line underwrite entrepreneurial activists' perceptions of their own effectiveness. Entrepreneurial activism thus represents a challenge to the form of democratization implicit in other forms of patient advocacy, which ostensibly brings the voices of "ordinary people" into powerful health institutions in the hopes that those voices will be heeded.

We have shown how entrepreneurial activism challenges standard sociological thinking about property and interests. Critical sociologists have tended to argue that patenting and other means of protecting genetic material and other intellectual property have the effect of limiting scientific research in the broad public interest.[77] But as we have shown, not all advocates support this position on property, arguing that it does not necessarily serve the interests of their disease communities. Some health activists instead favor creating and protecting intellectual property as a means to incentivize the commercialization of diagnostic techniques and treatments. In so doing, they strengthen the authority of commercial actors who might be more natural supporters of intellectual property.

Entrepreneurial health activism also unsettles standard critiques of conflict of interest. The conflict-of-interest framework presumes a system of expert authority where the interests and actions appropriate to particular roles—doctor, researcher, regulatory committee member, investor, advocate—are broadly defined and generally predictable. The formalized disclosure of interests is one of the ways this system attempts to police the behavior of its participants. Academic medical centers, scientific journals, and the federal government increasingly require disclosure of conflict of interest in funding applications, publications, and clinical settings.[78] State institutions governed by norms of disclosure like the FDA, CMS, or the U.S. Department of Agriculture are far from perfectly democratic.[79] Whether and how those disclosures are actually used in scientific, regulatory, clinical, or administrative decision making remains unclear. But disclosing interests has nonetheless been institutionalized as a technique of democracy that supposedly allows public statements and participation to be attributed, understood, and evaluated. The prostate cancer activists who accused FDA and CMS panelists of conflicting interests in therapies besides Provenge partook of a traditional version of conflict-of-interest accusation. But they also challenge the guiding assumption of disclosure by positing that economic interests can converge rather than conflict with interests in curing diseases. Some activists in fact reverse the traditional direction of accusations by implying that scientists' focus on research, funding, and academic careers can conflict with patients' interests in medical care.

What does it mean for the larger health care system if these activists undermine the conventional, albeit flawed, norms of disclosure in pursuit of their narrowly defined goals? A shortcoming of the conflict-of-interest framework is that it often assumes that a range of medical options exist and that conflicts of interest can cause decision makers to promote treatments that are medically suboptimal but economically more profitable. But in the cases discussed here, there may be no other options. For rare genetic diseases, patient groups typically work toward only one viable treatment or screening technology. Provenge treats only late-stage cancers that have stopped responding to other treatments. Activists may assume that nobody will ever profit from the last-ditch treatments and diagnostic techniques that they help to develop. But what happens when this "political economy of hope" runs up against success?[80] Though the diseases they target may remain rare, the research and technologies that entrepreneurial health groups own or license may find applications for other, more common conditions. Some of those who spoke in favor of Provenge, for example, expressed hopes that autologous cellular immunotherapies would be developed to target other cancers. These possibilities for cross-over research and broader applications may give activists latent economic interests in other patients' diseases, with potentially troubling implications for the broader health care system. An important agenda for future research will be to consider trade-offs that emerge from entrepreneurial activists' confluences of interests. How do these activists affect the larger landscape of innovation, commercialization, and profit? How do they change systems of expert authority, practices of participation, and the articulation of other publics' interests?

Entrepreneurial health activism will be important for social analysts to monitor because it has the potential to effect profound changes in the political structure of health care and biomedical research. This is not because it is necessarily widely prevalent. While we have no quantitative estimates, entrepreneurial health activism seems to be an emerging and still uncommon phenomenon. Yet some of the actors who engage in it have occupied important positions and received considerable attention.[81] By presenting a model of effective action for others to emulate and by intervening in crucial debates, entrepreneurial health activism works to elevate its own legitimacy and authority while challenging that of other arrangements.

Entrepreneurial health activism also has implications for health inequality. Health activists have often, though not always, been middle-class and educated.[82] Women and African Americans tend to have lower levels of advocacy and hence to be less successful at securing funding for the diseases that disproportionately affect them.[83] And entrepreneurial ethos, skills, and access to capital are additional aspects of mobilization that are likely distributed unequally.

But more crucially, health activism is usually organized around disease sufferers or social groups who feel that their particular medical needs have been neglected. As part of advocating for their needs, patient activists have consistently opposed government or private insurers' use of cost-containment or cost-effectiveness criteria in evaluating the effectiveness of health care technologies or in deciding whether they merit reimbursement. Advocates for diseases affecting children have important symbolic power in their fight against cost-effectiveness: The image of a child needing a $300,000-per-year enzyme-replacement therapy has more charismatic force than an elderly prostate cancer patient who wants to spend $100,000 for four extra months of life. Yet the image of the former helps make the case against cost containment for the latter. This creates a space where it is economically viable for manufacturers to continue developing expensive products that do not maximize the provision of appropriate, effective care across the population more broadly. It exacerbates the de facto rationing on the basis of cost that already exists for the uninsured and underinsured, while increasing cost pressures on everyone else.

The "public interest" is a notion that activists and many other actors—insurers, pharmaceutical companies, and regulators—invoke in various forms through their rhetoric of participation. But if we think of the public interest as served by broader access to high-quality, affordable health care, then it is being defended, albeit not always vigorously, largely by experts: policymakers, public health officials, regulators, and academics. By contrast, health activism, least of all entrepreneurial health activism, is almost never about this version of the public interest. Health activism arose in part as a response to paternalistic medical care, challenging the authority of physicians, researchers, and administrators.[84] Entrepreneurial health activism is not a definitive break with traditional forms of health activism, but it is an intensification of the interest-based challenges to authority that already limit capacities for providing better health care to more citizens.

NOTES

1. Sulik (2011).
2. Timmermans and Buchbinder (2010).
3. Neuman (2010).
4. Brill (2013).
5. Lee, McNulty, and Schaffer (this volume).
6. King (2006).
7. Walker (this volume).
8. O'Donovan (2007); Trumpy (2008); Rothman et al. (2011).
9. Brown et al. (2004).
10. Hoffman (2010); Nathanson (2010).
11. Epstein (1996, 2007); Zavestocki et al. (2002); McCormick, Brown, and Zavestocki (2003); Frickel (2004); Murphy (2006); Nelson (2011).
12. Bayer (1981); Lerner (2001).
13. Kedrowski and Sarow (2007).
14. Best (2012).
15. Levitsky and Banaszak-Holl (2010).
16. Bartley (2003); Hess (2004); Luders (2006); Wahlström and Peterson (2006); King and Soule (2007); Schurman and Munro (2010); Schleifer (2012).
17. Epstein (2008).
18. Leahy, Löfgren, and Leeuw (2011).
19. DuPuis (2002); Cohen (2003); Glickman (2009).
20. Panofsky (2011); Schleifer (2012).
21. Coeytaux and Pillsbury (2001).
22. Orsi and d'Almeida (2010).
23. Supreme Court of California (1990).
24. Greif and Merz (2007).
25. Hughes (2010).

26. United States Supreme Court (2013).
27. These patient advocate groups were the March of Dimes Foundation, Canavan Foundation, Claire Altman Heine Foundation, Breast Cancer Coalition, Massachusetts Breast Cancer Coalition, National Organization for Rare Disorders, and National Tay-Sachs and Allied Diseases Association. Other patient-oriented groups have submitted briefs on other grounds.
28. Liptak (2013).
29. Interview conducted by Panofsky, April 16, 2008.
30. Interview conducted by Panofsky, May 18, 2007.
31. Novas (2006).
32. Hughes (2010).
33. Anand (2006); see, for example, TransDerm Inc. (http://www.transderminc.com/).
34. Nestle (2001); Rowe et al. (2009); Stamatakis et al. (2013).
35. Stockdale (1999).
36. Anand (2006).
37. Panofsky (2011).
38. For a more complete discussion of various strategies that patient advocacy organizations use to direct research, see Panofsky (2011).
39. See, for example, Sills's classic study (1957) of how the March of Dimes struggled to shift its focus after successfully developing a polio vaccine and began to work on premature birth, maternal health, and newborn health.
40. Interview conducted by Panofsky, March 31, 2008.
41. Hughes (2010: 1148).
42. Centers for Medicare and Medicaid Services (2010).
43. United States Court of Appeals for the Sixth Circuit (2011).
44. Chambers and Neumann (2011).
45. Goozner (2011); Silverman (2011).
46. Foote (2002); Tunis (2004).
47. Prostate Cancer Roundtable (2010). The Prostate Cancer Roundtable includes several patient advocacy organizations and professional medical associations: the American Urological Association Foundation, Ed Randall's Fans for the Cure, Malecare Prostate Cancer Support, Men's Health Network, National Alliance of State Prostate Cancer Coalitions, Prostate Conditions Education Council, Prostate Cancer Foundation, Prostate Health Education Network, Prostate Net, Us TOO International Prostate Cancer Education and Support Network, Women against Prostate Cancer, ZERO—The Project to End Prostate Cancer, Prostate Cancer Research Institute, RetireSafe, and the Veterans Health Council (Prostate Cancer Roundtable 2010)
48. Prostate Cancer Roundtable (2010: not paginated).
49. Midthun (2011).
50. Brock (2012).
51. MEDCAC (2010b: 4).
52. MEDCAC (2010b: 62).
53. MEDCAC (2010b: 61–62).
54. Loncar (2011); Timmerman (2011).
55. MEDCAC (2010b: 38).
56. MEDCAC (2010b: 38).
57. MEDCAC (2010b: 38).

58. MEDCAC (2010b: 39).
59. Patel (2010).
60. MEDCAC (2010b: 39).
61. MEDCAC (2010b: 39).
62. MEDCAC (2010b: 39).
63. MEDCAC (2010b: 40).
64. Us TOO (2005–2011); Us TOO (2010).
65. MEDCAC (2010b: 41).
66. MEDCAC (2010b: 40).
67. MEDCAC (2010b: 40).
68. RetireSafe (2011: not paginated).
69. Source Watch (2011).
70. MEDCAC (2010b: 47).
71. MEDCAC (2010b: 48).
72. MEDCAC (2010b: 49).
73. United States District Court for the Southern District of Ohio (2010); Silverman (2011).
74. Censky (2011).
75. Berkrot (2011); Feuerstein (2011); Lopatto (2012).
76. Barker (2011); Rothman et al. (2011).
77. Kloppenburg (1988); Kleinman (2003).
78. United States Congress (2008); Chimonas et al. (2011).
79. Nestle (2002); Hawthorne (2005); Carpenter (2010).
80. Novas (2006).
81. Weiner (2004); Anand (2006); Hughes (2010).
82. Epstein (1996); Nathanson (2010).
83. Best (2012).
84. Epstein (2008).

PART IV

Unintended Consequences and New Opportunities

CHAPTER 9

Spirals of Perpetual Potential
How Empowerment Projects' Noble Missions Tangle in Everyday Interaction

NINA ELIASOPH

A newly prevalent kind of organization is spreading across the globe. It is supposed to, at once, both alleviate poverty and promote civic participation by involving disadvantaged people in solving problems rather than treating them only as victims. Beyond the goals of promoting civic engagement and helping the needy, these organizations' list of missions typically includes promoting transformation and innovation; appreciating grassroots, local, unique people and customs; and promoting sustainability. And above all, they have a mandate[1] to provide transparent accounts to funders and to do it all quickly.

I call these organizations *empowerment projects* and the language that they use to describe their work *empowerment talk*.[2] Scholars and practitioners have had high hopes for such projects, and, indeed, all of their goals are potentially laudable. But they are difficult to align with one another. All the multiple promises tangle with one another, but to keep everyday interaction possible, participants must find shared methods of smoothing out the tangles between each of the missions.

This chapter asks the following questions:[3] How, in one set of empowerment projects, did the goals of promoting civic participation and helping the needy come into tension with one another? How, in everyday interaction, did participants manage to make them harmonize? Empowerment projects are usually predicated on the existence of neediness and powerlessness. But the very instant that participants enter, participants are supposed to deny need's existence altogether, so that they can work together as civic equals. How, in everyday interaction, did participants manage to act as if they did not know about the very thing that brought their organization into existence to begin with?

Here, I will focus only on one of the most surprising, strange, but typical techniques for decoupling these two noble missions from one another—acting as if this inequality is already a thing of the past, as of the very moment that one begins to participate. This temporal leapfrog echoes the verb form called the "future perfect," the form of a verb used to describe an act in the future that will have already been finished: "I *will have* eaten lunch"; "We *will have achieved* equality," for example. In English, it takes the form "will or shall have" + "past participle." In these empowerment projects, this interactional sleight of hand did not usually solve the problem of inequality but only projected it into a utopian future when it already *will have been* solved. One result in the cases portrayed here is that in everyday interaction, both helping the needy *and* civic participation usually fell by the wayside. The emotional and political toll of this sleight of hand was often high.

This chapter draws on a nearly five-year-long ethnographic study of a network of such organizations. First, it will show that volunteers implicitly knew just how important inequality was to the very existence of their empowerment projects. It next shows that participants shared routines that allowed them simultaneously to rely on unspoken knowledge of inequality in order to decipher each other's speech and action, and to ignore this same inequality while interacting. To resolve the tensions between the mantra's missions of "civic participation" and "helping the needy" in practice, participants often focused relentlessly on this hoped-for, abstract image of a bright future, while giving no attention to the past and little attention even to participants' current conditions.

Decoupling One Goal from Another in Everyday Interaction

By understanding how this one set of missions—between promoting civic participation and helping the needy—come into tension, and how participants manage to merge them, we can see *how*, in everyday interaction, key rationales for empowerment projects often snarl with one another.

As we have seen in many of this book's chapters, empowerment projects' missions add up to a veritable *mantra*, calling for engagement that is:

Civic: Open, egalitarian, voluntary, makes the volunteer into a responsible independent citizen
Appreciative of unique people, customs, and conditions: Comfortable, hands-on, community-based, natural-feeling, grassroots; not reliant on distant, abstract experts; not bureaucratic, not hierarchical
Transformative: Innovative, soul-changing, multicultural, aimed at getting you to "break out of your box" and to "stretch your comfort zone"
Sustainable, rather than dependent on outside funding
Helpful to the needy
And they have a mandate to do it all with speedy accountability, to please multiple, distant, hurried sponsors

In the empowerment projects I studied, each of these aims frequently came into conflict with the others. For example, being "transformative" often meant challenging, rather than simply "appreciating" and celebrating people's unique customs. Promoting "civic participation" meant, to some organizers, being open to all, but organizers of programs that were conducted in Spanish for recent immigrant youth wanted to give their kids a "safe space" after a long day immersed in a foreign culture and language. Those organizers did not want to encourage their kids to mingle with diverse others at that moment. The mandate for "speedy accountability" does not cause *all* of the conflicts, but all the missions collide most pervasively, frequently, and forcefully when the mandate for "speedy accountability" was part of the collision.[4] Here, I focus on only the tension between promoting civic participation and helping the needy, and only on one method of reconciling them.

Many scholars have usefully pointed out that *no* organization simply lives up to its lofty, abstract promises, because the rules never completely match the unruly reality, so, to understand how people in an organization actually get things done, the researcher has to take their unspoken methods of "decoupling" into account.[5] Whether "loosely" or "tightly" coupled,[6] words never match actions.

As a backdrop to this chapter, I need to extend this argument, with two proposals. One is that an organization's missions might conflict with one another: An intensive care unit for babies evokes different kinds of responsibility from parents and doctors, for example, and the two approaches have to harmonize enough to come to agreements about treatment.[7] Second, we can expect that when people smooth out the tensions, in practice, they will develop everyday routines for doing so. It will be like other kinds of social order—relatively predictable and not simply random and ad hoc, but more patterned than scholars have usually understood. Participants have to master a *finite set of routine methods* for detaching and reattaching one mission from another, in everyday interaction. In my ethnographic research, I heard several such techniques.

The process of temporal leapfrog, of implicitly invoking the future perfect, was one particularly creative decoupling method. "Sustainable," "prevention," "at-risk youth": Many of the key terms that empowerment projects rely on are about a possibly risky, possibly wonderful future. Thus, Margaret Frye shows how young women in Malawi's NGO-sponsored education projects set their career sights high, sacrificing marriage and family for a while so that they can continue their educations.[8] The price of this relentless focus on a "bright future" will be worth it if the girl ends up with a steady job, but often, tragically, she ends up with neither marriage nor family nor job. The cases described in this chapter show face-to-face interaction that relies on this use of temporal leapfrog to reconcile divergent missions, but McQuarrie's chapter in this volume shows how whole cities build investment strategies that lean on a not-quite-yet existent, maybe-never-will-be-existent future. In them, the original question for many organizers—whether a general redistribution of wealth might fix the problem—vanishes.

This routine method of decoupling one mission from another could be called *temporal leapfrog*, invoking the future perfect before anything has been perfected. It is one illustration of the broader argument: These empowerment projects had not only typical tensions, but also typical methods for reconciling them. It is in these everyday, minute encounters that organizations, and the selves that can populate them, are made.[9] Perhaps when people develop typical, routine ways of smoothing out typical tensions, new organizational forms[10] start to solidify, thus making new kinds of "selves" possible.[11]

Rather than assuming that "civic participation" means what we like to imagine it meant two hundred years ago, when Alexis de Tocqueville described unpaid, self-organized local folks banding together to build roads and hospitals, we should learn what "participation" means in this newly prevalent kind of organization.[12] Empowerment projects are different from the image we might have of purely voluntary associations, or activist groups, in which unpaid, self-organized people get together without any sponsors to whom they are accountable. Some empowerment projects are part of city government programs of the sort Baiocchi and Ganuza describe in this volume.[13] Some are nonprofit or for-profit organizations that provide their services to cities and corporations to conduct "deliberation" and "dialogue," as described in Lee's and Polletta's chapters. In impoverished nations, many empowerment projects are funded by international nongovernmental organizations (NGOs), aimed at promoting development while also often aiming to promote women's rights, protect the environment, and do other things that westerners find worthy.[14] Many programs in the United States promise to empower youth, with varying degrees of success, depending on how they resolve the tensions between the various goals.[15] This is an admittedly far-flung set of cases, but they share many of the crisscrossed goals and tensions described here.

Empowerment projects do not work the same way everywhere, and some are more successful than others at resolving the tensions among all of these discordant missions, but they bear a family resemblance that can be seen when they try to put these mismatched missions into play.

Method and Field

To address these questions, this chapter describes three main kinds of activities that participants called "volunteering," found in these youth programs. All of the programs blended state, NGO, and corporate sponsorships:

Adult volunteers came to help in the afternoons, after school, with homework and other activities in free *community centers* that were, de facto, for low-income youth. Adults and university students came one or two hours per week, usually for less than a year. The two after-school programs described here are Community House, which met in a small building that also housed a food pantry and a couple of other social service agencies, and Casa Latina, which was an organization for mostly low-income, Spanish-speaking kids that sponsored a dozen after-school programs around town—the one Casa Latina program mentioned here met in an empty classroom for two hours an afternoon.

Many *disadvantaged youth* from after-school programs continued, some evenings, to participate in *civic engagement projects*, in which youth from socially diverse backgrounds met to plan and carry out service projects. One was the Regional Youth Empowerment Project (Regional YEP), which met monthly as a group and had projects between the meetings. The other portrayed here was the long series of planning meetings for local events such as Martin Luther King Day and Youth Service Day. These met monthly for several months at a stretch and then more frequently as the event drew near.

Nondisadvantaged youth volunteers who were not participants in the free after-school programs but came on their own, or in their parents' cars, were not considered "disadvantaged." These teens came from leafy suburbs and often expressed worry or dismay about the possibility that other teens like them were participating only for the purpose of adding lines on their curricula vitae for future college admission.

Snowy Prairie is a city of about two hundred thousand in the Midwest, with a majority white population and a relatively large middle class for an American city, but an increasingly large nonwhite—mainly African American, Latino, and Southeast Asian—population. It has good public schools, so unlike children in many U.S. cities, in which parents who can afford it send their children to private schools, children of all classes in Snowy Prairie mingle at school. It is, in some ways, a best-case scenario. If attaining equality is so hard here, how much harder might it be in a city with a larger gap between rich and poor? On the other hand, an intangible atmosphere of racial distrust here felt palpable to me. There is no easy way to measure this atmosphere, but at least two book-length studies corroborate my observation (to preserve my research subjects' anonymity, I cannot reveal the books' titles).

I spent four and a half years attending these organizations, along with several others like them, as well as many workshops and meetings for the adult leaders of these programs. Working as a participant-observer meant helping with everything from geometry homework to the Community House annual rummage sale, to entering data about youth volunteering into a countywide database that kept track of where and when kids volunteered, to deciphering federal grant forms, to volunteering alongside kids and adults in various youth-led service projects, such as gathering food for the homeless and decorating the Pediatric Hospital. I played soccer and capture the flag; painted posters; went to dances, movies, county budget hearings, and Halloween, Mardi Gras, and winter parties with volunteers, youth, and youth services administrators; and attended meetings, workshops and courses for adults who worked with young people.[16]

At each step, then, even the first step of finding research sites, there was a back-and-forth between data collection and analysis. Finding categories for comparison was especially puzzling, because I had initially come armed with the standard definition of civic associations that are "not market, not state, and not family."[17] These partly state-sponsored, partly nonprofit NGOs often engaged in money making, making them seem "market"-like; some attained a level of familylike closeness over time that exceeded that of many families and made them seem more like "family" than "real" families; some called themselves volunteer organizations but got funding from governmental and nongovernmental sources and often involved involuntary participation. In short, they could not easily be classified using normal sectoral divisions between "voluntary associations," "state agencies," "nonprofits," or even "family." As Martin points out in this volume, organizations across different sectors often imitate one another.

My task became to figure out what happened when the crisscrossed "logics" of the mantra were in play in these organizations that seemed to defy all established institutional boundaries.[18] Rather than starting with theoretical categories ("sectors," for example), I had to start with the practical activity and work my way up, to see how everyday promises and practices over time settled into routine, repetitive patterns of everyday interaction. Through this "constant comparative approach," ethnographers gather data in the form of fieldnotes and then return to the site over and over, to keep checking, confirming, or rejecting their hypotheses, depending on whether and how the same interactions repeat in the same way each time we return to the field.[19]

Inequality: The Presupposition of Empowerment Projects

When You, the Needy Participant, Are Supposed to Help Yourself by Becoming a Volunteer, You Learn That You Are the Problem

A dreaded future of neediness looms over many of these projects: Many are called "prevention" programs for "at-risk" youth, two terms that directly invoke a bad but expectable future. These empowerment projects were supposed to help youth overcome their disadvantaged beginnings by helping them to become self-propelled civic actors. Many were also supposed to help socially diverse youth bridge their differences. Much of their funding demanded that the projects address inequality. Behind the scenes, both in conversations among organizers and in conversations among youth participants, it was clear that members recognized this, but in conversations between youth and adults, or between disadvantaged youth and their college-bound peers, inequality could almost never be mentioned.

Nevertheless, youth participants often overhear the justifications for funding, and their taboo knowledge often reveals itself, in the form of mistakes, when they explicitly refer to the inequality that is supposed to be unspoken. For example, at an outdoor festival, a reporter approached a youth volunteer, hoping to give the boy a chance to display his generous volunteer spirit. The reporter asked the wispy black teenager, "Why are you here today?" The boy answered, "I'm involved instead of being out on the streets or instead of taking drugs or doing something illegal." His response was not quite a mistake. Others said they were volunteers so that they would not become obese, pregnant, dropouts, or drug dealers. Similarly, when another African American thirteen-year-old was asked to "speak from personal experience" about his own life in Snowy Prairie, he gave statistics about high school dropout rates among "African American males" in the city. Here is that impersonal future orientation in one of its many forms: Statistics predict grim fates for people like him, and he knows this, and he assumes, therefore, that his action today is aimed at preventing this predictable future. For disadvantaged youth, finding an implicit answer to the question, "Why am I in this group?" was easy. Statistics predict a miserable future for me: that I will do poorly in school and in life. *I am the problem.*[20]

Youth participants overheard the discussions about their neediness. In these programs, poor and minority youth often said that their civic volunteer work was good because it kept them out of trouble. At most public events that their organizations attended—Juneteenth, Cinco de Mayo, Martin Luther King Day events, for example—other organizations came, with fold-up tables covered with pamphlets giving advice about preventing domestic violence, tobacco use, or AIDS; offering free home insulation; advocating good nutrition on a budget; telling people how to recognize the signs of one disease or another; and generally addressing problems that people in their disadvantaged position tend to suffer. These empowerment project–sponsored events were supposed to be festive, but self-help instructions for prevention and treatment of diabetes, high blood pressure, and other diseases, and variations on these themes, were always part of the festivities.

Altogether, disadvantaged participants were called on to enter the programs to solve problems, but they knew that they were, themselves, the main problem that they were supposed to solve. A recurrent type of error occurred when youth participants mixed up the mismatched missions, then, as the example of the boy who told the reporter that he was preventing himself from becoming a problem illustrates.

We can hear how entrenched this pattern was when we hear what happened when one unusually politically minded adult organizer tried to break it. She invited her group of middle-school-age kids to go to a demonstration in favor of environmental policies, and she asked them to help make a banner to promote bike riding. She gave them a list of ten incriminating "Facts about the Car" regarding air pollution, sprawl, labor exploitation, and car-oriented use of tax money (this, as well as the messages that the kids wrote on the banner, were in Spanish—the program was nearly entirely for Spanish-speaking immigrants). These kids were so accustomed to seeing themselves as the problem, rather than seeing social policies as the problem, they wrote, "Ride a bike to lose weight" and "Don't get drunk while riding a bike" and "Don't smoke while riding a bike." Even though the organizer had started with the ten facts about the car, the problem the kids assumed that they were being asked to solve was not air pollution or tax payer–funded subsidies for highways and fossil fuels rather than public transit. Rather, the kids assumed that they themselves, and their bad habits, were the problems that they needed to solve. This mistake makes sense; empowerment projects are supposed to help the needy, and empowerment projects' main way of doing so is to correct their bad habits and prevent them from suffering the predictable problems that statistics predict for people like them. Usually, though, experienced participants and organizers had unspoken, routine techniques for *invisibilizing* inequality, powerlessness, and need.

When Future Potential Participation Is More Important Than Helping the Needy: It's All about Democracy and Participation!

With all of their crisscrossed missions, empowerment projects have to make sure to include many local grassroots volunteers, even when the volunteers are ineffective or harmful. Consider the logic: An empowerment project is supposed to empower the volunteers. In funders' eyes, a program is good if it has grassroots support, and having high numbers of volunteers is good proof of this support. The inclusion and empowerment of the volunteers have to be just as important as the concrete aid to the needy. The problem is that, sometimes, the organization cannot accomplish the goals of empowering the volunteers and helping the needy at once. Here, again, we see that there had to be a method of decoupling two of the missions from one another: civic participation for volunteers versus help for the needy. The temporal leapfrog was one such method.

For example, when youth volunteers gathered food for the needy, empowering the volunteers to become future leaders often mattered more than feeding the hungry today. Thus, organizers of the youth empowerment projects often complained that the head of the local food bank was "hard to work with," because she always insisted on the importance of food, and she had many requirements regarding the food that volunteers gathered, such as that the volunteers not gather more than she could distribute or store, that it be nonperishable, nutritious, and so on. In frustration, organizers would say that this food bank head never "got it" that the goals were "democracy" and "letting youth lead." She tried to control the flow and content of the food too much, rather than leaving it up to the youth volunteers to make decisions freely, on their own. After one meeting, for example, a county head of youth programming said, "*She's missing the point: It's all about leadership, and democracy*." This volunteering was supposed to make the volunteer into a better citizen tomorrow, without necessarily providing what the needy person needed today.

Food presents an especially striking problem for this approach, because it is hard, but not impossible, to treat eating as something that can wait for the future potential to come to fruition. At Community House, in Snowy Prairie, a nutrition educational grant allowed a nutritionist to come once a week one summer to teach kids about good nutrition. But aside from the weekly lunch that this nutrition education grant provided, there was no nutritious food in the after-school programs for disadvantaged youth. Community House had only an expensive vending machine, and one of the after-school programs distributed fun-sized bags of chips and greasy cookies. So, instead of spending the money for decent food now, on an ongoing basis, for more than one meal a week, the project funded educational programs *about* decent food, aimed at an indeterminate brighter future, when the participants already will have had enough money to buy it. Here again, the future perfect is in play.

In an overview of projects that aim to empower people around the United States, Sirianni and Friedland describe many nutrition and health education programs in impoverished areas.[21] Many are one-day educational events, "visioning" workshops, and other inexpensive efforts aimed at getting poor people who lack insurance to help themselves, with no mention of any expensive aid. Similarly, Haney described a hilarious, tragic scene of empowerment in a women's prison: The women are given educational workshops in which they are told not to eat Ramen noodles, but to eat Luna Bars instead, as if the price difference would be irrelevant when they get out of prison.[22] More tragically, the women are exhorted to get educations and are forced to express feelings of hopefulness about their future educations, but they are given neither classes nor tutors to help them get to that desired future. Instead, they are told that they are making bad choices.

"Choice" was a key term in this game of temporal leapfrog.[23] Empowerment projects often spent time teaching people to make good choices at some time in the future, when they have the resources, without giving them the resources to make the choices today. At one year's Martin Luther King Day event, a police chief, who grew up in one of Chicago's worst slums, gave a sing-song speech about all the "good choices" he made: avoiding bullies, going to a decent high school, avoiding gangs, getting a job. In the question and answer period, when asked how he had made those choices, he tried dodging the questions, saying with a chuckle that he had not told us about all the bad choices he had made. As the questions continued, his sing-song tone vanished, and he started angrily stabbing each word, saying, "I felt like I was *cheated* because not enough *volunteers* stepped in, and that's why I volunteer now," but he never mentioned the inegalitarian conditions that had made so many bad choices so easily available to him on Chicago's Southside. Instead, he said, "I teach the community how to self-sustain itself." His ability to leap out of his past came to seem unfathomable and magical.

Another key term for this temporal leapfrog was "leadership." Thus, when youth participants at one evening meeting were asked to discuss when they *had become* (notice the past perfect verbal construction—organizers' assumption being that if we call them "leaders," they will grow into the part) leaders and to discuss what the qualities of leaders are, most were baffled. Most youth participants said they were not leaders. Some decided that leaders were usually "tall" and "handsome." Adult organizers' faces and silences made it clear that these were incorrect answers.

Youth "leaders" often learned to act *as if* they were leading, when they were not yet leading. This was often necessary, given the adults' constant need to apply for grants during kids' summer vacations, *before* their youth programs started at the beginning of the school year. Like many empowerment projects,[24] these often operated on short-term "seed money," from multiple, distant hurried funders, so the organizations had to keep reapplying for new grants for new, often unrelated projects. Every few months, there had to be a different theme to the youth groups' projects, depending on whether the adults had secured a grant from an organization that supported tobacco prevention, the arts, health and nutrition, literacy, or stopping hunger and homelessness.

So the process of making the leaders lead in the direction of the funding required a delicate dance on discordant future timelines. Adults, scouting out funding possibilities, would select a theme—hunger, homelessness, literacy, arts—over the summer. Then, when the school year started and youth volunteers started coming to meetings, the adults would then subtly place the theme in youth volunteers' minds. And then the youth volunteers would magically take on the project as if they had thought it up.

For example, a week of youth volunteer projects was timed for an especially important moment in the county's budgeting cycle: early autumn. In a lunchtime meeting in the summer, six administrators and adults who worked in youth programs said that the point of the volunteering is "to showcase all the good work our kids [in local youth programs] are doing." Examples that the participants in the meeting had so far included were encouraging young people to conduct a food drive, a mitten drive, or a toy drive or visiting a nursing home or homeless shelter. But remember: The kids had not yet done any of this good work that was to be showcased yet!

Organizers had to negotiate a complex temporal map:

One youth worker: Let's not forget the county supervisors [*regional elected officials, in charge of some of the purse strings for these programs*]. We should do something for them, let them know kids appreciate the money, and that they want them to "up" it next year. We could even go to a county board meeting—do they have one that week? We could give them a "thank you note"—a note of appreciation.
[*more discussion of possible activities for kids to do that week*]
Darrell [a minister of a fundamentalist black church's youth program that gets government money]: This week is to show that we're doing these things, that kids are not out on the street, or causing trouble, that we need more money. That's what we're ultimately doing this for. Maybe we could get police records on lower youth crime that week, because youth are busy doing community service.
[*later that meeting*]
Georgia [a magenta-haired youth worker, dressed in shredded black clothes and boots]: I'm wary of planning everything for people who are not at the table [*her teens who would not start coming to meetings until school reopened in September, and this meeting took place in the summertime*] because it's not realistic.
Another youth worker: When you plan like that and they weren't there, and then you say, "Oh, but it was such a good idea!" but it wasn't *their* idea.

Adult organizers had to plan activities long before the youth volunteers arrived, but they did not want to stifle youth volunteers' creativity, so they often told the youth groups, in words that varied slightly from one meeting to the next, that whatever project was under discussion, it was "open and undefined, up to you to decide 'whatever.'" The ideas for community service had to seem to spring from the young people's inspirations themselves. Organizers wanted to make youth feel responsible, autonomous, and competent, that is, civic. But the result had to be good publicity for the organizations and fit with whatever the grant was that year, and the organizers had to show that the public money was helping the needy, preventing the young people from committing all the future crimes that statistics predicted for adolescents like them.

Given what Georgia says about timing, it would be hard to make the youth participants into leaders in these conditions. However, by juggling the mismatched temporalities correctly, adults and youth volunteers managed to make them appear to proceed in the preferred order: At the summertime meeting, adults decided to focus on the issue of hunger (there was a grant for it). A month later, Rob, the Snowy Prairie youth agency director, brought up the topic in a meeting with teen volunteers and some other adult organizers, indirectly suggesting that the teens start a subgroup to work on the issue of hunger, but nobody took the bait. A few weeks later, in late autumn, a youth volunteer named Samia gave a presentation to the other youth volunteers about the project, saying that her subgroup had decided to organize a project to work on the issue of hunger. Samia had managed to play along with the idea that it was a youth-directed project. As we will see below, there was something else going on, beyond the deployment of temporal leapfrog, that made Samia's face grow to fit the mask: There was a long-term, close relationship with Emily, the paid leader of Samia's after-school program. Emily was encouraging and supporting her at *every* step, not just naming her "a leader."

Organizers often indeed said that even the longest journey starts with the first step. But since civic projects like the Regional YEP met once or twice a month for the school year, with "ice-breaker" exercises that were supposed to speed up the process a bit; participants rarely had time to take a second safe step. In groups with this combination of infrequent, optional meetings and vast inequality, efficient bonding was necessary, so most meetings started with these parlor games aimed at *tempting* members to interact. But participants rarely had time to take the second step, a second chance to bond. In addition, taking a second step may have been upsetting, if participants were pressured to reveal and discover just how vastly different their lives were.

So participants had to act *as if* there would be a second step, but not to expect it at all. Again, it is the future perfect, without the equipment needed to reach that bright future. They learned to make small talk with strangers—a skill not to be underestimated in a world that involves quick turnaround time and short-term employment. A common ice-breaker, for example, was a musical chairs–type game, which the Regional YEP played before many meetings:

Everyone stands in a circle, with one kid in the middle.
 The kid in the middle calls out, "I am on a train, and I'm taking everyone who does *x* / has *x* characteristic / likes *x*!" and this kid runs to take someone's spot in the circle, as the kids who do *x* / have *x* / like *x* give up their spots in the circle. Whichever kid has not grabbed a spot goes to the middle, and the process starts over.

The point was just to have fun running around and learning a bit about each other. Participants always called out unthreatening, bland qualities: "everyone who is wearing blue jeans, come out," or "everyone who likes music, has been to California, has green eyes, has white shoes, is wearing underwear, is wearing short sleeves, has brown hair, has a ponytail, is wearing a jacket, likes basketball, likes ice cream." The qualities all had to be impersonal or visible matters of taste and not associated with any social divisions or troubles. "Is wearing jeans or sneakers or the color blue" were okay. In addition, "is blonde" was considered okay, because blondness was not considered divisive or controversial in this largely blonde city. "Has kinky black hair" or "knows a millionaire" or "gets straight A's" or "has a relative in jail" or "has traveled to Europe" or "has been to a welfare office" or "has ever gotten so drunk, they barfed" or "is gay" or "has parents who smoke dope" or "has been homeless" or "loves Jesus" were not okay. More precisely, no one ever tried ones like those. The closest anyone got to something personal or controversial was when one clumsy adult organizer, who dropped out after two meetings, said she would take on her train "anyone who farts in the bathtub." No one jumped onto her "train," and whenever I saw her after that, I imagined her bathtub farts. From this exercise, participants gained practice in mentioning inoffensive characteristics about themselves and others. They were "bonding" by staying nicely impersonal. This was not what organizers had in mind by bonding.

Still, the very act of speaking itself in that kind of situation was, in organizers' eyes, a triumphant gesture toward a more perfect future, a sign that we have launched the process of "making contact and bonding." The content of the speech was irrelevant as long as it stayed nicely impersonal, even if participants expected never to meet again. Paid organizers themselves often were clearly triumphant when they managed to engage a kid in small talk, even if they never saw the kid again. Conversely, organizers often forbade kids from talking about more troubling matters with one another. In one conversation among middle schoolers in an after-school program, for example, the topics were the brother on parole, the suspended friend, and the uncle in jail, until the paid organizer broke in to say, "Come on, guys, let's talk about something a little more 'positive' now!" On this principle, she tried, another day, unsuccessfully, to start a conversation about 1960s music.

Here is the future perfect again: The very act of having achieved a conversation was what mattered to organizers, because it seemed to presage a better future. The future orientation of this kind of speech was especially apparent when adults volunteered with young children. In many volunteer activities, an adult volunteer could feel sudden momentary closeness to any random child at any time, as they bonded over shared shoe sizes or shared tastes in candy, all without needing to know the child's name. In a week of free summer activities at a park in a low-income neighborhood, I seemed, on the face of it, to do what organizers would have happily called "forging a bond" with a girl when we both laughed hard together about a battery-operated talking necklace. Another volunteer managed to give off the appearance of bonding with a child over a Happy Meals toy. To accomplish this instant bonding, we had to assume that we are all the same underneath and that we very quickly can get to that "underneath" place. That way, we can plug in and out quickly and effectively, without getting to know the other person over time. Socially diverse, unequal participants were supposed to bond *quickly*.

Learning to make small talk is an important skill, but here it also served as a promise that diverse participants might come to appreciate each other someday *if they had the time*. But the second step never came, in these empowerment projects' short-term horizons, so kids from different backgrounds would work side-by-side for a year or more without learning anything about each other's lives except that they liked pizza and wore blue jeans. When, for example, the adult organizers held parties for them, the two sets of kids would "clump," in different parts of the room or in different rooms altogether as organizers complained among each other, away from the kids. Each set of kids would also complain about the adults' efforts at promoting bonding—one clump of college-bound kids said, for example, that the adults' efforts would "never work." Relatively affluent kids never figured out, for example, why the immigrant girl from Community House lived with so many adults who were not her parents and why each time they called her shared home phone, a different adult answered. They had to treat their bonding activities as *potentially* leading to something more, though they had to expect that the potential future would never arrive.

Two Harmful Uses of the Future Perfect: Promoting Plug-In Volunteering and Cutting Funds for Seriously Disabled People If They Do Not Become Active Volunteers

In the cases of the food pantry, the nutrition education projects, and the ice-breakers, participants were neither better nor worse off than they had been before people started being empowered. Sometimes, however, placing too much weight on participants' future potential for civic participation was a disaster. Here are two examples.

Adult volunteers came to help out in the after-school programs for disadvantaged youth, usually for an hour or two a week for a few months. They promised to become "beloved aunties" to the kids. But they did not know the kids, their homework, their teachers, their schools, or their families. They hoped to plug in and plug out quickly, like USB keys, so we call them "plug-in volunteers." They often ended up giving advice that contradicted the advice given the previous day, or hour even, by the previous volunteer. So, volunteer "homework helpers" on Wednesday often undid advice that the Tuesday's volunteer had given, who had, herself, contradicted Monday's volunteer's advice.

A typical day shows this: I was helping eleven-year-old Jeanette with a long-term homework assignment. It looked to me as if the previous day's volunteer had given her bad advice, to do the work in a way that did not respond to the teacher's assignment. So I undid the previous volunteer's advice and told Jeanette what I thought the assignment sheet really said she should do. Jeanette started working, but then I had to go make a phone call, and when I came back, another volunteer had taken my place, and I saw that he had already contradicted the advice I had given Jeanette fifteen minutes earlier. Jeanette was receiving a wealth of help, but in a mess of bits and pieces that did not add up to a coherent whole. Kids often complained to the paid organizers that the volunteers were unhelpful. In one meeting of a little middle-school governing body, populated by teens who were deemed "at risk," a girl said that she would rather wait until her mom got home from her second (minimum-wage) job than to try to get help from a volunteer who did not know her way of learning or her assignments. For these reasons, the three studious girls at Community House often hid in a private back room and shut the door, to get their homework done away from the chatty volunteers!

In one meeting, six recipients of an award for minority youth were supposed to stand in front of about thirty adult volunteers and potential volunteers. The volunteers kept asking how they could be helpful in one hour a week.

> *An adult volunteer: How does a mentor make a difference?* How does a mentor make a personal connection? I meet with my middle school kid once a week. What can I do with my kid to make the homework meaningful when I meet with him next Wednesday?
>
> *First girl [echoing the statement I so often heard]*: I know, just meeting once a week in the middle of the week is *not gonna be helpful*. I mean, I know if I have homework on Monday and Thursday, I'm gonna need help on it on Monday or Thursday. *Just once a week, that won't help.*

Another adult: It's about self-discipline. You can't always be there; he's gotta learn to organize himself so even when you're not there, he does what he needs to do.
First girl: So maybe you could meet with him on Monday and Thursday—because if he has homework on those days, that's when he's gonna need help.
Second girl: That's where motivation comes in. He needs to motivate himself.
Mentor: *My schedule doesn't allow me to come in more than once a week.*
Second girl: Maybe he should find a different tutor! [*everyone laughs nervously, a little shocked*]. No, not like that! Like [*people chime in, saying "in addition," "not instead of"*] an *additional* tutor.
Adult moderator: He needs to learn time management. We all do—need to plan, know what needs to be done when.

Eventually, in the future perfect, the boy will have learned how to manage his time, so the plug-in volunteers' work will be easy. But from the teens' perspective, it looked like volunteers thought they were helping them become self-sufficient by *not giving them the help they needed right now.*

These empowerment projects were designed to overcome inequality, and participants were supposed to learn about each other's lives, but with all the other missions in play, it was hard for anyone to take the time to understand inequality's effects on anyone's real life, much less figure out a way to prevent deprivation from harming these kids' futures or other young people's futures. The hurried volunteers and disadvantaged youth were supposed to encounter each other in the present, human to human, in the moment.

The plug-in volunteers were harmful, and yet these programs could not tell them to go home. For donors, these volunteers were symbols of a great potential, waiting to be unleashed, but before it was unleashed, valuing civic participation over the provision of needed aid not only did not alleviate suffering but also added to it. In one program, the teens who wanted to get their homework done hid in a basement to avoid the meddling plug-in volunteers.

In the next variation on the theme of harmful uses of the future perfect, we will see that even when the hope was undeniably unrealistic, participants had to act on the hope that needy people would eventually become self-sufficient and civically engaged, and that that would help them break out of a cycle of neediness. A large nonprofit umbrella agency, United Way, unveiled a new policy during the time of my fieldwork. Previously, it had distributed money to organizations that helped needy people, for things like food and home aid for the disabled. Now, it would give money only to organizations that could set their needy recipients on the road toward sustainability or at least toward "giving back to the community" through civic participation. These needy people, in other words, had to find ways to make their organizations lucrative or to make their participants contribute to society by becoming volunteers themselves. At the meeting announcing this change in plans, an organizer of a program for disabled senior citizens said that her organization would never become self-sustaining. Some of the seniors could not spoon food into their mouths independently. Some had dementia. The United Way head said she was sure there was *some* way that they could "give back to the community." Trying to finish a sentence saying that her disabled elderly people would never become self-sufficient, but just needed help now, the senior center organizer broke down, sobbing.[25]

The United Way's new formula was a very common form of empowerment project that I encountered while doing my fieldwork: "Asset-Based Community Development" (ABCD), which is based on the philosophy that all neighborhoods have "assets" on which local folks can draw and, by drawing on them, in turn, create a sense of wealth and of community, in a beneficial explosion of self-fulfilling prophesies. If local folks see themselves as civic problem solvers, rather than passive recipients of experts' aid, they will actually become more effective.[26] Whenever I participated in *any* meeting of an ABCD project, for example, I heard at least one local participant say that his or her particular poor neighborhood's assets include many loving grandmas, ready to help with gardening and babysitting. Yes, I thought, it would be very good to find ways for society to allow the grandmas to pass on their wisdom and know-how to the next generation. Feeling useful and needed is probably crucial for adults' psychological well-being,[27] and our society does not know how to use the genuine skills that we all share unless they can be packaged and sold for a profit. Still, I wondered if a place like Beverly Hills also had loving grandmas and whether they substituted for things that Beverly Hills residents might need—like dentists, surgeons; people to pay for the rent, electricity, and phone; pollution control experts, bus drivers, and earthquake safety engineers—or whether some public policies should change, to put less burden on those grandmas to provide for their communities' needs. I soon learned that organizers would have considered my puzzlement to be wrong in the first place: "Need" is almost a taboo word; rather, the word should be "choice." The idea with the grandmas was to provide a sense of hope, but not necessarily to address residents' main sources of deprivation. ABCD would leave that for another day, another discussion.

Tentative Solutions in Everyday Interaction

Some youth participants came to meeting after meeting not saying a word; for six months, or a year, or more, adult organizers waited patiently for them to become active participants. One boy, Raul, for example, came to the Regional YEP meetings and did nothing but make towers out of empty Doritos bags, and he shot Skittles at each other as if they were billiards. He spoke only once, when he mentioned visiting relatives in Mexico. Often, baffled organizers exclaimed to each other that they had no idea why kids like Raul kept coming to meetings and not saying a word for months at a time.

Some organizers stayed carefully tactful, saying to each other that asking directly would ruin the possible trust that the organizers hoped was developing. One proudly told me that she waited six months before one girl even said a single word to her—proudly because this organizer knew that her patience was starting to pay off. They were pleased that these Community House kids kept coming to meetings, because they assumed that it was preventing them from becoming a victim of domestic abuse, a drug abuser, or a criminal—for kids "like them," whom organizers (judging mainly by visible race) guessed to be disadvantaged, the Regional YEP was an important prevention program. The idea was to whet their appetites for volunteering, as organizers often put it—to give them a taste for it, so that at some time in the future, they might get "hooked."

In three disadvantaged volunteers' cases, this process worked. These three girls began to speak up in meetings, even though, as one said, it made her feel "salty." These three attended Community House's after-school program and civic engagement programs for the entire four years I was there, and Emily, the paid organizer, was always there, too. She was their confidante and accompanied them shopping, and she knew their parents, teachers, schools, and boyfriend situations—she was like a mother to them. Emily's implicit anticipation of the girls' future success was accompanied by a real relationship with them in the present, so it was not just a temporal leapfrog; rather, Emily filled the gap between the present and the hoped-for future with an ongoing relationship.

Ironically, once these three disadvantaged girls developed into genuinely active volunteers, organizers had to start showcasing other, *more needy* youth. Otherwise, it would start to look as if the program had only helped one or two people, which was not enough. In a discussion between adult organizers about how to plan an event that would "showcase positive youth involvement," Emily offered her three most dedicated youth volunteers (plus another girl who ended up dropping out of the civic engagement projects), saying they could help. Rob, of the Snowy Prairie youth agency, glared at her, saying, "And maybe we can get some people beyond 'the usual suspects.'" Emily had hoped to develop the talents that these four brave, dedicated volunteers had begun to cultivate. These four teens were *no longer considered needy*. They were on the road to becoming genuinely civic actors. But in these programs, such competent youth volunteers had to keep getting dumped off the waterwheel so that new, fresh, needier volunteers could pour in the top. This echoed a larger theme: Everything had to be "seed money" for future, potential projects. Refining a project was always left for the indefinite future, with no support for the voyage to it (though in this case, Emily slyly devised another way of resolving the tension between helping the needy and promoting civic engagement: She coached one of her girls, Samia, so that Samia eventually did lead the meeting anyway, despite Rob's suggestion). Emily defied the usual approach; she assumed that after coaching Samia to take the first step, staying with her while she took a second, third and fourth would be necessary before she learned to walk.

Sometimes, focusing on the hoped-for future could help bring it into existence. In empowerment projects, participants might be able to lay the past aside and just work together, side-by-side, if organizers offered real help that allowed weaker participants to learn to speak and make decisions as equals, gropingly, over a long stretch of time. But this was not a simple assertion of the future perfect. It was a slow, ongoing walk toward an uncertain but hoped-for future. In contrast, the use of the future perfect was a way of obscuring problems by just making them seem as if saying is doing—as if all one had to do to make them disappear is act as if they had disappeared already. Poof.

The following final example will show how the image of the empowered volunteer can easily short-circuit the possibility of imagining that another solution to poverty is possible. Ignoring individuals' pasts and relentlessly focusing only on a hoped-for, potential future made it impossible to see that neediness is damaging and that the damage could easily have been avoided by social organization coming from the state, specifically. The only solution to poverty that appeared on the horizon is based on self-improvement, and in one very specific way, this solution worked, when scholarship funders believed that volunteering creates better future citizens. Knowing about this assumption, disadvantaged high school kids worked hard to focus on volunteer work, even if it cut into the time they spent doing homework.

Thus, when Samia, the disadvantaged girl we met earlier, became a very active volunteer, it was partly with the intention of being able to describe her selflessness when she applied for a scholarship for college. This volunteer work ended up making it possible for her to go to college, not necessarily because it "empowered" her to be a good citizen but because it earned her scholarship money to pay for some of the tuition.

Volunteers like Samia work for free, working on themselves, improving themselves, and ridding themselves of deficiencies so that they can become good-enough people to *deserve* an education. In most wealthy nations, tuition is free for all qualified students. Education in those nations is considered a "right." In the United States, it is not considered a right, and only people whose parents can afford the tuition, or people who are lucky enough to get scholarships, can go to college. But even in the United States, in the mid-20th century, lack of access to education was considered an unjust symptom of social inequality. The solution at that time was "social citizenship," to make the society more egalitarian by redistributing wealth or by giving people free or very low tuition, as the University of California did for most of the 20th century but no longer does.[28] Here, in an empowerment project, on the contrary, the inequality is not treated as an injustice. The problem is seen as emanating from the person, who needs to improve himself or herself in order to deserve access to the education that more privileged peers enjoy. So, in Samia's case, with constant attentive support, she got something she needed, but in a roundabout way, by shaping herself around an image of future good citizenship that would attract scholarships by the time she got to college. In this way, the prospect of "social citizenship" recedes into the very far distance.

Conclusion: Variations of Temporal Leapfrog with Varied Potentials for Ameliorating Inequality

Civic participation and helping the needy are two of the many tangled missions of empowerment projects. Participants have to find ways of meshing them, at least enough to keep interaction afloat. One method for converging civic participation and helping the needy was to pretend that we are already equals in this civic forum. This sometimes eventually worked, to make the not-yet-civic actor into one. More often, though, ignoring people's pasts and focusing on a hoped-for future made the mission of "helping the needy" difficult, because slicing off the person's unique past meant ignoring inequality and ignoring social conditions.

Of course, all organizations rely, in some ways, on gluing people's emotions and actions to hoped-for futures that may well not materialize[29]—that is what stock markets and crashes are about, and it is what happens when states invest in infrastructure that might never be used or might be used by an invading power. One might guess that there is usually more of a step-by-step path connecting the present to the hoped-for future than we see in empowerment projects; nevertheless, empowerment projects show, in a particularly clear way, a trend that one could study in many kinds of organizations. In this conclusion, I wish to sketch some possible ways that visions of a future shape an organization's present actions and present "structures of feeling," and I then tie that back to this volume by asking which kinds of paths toward the future might be most promising for addressing social inequality.

When Saying Is Doing:[30] Sometimes, "saying" simply *is* "doing." If I say, "I christen thee the *Queen Mary*," and I am the mayor whacking a champagne bottle against the side of the new ship, why, then, the ship *is* the *Queen Mary*. If I am a police officer and I say, "You are under arrest," then you *are* under arrest. If I am a priest and I now pronounce you married, then you are. These empowerment programs tried to work this way. But if I say I am going to be a beloved auntie but do not spend the time to become one, I will not become one; if I tell you how to eat healthy food but do not give you access to it, it will not magically be available. The problem is that if I am not a mayor, officer, or priest, all the whacking and the pronouncing in the world will not make it so. The mayor, officer, and priest occupy institutionalized positions that give them the power to make their words into realities.

Prospectancy: We saw another way that anticipating a hoped-for future can help make that future become real. A long-term caregiver like Emily can stand by patiently, for months or years, waiting for the truth to surface—waiting for the three youth volunteers to "realize," in both senses of the word, their capacity to be competent civic actors. With these three volunteers who started off silent and eventually became active, decision-making, speaking participants, focusing on a hoped-for future worked well, as long as it also included a real relationship over time, in a continuous present. "Prospectancy" is a good term for this feeling of hope that a caregiver exudes, when faced with all of the details of the life of this person who is not yet responsible as, not yet as self-sufficient as the caregiver.[31] With those three disadvantaged youth volunteers, a prospectant, attentive caregiver made very tiny, careful, happy self-fulfilling prophesies about their independence precisely at the very moment *before* the prophesies were *about to* come true. Good care makes itself as *invisible* as possible, to seem to be not a burden to the caregiver, making it seem that the person who is being cared for is just on the verge of being able to do it himself or herself.[32] Feeding toddlers, adults proclaim the yumminess of strained yams, thus helping to make it seem yummy; one toddler-sized step before keeling over is happily called "walking." Using this kind of predication can become a happy self-fulfilling prophecy at best or at least preserves the recipient's sense of dignity.

In contrast, in empowerment projects, this happy prophesizing is part of a whole organization's machinery, including hundreds of people who are rarely in intimate, one-on-one relationships with one another. The organizers *have to* assume that kids like Raul are steadily marching forward along the road to self-sufficiency. To be tactful, organizers have to assume this without necessarily knowing Raul personally. Empowerment projects' prospectancy is often done universally and relatively impersonally, on a group level, with members who have not developed a feel for one another over a long stretch of time. It is done in a big, public forum, in an organization that requires management and accounting, and multiple, crisscrossed public justifications, in the potentially harsh public spotlight, gazed on by many hurried, distant audiences. Youth participants often assume that they have indirectly been invited to proclaim their dependence and neediness publicly (and indeed, sometimes, this invitation was quite direct). Despite empowerment projects' promise to appreciate unique people, this hurried, public mass production of intimate care often becomes the opposite of prospectancy.

Symbolic Realism: For plug-in volunteering to work, participants had to have another approach to the future other than prospectancy. Religious language often works by invoking a hoped-for future as if it has already arrived: "Here, there is no rich or poor, master or slave, Jew or Greek: all are one in Christ Jesus." When plug-in volunteers assumed that we are all interchangeable, that anyone could do what anyone else could do, as long as someone did it, intimacy had to become impersonal and universal, available equally to everyone quickly, no matter how far apart their starting points in everyday life are.

This hopeful universalism has sometimes inspired activists to press for social change. When shoeless, dishonored Christian slaves in the United States sang, "I got shoes, you got shoes, all of God's children got shoes! When I get to heaven, I'm gonna walk all over God's heaven! I got a crown, you got a crown! When I get to heaven, I'm gonna shine all over God's heaven!" it reminded them that, in a metaphorical sense, they *already had* what all humans have, despite their current barefoot and crownless circumstances. They recognized, however, that they did not have shoes or a crown at that moment. When religions speak like this, it is metaphorical, predictive language that Robert Bellah calls "symbolic realism."[33] It reminds us of something that we know is not realized in our current society but should be; it serves as a dream, a hope, that this submerged, veiled equality will someday *become* as real socially as we know—on another plane of reality—it is. In the case of the shoes and the crown, faith in the existence of another dimension of reality eventually became fuel for the civil rights movement. But just saying that you had shoes did not, by itself, give you shoes; political organizing helped. The organizing drew its energy partly from this projected future of greater equality, but there was nitty-gritty work to do as well, and organizers did not assume that the dream of perfect equality could become real on earth.

To make symbolism useful for activism, the trick is to *preserve the tension*[34] between the two planes of reality—to make plans in this world, instead of assuming that the future perfect will inevitably arrive. In contrast, adult organizers in Snowy Prairie tried to collapse them and make the transition from one to the other instantaneous. They hoped that focusing on the future would easily open up creativity and would allow people to stop dwelling on the past. But what looked to the organizers like an invitation to creativity sometimes felt, to the youth participants, like abdication. For example, when youth participants asked how they should organize Martin Luther King Day, one of their first questions was always about what has been done in the past, how the holiday began, and what other people have done. A typical answer was "it's open and undefined, up to you to decide whatever," so youth participants frenetically guessed about the future, by overhearing, second-guessing, indirectly asking. By inviting young people to dream up ideas as if they "have a magic wand and anything is possible," organizers hoped to empower youth. This anti-hierarchical message was supposed to make youth see that society and material conditions were irrelevant. But youth participants second-guessed what is possible, without the benefit of a warm-bodied, familiar intermediary's step-by-step guidance. Often, they were armed with a magic wand but no loyal, familiar adult acting as a *realistic* guide. Prospectancy would involve the more experienced, able person invisibly guiding the less experienced or able one. Invoking symbolic realism to leaven action would include practical planning to get hats before we all get crowns. The problem in these empowerment projects was not the planning; instead, it was the attempt to make planning seem irrelevant.

Declaring an Inevitable Relation to a Hoped-for Future: Another way that anticipation of a future can direct personal and social change occurs when a seemingly *inevitable* future starts to drag everyday interaction forward too urgently, implacably and unequivocally toward an imagined utopia or an apocalypse. People in this situation do *not* preserve the tension between the wish and the reality; instead, they attempt to collapse them. Many times over the course of history, people have become convinced of the projected future's inevitable reality, leading to war, massacre, rebellion, suicide, or revolution.[35] This kind of prediction short-circuits debate. In contrast, we have to *proclaim*, "We hold these truths to be self-evident that all men are created equal" because, as Hannah Arendt argues, simply asserting the seemingly self-evident truths would require relying on a ruler who could rule by decree. By prefacing these "truths" with "we hold," the founding fathers implicitly acknowledged that their nation would have to rely on agreements, hopes, and promises *between humans*—the provisional "prospectancy" that describes a hoped-for future as a belief, not yet a fact.[36]

Empowerment projects use hopeful speech of this last sort, in quotidian, everyday situations, not in distant documents like the Declaration of Independence. The problem is that empowerment projects assert a future without providing any means of getting there, but they are charged with the reliably long-term, daily work of taking care of people who depend on them now, today, not just in an inspiring dream world of the future. Nations are supposed to have long time horizons, and they operate partly based on shared, abstract aspirations, whereas empowerment projects are supposed to be temporary and help people immediately. In this context, speaking *as if* all people already are equal and already have shoes can obstruct their ability to get shoes today. Speaking this way does not help them plan just how they will overcome inequality. Instead, in the youth programs, this kind of speech tended to eviscerate the present.

Of course, for most political theory, democratic dialogue has, by definition, meant laying inequalities aside momentarily; the fiction of equality has been considered a necessary fiction that makes respectful dialogue possible. This volume shows how to ask such questions empirically. Our questions are how and when this fiction is useful, and when it should be pierced. When, in Walker's chapter in this volume, for example, corporations sponsor so-called activism that is aimed at making the company better able to make profits, citizens and legislators need to know how to ask questions about those activists' particular pasts and pathways to activism.

Without the enduring institutional power of the priest, police, or mayor, or the tender and intimately individual tact of the long-term relationship, or the shared universalism of some religions combined with realistic planning in the shorter term, the hopeful pronouncements easily become painful abstractions.[37] In these empowerment projects, there was rarely time to see the prophesies come to fruition, because the organizations had to keep inviting new members, inventing new projects, not getting "old and stale" and "entrenched" for a long-enough time to make all those potentials into realities. Participants were treated as perpetual future potentials: potential leaders, potential feeders of the hungry in the future, potential future risks, potential intimate acquaintances.

Partly, this temporal leapfrog was a result of the constant chase for money, and partly, it embodied a desire to keep moving forward into that glowing future. Everything had to be done quickly: before the "usual suspects" grew tiresome and started to make it seem as if the programs had helped too-few needy youth; before the grant period was over and the organization had to fill out another application for another short-term grant for seed money to accomplish an innovative project. Not all relationships can survive such speeding up, though, so it makes sense in these organizational conditions to treat relationships as perpetual future potentials. Youth participants were continually asked to put on public events that showed how much good their youth programs did, before the youth participants had a chance to see if the program really did do any good. Underprivileged participants had to put on these public presentations about "all the good things" that they *will have done*, instead of doing other activities that they themselves might have preferred, such as learning to fish, swim, do chemistry experiments, or play electric bass—learning anything that might take time or money other than how to do good PR for their programs. If they do learn anything, it must not take too long to learn, must be immediately "showcase-able," and is treated as a cure for their problems. In this way, the potential future starts to feel more real than the present.

NOTES

1. On the distinction between "mission" and "mandate," see Minkoff and Powell (2006). Here, the "missions" were "mandated" by funders, but organizers made it clear that the only demand that felt like a mandate imposed from the outside was the mandate for accountability.
2. Eliasoph (2011).
3. Katz (2001, 2002); Lichterman (2002).
4. Lee's, Walker's, and Meyer's contributions to this volume show some of the most terrifying ways that the need to please donors undermines the prospects both for civic participation and for helping the needy.

5. Meyer and Rowan (1977).
6. Hallett and Ventresca (2006a, 2006b).
7. Heimer and Staffan (1998); see also Binder (2007). A massive literature in management examines "hybrid" organizations that have mixed missions—for example, microcredit banks that sit halfway between the fields of social work and finance (Batillana and Dorado 2010).
8. Frye (2012).
9. Goffman (1959); Collins (2003).
10. Clemens (2006).
11. Swidler and Watkins (2008).
12. Smith (1997); Eliasoph (2009). Many aspects of these are not new, as Clemens and Guthrie (2011) clearly show, but my point is that they are newly prevalent.
13. Bacque and Sintomer (2001); Baiocchi (2005); Gret and Sintomer (2005); Berger (2008); Talpin (2011); Charles (2012).
14. Bob (2001); Swidler and Watkins (2008); Dale (2010).
15. Baizerman et al. (2008).
16. The book from which this chapter is drawn (Eliasoph 2011) follows this web of youth volunteers, adult volunteers, and paid adult organizers.
17. Wolfe (1989); Anheier (2007).
18. Thornton and Ocasio (1999).
19. Glaser and Strauss (1967); Ragin and Becker (1992).
20. How little has changed since W. E. B. Du Bois asked, referring to the experience of being black in the United States, "How does it feel to be a problem?" in 1898!
21. Sirianni and Friedland (2001).
22. Haney (2010).
23. See Cruikshank (1999) and Lee (this volume).
24. Swidler and Watkins (2008).
25. For a similar scenario, shutting out old people, see Sampson (1996) on building "civil society" in Albania.
26. Kretzman and McKnight (1993, 2005).
27. Erikson (1959).
28. Marshall (1950).
29. Tavory and Eliasoph (2013).
30. Austin (1965). His book's title in English is *How to Do Things with Words*, but in the French translation, it is *Quand dire, c'est faire*, which means "when saying is doing."
31. Gorney (1972).
32. Molinier (2005).
33. Bellah (1970).
34. Dumont (1986).
35. Hall (2009).
36. Arendt (1990).
37. As Vallas and coauthors show in this volume, abstract terms like "human rights" might help Americans' solidarity efforts toward workers in labor struggles in the global south. At a distance, it may well not matter if helpers understand the particulars of the lives of workers whom they want to help. But in everyday interaction, the particulars of each party's life do matter.

CHAPTER 10

Becoming a Best Practice
Neoliberalism and the Curious Case of Participatory Budgeting

GIANPAOLO BAIOCCHI AND ERNESTO GANUZA

The rapid globalization of people and ideas characteristic of our era has posed a number of interesting challenges for critical scholarship, one of which has been the circulation of ideas and blueprints for things that would have once been described as progressive. The appeal of participation described in the introduction is in fact a quite global phenomenon. Among international development agencies there is a near-identical counterpart to the way that participation has become mainstreamed, professionalized, and, according to many, depoliticized in the United States. Though *officially* endorsed by International Development agencies like the United Nations (UN) since the 1970s,[1] "participation in government" has been advocated with particular vigor by a wide cast of characters since the late 1990s as a panacea for an ever wider set of ills. That participatory ideal, in many cases genuinely emerging from social movement actors, has lent them a veneer of authenticity, and they now are part of a constellation of concepts: good governance, nongovernmental organizations (NGOs), civil society, grassroots action, decentralization, sustainability, local innovations, social entrepreneurship, among others.

Critical global scholarship has followed, much like the contributions in this book, challenging the "heroic claims" made on behalf of participatory approaches,[2] while taking "participatory boosterism" to task for failing to address questions of power, inequality, and politics.[3] More pointedly, scholars have begun to point to participation, and participatory prescriptions in particular, as part and parcel of neoliberal governmentality. As part of a new rationality of government that calls forward an entrepreneurial citizen, participation emphasizes some of the most important characteristics of that citizen: self-regulation, responsibility for his or her own problems, and non-conflictive partnerships with the state.[4] Because participation in government is seen as an alternative to conflictive mobilization and disruption, it is argued, it becomes part of a set of strategies that depoliticize conflicts and thus pave the way for ever more aggressive neoliberal reforms of the state. Leal, who calls participation a "buzzword in the neo-liberal era," argues that it is no "coincidence that participation appeared as a new battle horse for official development" just when the impacts of earlier shock treatments were being felt.[5]

The problem, of course, with blanket condemnations is that they mirror the earlier blanket celebrations (the "participatory boosterism") in their lack of attention to particular instantiations. To paraphrase Lee (this volume), what is needed is to remove the "halo" around certain kinds of participation in order to empirically study them. But to simply replace the "halo" with another kind of prior judgment is less helpful, even if that judgment is more critical.

In this chapter, we tell the story of the curious case of participatory budgeting and its global take-up. A relatively straightforward idea, that citizens ought to decide on public budgets, it has been taken up by more than 1,500 cities around the globe through serpentine paths. It emerged out of the cauldron of leftist experimentalism in Brazil in the early 1990s as a particularly successful instrument and diffused to neighboring countries before being awarded a prize as a "best practice" by the UN Development Programme in 1997, and featuring prominently in the *Human Development Report* in 2001. But at the same time it was heavily discussed and promoted at the first World Social Forums in Brazil (starting in 2001) and made headway in Europe through the institutional Left and through networks of alter-globalization activists. By the time it finally arrived in the United States in 2009, participatory budgeting (PB) had completed a twenty-five-year journey from social movements in Brazil during the end of its military dictatorship, via international development agencies and global social justice networks alike, to what its original architects would have no doubt described as "the heart of Empire."

We tell the story of this travel, seeking to unravel the puzzle of its seemingly endless adaptability. The argument we make is that the best-practice version of PB differs from its original version in one way: In its original version it was but *one part of a set of institutional reforms*. In addition to open meetings where citizens decided on priorities (the more visible part of PB, and the one that is emulated), there was a (much less visible) institutional architecture that linked those preferences to the centers of decision making so as to give them impact. That is, the new version can sit *outside* of the state and be very easy to implement. It is what the sociologists of science John Law and Annemarie Mol would call a *mutable mobile*, a kind of object that maintains some visible similarities as it is translated from context to context but where less visible arrays of connections change considerably.[6] It is not a simple "neoliberalization of participation" story that we tell here as much as it is a story of institutional delinking as a precondition for its travel in the neoliberal era. In spite of invocations of social justice by some of its implementers, over time PB became *delinked* from progressive institutional projects.

PB is, of course, not unique in its status as a traveling democratic technology. Other traveling best practices could be the subject of investigation, like Truth and Reconciliation Commissions, the solidarity economy, citizen juries, users' councils, microcredit schemes, gender budgeting, urban cooperatives, and fair trade. It is our intuition that they, too, have undergone mutations in their travel that have rendered them mobile. In the case of PB the principal condition for its travel was its decoupling from the state or state reforms. It instead joined the loose toolkit of ideas for innovative good governance, part of the "fast policy transfer" that has been described as characteristic of our moment.[7] As such it can be reassembled and rendered compatible with the most diverse projects. In the 2000s, for example, in the Andean region, PB was promoted by *both* the USAID and Internationalist activists of the Chavez government (which also adopted it as a national policy).

Before making these points, however, we first turn to PB's origins in Porto Alegre, in the mid-1980s, where we discuss the genesis of the "thing that worked," in particular its innovation of rejecting associational representation in favor of universal individual participation and its administrative reforms. We then address its travel throughout Brazil in the 1990s, before discussing its global travel as a best practice and as part of international toolkits.

The Thing That Worked

In October 1985, when community activists met with mayoral candidates in what was to be the first free election in the city of Porto Alegre since the military coup in 1964, they must have had little idea of how the discussion that evening would resonate around the world over the next quarter century. The minutes from the meeting describe how activists who had come together under the umbrella of UAMPA, the Union of Neighborhood Associations, had prepared a slate of questions for each of the candidates. These covered many of the concerns of urban social movements at the time: For example, "How would the candidate, as mayor, improve public housing or transportation?" But one of the questions also was whether, and how, the mayor would implement community control over municipal finances, an idea endorsed earlier that year by the neighborhood associations in its yearly congress. The mayor elected later that year *gestured* toward participation but in the end did not create the imagined institutions. The mayor elected in the following election, however, Olívio Dutra of the Workers' Party (PT), eventually set in motion a process called "participatory budgeting," so that by 1990 and 1991 it was implemented, took hold, and by 1992 could be said to have worked. Porto Alegre's administrators managed to do something that had eluded leftists up to that point: Combine good governance, redistribution, and political good fortunes.

The story, so far, is well known. A PowerPoint presentation on the history of PB that precedes its introduction anywhere usually has a slide that makes the same point: Social movements introduced an idea, the government of the Workers' Party took it up, it *worked*, and it traveled the world. There are two elements often missing from presentations that we discuss here. First, there is one crucial difference between the proposal that came from social movements and the thing that worked. The *translation* of the idea, the realignment of meanings and interests as new allies are brought on board, changed it in one fundamental respect: It *deemphasized the role of existing associations and their leaders in favor of the individual citizen*. Second, PB was an integral part of the *whole administrative project that worked*. It was perhaps its most visible part but was not its only, nor even perhaps its most important, part. Here we thus discuss the emergence of these two elements of the thing that worked.

The Individual-Association Pendulum

Though today seen as a natural, and self-evident, feature of participatory budgeting, the break with associational democracy would have been unexpected from the vantage point of observers of Porto Alegre or the Workers' Party in the late 1980s. Though the Workers' Party is *today* credited with creating a system of direct, individual participation in budget matters, then it was strongly identified with social movements and unions. Strongly rooted in the new, democratic unionism of the era, this was a party with a broadly socialist platform that was constantly evolving as it weaved in more movements into the tapestry of its constituency: the progressive church and student, urban, environmental, and feminist movements.

The proposal from civil society was based on associations. If we return to the original document from the neighborhood associations, it called for a system "where the investment priorities of each district would be discussed with *popular leaders of each district,*" where there would be "Popular Councils throughout with proportional representation of the community movement to discuss the municipal budget." The UAMPA proposal was one in which *representation of associations* was central. In it, representatives of clubs, churches, associations, and "others" would come together in a forum to debate proposals.

The participatory budget that was implemented in 1990, in contrast, had as one of its *key* principles, if not *the* key principle, the fundamental rule of "meetings open to anyone" without any privileging of existing associations or movements. Any citizen—associated or not—could come to the meeting and have equal voice. The distance between the two ideas was immense and profoundly consequential.[8] The changes had to do with early difficulties with organized movements as the administration attempted to institute the new participatory process that is well described elsewhere. It is important to note that the administration's position was that city hall ought not to respond only to its allies or even to working classes and the poor, but to think "*of the whole of society, and not only one segment.*"[9]

The mayor would begin to repeat the message that this was a way to govern "for all" and not "for one group, for one class, or for one social sector."[10] For PB, the administration emphasized the *participation of individuals*. It divided the city into sixteen districts, with the intent to reach areas with unorganized participants. The rules for the process were rewritten to clearly specify that associations played no formal role in the process. And citywide the Union of Neighborhood Associations would now only play a minor role.

This process was something of a novelty: These were to be procedures based on the participation of "ordinary" citizens allowed to debate the general interest, as a new form of management of public affairs. It did not go *against* associations per se—as many imagined this process would empower civil society, as much as it was a *challenge to their monopoly of representation of the people or the idea that they represented all citizens*. But it also required new administrative habits to handle this new political subject (all citizens), which implied a big change for an administrative apparatus developed around privileged interlocutors.

Administrative Reform and a New Public Sphere

As the administration began to change its discourse in terms of a *city for all*, it also began to reorganize its administrative machinery. In order for a "new public sphere" to emerge, it was necessary to reach all citizens and to develop transparent spaces of interactions with the administration.[11] PB was understood not only as an invitation for people to participate, but also as part of a thoroughgoing set of reforms to devise a wholly new way of governing. The reform consisted of three lines of action.

First, all social demands were channeled through PB, and all other channels were essentially closed. Contact with the administration on the part of the population was to be made almost exclusively through PB in such a way that it was impossible to receive any funds, investments, or projects outside of the participatory process.[12] This was a rupture with old traditions on the political right *and* the left. It was meant as a way to avoid cronyism, circumventing politicians, but it also circumvented social movements. It was meant as an entirely new way of social and political relations. They bet on a new system in which all could participate (both the poor and the wealthy, the associated and the nonassociated), but, importantly, in which *all decisions* were going to be made this way.

Second, in order for "participation to come into the administration" it was necessary to create new patterns and practices *within* the administration. This was a combination of "political centralization with administrative decentralization."[13] Centralization was achieved by the creation of a new cabinet-level department that centralized all participatory inputs and coordinated these efforts. Also, as an administrative body above municipal departments, this was a way to ensure impartiality in implementation. This was combined with decentralization efforts and with a series of administrative reforms to prepare the administrative machinery to receive the inputs from the participatory process. For example, all municipal departments were required to create positions of community facilitators. Community facilitators were to be the "face" of each municipal department in each of the city's districts and were required to attend PB meetings with the express purpose of helping participants prepare technically viable projects and to be accountable for the ongoing projects. There was an effort to subsume technical expertise, what has been well documented and described as "techno-democracy."[14] As much as possible, "technical expertise was to be made subservient to the popular mandate, and not the other way around," as one of the facilitators described it in an interview in 1999.

Third, there was a significant tributary and fiscal reform to increase revenues. This was described by its architects as "a rigorous policy of cutting current expenditures," combined with tax reforms and measures to improve tax administration. The city's financial capacity increased as a result. The reforms introduced tax progressivity in the most important municipal taxes, and utility rates were updated and indexed to inflation. These reforms essentially doubled the city's income over the next ten years.

The Remaining Opposition of Neighborhood Associations

It is also important to mention at this point that organized neighborhood associations in many parts of the city, and its federation, actively resisted much of the implementation of PB. For neighborhood leaders accustomed to the "dance" of protest and favor trading (and privileged access to clientelist politicians), the process threatened to challenge privileged channels of communication. But more radical activists found the process too limited. For some within UAMPA, the experience meant imbuing participation with a different logic, focused on resolving the specific issues of life in the city, rather than "attacking the core problems: how the city was financed, what state model was desired." According to one of its leaders at the time, it was seen as "a space of joint management with the government in which demands could *not* be made. . . . It seemed a contradiction to be discussing how to share out a scant municipal resource, fighting for a piece of the budget, instead of debating the financing of the cities."[15]

The sentiment of activists within UAMPA at the time highlights some of the unintended consequences of this invention. As a *form of democratization from above*, based on transparent devices and supported by citizens' participation, the process was not without contradictions. First, as it was supposed to transform the collective action from protest to proposition, it meant to give to civil society a new role in public affairs. If we imagine, for a moment, an idealized Habermasian sequence in which informal debate in the public sphere is followed by structured deliberation of formal positions that are then passed along to authorities,[16] PB radically changed the first step. Instead of an informal debate, PB set up a structured debate among people and this formal deliberation was translated directly to administration. This took place in a horizontal public space where citizens gained influence over public decisions. But this is premised on accepting certain limits of the public debate, mainly based on administrative limits and schedule. The concern from activists was that this would make resistance to city managerialism less likely.

A second contradiction had to do with the recognition of collective actors. As we have discussed earlier, one of the points of contention between neighborhood activists and the administration had been the administration's refusal to grant special status to associations. At various points UAMPA removed its participation from the process over this point.[17] There was a disconnection between the official and the legitimate representation of the citizenry. That is, the allowed, official representation of the citizenry in PB (all citizens on equal footing) was not the same that had organically emerged over the years in neighborhoods (certain individuals as selected representatives). This, for many neighborhood leaders, represented an administrative attempt to break the back of associations and their autonomy by disrespecting their criteria for participation and representation. One recalled that "it had taken me a lot to become president of the association . . . and they wanted me to go and discuss things with other people who had done nothing to get there."[18] The PB invention was a different process in the collective action logic as we can see through McQuarrie's chapter in this book about the evolution of social movements in Cleveland over the last thirty years.

Successes

During the 1990s, besides social movement criticisms, PB was a success. Porto Alegre's poorer citizens participated in droves in a relatively simple system that promised, and delivered, results. Many poor urban denizens, otherwise having little voice in government or political affairs, became apt and loyal participants, diligently coming to meetings week after week to debate the arcana of municipal finances and regulations as they decided on investment priorities for their neighborhoods, boroughs, and the city itself. The administrative reform improved the administrative machinery, improved the conditions of poor people, and established a new way of administering that would eventually cause admiration elsewhere. And it proved politically efficacious: The PT administration was comfortably reelected in 1992, 1996, and 2000, each time advertising PB as the centerpiece of a mode of governance that benefited the "whole city." The ideas of universal participation and a new public and transparent management fit well with new ideas of change coming from international agencies and scholars who talked about the deliberative turn in politics. Everything was new, but it quickly met an international audience that turned PB into a novel, traveling blueprint.

Becoming a Best Practice

The spread of PB took place very fast, and we can identify at least two phases. First, there was the diffusion through Brazil—and to a lesser extent Latin America—up to the mid-1990s. During this period it was through networks associated with the PT and allied NGOs that the idea traveled as a success story of "how the left can govern." The "Porto Alegre story" became emblematic in the 1990s of the way that the PT—and, by extension, the left—could govern and govern well.

Becoming a Modifiable Model—Leftism That Worked

The 1990s saw Porto Alegre's PB become the preferred prescription for leftist city administrations in Brazil. If Porto Alegre showed that leftists could govern by distancing themselves from associations and by reinventing the municipal administration, the adoption of Porto Alegre–inspired PB throughout the country showed that as a tool it was eminently adaptable. That is, it was possible for it to achieve results in contexts outside of the original city. It was adopted by some 103 municipalities by the late 1990s, most of them adaptations of the "Porto Alegre model."[19]

The political efficacy of PB in Porto Alegre (described above) stood in sharp contrast to several of the other PT administrations that had self-destructed under conflicts in the late 1980s and early 1990s. The early experiences of the PT in power were not successes, but the commitment to participation was sustained because of demands of social movements, as well as an enduring leftist vision of popular power that animated cohort after cohort of elected officials. But this participatory thrust was very much tangled up in more mundane politics and very visible failures, like the practical collapse of the marquee administration of Luiza Erundina in São Paulo a few weeks before the 1992 election. Acrimony within administrations, often pitting the PT against its own social base—social movements and unions—was also endemic in early PT administrations. The PT's vision for participation during this period was deeply ambiguous: Was participation an end in itself or was it a means to broader social change? Was it to privilege organized bases of support or was it to reach out to the rest of society? But a central problem for elected officials was how to make participation compatible with governance and reelection. In many cases, the party-administration-movement combinations that were meant to congeal in "popular councils" (forums of discussion and debate for the popular sectors: social movements, unions, neighborhood associations, as well as citizens) proved unworkable and often led to open conflicts. In these cases, councils tended to privilege organized movements, which often came at the expense of the administration's legitimacy with the broader electorate. Upon reflection, many administrators came to reject the idea that PT governments should be instruments of mobilization and came to question the feasibility of governing with movements.[20] Eventually, new, more pragmatic views of participation would become dominant as a result of these early trials.

Porto Alegre's relative success stood apart. In sharp contrast to other cities, its participatory process was one that emphasized individuals and distanced itself from social movements. Unlike in other cities, negotiating with presumed bases of support—unions, social movements—was something that emerged out of the participatory process. Its administrative reform was one that helped shield the administration from charges of favoritism.

The transition from success to replicable model took place in national conversations about Porto Alegre. PT administrators, along with academics and movement and NGO activists had, in 1990, formed a national network to exchange experiences and debate the merits of different participatory experiments. By 1996 they had reached a consensus on PB as its principal prescription, and by then, it was possible to speak of the "Porto Alegre model" as the primary inspiration. In 1997–2000, 103 administrations introduced PB, and at least 150 did in 2001–2004. Almost all of these drew direct inspiration, if not downright technical assistance, from Porto Alegre.

As PB became the preferred prescription for the left, two elements are important to remember from this time. First, it was shown that PB could travel and that it could work in a number of contexts. That is, it was *modifiable* and could succeed in several other contexts. Second, PB itself was promoted as having a number of potentially beneficial impacts on city government other than redistribution and empowerment. That is, it was likened with good governance.

PB had broken with the imaginary that associated participation with populism and economic inefficiency, though without ceasing to uphold social justice. The benefits of PB in this version are a mix of good governance (transparency, increased resources, the reduction of clientelism), social justice (redistribution of resources), and civic goals (legitimacy, dialogue, cooperation, and solidarity). All of these attributes are, of course, attractive to both local state officials and politicians seeking an advantage in Brazil's highly competitive party system.[21] It is also important to note that Forum Nacional de Participação Popular (FNPP) documents emphasize the importance of "adapting to a local context." Indeed, many experiments began as exact copies of the Porto Alegre experiment, down to the names of the municipal departments responsible for the process, only to be modified after a year or two.[22] The list of "best PB practices" increased a lot in the late 1990s to include modifications in other cities. It is also important to note that, by the 2000s, PB began to lose its exclusive identification with the PT. Most earlier experiments were associated with the PT, but an increasing number of other political parties began to carry out PB in the 2000s.[23]

The Making of a Legend: International Networks

In the 2000s, the idea traveled much farther. After implementation in Europe, and then the rest of Latin America, PB arrived in Africa, Asia, and North America. If the travel within Brazil had shown that PB was successful, modifiable, and not necessarily only good for redistribution, in this second stage the idea traveled as a success story of primarily "good governance" and one divorced from administrative reforms. The PT's innovation, in separating it from any identification of participation with social movements and associating it with a transparent and efficient administration, made it an attractive device. The fact that it seemed to work in different contexts also helped. But it was the process of translation, which turned PB into an instrument abstracted from a political project altogether and separable from administrative reforms that propelled the transnational journey in which PB crossed national, cultural, and political boundaries. By the late 2000s there were consolidated networks promoting PB on all continents, and more than 1,500 cities throughout the world claimed to do PB.[24]

There are a number of milestones in this international journey. As is well known, the late 1990s were a period of increased attention to participation and good governance among development agencies. The first time it truly attracted global attention was in 1996. That year it was one of forty-two best practices recognized by the UN Habitat Prize, awarded in Istanbul. Shortly after, the Urban Management Program of the United Nations in Latin America and in the Caribbean (PGU-ALC) was launched, promoting a number of studies and the publications of manuals for practitioners.[25] In 2001, the World Social Forum was held in Porto Alegre for the first time. Hundreds of thousands of international activists visited the city through its first four editions in that city.[26] The European Union program with Latin American local governments (URBAL) was another important conduit, especially its "Network 9," dedicated to PB, launched in 2003.

Between the UN-sponsored programs, the loose networks coalescing around the World Social Forum, and the EU programs, an international network of practitioner-experts began to come together around PB in the early 2000s. The same dozen or so principal experts circulated between all of these settings, sometimes seeing each other several times a year. There were a few attempts to formalize into an international PB network, none successful. Nonetheless, this loose-knit group came together around different projects that sometimes mobilized millions of dollars.

There was a loose transit between the academic world and this new group of experts. Some of the experts came from the academy, and favorable scholarship on PB played an important legitimating role in this international travel. Several of the reports published on PB were based on academic work, and sometimes report work would find its way to becoming masters' and PhD theses. The first MA and PhD on PB were written at the Federal University in Porto Alegre in the mid-1990s and were soon followed by literally *hundreds* more throughout Brazil and, later, Europe and the United States in the early 2000s. Some of the more prominent names in the world of PB expertise got their start by doing PhD fieldwork on PB, while others, after working on PB in the Porto Alegre administration, would return to graduate school to reflect on these experiences.

The PT administration in Porto Alegre played no small role in this internationalization, actively promoting PB in a variety of ways. One of the issues of perceived electoral vulnerability in the mid-1990s, especially with middle-class voters, was that the PT was in danger of being seen as a parochial, leftist party, out of touch with global trends. Other political parties capitalized on this, presenting themselves as modernizers. So, in 1996, there was a concerted effort to gain international visibility; an "international relations" department was instituted within the administration, closely linked with PB. Projects were sent to international competitions, and top administrators sought out international, high-profile visits to promote the "PT way of governing" and, in particular, PB, which was "the administration's calling card," as one administrator recalled. The Porto Alegre administration during this period regularly received visits from administrators from other cities and dispatched its own functionaries to other cities. In interviews with members of the "community relations office" and the "planning office," some recalled taking *dozens* of international trips a year in the early 2000s.

Altogether, the UN and EU sponsored efforts, alongside the interest generated by the World Social Forum and the academic research, helped launch hundreds of experiences outside of Brazil at this time. The Progama de Gestion Urbana (PGU), the UN-sponsored network, for example, sponsored dozens of international events, while producing "practical tools and materials," as well as "training programs."[27] Partner cities and recipients of training included cities in Chile, Colombia, Argentina, Ecuador, Peru, the Dominican Republic, and Venezuela. The latter three countries actually developed national laws promoting PB in municipal governments. Activists who visited the World Social Forum, where hundreds of workshops on how to do PB were held, returned home to implement versions.[28] The first fifty European PB examples, established between 2001 and 2005, in Spain, Italy, France, and Germany, were directly attributable to World Social Forum–inspired exchanges. EU-sponsored efforts were even more ambitious. Starting in 2003, its "Network-9" developed partnerships with city governments, NGOs, and universities to facilitate exchanges of best PB practices, commissioning countless studies and how-to manuals and convening several meetings. At its height, Network-9 had a budget of five million Euros and involved 450 local governments. In 2008 it went so far as to offer an international online master's degree in participatory budgeting (based on stays in Porto Alegre, and then other participating partner cities).

Although PB had featured prominently in the 2001 *Human Development Report*, it was only in the latter half of the 2000s that the World Bank became heavily involved with its dissemination and its involvement. This helped propel PB to Africa, usually in partnership with NGOs and other development agencies. The first experiences were in Cameroon, where an NGO first organized a conference on PB in partnership with a World Bank–funded Municipal Development Partnership and UN Habitat. A letter of intent for the promotion of PB in Africa, from 2004, signed by these organizations, signaled the beginning of a large effort; this would come to include several workshops, training manuals, a radio show, and an online component. Together, this facilitated the start of dozens of experiences in most African countries by the late 2000s.

The expansion of PB to Asia came slightly later and with less of a coordinated strategy; rather, it came as a series of direct exchanges between city governments sometimes sponsored by UN Habitat or the World Bank; between Brazil and the Philippines, sponsored by Transparency International in 2003; between Korean and Brazilian municipalities in 2004; and between China and Brazil in 2005.[29] PB is found today in cities in Japan, South Korea, China, India, Indonesia, and Thailand. And in 2009 a German foundation within the orbit of the Social Democratic Party (Friedrich Ebert Foundation), the Marc Bloch Center (Berlin), and Zhejiang University in China promoted the first Asian-European Congress on PB in the city of Hangzhou in China.

The numbers for the spread of PB are impressive. By 2005, there were roughly 200 PB experiences outside of Brazil; by 2008, there were at least 500; and by 2010, the sum total of PB experiences is at least 1,500. These experiences are today concentrated in Latin America and southern Europe, with a strong presence in northern Europe, and a significant number of cases in Africa, Asia, and Eastern Europe. North America has a half-dozen experiences at the time of this writing.

The very first striking feature of these toolkits is their uniformity. There is very little substantive difference between versions produced by different organizations (such as the UNDP or the World Bank) or even between toolkits that come out of the World Social Forum and those of development organizations. They typically provide a concise history of PB's origins and a brief discussion of its political and/or social merits. This promotional element, however, is secondary to their primary purpose as implementation guides for potential promoters. Most provide a step-by-step methodological manual, outlining each stage of the implementation process, from design (dividing the municipality into geographical regions, deciding the rules etc.) through to a monitoring stage. They offer advice to government officials carrying out the process, such as what challenges to expect to what content to include in manuals for citizens and trainings for government employees involved in the process. Some (UN-Habitat's Africa Toolkit Volume II is a formidable example) even include template documents to be used while running a PB process, such as sample surveys of citizen interests, budget allocation schematics, and self-assessment questions, summarizing key issues to which readers should pay particular attention.

PB is presented as a politically neutral, technical intervention. Toolkits highlight the universalizing ("giving voice to all"), rational, and transparent procedures of PB. It transforms the wishes of the grassroots into sensible, quantifiable, and comparable demands. It also abstracts the visible procedures of PB from the less visible administrative reforms of which it was once part. Instead, it offers an isolated image of PB, one that can fit well with any kind of administration. In toolkits, PB seems not to depend on it. Instead, the success of participatory budgeting depends on the willingness of the administration (politicians and civil servants) and the civic effort of citizens. Instead of depending on administrative reforms, in toolkits the hope is presented that PB could foster administrative reforms. The promised results are tangibly desirable: better distribution of public money, as well as a greater concern about citizens by the public, which would result in increased tax revenues and increased solidarity among the population. All are winners: Politicians can become more legitimate and potentially more popular; citizens can gain civic virtues and control over public space; the administration itself will be better off.

A Tool for Good Governance

One clear consequence of the transformation of PB into a best practice has been the marginalization of social justice principles that inspired the initiative in the first place. Its principal justification now has to do with good governance and universal participation, which fits well with the neutral and technical language of PB. PB, in this way, comes to be one of many tools available to make for good governance. "Good governance" has come to signify those "things that enable a government to deliver services to its people efficiently," made possible by a "combination of transparent and accountable institutions, strong skills and competence, and a fundamental willingness to do the right thing."[30]

From this perspective, PB becomes a good tool to promote greater accountability and give voice to citizens in public decisions, improving good governance from outside of the administrative machinery. Like many other tools for good governance, it is prized for its value-neutrality, its ease of implementation, and its ability to attract many different kinds of institutional stakeholders. PB is called for when there is a deficit in good governance. It is not surprising, then, that PB is sometimes also treated as a redundant process. Anwar Shah, a World Bank expert on PB, argues that in a democratic setting, where there is the rule of law, PB can be a costly repetition of institutions of representative democracy. He argues that "if there is a democratic process, participation, if there is rule of law, then participatory budgeting is not needed." Only in the absence of democratic participation, "*then* one has to have some sort of participatory process to hear the voices that have not been heard."[31] Shah's perspective is shared by many politicians in local governments elsewhere.

Democracy in Motion

To return to the concerns with which we opened the chapter, the puzzle of the seeming polyvalence of something formerly associated with the left should be easier to understand. We have traced the origins of PB in the late 1980s among social movements to then consider its movement over the next twenty-five years. We showed how PB emerged in Porto Alegre out of an open-ended experiment by a leftist political party; its search for a model of participatory democracy ended with a new invention, a novel translation of social movement ideas: a model of participation that deemphasized associations and collectives in favor of the individual citizen. This, anchored in a thoroughgoing administrative reform, seemed to provide an answer to the elusive quest of combining good governance, legitimacy, and redistribution for the Workers' Party. Throughout the 1990s, this leftism that worked became the preferred prescription for other Workers' Party administrations throughout Brazil, beating out other models based on councils, for example. It traveled throughout the country, showing that it was an adaptable tool and one that seemed to provide good governance and help the party's electoral fortunes. In the late 1990s, however, it attracted international attention, becoming a best practice that was taken up by a number of international networks. The best-practice version, however, was one decoupled from the administrative reforms and from the machinery of the state. By not defining participation as part of the administration, but as an external tool that can influence it, its implementation became much easier. It also became compatible with any number of political projects and was now understood almost exclusively as a tool for good governance, as social justice and redistribution became less important.

Clearly, there is something about PB that resonates with the current moment of retrenched national states and dissatisfaction with governments (see the chapter by Vallas and colleagues in this volume). The rapid diffusion of PB through the world also no doubt speaks to the nature of our rapid communications and increasingly intermeshed networks in the globalized era.[32] But looking at this story also earns us purchase on the question of how ideas—specifically ideas about governing and running social affairs—travel. At least the story challenges the notion that a characteristic of our era is the exclusive diffusion of institutional blueprints from north to south and the dominance of northern-based actors and institutions in generating those blueprints, as has been documented for the fields of economics, for example.[33] And the story, in some ways, bears the mark of "counter-hegemonic globalization," the notion that "transnational connections can potentially be harnessed to the construction of more equitable distributions of wealth and power."[34] If anything, it challenges us to look beyond "neoliberalism" as a taken-for-granted descriptor of recent shifts in policy.[35]

The story confirms the general idea that, indeed, policies "move in bits and pieces—as selective discourses, inchoate ideas, and synthesized models," rather than as complete and coherent blueprints.[36] In our case, what has moved around the world is something in between a *policy instrument* and a *device*.[37] A *policy instrument* "is a means of orienting relations between political society (via the administrative executive) and civil society (via its administered subjects), through intermediaries in the form of *devices*."[38] A *device*, more humbly, is a "mix of technical components (measuring, calculating, the rule of law, procedure) and social components (representation, symbol)." Policy instruments produce effects, carry meanings and representations, have aims ascribed to them, and embody a "concrete concept of the politics/society relationship and sustained by a concept of regulation."[39] PB in its earlier stages would have been a policy instrument, for it implied a very specific way of orienting the relationship between political society, civil society, and the state. As a best practice, however, it was reduced to a set of procedures, and the relationship between these procedures and the state, or between civil society and government, became completely dependent on local implementation. As McQuarrie suggests in a previous chapter, it helps to expand participatory technologies, but it's difficult to acknowledge at this stage their transformative spirit. As we have suggested earlier, this makes PB closer to a *mutable mobile*, kinds of "objects that have to adapt and change shape if they are to survive" while maintaining a surface similarity. Law gives the example of the diffusion of the Bush pump in Sub-Saharan Africa, which serves as a useful image here.[40] These pumps were very widely adopted and taken, at one point, as evidence of a kind of diffusion of cultural modernization; yet, upon closer inspection, it was only the surface features of the pump that remained constant—its handle and its outward appearance. Subterranean features (plumbing and pipes), who used the pump, and what a definition of a successful pump was, were quite different in each village.

Political Openings and Possibilities

This chapter is about Latin America and a particular participatory prescription, though one that is certainly among the prescriptions that has taken on the widest appeal and probably generated more conferences, consultancies, and dedicated institutions than any other. But other similar investigations could be undertaken on the trajectories of the solidarity economy, citizen juries, users' councils, microcredit schemes, gender budgeting, urban cooperatives, and fair trade, among many other traveling best practices. We conclude with the suggestion that, as for those other best practices, there are profound contradictions and ambiguities in the travel of participatory budgeting, and it is there, exploiting those, that we see openings for progressive interventions.

First among them has to do with the limits imposed on participants. If earlier, utopian versions of civil society theory imagined social movements as connectors between public opinion and public policy, with PB, it is the administration that establishes and regulates those communication channels.[41] But it does so on its own terms. PB translates the wishes that emerge in grassroots democracy into a technical and rational language, into sensible projects that can be weighed against each other in a transparent way, helping citizens to present their needs. PB promises to solve problems of democracy, namely its unruliness and unpredictability, substituting them with rationalization of demand making. Within PB meetings, demands do not exceed the boundaries of the process, individual participants are not unfairly swayed or overwhelmed by organized groups, and there is a value-neutral way to adjudicate between competing demands. That is, through procedure, democracy is more bounded, more fair, and more objective. But PB, by definition, excludes demands, projects, and ways of making claims. In Porto Alegre, a case in which social movements originated the idea in the first place, the government *still* had to face the protests of urban social movements. In most other contexts, the introduction of PB constitutes a kind of "democratization from above," in which limits may come to be experienced as external impositions by civil society organizations. As a best practice, and codified in toolkits and instructional manuals, these more messy features disappeared.

Second, there are profound ambiguities in what PB is and what it is supposed to do. In the practitioner and scholarly literatures there are often disputes about how to define PB, or whether a particular experience "is or isn't really" a case of PB. For many practitioners, the bright, dividing line has to do with decision making. Is decision making within a particular experience of PB "binding" or merely "advisory"?[42] For others, the dividing line has to do with a minimum quality of participation. But attempts to parse out a general definition can make us lose sight of the features that make it a good tool in either China and Brazil or France. In one way, as we have documented, PB travels through quite specific and narrow networks of experts, is codified in how-to manuals and toolkits, and often winds up with many surface similarities, such as a yearly cycle, universal participation, deliberation, and symbolic connection to Porto Alegre. But there is also an unpredictable element. Loose ideas about "participation" and even about PB are like other things that travel in "ideoscapes," those constant flows of "ideas, terms and images, including 'freedom', 'welfare', 'rights', 'sovereignty.'" The sources of these ideas can be manifold, their coherence is loose, and multiple local interpretations are always possible.[43] Particularly because the proponents of PB can be so different, it is possible, at any one site, for experts and implementers to run up against quite divergent local interpretations of what PB can be.

Third, and perhaps most salient, is the ambiguous relationship to the administration. As we have mentioned earlier, the relationship between participation and the administration was black-boxed in the international travel of PB. In most cases, the implementation of PB has been outside of the administrative machinery. But the logic of a participatory experience anchored in a direct process of decision making can come to collide with institutional structures set up for something else. Many administrations promoted PB as an alternative to the existing connectors between civil society and administration, but without transforming the latter. PB was then expected to achieve desired outcomes (to improve the administration, for example, or to increase citizen trust), regardless of changes in administrative organization. This has been a source of tremendous confusion. As the boundaries between "state" and "society" are not always self-evident, the question of where the citizen mandate ends and where expert prerogative begins with participatory decision making, for example, is a final source of ambiguity.

Returning to these ambiguous aspects can occasion, in our view, productive tensions and the potential to repoliticize participation. Each of these ambiguities can provide the space for claims making by participants and others to resist "expert closure" and push the boundaries of participation toward meaningful decision making about the conditions that affect their own lives.[44]

NOTES

1. The UN endorsed participation in two documents in the 1970s: Popular Participation in Development (1971) and Popular Participation in Decision Making for Development (1975).
2. Cleaver (1999: 597).
3. See Harriss, Stokke, and Tornquist (2004); Hickey and Mohan (2004).
4. See Li (2005); Ong (2006).
5. Leal (2007: 543).
6. Law and Mol (2001).
7. Peck (2011).
8. In terms of political theory, it is the difference between associational democracy (or corporatism for that matter) and direct democracy. It is the difference between placing special value in autonomous spaces in civil society and their capacity to generate demands, and placing special value in spaces where all citizens can participate in equal footing. See Cohen and Rogers (1995), for example.
9. Genro (1990: 57).
10. Cited in Harnecker (1993: 9).
11. Genro (1999).
12. Baiocchi (2005).
13. Navarro (1996).
14. Santos (1998).
15. Interview with one of the founders of UAMPA, August 21, 2008.
16. Habermas (1996).
17. Interview with one of the founders of UAMPA, August 21, 2008.
18. Interview conducted on August 10, 2008.
19. Grazia and Torres Ribeiro (2002).
20. For example, in 1989, when thirty-six PT mayors won elections, most of their government centered on giving movements voice. The centerpiece was the "popular council"—a forum of discussion and debate for the "popular sector": social movements, unions, neighborhood associations, as well as citizens. These often failed, sometimes spectacularly, as administrations encountered difficulties with their own base of support in social movements and unions. In what was later described as a "shock with reality," two-thirds of these PT administrations did not manage reelection, with a full one-third of the mayors in question leaving the PT before completing their term.
21. Wampler (2007).
22. Teixeira (2002).
23. Wampler and Avrtizer (2005).
24. Sintomer et al. (2010).
25. Cabannes (2006).
26. Baiocchi (2005).
27. Sintomer et al. (2010: 25).
28. Sintomer, Herzberg, and Röcke (2008).
29. Sintomer et al. (2010); Allegretti (2011); He (2011).
30. Wolfowitz (2006: 3).
31. Interview with Shah, August 3, 2009, in the World Bank, Washington, D.C.
32. Strange (1996).
33. Babb (2005).

34. Evans (2003: 1).
35. Ferguson (2010: 171).
36. Peck and Theodore (2010).
37. Lascoumes and Le Gales (2007).
38. Lascoumes and Le Gales (2007: 5).
39. Lascoumes and Le Gale (2007: 4).
40. Law (2002).
41. Cf. Cohen and Arato (1992).
42. In Europe, for example, most experiences are advisory with the exception of Spain. If we take into consideration these procedural characteristics, the PB in Brazil (Avritzer 2006) would have nothing to do with what would happen in Europe (Sintomer et al. 2008) and none of these with what happens in China (He 2011).
43. Appadurai (2004).
44. Latour (1987).

CHAPTER 11

The Social Movement Society, the Tea Party, and the Democratic Deficit

DAVID S. MEYER AND AMANDA PULLUM

Keli Carender started blogging in January 2009, just after Barack Obama took the oath of office. An underemployed math teacher and improv comic, she adopted the pen name, "Liberty Belle," and called for conservatives to come out and oppose the Obama administration and take back America. She described herself as

> a girl who has come to realize that the people of the USA are in dire need of a basic Economics lesson as well as a review on individual rights and freedom. I am a girl who is dedicated to filling that educational void. I will not sit idly by and watch as social democrats, socialists, or communists attempt to dominate this country. I am ready to do my part and fight for liberty. Join me?[1]

She expressed distrust of government, arguing that Republicans could offer better answers to the nation's pressing problems and that their success in doing so was predicated upon pressure from the grassroots. In her first post, she described her goals and her strategy for achieving them:

> I believe we should have a "Solution Revolution." No more flowery language, no more rhetoric. GOP Solutions are straight-forward, real, alternative solutions to the problems we face. We need to sit down and actually create SOLUTIONS that are based in OUR principles like the free market, fiscal conservatism, individual freedom and liberty, self-responsibility, and the importance of family. From there we put it on every website, talk show, hold press conferences, send email alerts, pamphlets, calls, door to door, send out groups of "educators" into communities to have meetings where we describe and discuss our SOLUTIONS to their problems, etc.... BOLD and DIFFERENT and REAL.
> ... Once we have solutions for all of the hot button issues (energy, healthcare, education, etc.) we put it together in a simple, user-friendly format which states the problem, our solution, the Democrats' solution, and why ours is better, all side by side. Let's rush the field in every medium—like comedy, viral videos, and merchandise (i.e. "agitprop").[2]

Articulate and dramatic, yet a novice to politics, Liberty Belle became an icon for the emerging Tea Party movement.[3] She organized demonstrations in Seattle, and she theatrically confronted Congressman Norman Dicks in a town meeting about health care. Waving a $20 bill, she demanded that Rep. Dicks take her money if he thought it was legitimate for the government to take money from American citizens for health care. Dicks refused the offer, and the video of Carender confronting him went viral, generating more than 70,000 hits on YouTube, more on conservative websites.[4]

The image Carender projected is a familiar one in American politics and American social movements: She is the average citizen, not particularly engaged in politics, provoked by threats from government into political action. She expressed no interest in a long-term career in politics, electoral or otherwise, but saw herself as a participant in a growing movement that can restore a vision of limited constitutional government that respects the rights of individuals. Carender is also not alone.

Since President Obama took office, activists have organized demonstrations to "Take Back America" across the United States. Sometimes donning colonial costumes, self-described Tea Party activists appropriated a version of American history that cast themselves as patriots fighting against a tyrannical government: a government that bailed out large banks, that mandated and regulated health care, that might regulate greenhouse gases, and, most vehemently, that taxed. (Placards used TEA as an acronym for "Taxed Enough Already.")

Vigorously embracing a populist democratic rhetoric, Tea Party activists were insistent about restoring an America that was responsive to the needs of "We the People." The rhetoric and activities of the broad Tea Party movement promise a campaign to *redemocratize* the United States, although the definitions of democracy are generally vague, implicit, or contradictory, and tend to exacerbate existing inequalities. Tea Partiers promised a staunch defense of free speech rights, while simultaneously shouting down members of Congress at town hall meetings; they decried Obama's "socialized" health care bill while searching for ways to preserve Medicare and Social Security, which many Tea Partiers receive.[5] National Tea Party groups received considerable financial support from capitalist interests, such as the Koch brothers.[6] Tea Partiers want lower taxes and more jobs, but unlike their Occupy counterparts on the left, they favor fewer restraints on big business and oppose most government support for the poor and the working class. Many local Tea Parties, claiming that undocumented immigrants were voting in droves, supported voter ID legislation that would complicate access to the polls for legally allowed voters without identification. Such laws, opponents argued, would disenfranchise a wide range of voters who are relatively less likely to have acceptable ID: the young and the elderly, low-income people, people of color, transgender people, and more.

The notion that a social movement can be a source of democratic renewal, even in America, is hardly new. The question is whether the resources necessary to promote a campaign like the Tea Party make the promotion of any classical vision of democracy unlikely. The social movement is historically a form sometimes used by constituencies to redress democratic deficiencies, but the form has also been used by constituencies with very different aims. We mean to explore the tension between grassroots mobilizations animated by democratic rhetoric and potentially less democratic claims on policy.

We situate our study of the Tea Party in the larger world of social movement theory, established in both sociology and political science. The Tea Party represents an analytical challenge for such theories, which generally view social movements as the province of groups of the otherwise disadvantaged, who cannot get what they want without protesting. Such approaches focus on the relationship between a challenging movement and the world around it.[7] We begin by sketching out some of the concepts helpful in making sense of the Tea Party established in theory, particularly the notion of a "social movement society" (Meyer and Tarrow 1998), which emphasizes the spread of movement forms and tactics across a broad range of constituencies and issues. We then look at the mobilization of the Tea Party movement and its relationship to the political context. We note the linkage between grassroots activism and well-heeled funders supporting activism as their best political strategy—for the moment, noting the peculiar and evolving relationship of the Tea Party movement and the Republican Party. We observe potential rifts within the Tea Party, generally based on differences on critical issues between the grassroots and the professionals. We conclude by returning to the social movement society hypothesis, noting that an ostensibly populist democratic movement, like the Tea Party, depends on elite sponsorship that may have no long-term interest in democratization.

Social Movements and the Social Movement Society

The history of social movements in the United States is animated by fights for political inclusion lodged by (and on behalf of) groups without the political access or resources to exercise influence without protest. For the most part, the largest movements of the first two centuries of American life represented people who were visibly excluded, most notably workers, African Americans, and women. But nativist and populist conservative groups have also episodically mobilized in opposition to threats from these and other marginalized and minority groups, and the Tea Party is no exception. We can find within the Tea Party a backlash to rising populations that its members view as threats. Muslims and Latino immigrants are most commonly mentioned, and the Tea Party has attracted more than its share of "birthers"—people who believe that President Obama is not a natural-born U.S. citizen and is therefore ineligible to serve as president—or those who believe that Obama is secretly a Muslim.

After the Second World War, large and sometimes sustained mobilizations by groups of people who ostensibly enjoyed access to mainstream American life and politics emerged. Antinuclear weapons, environmental, and antiwar campaigns, to name a few, were animated by the members of the middle class, who claimed that they lacked meaningful access to decisions that affected their lives. In effect, their efforts argued that the availability of conventional democratic remedies for redress (party activism, election campaigns, lobbying, and more routine civic engagement) were insufficient means for making claims. On the left and the right, activists identified similar categories of culprits: self-interested politicians who ignored them, well-established interest groups who looked after narrow concerns, a nonresponsive government, and mobilized opponents.

Over the last fifty years, in the United States, and indeed in other wealthy countries, it seems that the routine means of access to political influence are inadequate and unsatisfying for virtually everyone. The culprits include the growth of the administrative state and the decline of meaningful political parties.[8] Thus, we have seen the permanent establishment of groups that represent interests that are only occasionally visible to the larger public (e.g., various corporate and trade associations; peace concerns, abortion rights [for and against], gun rights [for and against]).

Ironically, the growth of mobilization leads to more mobilization, through demonstration effects and countermobilization. Nearly fifteen years ago Meyer and Tarrow proposed the concept of a "social movement society" to unify a series of such observations about social protest in the contemporary era.[9] They claimed that social movement tactics had widely diffused across causes and constituencies and had become a routinized part of modern politics, more accepted, and less disruptive. They argued that increased frequency of protests was accompanied by other changes in politics and life that made the social movement less disruptive: (1) the general public became more tolerant to protest as a political tactic; (2) police and other state authorities developed negotiating strategies to manage protests to increase predictability for all concerned and minimize disruption; (3) social movement organizations formalized, bureaucratized, and established themselves as more or less constant presences in political life; (4) organizers created a professional identity; (5) as protest was increasingly accepted as a tactic of political influence, it was no longer confined to those holding intense passions or lacking institutional means of redress; and (6) activists employed a narrower range of social movement tactics, emphasizing less disruptive, threatening, or costly approaches to invite broader participation (for example, staging a large and colorful demonstration on a weekend in a public location negotiated with authorities rather than staging ongoing civil disobedience campaigns).

Meyer and Tarrow noted that the implications of such changes were largely unexplored, and they posed fundamental questions about contemporary democracy. They asked whether the social movement society represented an increased democratization of political life in advanced industrialized societies or the effective neutering of a tactic that had sometimes been useful to those without other access to political influence. They suggested that the more crowded social movement landscape made it harder for any new cause or constituency to break through the clutter of movements. If social movements become a part of routine politics, they asked, can they also be an effective means of redress for those normally excluded from mainstream politics?

Previous understandings of social movements have viewed social protest as an effort to even the odds by those who are poorly positioned to make claims effectively through conventional politics.[10] The disadvantaged could use disruption to bring attention to their cause, to engage latent support, and to mobilize countervailing resources. In relatively closed or repressive polities, this meant that anyone outside the ruling group might try to launch protest movements. In advanced industrialized democracies, however, people who were disadvantaged politically, economically, or socially would use protest to try to make gains. Either way, movements were a tool for enhancing democratic participation in politics.

The social movement society theory focused on those advanced industrialized democracies. The signal social movements of the 1960s, particularly in the United States, supported the notion that people who could get what they wanted in other ways would avoid protest. The large movements of the time were animated by ethnic minorities seeking civil rights and inclusion; young people seeking to end the war and enhance their opportunities to participate in decisions about both political life and higher education; and women seeking meaningful inclusion in politics and economic opportunities.

But by the 1970s, social movements emerged representing constituencies that had more tenuous claims to disadvantage, often organizing and mobilizing on issues that might have little direct effect on their lives. Additionally, conservative movements employed the tactics and rhetoric of the civil rights movement to battle government action intended to promote egalitarian policies. As an example, white, mostly working-class people in Boston neighborhoods used protest to stop racial integration of their schools—in the name of democratic control.[11] By the 1980s, the repertoire of social movement actions, including demonstrations and even civil disobedience, had extended to people and causes that were not dramatically disadvantaged, and they often made claims on behalf of others. The peace and environmental movements, for example, were led by educated and middle-class people who could engage in more conventional politics, including participating in electoral politics; indeed, they often did, in addition to movement tactics.

The Tea Party and Social Movement Theory

The Tea Party movement provides a fascinating case of right-wing populism in the social movement society, and it is an illustration of much that is well established within social movement theory. Tea Party activists attacked the policies of the Obama administration, claiming a democratic lineage that started with the founders of the American republic. Employing the usual social movement repertoire, including demonstrations, lobbying, judicial challenges, and electoral activism, they charged that the Obama administration's efforts, particularly on health care, violated both the Constitution and basic notions of democracy.

The Tea Party's sudden emergence and generally unexpected mobilization led to a flush of attention. When directed to the midterm elections, mainstream media coverage was extensive and often hyperbolic, as reporters and analysts tried to make sense of an ostensibly new force in American life. Of course, contemporary political figures with all kinds of axes to grind seized upon the Tea Party to find the following: authentic American democracy; horrific American nativism; regular citizens newly engaged in politics; marginalized crazies newly legitimized; an "astroturf" lobby for wealthy interests;[12] a backlash against government intrusions on health care, bank bailouts, gun regulation, taxation; or antipathy to the election of the first black president. An analyst can find evidence to support any of these claims. Given the sloppy and diverse nature of social movements in America and elsewhere it really isn't surprising that we can use any volatile social movement as a kind of Rorschach test on which to project our preferred political interpretation. This, of course, *isn't* new.

Tea Party activists, journalists, and public opinion pollsters claim that the Tea Party represents people who do not normally depend on social protest to try to get what they want from the political process. Polls show Tea Party supporters to be better educated, more affluent, and whiter than the American population at large—not unusual for some kinds of social movements.[13] But those are exactly the sorts of people who animate protest campaigns in the social movement society.[14]

Like most movements in America, the Tea Party is diverse and divided, comprising multiple organizations and more or less loosely associated individuals who agree on some things and disagree on others. It is actively wrestling with negotiating a relationship with mainstream institutional politics, including presidential elections and the establishment of a caucus within Congress, while simultaneously decrying both parties as unresponsive to the demands of "We the People." We see this in the electoral realm, as Republicans argued about the wisdom of primary electorates choosing purer Tea Party candidates who may be weaker in general elections than their less pure opponents. Both monied interests and voters at the grassroots have repeatedly confronted the dilemma of supporting the purer advocate or the stronger candidate.

For participants, the Tea Party is about more than its expressed claims—which have been mostly vague anyway—and participants disagree about exactly what it means to be a Tea Partier. This isn't unusual among movements in America. The success of the Tea Party in sustaining itself and exercising influence on politics and policy will reflect the extent to which activists and organizations are able to agree to cooperate on proximate goals and strategies.[15] Even with all the uncertainty about the Tea Party and its development, there is much that we do know, and it fits squarely with what existing theories about American social movements would have us expect. Here we direct attention to political opportunities, resource mobilization, coalitions, and public policy.

Political Opportunities

Political opportunity theory is supposed to help us understand how the claims, tactics, and trajectory of a movement are affected by the world outside that movement, with a particular focus on formal politics.[16] Research focuses on both formal institutional characteristics as well as political alignments. In its short life, the Tea Party has spoken back to an ongoing debate in the field.

In one of the most influential statements of the political opportunity approach, Doug McAdam argued that African American activists responded to positive signals and the presence of powerful allies in institutional politics, or, more generally, political openings.[17] Costain found the same story in reference to women's movements.[18] But in reports on other movements, we can see mobilization in response to policy setbacks and the exclusion of allies from institutional power.[19]

We can generalize from these observations to suggest a broader theory based on the notions that different groups turn to protest from different structural conditions, specifically: Movements of people generally excluded from political influence would depend on openings, whereas movements of people who are used to institutional access would respond to policy provocations and political exclusion. This means that groups of the excluded will mobilize when they are poised to influence policy, but those who are not excluded will mobilize when they feel that they are losing political influence or that their interests are being threatened. Paradoxically, however, some kinds of movements are likely to mobilize when they are least likely to get what they want, reasoning that perhaps they can stop or slow initiatives they find abhorrent. (This approach looks more like the curvilinear relationship between opportunities and mobilization that Charles Tilly offered than like subsequent iterations of political opportunity theory emphasizing openings.)[20]

The Tea Party movement provides a clear case of a constituency mobilizing in response to bad news (that is, perceived exclusion) and the threat of unwanted policy initiatives. The Tea Party represents both the mobilization of conservatives in the face of defeats and threats and the absence of viable institutional alternatives for influence. After the 2010 elections, however, when the Republicans took control of many state legislatures, governorships, and the House of Representatives, the dynamics of protest mobilization became more complicated, and grassroots Tea Party activism atrophied.

Note that, even with such a short life, there are different narratives for the emergence of the Tea Party, all starting with defeat. Some trace the beginning to mobilization of Ron Paul supporters in 2007, who were disaffected with their candidate's slim prospects for winning the Republican presidential nomination. Others mark the Tea Party's emergence with Carender's blog or with CNBC correspondent Rick Santelli's February 2009 rant against the government bailout of the financial industry and mortgage holders. Alternative narratives focus on Glenn Beck's "9 Principles and 12 Values," Tax Day protests, or the health care town meeting shutdowns. In all of these stories, the Tea Party is a response to a government (and in Beck's case, a culture) *that is not listening* to at least one large segment of the citizenry.

There is a reasonable case to be made here. Barack Obama, running on a progressive platform that emphasized health care reform and tax increases on the wealthiest Americans, was elected with a decisive margin in 2008, and his candidacy demonstrated coattails that far exceeded those of his predecessor, George W. Bush. Democrats picked up nine seats in the United States Senate, going from a bare majority dependent on the support of two independents to a filibuster-proof sixty votes (after Pennsylvania Republican Arlen Specter changed parties). Democrats also picked up twenty-one seats in the House of Representatives, as well as a margin of sixty-nine votes. This meant that the liberal wing of the Democratic Party enjoyed firm control of the House and that the center of gravity in the Senate had shifted substantially to the left as well. Conservative voters suddenly found themselves with far less political access than they had enjoyed during the Bush administration.

People opposed to the financial bailout (an approach supported by the Bush administration and many visible Republicans) had few institutional routes to influence. With little prospect for any kind of influence within the House, booing or heckling a presidential speech was about as much as any House Republican *could* do. If the archaic rules of the Senate afforded the minority relatively more political leverage, it was still leverage only to block or stall the Obama administration's initiatives. Conservatives faced a national executive and legislature that were both unusually insulated from their direct influence. Even if the judiciary were more explicitly conservative, it is not an institution obviously responsive to citizen advocacy. In short, there were no conservative allies in a position to deliver very much to dissatisfied citizens.

Untethered by the responsibility of governance, conservative rhetoric was untempered. Frustrated conservative voters shifted their attention from the minority leaders in the House or Senate—who really couldn't do much more than talk—to advocates better positioned to speak more clearly and more provocatively. Radio and television personalities, particularly Rush Limbaugh and Glenn Beck, became the most colorful, prolific, and provocative opponents of the Obama administration. The hundreds of Republican legislators were a less promising target for influence than the more diffuse politics of the streets and social movements. Most people take to the streets only when they believe that protest is the best strategy for them to get what they want from politics, and this is a clear case in which interests and advocates who would normally work through lobbying and electoral politics were essentially forced into the light, politics outdoors, with the more polemical rhetoric that flourishes in such settings.

Resource Mobilization

Although narratives emphasize a provocation or disappointment in spurring the Tea Party, it is important to stress that the Tea Party advocates were not starting from scratch. The large business interests that later provided funding and support for the Tea Party were organized against some of the Obama administration's initiatives years before Obama came to power. Most notably, FreedomWorks (fronted by the former House Republican leader Dick Armey), the libertarian Club for Growth, pro-business Americans for Prosperity, and American Majority were all established before Obama's election and funded by very wealthy sponsors who sought both to promote an ideological vision and to protect a financial interest. As Jane Mayer's profile of the billionaire Koch brothers notes, the promotion of a conservative ideology with hundreds of millions of dollars serves business concerns worth many times that.[21] Moreover, she points out that the Koch brothers had accepted the input of big government initiatives when they were helpful to the business.

This is not to say that the people who assembled in town meetings across the United States to shout at members of Congress who might support health care reform were insincere or that their local Tea Party groups were directly funded by big business interests. Rather, we want to emphasize that coordinated campaigns and social movements more generally are not spontaneous affairs but are organized. Well-heeled financiers and professional organizers dedicated themselves to stoking activism in the town halls, on the Washington mall, and in the streets more generally, and activists at the grassroots may not know—or have reason to care—about these larger business interests. Conservatives were also adept in using websites and social networking, conservative radio shows, and Fox News to promote their analyses and their activities. Populist mobilization and large money interests formed a mutually dependent and beneficial relationship: Frustrated citizens with grievances about taxes or health care found support—material, organizational, and ideological—for their opinions, while large established interests found common cause with populist anger and lacked alternative approaches to influence. Groups like FreedomWorks invested in grassroots mobilization because it was their best opportunity to express their claims visibly and effectively. Extensive populist mobilization, in this case, depended on the engagement and investment of the elite interests that are normally the targets of populist movements.

The alliances between the grassroots and their business sponsors, however, are something that cannot be taken for granted but must be renegotiated from issue to issue. Sometimes these negotiations are successful, but as we discuss below, there are also some ideological disconnects between grassroots Tea Partiers and the larger, well-funded organizations that promote their interests through Tea Party campaigns.

Tea Party Coalitions

At the national level, the Tea Party has been represented by several different organizations that share some short-term concerns but offer very different visions of the future. On a local level, scores of grassroots-identified Tea Party organizations and individuals do not always agree on either short-term concerns or long-term solutions. Such local organizations are often founded by retired and/or economically comfortable individuals—people with the time and resources to devote to Tea Party activism. Unlike the usual model of mobilization through existing social networks, local Tea Party activists often did not know one another before meeting at protest events.[22]

This disagreement and tension are common for American social movements, which are made of coalitions of groups and affiliated individuals united, for a time, on a program of common concern. For reactive movements that respond to bad news, such movements generally focus on a set of pressing issues, such as nuclear power, access to abortion, or opposition to a war. Within such a coalition, groups will share a common short-term agenda but often differ in their analyses and on affiliated issues that matter to them. As an example, the Nuclear Freeze movement represented a coalition that spanned absolute pacifists, far left groups, and advocates of an older tradition of nuclear arms control.[23] Such a coalition functions only in opposition, fragmenting when political authorities start to respond in any way.

The Tea Party demands are somewhat less defined, with the appellation glossing over a broad range of concerns and substantial differences on matters of policy and politics. Over time, the Tea Party label evolved from a general reflection of fiscal conservatism and antitaxation rhetoric to an all-purpose designation for mobilized opposition to President Obama's political agenda. Although several groups claiming to represent the Tea Party have been created, here we discuss four of the most active and publicly visible organizations.

Of all the national groups, the *Tea Party Patriots* seems best to embody the conservative democratic ethos the movement claims. Organized by a small number of

with preventing environmental regulation that may stifle their coal and oil business. Americans for Prosperity, created in 2004, is focused on "fiscal responsibility," and it emphasizes cutting taxes, reducing regulation of business, and limiting the reach of the judiciary. It does not stress a social agenda.

Similarly, FreedomWorks "fights for lower taxes, less government and more economic freedom for all Americans . . . it drives policy change by training and mobilizing grassroots Americans to engage their fellow citizens and encourage their political representatives to act in defense of individual freedom and economic opportunity." Led by former Congressman Dick Armey, who served as Republican Majority leader in the House of Representatives, it has worked with Tea Party Express to support conservative Republicans. Armey has urged grassroots groups to focus on the electoral payoff and to avoid divisive social issues. Tea Party activists have criticized Armey and FreedomWorks for being more interested in Republican fortunes than American values.[28]

The Tea Party has become a catchall label for conservative activists who disagree among themselves about both substantive and strategic matters. In the early part of the Tea Party's emergence, groups and activists differed on priorities and on candidates but were able to work in cooperation *against* President Obama, his agenda, and Democrats more generally. While Obama provided a symbolic unity for the movement, this was maintained by cooperation, often implicit, on key issues. To appeal to the diverse constituency of the Tea Party, specific candidates must articulate policy preferences on the whole range of issues that often separate Tea Partiers into libertarian and social conservative camps.

Policy Debates and Political Coalitions

The initial battles for the Tea Party were rather simple ones in terms of political coalitions. Tea Party citizen groups and well-established conservative groups agreed on opposing the financial bailout after it had been passed. Opposition to taxation (in general, on principle) was also an easy area of agreement, as was opposition to President Obama's health care reform effort. The tactic of shouting down efforts to explain the proposed reform at town meetings was a vision of democracy based on assertion rather than dialogue. No doubt, some elements of the populist critique of government health care in general, most notably support for Medicare, would have a hard time surviving in an open and informed dialogue.

After the 2010 elections, however, Tea Party activists found themselves trying to promote a populist, grassroots image while advocating policies that benefit business interests and wealthy funding organizations. To be sure, these groups might forge alliances to support gun rights (not particularly salient for big business) or oppose legislation on climate change (not immediately salient for right-wing populists), but these issues have not been at the top of the Democratic Party's active agenda and provide little impetus for mobilization as long as they are on Obama's back burner.

Other issues are more difficult and complicated. As it has been since the 1970s, conservative populism is split between libertarians and social conservatives. If some issues, like taxation generally, can paper over differences on the populist right, others experienced activists, the group's initial goal was to support grassroots activism. It has styled itself as something of a clearinghouse for its more than 2,500 local allies. Articulated in terms of limited federal government, free markets, and fiscal responsibility, it also prizes personal liberty and the rule of law. The Tea Party Patriots have self-consciously tried to develop a model of organization based in the grassroots, immune to co-optation or decapitation.[24] The activist leaders read and recommend Saul Alinsky as a model for grassroots organizing, and they explicitly reject the notion of building a stable Washington-based institutional structure.

In contrast, the *Tea Party Express* is a somewhat older group established by a long-time Republican political consultant named Sal Russo. Originally a political action committee (PAC) called "Our Country Deserves Better," Russo renamed the group when grassroots Tea Party activism took off. It is far more focused on candidates than any particular policy position, save for safe positions against taxes and against the "nationalization of industry." The group funneled money and expertise into several campaigns, notably those of Joe Miller (Alaska) and Sharron Angle (Nevada). It is the largest independent group supporting Republican candidates, spending more than $5 million on the primary campaigns of candidates it endorsed. More than half of this money has gone to consulting firms controlled by Russo or his wife. The group has effectively functioned as a conduit for grassroots money given to conservative Republicans and translated into consulting service by Russo and his allies.

Tea Party Nation is a for-profit organization that has been visible only in organizing national conferences, at which delegates who pay relatively high registration fees can participate in workshops on politics and issues and can hear well-compensated speakers. It operates as a business more than as a movement group, offering services or entertainment to the Tea Party movement. The first national conference in Nashville featured Sarah Palin, speaking for a reported $100,000 fee. One observer emphasized the ideological diversity and demographic similarities (affluent, old, and white) of the participants.[25] Several conservative members of Congress canceled commitments to attend. Subsequent conferences have been canceled, presumably because of the failure to attract large paying audiences.

The most visible group was probably Glenn Beck's *9-12 Project*, designed to build national unity around Beck's "nine principles and twelve values," which endorse spiritual/religious values that resemble self-help rhetoric. Principle 2, for example, announces "I believe in God and He is the Center of My Universe." Principle 4 expresses personal goals with a bit of a political edge: "The family is sacred. My spouse and I are the ultimate authority, not the government."[26] Beck clearly has concerns beyond political mobilization. Beck himself renounces the identity of a Tea Party supporter, explaining that he will work with Tea Partiers when they have common purposes.[27]

Underneath these Tea Party sites are longer-established interest groups and think tanks, which are often more specific in their claims, more tightly organized, and less directed to the grassroots mobilization of the moment. The two most visible organizations, *FreedomWorks* and *Americans for Prosperity*, are groups that spun off from Citizens for a Sound Economy, an organization founded in 1984 by the Koch brothers, billionaires who own several large business interests and are particularly concerned can exacerbate them. To date, the Tea Party groups have, for the most part, avoided taking strong positions on divisive issues, including drug law reform, same sex marriage, or United States foreign and military policies.

As the Tea Party's electoral efforts have been in support of selected Republican candidates for office, activists had to deal with the range of forces in the Republican Party coalition. This meant working to purge some moderate Republicans: Senator Arlen Specter (Pennsylvania) and Governor Charlie Crist (Florida) left the Republican Party in anticipation of difficulties in party primaries; this is surely happening at the rank-and-file level as well. Social conservatives pushed Tea Party activists to pay attention to their issues as well, demanding attention for their critical electoral role.[29] This means that Tea Party candidates who win Republican primaries oppose abortion rights and gay marriage, and activists who don't share those views must decide the issues they will be willing to neglect.

Particularly problematic is the immigration issue. American populism has always contained a nativist streak,[30] and nativists have mobilized across the country to promote a harsher immigration regime. As an example, consider Arizona's controversial SB 1070, which required police to inquire about the immigration status of those suspected of being in the country illegally. Tea Partiers rallied in support of the bill and its stance on immigration, and they countered protests against SB 1070.[31] In response to calls for boycotts of Arizona-produced goods and services, Tea Partiers organized a "buycott," encouraging supporters to purchase from Arizona-based companies and to vacation in the state.[32]

At the same time, large business interests have historically supported relatively open borders and free labor. FreedomWorks, as a notable example, lists immigration reform among its lower-priority issues, and it calls for a guest-worker program to facilitate the legal movement of labor across borders, while Americans for Prosperity does not list immigration as one of its concerns at all.[33] In essence, the institutional conservative plan is to provide a legal way for American employers to access the global labor market, but this is not the position articulated by nativist groups at the grassroots or what specialist groups like FAIR (Federation for American Immigration Reform) advocate.

Structural differences between national Tea Party organizations make navigating these issues even more complicated. Tea Party Patriots, for example, has built a network of local, grassroots organizations across the country, and, especially in the smallest of these groups, the voices of a few members can more easily direct the work of the entire group. Groups like Tea Party Express, on the other hand, don't have such direct connections to the grassroots, but they do need to sell high-priced tickets to political events, making some degree of compromise on the issues necessary. However, as with any coalition, the Tea Party has faced pressure from political allies, targets, and onlookers to articulate a unified set of claims. National organizations and self-appointed Tea Party leaders have stepped up to provide their versions of answers, shifting the balance of power in the movement away from the grassroots.[34]

Like many social movements, the positions articulated within the diverse Tea Party coalition create conflicts and contradictions. We've seen expressed concern with the deficit, but that concern is often overwhelmed by opposition to taxes in general, and opposition to government-run health care at the grassroots was notable for excluding Medicare. The immensely popular Medicare system, however, has been largely unchallenged by grassroots Tea Party activists—perhaps because many Tea Partiers are themselves of an age to be recipients of Medicare. In fact, Americans for Prosperity includes perceived threats to Medicare in its reasons for opposing "Obamacare."[35] When Rep. Paul Ryan, chair of the House Budget Committee, proposed a highly controversial budget that would entail large cuts to Medicare and turn the program into a voucher system for the purchase of private insurance, he exempted current recipients—and everyone over fifty-five—from any program cuts.[36] Here the base and the grassroots are at odds, and jury-rigged political compromises display dramatic disconnects between expressed ideology and proposed policies.

Opposition to restoring tax rates to their pre-Bush levels provides another example of potential conflict. Although Tea Partiers campaign against the deficit, resurrecting the tax rates of the Clinton era is a clear step that the institutional Tea Party rejects. And railing against tax hikes is a safe mobilization strategy, if not a program to reduce the deficit. It's hard to imagine a focus on controlling federal deficits—a focus of some small specialist groups for several decades—animating populist mobilization for very long. Foreign policy may be even more problematic: The Tea Party includes both Ron Paul–style America-firsters on foreign policy, as well as traditional interventionist conservatives, and both FreedomWorks and Americans for Prosperity are notably quiet on foreign policy concerns.

In pursuit of restoring the centrality of constitutional principles to governance, some advocates have argued for reforming the Constitution. Of course, campaigns to amend the Constitution are long, expensive, and rarely successful.[37] And then there's the content: Some Tea Party activists have called for repealing the Seventeenth Amendment, which provided for the direct election of senators rather than having state legislatures choose senators. Such activists argue that this limitation on democratic elections would strengthen states' rights and increase oversight of potentially corrupt and wasteful Washington politicians.[38] This demand doesn't square with a populist orientation or the democratic rhetoric the Tea Partiers employ.

More provocative, but hardly more promising, are efforts to amend the Fourteenth Amendment. This amendment provided the justification for a policy (birth citizenship) and a judicial decision (supporting same sex marriage) that Tea Partiers oppose. But taking on the amendment, passed in the wake of the Civil War to ensure equal citizenship for persons who had been slaves, carries even more obstacles. Certainly, it will be impossible to attack the Fourteenth Amendment and avoid divisive politics about race.

As issues cycle through government and public attention within government, the nature of alliances Tea Party activists can build, with both well-established, well-funded groups and with other citizen groups, will change. Helpful analysis of emergent movement coalitions depends on taking the interests of the organized seriously and paying careful attention to the policy process.

American Political Institutions and Movement Schisms

Tea Party partisans run risks in focusing on particular issues, but engagement in the normal conventional politics of representative democracy, including elections and legislative coalition building, are equally problematic. Like members of other movements, Tea Partiers have tried to gain a voice in Washington by supporting allies—conservative Republicans who align themselves with the Tea Party—in their electoral bids. So far, these efforts have generated some success and many dilemmas. Once elected, those institutional Tea Partiers must confront the reality of legislative life in a pluralist polity.

The American political system offers frequent elections that force advocates to compromise on issues in order to elect champions to office. The Tea Party's moment of potential influence arrived very early in the 2010 midterm elections. Because Tea Party supporters are overwhelmingly concentrated in the Republican Party, and because they represent one of the most energized factions in contemporary politics, they were extremely well positioned to exercise influence in party primaries, where voter turnout is generally very low. Thus far, they have done so, helping nominate favored candidates often opposed by the party's establishment. Many, however, lost to Democrats who seemed beatable; for example, Sharron Angle (Nevada), Christine O'Donnell (Delaware), and Ken Buck (Colorado) all ran unsuccessfully despite winning their Republican primaries and garnering considerable Tea Party support.[39] It's not that all of the Tea Party favorites lost, but they won in states that were already Republican (for example, Utah and Kentucky).

And movement candidates virtually always disappoint in office. If they hold to the purist rhetoric, they will be unable to make inroads in Congress. If they eschew porkbarrel politics, they will disappoint constituents who *know* that other elected officials deliver earmarks to their districts. If they compromise on principle to make deals, they will alienate many of the people who put them in office, because they will become the successful institutional politicians they railed against. This is a feature of the institutional design of the United States, and it is one that challenges all social movements. The nature of representative democracy, especially as embodied in American politics, necessitates the kinds of compromises that populists at the grassroots abhor. If compromise and dialogue are anathema to some elements of the Tea Party, it bodes badly for the democratic resurgence that activists seek to promote.

Once gaining political office, Tea Party supporters must face the dilemma of translating attractive rhetoric into influence on policy. Like most social movements playing on the field of American politics, they are likely to be more successful in frustrating initiative than in taking it. The health care shutdowns, followed by the election of Republican Scott Brown to the Senate in Massachusetts, were effective in slowing Democratic progress on the health care bill; once the bill passed, Tea Partiers and their allies focused on bringing lawsuits that could delay its implementation.[40]

Paradoxically, however, the shutdowns may have been more effective in warning Republicans off compromise with the Obama administration, as well as minimizing their direct influence on the resulting bill. Absent the prospect of cooperation with

Republican allies, institutional Democrats had no real reason to trim their ambitions to gain votes, and they sought compromises within their coalition, rather than across partisan boundaries. By shouting down proponents of health care reform during town hall meetings and refusing to compromise with adversaries, Tea Party activists sought to hinder or prevent open dialogue and debate with opponents—a key component of deliberative decision making. But in attempting to frustrate debate and deliberation, Tea Partiers and their allies, rather than thwarting it, may have excluded themselves from the democratic decision-making process.

It may well be that President Obama was unnecessarily timid in his health care stance (dropping insistence on a public option in the bill) or in his stimulus request (roughly half of what many economists said was necessary), but it's hard to credit the Tea Party with eliciting such concessions. By continuing to erode any space for moderates in the Republican caucus in the primaries, and by helping to defeat conservative Democrats in conservative districts, the Tea Party allows Democrats in government to move a little further to the left.

The most visible activism of the Tea Party has eschewed compromise or even a competition among politicians on anything less than an apocalyptic, scorched earth landscape. President Obama and the Democratic Party are derided as socialist or even fascist, not as opponents in a democratic process. One oft-repeated goal of the Tea Party coalition has been "taking back" the country, with the argument that a group of liberal, elitist, and/or socialist politicians have stolen away control of the government from the American people. In short, the purported enemies of the Tea Party are portrayed as enemies of democracy: elected officials who, once in office, make laws and spend tax dollars with no concern for the will of the people. Ironically, officials elected through the constitutionally prescribed process—by majorities—are described as threats to American democracy and therefore not worth engaging in dialogue, much less negotiating compromises, with.

The familiar processes of negotiating legislation inside mainstream political institutions, including even the Republican Party, are described as threats to American honor, heritage, and democracy. It is through this lens that we can understand the efforts to dismiss President Obama's claim to office and respect because of clearly false assertions about his birth or his religion. By insisting that he is somehow lying to the American people about these aspects of his life, some Tea Partiers want not only to invalidate Obama's election, but also to paint him as an enemy of the people and a usurper of the presidency, threatening the democratic processes that Americans hold dear.

Conclusion

The Tea Party is another version of the sort of reactive politics that has animated social movements in America on both the left and right. Conservatives who have been shut out of government have taken to the streets to express their displeasure, and they've been aided by a weak economy and a few provocative initiatives from the Obama administration. Without doubt, an atmosphere of crisis has animated their efforts and has aided activists in gaining both mass and specialized media attention.

Democratic rhetoric animates the Tea Party, as it does many social movements, for obvious reasons. Tea Partiers claim that government has been unresponsive to their needs, values, and concerns (thus, nondemocratic). They argue that citizens, like themselves, should play a critical role in making (or stopping) policies that affect their lives (thus, embodying democracy). They employ the Constitution as a justification for their claims, arguing that their efforts harken back to a better time for people like themselves. Without allies in power, the only meaningful expression for their concerns is through grassroots activism, which, with increasing frequency, focuses on the electoral process.

In the contemporary social movement society, however, we've seen that substantial sponsorship is necessary to build the infrastructure of a movement, even one that emphasizes democratic participation at the grassroots. If those wealthy sponsors are comfortable employing grassroots activism to serve their own ends, their willingness to allow the grassroots to define those efforts is not yet apparent. This linkage to considerable and well-established resource flows may result in some co-optation of the grassroots, but it may also be the best option for producing the political leverage that the grassroots wants, creating a dilemma for local groups and individual activists, as well as a contradiction in terms of democratic participation. When social movement activism becomes widely diffused, used by the advantaged as well as the excluded, it may be that viable paths toward influence for the excluded have become even harder to find and follow, and the paths that exist may have been shaped by those with the resources to fund protest in the first place.

Meanwhile, Keli Carender's personal trajectory illustrates all of the dilemmas inherent in the routinization and professionalization of activism. At one point, she proposed working with the liberal group, Moveon.org, on a set of common issues: transparency in government; ending legislative earmarks; balancing the budget; reducing the influence of lobbyists; and protecting free speech.[41] But such issues are not the priority of the large institutional sponsors who made the meteoric growth of the Tea Party and the signal candidacies of Tea Party activists possible. And Carender is not the ally that liberal groups seek to cultivate. Early on, she was spotted by the talent scouts in FreedomWorks, who flew her from Seattle, Washington, to Washington, D.C. Within a year, she wound up as a staff member of the Tea Party Patriots, and she spends her professional time speaking and writing to mobilize the grassroots.

There is a democratic irony here. Successful mobilization has been contingent on the linkage of populist anger with establishment resources. Mobilization to take back American politics, bringing some vision of the people and democratic control, is contingent on the sponsorship of interests that want only to use those people and that mobilization for their own ends, which often, for good and ill, has little to do with democracy. Absent the professional resources and funds of well-established groups like Americans for Prosperity or FreedomWorks, it's doubtful that frustration at the grassroots could have grown into a national movement so quickly. Absent real grassroots frustration with the economy and the Obama administration, it's unlikely that these groups could have built or bought a movement. The alliance negotiated between grassroots anger and frustration, partisan opportunism, and the elements of elite interests is inherently unstable, as it has always been. Both successes and failures will strain these connections, and what emerges is likely to be more chaotic and unfocused than what has come before.

NOTES

1. Carender (2009a).
2. Carender (2009c).
3. Ward (2010); Zernike (2010).
4. Carender (2009b).
5. Skocpol and Williamson (2012).
6. Mayer (2010).
7. We develop these arguments further in Meyer and Pullum (2014).
8. Ginsberg and Shefter (2002).
9. Meyer and Tarrow (1998).
10. Lipsky (1970); Tilly (1978).
11. Lucas (1986).
12. Garcia Bedolla (2010). "I can think of no other social 'movement' that can claim political patrons of this magnitude," Garcia-Bedolla writes. We can. The civil rights movement, for example, enjoyed the support of elected officials in the north and top-level officials in all presidential administrations from Truman to Johnson. More recently, advocates for gays and lesbians being allowed to serve openly in the military have been able to call on the support of the secretary of defense and the chair of the joint chiefs of staff, and supporters of government funding for stem cell research have drawn on the almost unanimous support of both academic science and drug and biotechnology companies.
13. *New York Times*/CBS News (2010).
14. Meyer and Tarrow (1998).
15. Meyer and Corrigall-Brown (2005).
16. Meyer (2004).
17. McAdam (1982).
18. Costain (1991).
19. Meyer (1990).
20. Tilly (1978).
21. Mayer (2010).
22. Snow et al. (1980); Skocpol and Williamson (2012).
23. Meyer (1990).
24. Rauch (2010).
25. Raban (2010).
26. The 9–12 Project (2009).
27. Leibovich (2010).
28. Vogel (2010).
29. Martin and Hohmann (2010).
30. McVeigh (2009).

31. Schappert (2010).
32. Buycott Arizona (2010).
33. Americans for Prosperity (2011b).
34. Skocpol and Williamson (2012)
35. Americans for Prosperity (2011a).
36. Khimm (2011).
37. Mansbridge (1987).
38. Bai (2010).
39. Harris (2010).
40. Richmond Tea Party (2010).
41. Ali (2010).

CHAPTER 12

Public Deliberation and Political Contention

FRANCESCA POLLETTA

On November 15, 2003, residents of Washington, D.C., gathered to deliberate about budget priorities for the city. Organizers of this citizen summit, the third in a series, had recruited a demographically representative group of 2,800 citizens and had gotten the mayor's commitment to include the summit's recommendations in a citywide strategic plan. Seated at tables of twelve with a professional facilitator at each, participants traded ideas for reforming police-community relations, discussed the need for more senior housing, and debated with city officials about who should control the public schools.

Meanwhile, outside the Washington summit, sixty people with banners and a megaphone had gathered to protest the mayor's policies on housing and education. When the mayor himself appeared, demonstrators yelled to him that the city had favored developers and the rich at the expense of poor people, the elderly, and the young. "Fund schools, not a stadium," one protester called into the megaphone, while others took up a chant: "Tony is a phony!" The mayor nevertheless invited protesters to join the summit. According to the *Washington Post* reporter who was covering the altercation, a few minutes later, several protesters did.[1]

The question for students of deliberative democracy is this: Should the mayor have invited the protesters to join the forum? The question for students of social movements is this: Should the protesters have accepted the invitation? The questions for both are these: What is the relation between deliberation and protest? Should deliberation make protest unnecessary? Or does the institutionalization of deliberation make protest even more necessary? Should protest and deliberation coexist in a vibrant democracy, and, if so, what should be their relationship? Given the current enthusiasm for public deliberation, these questions are of more than intellectual interest. With public deliberative forums proliferating and tens of thousands of Americans participating, variously, in citizen summits, Deliberative Polls, 21st-century town meetings, study circles, National Issues Forums, and countless local deliberative exercises, the issues they raise are practical ones.[2]

One answer that is common in the literature is that deliberation and protest are at odds.[3] Deliberators try to persuade each other of the merits of their views through reasonable appeals to shared values. They are open to changing their minds. They are convinced that the opinions they arrive at jointly will be taken seriously by decision makers. Protesters try to shake people out of their lethargy through acts of disruptive action. They refuse to participate in forums organized by decision makers because to do so will legitimate the status quo and foreclose their ability to act outside it. A different but not uncommon answer to the question of the appropriate relationship between protest and deliberation is that each mode of political action has its place in contemporary democracies.[4] Protest is warranted when deliberation fails to live up to its claims of fairness.

Both perspectives make important assumptions, however, about how protest works, how deliberation works, and how political change works. Empirical research on real instances of protest and deliberation undercuts each of these assumptions. It suggests that the tension between protest and deliberation is overrated. To be sure, there simply is not much empirical research available. We need a much fuller understanding of how episodes of public deliberation figure in contentious political processes. The findings that I draw from what little research there is are partial and tentative. But they suggest that activists are often served well by deliberation. Deliberative forums, especially well-publicized ones, gain activists publicity for their cause and access to decision makers that they would not otherwise get. Research also indicates that deliberation may not be harmed by the presence of activists. Indeed, far from being jeopardized by activism, deliberation's impacts may depend on activism. Insofar as decision makers are susceptible not only to the persuasive force of the recommendations that emerge from a forum, however, but also to pressures from economic and political groups that may have quite different interests, deliberation's sponsors may need to take an assertive stance to compel decision makers to be responsive. If the larger point, however, is not only that both deliberation and activism are necessary to a vibrant democracy, but also that activists should be deliberativists, and deliberativists, activists, then the question is what prevents them from shifting between those roles. I draw attention to obstacles that are both structural and cultural: organizational inertia, the constraining power of tactical repertoires, and the striking reach of the structures of deference that govern everyday life.

To make these arguments, I draw on published case studies of deliberation around municipal budgeting in Porto Alegre; container-deposit legislation in Australia; gene technology in Germany; environmental assessment in South Africa; health care reform in Oregon; the budget deficit in cities across the United States; and my own research on the rebuilding of Ground Zero in New York City.

Public Deliberation and Inequality

Proponents of public deliberation contrast deliberation to aggregative modes of political decision making. They argue that, given the opportunity to discuss matters of public concern in a setting of equality and mutual respect, citizens are capable of altering their original preferences.[5] Even if citizen deliberators do not reach consensus, they are more likely to accept the legitimacy of decisions that do not match their preferences exactly.[6] As proponents see it, public deliberation tends to produce policies that are more sensitive to informed public opinion, citizens that are not only better informed but also more trusting of political processes, and, as a result, more legitimate and stronger polities.[7]

Protest is another alternative to aggregative politics. Like deliberative politics, protest privileges the common good over the sum of narrowly defined interests. And like deliberative politics, it champions the talents and capacities of ordinary citizens against those of experts. In other respects, however, protest and deliberation are at odds. Iris Marion Young, in a much-cited piece, draws attention to two objections to deliberation from the perspective of an activist.[8] One is deliberation's premium on a narrow definition of reasonableness. Deliberators are supposed to back up their views with reasons that all can accept as legitimate. But the structure of the discourse available rules out a priori certain possibilities. The issues to be discussed may be formulated in a way that admits only a limited range of solutions; as, for example, in a forum on welfare where women's familial caretaking work is not treated as real work. Or what may pass as legitimate reasons could be biased. Ostensibly universal values and neutral standards may actually universalize and naturalize the experience of the privileged. The danger, then, is that already marginalized speakers and positions are further marginalized.[9]

The second activist objection to deliberation is that insofar as deliberative forums are either run by the state or are run by people who believe that existing institutions can remedy social problems, then activists' participation in such forums limits their ability to protest the system from outside it. The danger here is of co-optation. By explicitly or implicitly endorsing the legitimacy of the deliberative forum, activists are ill-positioned to then challenge its legitimacy. Insofar as deliberation is controlled by the state or other authorities, the equality they promise is illusory. Democracy becomes a spectacle of democracy rather than a means of holding decision makers accountable.[10]

Young's charges have not gone unanswered. Talisse argues from the side of a deliberative democrat that the sticking point is not deliberative democrats' narrow definition of reasonableness.[11] Rather, it is that activists are unwilling to take seriously any arguments that are advanced against their position. They want to persuade but not to be persuaded. Guttmann and Thompson argue that members of disadvantaged groups are quite capable of making persuasive appeals in a deliberative forum, and they are more likely to be heard there than outside the forum.[12] Other scholars have taken a different tack: arguing that protest is legitimate in certain circumstances, namely when deliberation has failed to live up to certain standards. For example, Smith argues that civil disobedience is appropriate when deliberation has been insufficiently inclusive, overly controlled by the powerful, or biased.[13] Sparks argues that dissenters' legitimacy comes from the fact that they lack access to institutional channels of opinion.[14] Habermas argues that protest is warranted when it exposes the gap between legality and legitimacy.[15]

Despite their diversity, there are several striking commonalities in these arguments, Young's included. One is that they treat protest as direct action. Young refers to "demonstration and direct action" and to "typical tactics of activism such as street marches, boycotts, or sit-ins."[16] Sparks refers to "marches, protests, and picket lines; sit-ins, slow-downs, and cleanups; speeches, strikes and street theater";[17] Talisse, to "direct action in response to injustice";[18] Habermas, to "civil disobedience." Furthermore, all conceptualize direct action as persuasive rather than coercive in intent. For Young, the activist aims "to make a wider public aware of institutional wrongs and persuade that public to join him in pressuring for change in the institutions."[19] Smith: "A citizen engages in civil disobedience to persuade the state to enter into a dialogue about law and policy in the light of perceived failings in existing deliberative procedures . . . [and] to communicate concerns to other citizens in civil society, to raise awareness of issues and to secure support for his or her viewpoint."[20] (One exception to these conceptions both of direct action and protest more generally is Fung, who emphasizes instead the coercive power of direct action and, as I will, the variety of strategies that make up activists' arsenal. I will take up his argument later in the chapter).[21]

What is wrong with conceptualizing activism as direct action? After all, many movements engage in direct action. Many do so effectively, and many do so with the aim of persuading people to support their views. The theorists I quoted would not deny that movements do other things, too: They recruit participants and supporters; raise money; seek favorable media coverage; lobby officials; bring legal cases; support or oppose legal cases; build coalitions; sustain the loyalty and commitment of their members; and test goals, slogans, frames, and images. But what if direct action is a strategy that depends for its success on an audience that a deliberative process can secure?

Obviously, direct action will only persuade the public of the merits of the movement's views if the public is aware of the direct action. This is one of the reasons, of course, that movements use attention-getting tactics. Media coverage raises the public's awareness of the movement and its goals. Reading about or seeing coverage of a group of people who are sitting-in or marching—who are willing to sacrifice their time and energy, and sometimes, their safety, freedom, or reputation—may persuade the public of the worthiness and urgency of the cause. Indeed, movement scholars have argued that media coverage is an important route to movement impact.[22] However, recent research suggests that direct action is not the main way, or perhaps even a good way, to get that coverage. Analysis of a century's worth of *New York Times* coverage of movement organizations by Amenta and his colleagues shows that most coverage is not prompted by movement-initiated protest events. Instead, movement spokespeople are likely to be quoted or written about when they are responding to—simply talking about—something else: the passage of a new law that relates to their mission, a campaigning politician's speech that is offensive to their membership, or their plan to protest at a hearing, speech, or meeting.[23] This is what happened at the Washington citizen summit I mentioned earlier, where protesters were able to capitalize on the fact that a reporter had been dispatched to cover the forum, not their protest. But activists need not protest a forum in order to get coverage by being associated with it. The forum may provide a public platform, or access to a platform, in diverse ways.

A second assumption shared by the three perspectives is that activists jeopardize deliberation because their minds are already made up. Deliberation, by contrast, depends on people's willingness to scrutinize their assumptions and possibly change their minds.[24] If this were not the case, it would be more efficient simply to aggregate people's preferences. Talisse is most explicit about deliberation's dependence on what he calls "epistemic modesty" but the other theorists operate on a similar premise.[25]

But what if deliberation does not, in fact, work that way? What if people participate, and gain something valuable from their participation, even if they do not change their minds? Or what if changing one's mind does not depend on questioning and altering one's assumptions? If either or both of these are true, activists may not pose a threat to deliberation.

Finally, all three perspectives treat deliberation's impact on the policy process as depending on decision makers' willingness to be persuaded by the recommendations that emerge from the deliberative process. As Young puts it, the difference between the deliberativist and the activist "may reduce to how optimistic they are about whether political agents can be persuaded that there are structural injustices, the remedy for which an inclusive deliberative public ought to agree on."[26] But what if there are other, and perhaps better, routes to impact? What if such routes to impact depend on conditions that activists are well equipped to identify and capitalize on? If that is the case, far from threatening deliberation, activists and their methods may be important to deliberation's success.

In the following, I explore these possibilities. There are still relatively few case studies of activism in and around deliberative processes, let alone the kind of comparative studies that we need. In drawing on these case studies, I am lumping together very different kinds of deliberation and very different kinds of activism. The stakeholder deliberative processes in which representatives of interested parties are selected to participate are quite different from the public forums in which everyone is invited to participate (and organizers work behind the scenes to recruit members of typically underrepresented groups). Local community organizing is very different from national advocacy. The political contexts of these cases also differ significantly. So lumping them together is risky. But doing so does point to questions we should be asking and research we should be doing to answer those questions.

The case I know best, and the one I draw on most, is the public deliberation that followed the destruction of the World Trade Center Towers in New York City in 2001. That politicians and planners decided to make the rebuilding of the World Trade Center site a public and participatory process was, to many, surprising.[27] After all, New York City urban development had long been criticized for being driven by real estate interests and periodically paralyzed by battles between community groups and developers.[28] In that context, it seemed surprising that the Lower Manhattan Development Corporation (LMDC), an agency led by developers, financiers, and officials for economic development, should talk so enthusiastically about giving power to the people. Yet in the months after the terrorist attack, public forums were organized by a variety of civic groups and rebuilding agencies. Among them, in April 2002, the Municipal Art Society spearheaded a series of 230 "visioning workshops" around the tristate area, with 3,500 participants generating ideas for memorials, job-creation programs, and livable neighborhoods. In July, the LMDC collaborated with the Port Authority, the interstate agency that owned the site, and the Civic Alliance, a coalition of civic groups, to convene possibly the largest "town meeting" ever held in this country. Some 4,500 people met in a midtown convention center to jointly review the preliminary plans for the World Trade Center site as well as to deliberate more broadly about the future of Lower Manhattan. "Listening to the City" attracted international coverage and was credited with sending decision makers back to the design drawing board. It was followed by an online dialogue, more public hearings, an exhibition of new architectural design plans, and numerous public workshops.

Using participant observation, I studied the planning and operation of several of these efforts: Imagine New York, Listening to the City, and Listening to the City Online. With graduate student collaborators, I also interviewed participants in Imagine New York and Listening to the City immediately after the forums and then again a year later. Online dialogue participants were surveyed by the organizers immediately after their participation and my team re-interviewed them a year later. We also conducted several kinds of content analyses of twenty-five group discussions that made up the online forum. Finally, we interviewed planners of the three deliberative exercises as well as those charged with redeveloping the site and representatives of advocacy groups. In the following, I draw only selectively on portions of that research; the research design and findings are described elsewhere.[29]

Deliberative Democrats and Activists

There is an assumption made by all three perspectives that I have not yet mentioned. It is that activists and deliberativists are different people. That may not be the case. When Caroline Lee and I surveyed deliberation practitioners—facilitators, organizers, and staffers at the organizations that run deliberative forums—45 percent reported a background in organizing or activism. Respondents with less than twelve years' experience in the field were even more likely to cite a background in organizing/activism.[30]

Claims like these may reflect what Meyer and Tarrow refer to as a "movement society" in which the methods of activism have become popularized outside the sphere of contentious politics.[31] Deliberativists may call themselves current or former activists to indicate their political consciousness, not the methods they use. But deliberativists' activist ideals may also reflect the distinctive ways in which the field of public deliberation has developed. Elsewhere, I have argued that the American field of public deliberation was launched mainly by men with backgrounds in federal government, academia, and public opinion polling who saw deliberation primarily as a means of civic education.[32] However, as public deliberation developed into an institutionalized practice, it merged with already-institutionalized practices of dispute resolution and especially intercultural dialogue. Deliberation drew personnel and an idiom from those fields, and, in the process, a masculinized practice and discourse became feminized. As a result, and contrary to standard feminist criticisms of deliberation as devaluing the contributions of women, my research showed that women are as active and influential participants in deliberation as men.

Another dimension of the field's evolution may have been its integration with an idiom and practice of community organizing. McCoy and Scully refer to the "marriage" of deliberation and community organizing.[33] Sirianni and Friedland argue that a group of activists moved from contentious participatory democracy in the 1960s to pioneering collaborative participatory democracy in the 1990s.[34] Leighninger lists among the initiators of deliberative experiments government and nonprofit leaders such as school superintendents, human relations commissioners, and leaders of interfaith groups but also "community organizers . . . and activists."[35] In Ryfe's survey of sixteen organizations sponsoring deliberative forums, all but four emphasized deliberation aimed at achieving demonstrable impacts, rather than at educating their constituencies. Organizers said that the pressure came from participants who believed, as Ryfe puts it, "deliberation is useless unless it results in tangible change."[36] This belief, too, may have led to alliances with community organizers. Indeed, in a recent conference bringing together deliberation practitioners and community organizers, participants spent a lot of time arguing that the divide between the two that existed at the national level was nonexistent at the local level. Deliberation, a participant said, was a "subset of community organizing."[37]

Clearly we need a better understanding of the field's evolution to decide whether the trend I have described is actually occurring. I offer it, however, as one point of challenge to the notion that activism and deliberation are necessarily at odds. I want to concentrate, however, not on overlaps of ideology, practice, or personnel, but on overlaps of strategic interest. There may be good, instrumental reasons for activists and deliberativists to collaborate. And they do collaborate. In his study of Porto Alegre's famous participatory budgeting process, Baiocchi found that activists recruited people to forums, negotiated among parties before, after, and during meetings, and gathered the information that residents needed to deliberate effectively.[38] In neighborhoods where activists were not involved, the process was both less deliberative and less effective in getting residents what they wanted. For activists, the forums were a place to demand government concessions, promote political learning, build grassroots leadership, and recruit members.

In Porto Alegre, activists had pressed for the participatory budgeting system to begin with, which may explain their investment in it. Still, there are ways in which deliberativists and activists not in that situation are mutually served by their relationship. As I noted earlier, activists need publicity. But not any publicity will do. Activists need a public stage from which they can draw attention to their issue, make their claims, and rebut the claims of authorities and other influential actors. They need to be seen as representing not just themselves but a much larger group of people who could be mobilized to act on behalf of the movement.[39] Activists' claims to accurately represent that larger group's views must be believed. In addition to public attention of a certain kind, activists need access to those with power, whether that means direct access to decision makers or to influential allies. Deliberativists, for their part, also struggle to claim representativeness, in two senses. If they do not seem to have some demographic representativeness, they can be attacked for being exclusive.[40] If they are seen as marginalizing not certain people but certain points of view, they can also be discredited.[41] When these two sets of needs are considered, one can see rationales for collaboration.

Only a few deliberative forums rely on random sampling. Instead, the groups sponsoring forums often depend on members of their advisory boards to recruit through their organizations. For that reason, advisory boards often include organizations representing people of color, working-class people, immigrants, and home renters, organizations that often have a community organizing and social justice bent. Organizers and activists can find themselves asked to serve as recruiters for deliberative forums.[42] In Lower Manhattan, for example, Civic Alliance staffers were sometimes frustrated by members of the Labor Community Action Network (LCAN), an advocacy group representing workers and low-income residents, who were relentless in their press to get jobs and housing on the redevelopment agenda for Lower Manhattan. But LCAN was valuable to the Alliance for its ability to recruit people of color and low-income workers to participate in the Listening to the City public forum.[43]

What do activists get for doing that recruitment? A seat at the table. One of LCAN's organizers explained that they had agreed to sign on as one of the sponsors of Listening to the City in part because doing so legitimized them with decision makers, with the press, with the other civic groups engaged in the rebuilding coalition, and with potential recruits and supporters.[44] In addition, by participating in planning a deliberative forum, activists can get their issues included on the agenda. This was the possibility that the Civic Alliance offered to LCAN, for example, in recruiting it to Listening to the City.[45] Helping to plan a forum may also put activists in a direct, collaborative relationship with the decision makers they target.

Hendriks studied three citizens' forums—one on a proposed waste-recycling policy, one on gene technology in the food chain, and one on consumer-protection policies—in which representatives of activist and public interest groups, along with representatives of commercial groups, government agencies, and professional organizations, were invited to address the randomly selected groups of citizens.[46] She found that activists and public interest organizations were the most likely to engage in the process. The commercial representatives were the only ones who actively refused to participate. Activists' decision to participate, like that of the other groups, was thoroughly strategic. No one participated mainly to contribute to the common good. Rather they saw an opportunity to press their case. Activists saw an opportunity to correct what they considered to be industry-promoted misinformation about the safety of genetically modified food. Citizen forums were a "platform for advocacy," Hendriks argues.[47] In Durban, South Africa, local environmentalists partnered with a Danish environmentalist group to develop expertise around the environmental impacts of development projects. That expertise then became the basis for their role in deliberative environmental impact processes.[48]

Participating in a forum that activists neither helped to plan nor were invited to address may also have benefits. Other activist groups beside LCAN found Listening to the City a fertile ground for securing publicity and recruiting new members: proponents of rebuilding the World Trade Center Towers to their original height, small business owners lobbying for a greater share of federal funding, and groups seeking to raise awareness about environmental dangers at the site. Activists did not have to stand outside the forum and protest against it. Instead, they only had to wear t-shirts publicizing their cause to be interviewed by reporters who already had enough footage of tables of citizens deep in conversation. In their discussion groups, activists were able to make their case and provide potential supporters contact information to get more involved. They put a human face on causes that might otherwise be seen as trivial, abstract, or distasteful.

Changing One's Mind

The picture I just presented of activists at Listening to the City would undoubtedly raise objections from the deliberativist. If activists are leaving the discussion to seek out reporters, how seriously engaged in the conversation are they? More important, if activists are there to make their case, just how committed to deliberation can they be? Deliberation depends on a willingness to change one's mind. It requires that one scrutinize one's own assumptions and try out alternatives. Activists, however, cannot but be evangelicals for their cause.

The argument is plausible. But it rests on the notion that people change their minds in deliberation and that they do so as the result of give and take with people who have different opinions but are equally willing to revise them. Is that rendering correct? The jury is still out. Experimental research on opinion formation has yielded partial and conflicting results. Some research has suggested that people do change their opinions as a result of participating in a deliberative forum, but the change usually results from getting new information and, according to some researchers, from internal reflection rather than group dialogue.[49] Some researchers have found evidence of increases in the clarity or consistency of opinion after deliberating; others have not.[50] Much research has identified social pressures to conformity.[51]

What do these findings imply about the likely consequences of admitting activists into deliberative forums? On one hand, the fact that gaining information seems to drive opinion shift means that activists might undermine that process by presenting information that is inaccurate. On the other hand, the danger may be less that people are presented with obviously partisan views than that they acquire partisan views that are passed off as information. In my group's analysis of how online deliberators made use of information about the rebuilding of the World Trade Center site that they sought out and shared online, we found that one of the most commonly shared URL links was to a proposed design for the site.[52] Participants described the design simply as an attractive idea for rebuilding. What no one mentioned, and what was not made clear anywhere on the site, was that the design had been commissioned by a conservative think tank that was alone in proposing that more commercial space should be built at Ground Zero. Other websites similarly concealed their partisan agenda and were circulated without commentary as information. This suggests that activists' participation in a forum not as ordinary citizens but as activists might have the benefit of exposing people to points of view not represented in the mainstream, while making clear that the information presented was from a partisan point of view. The fact that it was offered by an activist might encourage participants to question its accuracy and to seek out alternative sources of information. If the best information is that which stands up to challenge, then the presence of an activist would assist in that process.

In further support of the notion that the activist with a position might aid rather than undermine deliberation are the observations offered by Listening to the City participants. Interviewed after the event, most denied that they had changed their opinions about anything. But they had come because they wanted to clarify their opinions, they said: to figure out what they felt about questions they knew were both important and complex. "It's not that I didn't feel this way and now I do," one interviewee explained. "I clarified something. I was torn between do we rebuild the towers, how much business do we put there, do we make it all a memorial—I was hearing all these things. Where were my thoughts in all this?" Interviewees wanted, they said in different ways, to make sure that their opinions were based on a grasp of all the issues at stake, which included the priorities of different groups.

Participants referred repeatedly to the impact of their interactions with others in their groups. One said, "The fact that I was willing to listen to other people's point of view was very exciting and to really see other people's point of view [was, too]." Describing herself as politically conservative, she said she was "amazed at what came out of my mouth. I said there should be low-income housing down there." Another participant explained, "Much of my thinking prior to the event had been solo thinking. The experience made me aware of other people's experiences." Remarks like these suggest that being exposed to *people* espousing different views had a value that just being exposed to different views by, say, reading about them would not have had.[53] In addition, however, participants defined their own views against those of other people, as much as in line with other people. After saying "I was amazed at what came out of my mouth," the respondent I just quoted continued with "because there was one man at the table who I thought was a trifle racist and I was amazed I said there should be low-income housing down there." She had developed her enthusiasm for low-income housing against the opposition of the member of the group she perceived as racist. Presumably, the more differences in position expressed in the group, the less likely people would be to feel pressure to conform to any one position. The presence of a self-consciously partisan viewpoint would help to provide that.

Finally, the presence of activists who are used to challenging the norms of polite behavior may have a valuable impact on deliberation. Deliberativists argue that forums in which elected officials are present are ideal for both citizens and officials. Officials' presence makes officials more likely to act on citizens' recommendations and makes citizens more likely to come to trust their representatives. But Button and Mattson found that when public officials joined the room, forum participants consistently shifted into a listening mode: asking the official questions and listening respectfully to his answers.[54] Some participants had been coached in advance: They had been provided informational materials so they would be up to speed technically and they had been repeatedly reminded that this was a roundtable rather than a lecture. Still, they adopted a deferential stance. Officials, for their part, in Button and Mattson's observation, never seemed to learn anything from citizens.[55] In a situation like this, activists, who may have experience in challenging officials, could, by their example, encourage others to do so.

Now, the presence of an activist certainly could have downsides. An activist might monopolize talk or hijack the agenda. His or her presentation of evidence might be so compelling as to foreclose rather than inspire challenge. An activist might intimidate people into agreement or, conversely, might serve as a lightning rod for challenge, discouraging other members from airing their disagreements with each other. Activists who originally endorsed the deliberative forum might drop out when they saw things were not going their way, eliminating any potential for reconciliation, compromise, or alternative solutions. These are reasonable possibilities, and the presence of effective facilitators, while surely a help, cannot be expected to deal with all of them.

Finally, what if activists changed their minds? Would that be so bad? Talisse argues that the social dynamic of polarization can work against activists if they limit themselves to discussions only with supporters.[56] Pushed to become more extreme in their positions, they may lose their ability to connect with people who might share their original commitments but not in their extreme form. Whether or not this is true, one can imagine activists treating deliberative forums as opportunities to try out ideas and ways of justifying them (just as the government has treated such forums as focus groups for contemplated programs).[57]

Decision Makers and Impact

Deliberativists, of course, would be delighted if activists changed their minds in the course of a deliberative forum. This would demonstrate the power of rational persuasion and also help deliberativists to convince decision makers to listen to the forum's recommendations. After all, the recommendations resulted from a process that began with radically opposed views. Here, activists would be skeptical, and for good reason. Decision makers might well credit the forum with influencing policy—if it was the policy that decision makers already wanted or if the policy was so unimportant as to not count as a concession of any kind. Decision makers would get credit for having followed the will of the people while not having done so in any real way.

I believe that both views rest on a questionable assumption: that policy impact is mostly a matter of decision makers' willingness to listen to the recommendations that issue from the forum. Part of the problem is that discussions of deliberation's impact have tended to conceptualize deliberation as a sphere or zone that is somehow removed from politics. An alternative perspective holds that deliberation is political all the way through. This means that deliberativists have to fight for influence from the get-go, but it also means that there are multiple avenues for impact.

We can take a page here from recent research on the conditions for social movements' impact. Movements' impact on policy is usually not a function of their having disrupted the system enough to extract concessions from those in power. Nor is it a matter of activists having persuaded decision makers of the merits of their views. Rather, impact depends on activists' capacity to take advantage of favorable political and cultural situations. Let me highlight three such situations. Whatever a politician feels personally about an issue, if she is running for office and an activist group manages to convince her, convince the media, or convince her opponent that the issue is a public litmus test of the politician's seriousness or ideological consistency and that she will lose votes if she pledges to support one or the other side of the issue, she is likely to take a stand on the issue. She is also likely to press for the legislation or policy change that is consistent with that stand.[58] Her personal opinions about the issue are somewhat beside the point.

Activists have also taken advantage of the fact that decision makers are rarely a unified group. Activists can draw on support from one administrative agency, or they can exploit cleavages among administrative agencies or political elites to gain leverage.[59] As I noted earlier, media coverage is an important route to impact and, like the other routes I mentioned, it both is and is not within activists' control. Getting in the press can mean getting an issue onto the public and policy agenda. Unfavorable coverage, of course, can make a movement and its cause seem misguided, silly, or dangerous. The trick, then, is to get the cause framed in the media in ways that align with valorized modes of action.[60]

Each of these routes to impact combines favorable circumstances with strategic action that capitalizes on those circumstances. Each depends on decision makers, but none relies on the goodwill of officials. Rather, the model is one of decision makers responding rationally to political pressure. I believe that the model, which is intended to account for movements' impact, may also account for the impact of deliberative forums. Such forums are rarely sponsored by decision makers alone. Usually they are put together by coalitions of groups with diverse interests.[61] Decision makers also have diverse interests. Moreover, decision makers can rarely implement recommendations without scaling hurdles of time, funding, and staff; competing commitments; and bureaucratic rules. For all these reasons, even a willingness to listen, in the absence of pressure to do more than listen, is unlikely to accomplish anything. Several scholars have talked in this vein about the importance of deliberative "entrepreneurs": people who work with and within existing institutions to make deliberation effective.[62] The term "entrepreneur" valuably points to the energy and creativity necessary to the role. However, the term may not fully capture the political assertiveness that is also necessary.

The Lower Manhattan rebuilding process illustrates several of these dynamics. By all accounts, Listening to the City influenced the initial site planning. The public's emphatic rejection of all six site plans that had been commissioned by the LMDC sent the agency back to the drawing board and led them to launch an international design competition. The public's support for re-creating the street grid that had been built over by the original towers, for broadening a thoroughfare that connected the neighborhood to an adjacent residential area, and for an iconic tower that would redefine the Manhattan skyline, was influential for members of the LMDC and shaped its subsequent planning.[63] That public deliberation had these impacts is surprising for several reasons. The LMDC had already invested time and money in site plans that, even before Listening to the City, had come under attack and undoubtedly would again at the public meeting. The governor, who controlled the LMDC and the Port Authority, was under intense pressure by Lower Manhattan corporate and real estate interests (as well as the *New York Times*) to move quickly on planning, and it was likely that a public process would slow things down.[64] The Port Authority was notoriously uninterested in public input and determined to go its own way.[65]

So why did decision makers agree to the public forum? Why did they not control it? And why did they follow any of its recommendations? The conditions for (movement) impact that I cited above seem to have played a role. First, decision makers were not unified, and the forum's promoters were able to take advantage of cleavages among them. The LMDC's role in relationship to the Port Authority was unclear and the subject of contention. While the Port Authority's primary concern was to replace the commercial space that had been destroyed and to secure its revenue streams, the LMDC, though run by loyalists to the governor, was staffed by people with ties to New York's city planning and design networks. Many within LMDC saw an opportunity to better integrate the site into Lower Manhattan and they were frustrated with the preliminary site plans that hewed to the Port Authority's requirements. Alex Garvin, who was vice president for planning and design at the LMDC, said later that the "public, in a funny way, became my personal ally all through this process."[66] Members of the LMDC were thus open to the idea of a public forum and they secured the cooperation of a reluctant Port Authority.

As I noted, the LMDC and Port Authority were headed by people who were loyal to the governor. However, the fact that the governor was running for reelection probably made him unwilling to be seen as pressing for the site's redevelopment in the face of victims' families' call for a slower pace. In fact, before his election, the governor's only direct intervention in the rebuilding process was to assure victims' families that the footprints of the towers would not be built on. The governor's reluctance to take a more hands-on role, at least initially, opened the way for public influence. Finally, Listening to the City enjoyed extraordinary media coverage. The event was covered by more than two hundred media outlets, including the major television networks, dailies from around the country, and international media.[67] Importantly, the opinions that were voiced there were cast in the press as the people's voice. *New York Daily News* columnist Pete Hamill wrote enthusiastically, "At each table, they debated in a sober, thoughtful, civil way. They voted, offered comments, and moved on to the next item on the agenda. We have a word for what they were doing. The word is democracy."[68] From the point of view of the Civic Alliance, which had cosponsored the event, the media coverage gave it a role in the decision-making process that it had not enjoyed before. "Because Listening to the City was such a phenomenal success from a media standpoint, the club we were swinging was bigger than anyone was used to," one Civic Alliance staffer explained later.[69]

The impact of Listening to the City can be interestingly compared to that of Imagine New York, the series of workshops that were held around the city in the spring of 2002. Like Listening to the City, Imagine New York was planned and organized by a coalition of prominent New York civic groups, in this case, spearheaded by the venerable Municipal Art Society. Like Listening to the City, officials signaled their support for the forum early on and the LMDC vice president Alex Garvin appeared at the press conference at which the findings were presented. However, Garvin later said that the fact that Imagine had been developed without any relation to the current issues on the table made it altogether uninfluential.[70] The six site plans had not yet been unveiled so there was no clear target for public disapproval. Perhaps most important, Imagine secured nothing like the publicity that Listening to the City did, in part because of Listening to the City's size and scale, its technological sophistication, and its timing.[71]

My hunch is that similar conditions may precede other cases of deliberative impact. Again, these conditions have little to do with political decision makers' personal enthusiasm for deliberation. They are an electoral context in which political decision makers have a special stake in being associated with the will of the people; cleavages among decision makers give some a competitive interest in supporting deliberation; and deliberation sponsors can frame a forum as reflecting the people's will. For example, when Oregon convened a series of public forums intended to prioritize medical services that would be covered by Medicaid, critics drew attention to the forums' domination by health care workers. These were hardly representatives of Oregon's citizenry. But reformers were able to frame the forums as consistent with Oregon's long tradition of citizen participation in policymaking. The point of the forum was to create "public buy-in" to a potentially controversial program that would extend Medicaid benefits to more poor people at the cost of reduced services.[72] In other words, reformers were able to capitalize on a resonant narrative of Oregonian democracy by framing the forums as the people's will.

The larger point is that deliberation sometimes may *require* advocacy in order to have real impact.[73] In that sense, then, both activists and deliberativists may be best served by an ability to switch from one stance to another. As an environmental activist in Durban, South Africa, put it, far from being at odds with deliberation, activism "*means* having regular public forums, it means writing regular letters to these government officials and politicians, it means when people don't respond and are afraid to deliver it means taking to the streets and doing a protest and, you know, constantly being in the media and showing them for what they are."[74]

Or, as a participant in Listening to the City put it, "We need to protest, shut things down if we have to, to make sure they commit to really taking our—the stuff we did with the selection process and voting and the whole democracy thing—taking it seriously." An LCAN organizer, David Kallick, said that his group had seen its role in Listening to the City as simultaneously "inside and outside; to help shape the agenda of the day, to give our input into that agenda, and to protest from outside the fact that a lot was being left off that agenda." So as forum participants followed a program that LCAN had helped to craft, LCAN activists demonstrated outside the forum with a giant papier-mâché ear asking George Pataki, "Can You Hear Us Now?"[75]

In chapter 3 of this book, Vallas and his coauthors describe another kind of hybrid strategy. Contrary to criticisms that anti-sweatshop campaigns have abandoned a focus on the state for "name and shame" strategies targeted exclusively at retailers, the authors found that many campaigns successfully combined a name and shame strategy with efforts to press national and international governmental institutions to regulate firms denying workers' rights. However, the authors underscore the widespread perception that fighting for workers' rights is incompatible with fighting for human rights. Similarly, there are obstacles, real and perceived, to a group's ability to shift between activism and deliberation.

Why Deliberative Activism Is Difficult

As I noted earlier, theorists of deliberative democracy who reject Young's view of activism and deliberation as irreconcilable argue that activism is warranted—*becomes appropriate*—when deliberation fails to live up to certain democratic standards. Fung describes "deliberative activists" who take up increasingly coercive methods to secure the minimal conditions for deliberation.[76] I have made a different argument: a deliberative forum, even if run according to the highest standards of equality, publicity, and autonomy, may require that its sponsors advocate on its behalf.

Interestingly, the Listening to the City participants we interviewed, like the one I quoted above, were enthusiastic about the need for advocacy on behalf of their recommendations. Asked whether he thought Listening to the City would influence decision makers, one participant answered, "It depends on the people who put Listening to the City together, how vigilant [they are]. . . . If they back off and let them maneuver and manipulate this situation, it will be null and void what we did." Participants hoped, and sometimes expected, that they would be involved in advocating for the recommendations they had arrived at. One participant became less confident of the possible impact of the forum, she said, when she saw that "they weren't talking about expanding the process." Indeed, when interviewed a year after Listening to the City, participants complained that organizers had not capitalized on their enthusiasm. "We were never invited to participate again. I think there should have been a second or a third follow-up with the rest of the plans." Participants evidently operated with a model of political influence that combined pressure with persuasion.

By contrast, AmericaSpeaks, the national nonprofit that organized Listening to the City (as well as the Washington summit I described at the beginning of the chapter), described its role in general as one of a "neutral, honest broker." It emphasized that "any organization attempting to involve the public must position itself so that citizens have confidence that the forums they are participating in are unbiased and meaningful."[77] The question, though, is whether guaranteeing "meaningful" forums may require that the sponsoring organization move from serving as "broker" to serving as public advocate for the positions arrived at in the forum.

Deliberativists in Lower Manhattan struggled with the question. Initially, both the Municipal Art Society and the Civic Alliance, the organizers, respectively, of Imagine and Listening to the City, saw their role as one of expert consultant to rebuilding authorities. In an interview, an Imagine organizer, Holly Leicht, describes the Municipal Art Society's initial approach as "having a quiet relationship—influential board members talking to people in LMDC."[78] The Civic Alliance head Robert Yaro explained in February 2002 that their "role is not to be directly part of the public process but to be a resource to people who make decisions."[79]

When Imagine's recommendations were ignored by the LMDC, the Municipal Art Society did not move immediately into an adversarial role. Rather it struggled with whether to be an "outside advocate or a monitoring partner" Leicht explains. Informal lobbying was an "MO that [the Municipal Art Society] uses all the time" and they were effective at it. Striking a "balance between staying public on issues and having a quiet relationship" was no easy task. Imagine's organizers repeatedly told participants that they were committed to ensuring that participants' voices "were heard by decision makers." But at the Imagine summit, organizers shifted gears somewhat, encouraging participants to write letters to rebuilding authorities rather than proposing any collective strategy for political influence.[80]

Eventually, Imagine's organizers became more comfortable with a role as public critic. They joined with advocacy groups to outline nine principles that had not been addressed by the LMDC's guidelines. Then they invited Imagine workshop participants back to comment on the second set of design plans and presented a summary of those findings at LMDC formal hearings. They convened another set of workshops to solicit public input about transportation issues at the site, and held educational seminars and workshops for people to weigh in on the proposed designs for a memorial at the site.

The Civic Alliance had more success in gaining officials' ear early on, and the group was successful, at least initially, in a consultative role. The Alliance had intended Listening to the City to solicit public input into broad priorities for Lower Manhattan rather than focusing on the site plans. However, it was able to get some larger planning issues into the agenda, as well as to secure the financial support, attendance, and endorsement of members of the LMDC and Port Authority.[81] When, in spite of the huge amount of publicity that was generated by Listening to the City's participants' rejection of all the preliminary plans, the LMDC made no immediate plans to shelve the plans that had provoked such antipathy (they would do so shortly after), the Civic Alliance began to be more vocal in criticizing rebuilding authorities.

That shift was a difficult one, however. Some critics of the Civic Alliance argued that the personal ambitions of its leaders were getting in the way of its willingness to oppose the powers that be. But it seems more likely that the issue was a practical one: Would the Alliance have more impact by challenging the process from outside it or trying to redirect it from inside? Listening to the City had been the Civic Alliance's "club," and so Alliance staffers tried to raise funds for another incarnation of the event. This one would invite public comment about the second round of site plans—and, more important, about some of the other issues that had been quietly pushed off the table by rebuilding authorities, issues such as the amount of office space at the site, affordable housing, and rebuilding authorities' plans for distributing federal block grant funding. However, Alliance staffers were unable to raise the money for such an event.[82]

Along with strategic concerns, the Civic Alliance, like many groups in the process, was unwilling to come out swinging in a context still marked by the loss of so many lives. David Kallick says that there was also real reluctance to be perceived as "obstructionist," given New York City's long history of community advocacy derailing development projects. Everyone knew how easy it was to stop something. "We really, really wanted to find a way to have community and activist concerns included in a process that made the project better," Kallick explains.[83] In other cases, the norms against adversarialism have less to do with a local history of contention, and an effort to break free of it, and more with institutional norms of interaction. In this vein, Hendriks describes the norms against adversarialism that operated in Germany but not in Australia; also, Bevington shows how such norms operated in the case of environmental activists who had gained access to powerful congressional representatives.[84]

Six months after Listening to the City, the Civic Alliance was willing to embrace an oppositional role. Listening to the City participants received an email from the Civic Alliance declaring that "the public agencies have ignored our call for a thorough public process" in reviewing the new design plans and urging them to write officials demanding more public input.[85] However, according to observers, the Civic Alliance was out of the consultative loop with the LMDC by that time.[86]

By that time, too, opportunities for public input were diminishing. The governor, after selecting the heads of the new development agency, had been minimally involved in the rebuilding process. But he intervened rather suddenly to override the LMDC's pick for the master planner of the site. As the chair of the LMDC's site-planning subcommittee put it, the issue was "pride and who calls the shots."[87] Soon after that, the leaser of the site, Larry Silverstein, announced that his own architect would be designing the site. That architect, David Childs, and the official master planner, Daniel Liebeskind, were forced into what was by all accounts an awkward marriage, and Liebeskind was left claiming to still have some influence while his design was, for all intents and purposes, scrapped.[88] Planning for the memorial was completely closed to public input, and by the end of 2005 editorialists for the *New York Times* referred nostalgically to Listening to the City when they talked about the public's disappearance from the rebuilding process.[89]

There may have been no way that the civic groups sponsoring public deliberation could have secured a continuing role for the public. With the governor's reelection and increasing involvement in the rebuilding process, some of the ambiguity of authority that had allowed the civic groups to press for public input had receded. The public's attention was understandably focused on the high-profile international architectural competition, which diverted attention from the fact that the specifications for rebuilding, and in particular the requirement for the full replacement of commercial space, had not much changed.[90] It is worth asking, however, whether the civic groups involved in Listening to the City and Imagine might have missed a valuable opportunity for effective advocacy.[91] Right after Listening to the City, the public was cast as having virtuously forced narrow-minded rebuilding authorities to change course. What if, at that moment, Listening to the City's organizers had pressed hard, and perhaps mobilized participants to press hard, for more of the recommendations that came out of the forum? What if organizers had repeatedly reminded authorities that "the people" wanted not only an iconic tower but also affordable housing at the site; not only the restoration of the street grid but also a reduction of the amount of planned office space? Might things have turned out differently?

For my purposes here, the important point is that the New York City case points to some of the obstacles to the kind of flexibility that would allow sponsors of public deliberation to capitalize on activist methods. In this case, of course, the high emotions still attached to rebuilding and the gravity with which people approached the rebuilding process made everyone understandably reluctant to shift into a confrontational mode. In a decision-making process that was complex and often obscure, it was difficult to determine the best route to influence. For organizations with a standard repertoire for dealing with decision makers (as the Municipal Art Society's Holly Leicht described her organization's "MO" of a "quiet relationship"), it was hard to shift to an untested and unfamiliar mode. In their study of deliberative initiatives around school reform in South Carolina, Weatherford and McDonnell point to the difficulty of sustaining largely volunteer organizations long enough to keep up the pressure on officials.[92]

Moreover, barriers to flexibility operate on the side of not only deliberativists but also activists. The South African environmental advocates I mentioned earlier who effectively partnered with a Danish group to present themselves as experts in the deliberative process came under fire from activists in local townships.[93] Local activists equated the group's abandonment of the disruptive protest tactics inherited from the apartheid era with an abandonment of their radical commitments. Hendriks describes marginalized groups' wariness of participating in a deliberative process when they were used to being locked out of the politics that mattered.[94] In both cases, the risks of moving away from a familiar protest repertoire were better known than the potential gains.

I want to raise an even thornier challenge to the compatibility of deliberation and activism. It is possible that deliberation's effectiveness depends on it being seen as not political. Even if, in fact, the notion of a zone of interaction free of politics is illusory, that notion may still be politically useful. The Listening to the City participants I interviewed said over and over again that they had appreciated the fact that the forum was not "political," by which they seemed to mean driven by partisan interests. They did not see liking the forum's neutrality as at odds with believing that its organizers should become advocates for the positions they had arrived at in the forum. And I would argue that the two are not necessarily at odds. But undoubtedly the balance is difficult to strike.

Likewise, it is easier for decision makers to ignore a forum's recommendations if they can say that the process was tainted by advocacy groups or special interests seeking to manipulate people's opinion. Reporters, for their part, may find more newsworthy the allegations that a forum has been rigged than the results of the forum. AmericaSpeaks encountered just this problem when it ran a nationwide series of forums on the budget deficit in 2010. The effort was widely criticized when it was reported that a conservative foundation was funding the forums and had set the agenda.[95] Organizers protested futilely that liberal foundations had also funded the forums, that left-of-center groups had participated in setting the agenda, and that the citizens who participated ended up staking a strong *liberal* position on the deficit.[96]

In this case, organizers were not successful in framing the forums as the people's will. In the case of Oregon's health care forums, as I noted earlier, organizers were successful in doing so and managed thereby to counter widespread attacks on the forums' unrepresentative character. Political skill undoubtedly plays a role in securing a public perception of deliberation as nonpolitical. There is no reason, however, that political skill cannot also be used to advocate for the recommendations that are arrived at by way of public deliberation.

Conclusion

The notion that deliberation and activism are at odds, or that activism is warranted only when deliberation is improperly conducted, is based on a misleading picture of activism, a misleading picture of deliberation, and a misleading picture of political change. Because activism depends not just on challenging the powers that be but also on doing so with a public audience, activists sometimes have good reason to help plan and participate in public deliberative forums. Because deliberation works for individuals more by providing them information, and the capacity to assess information, than by providing persuasive arguments, and because it is jeopardized by people's tendency to be deferential, the presence of activists can foster good deliberation rather than threaten it. And because political change is often less a function of decision makers' personal commitment to a particular course of action than it is their vulnerability to pressure on behalf of a course of action, deliberativists can profitably capitalize on activists' strategic repertoire for creating that kind of pressure. Together these suggest that activism and deliberation are not only compatible; sometimes they may be necessary to each other. Activist groups may be shut out of public debate on an issue by shunning opportunities to be involved with a high-profile forum. And groups that sponsor forums may find that they need to go to bat for the recommendations that emerge from the forum—or risk the forum remaining just a feel-good exercise in talk with little political impact.

To be sure, I do not want to suggest that there are no tensions between deliberation and activism. Activists are right to suspect that decision makers will not readily accede to the recommendations that come out of a forum if those recommendations are not what they had expected. Deliberativists are right that activists' commitment to a single issue and single position may end up stifling deliberation rather than encouraging it. The tensions are there. Alongside those tensions, however, there are also strong continuities of interest. Recognizing them should open up new avenues for the public to have an effective role in policymaking.

NOTES

1. Fernandez (2003).
2. See, e.g., Gastil and Levine (2005); Fung (2007).

3. Young (2001); Talisse (2005); Levine and Nierras (2007); Sirianni (2009).
4. Habermas (1985); Sparks (1997); Smith (2004); Fung (2005).
5. Habermas (1984); Dryzek (1990); Elster (1998); Bohman (1996).
6. Cohen (1989).
7. Barber (1988); Fishkin (1991, 1995); Roberts (2004); Gutmann and Thompson (2004); Fung (2007); and for good reviews of the now vast literature on deliberative democracy, Chambers (2003); Delli Carpini et al. (2004); Rosenberg (2007).
8. Young (2001).
9. See also Fraser (1992); Benhabib (1996); Mouffe (1996); Sanders (1997). More broadly, the orientation to abstract reasons that deliberation requires disadvantages women, people of color, nonnative English speakers, and working-class people, who are not only less comfortable with an abstract rational discourse but are less likely to be seen as capable of that form of discourse, no matter how they actually speak (see Young 2000).
10. See also Whelan and Oliver (2005); Mansbridge (2007).
11. Talisse (2005).
12. Gutmann and Thompson (2004).
13. Smith (2004).
14. Sparks (1997).
15. Habermas (1985).
16. Young (2001: 670).
17. Sparks (1997: 75).
18. Talisse (2005: 426).
19. Young (2001: 676).
20. Smith (2004: 363); see, for similar formulations, Talisse (2005: 436) and Sparks (1997: 75).
21. Fung (2005).
22. Lipsky (1968); Ferree et al. (2002); Koopmans (2004); Vliegenthart et al. (2005).
23. Amenta et al. (2012).
24. Elster (1998); Bohman (1996); Rosenberg (2007).
25. Talisse (2005: 430).
26. Young (2001: 681).
27. Polletta notes at Imagine New York press conference, June 10, 2002; remarks by Alexander Garvin (LMDC) and Ron Pisapia (Port Authority): Lower Manhattan Development Corporation (2002).
28. Pedersen (2002); Sanders (1997).
29. Polletta and Wood (2005); Polletta and Lee (2006); Polletta (2007).
30. For more information on the survey, see http://sites.lafayette.edu/ddps, and Lee (2011).
31. Meyer and Tarrow (1998).
32. Polletta and Chen (2013).
33. McCoy and Scully (2002).
34. Sirianni and Friedland (2001).
35. Leighninger (2006: 18).
36. Ryfe (2002: 366).
37. Quoted in Leighninger (2009a).
38. Baiocchi (2005).
39. Tilly (1999).
40. Goodin and Dryzek (2006).
41. Hendriks (2002).

42. McGrath (2009).
43. Petra Todorovich interview, June 17, 2003.
44. David Kallick interview, October 19, 2002.
45. Goldberg (2005: 124).
46. Hendriks (2006).
47. Hendriks (2006: 581).
48. Barnett and Scott (2007).
49. Goodin and Neimeyer (2003).
50. See Pincock (2012) for a review.
51. Mendelberg (2002).
52. Polletta, Chen, and Anderson (2008).
53. Pace Goodin (2000).
54. Button and Mattson (1999).
55. See also Ryfe (2002).
56. Talisse (2005).
57. Goodin and Dryzek (2006).
58. Meyer and Minkoff (2004).
59. Amenta et al. (2012).
60. Snow (2004).
61. Button and Mattson (1999).
62. Fagotto and Fung (2006); Sirianni (2009).
63. Goldberg (2005); Goldberger (2005); Sagalyn (2005: 40); Polletta interview with Alexander Garvin, July 3, 2003.
64. Sagalyn (2005).
65. Sagalyn (2005); Fainstein (2005).
66. Alexander Garvin interview, July 3, 2003; see also Goldberg (2005); Goldberger (2005: 101).
67. Lukensmeyer and Brigham (2002).
68. Hamill (2002).
69. Civic Alliance staffer interview, June 17, 2003.
70. Alexander Garvin interview, July 3, 2003.
71. Leighninger (2006: 144) describes a large-scale deliberative initiative that received little media coverage—and had no legislative impact—because, he argues, its size was not matched by a perceived diversity of participants.
72. Jacobs, Marmor, and Oberlander (1999).
73. Kadlec and Friedman (2007) make a similar point, while also noting that few discussions of deliberation have covered what happens after the forum.
74. Barnett and Scott (2007: 2619); emphasis added.
75. Kallick, email correspondence, November 14, 2011.
76. Fung (2005).
77. AmericaSpeaks (2002: 1, 2).
78. Holly Leicht interview, October 17, 2002.
79. Quoted in Pedersen (2002).
80. Polletta notes from Imagine New York summit, June 1, 2002, New York City.
81. Petra Todorovich interview, June 17, 2003.
82. Petra Todorovich interview, June 17, 2003.
83. Kallick, email correspondence, November 14, 2011.

84. Hendriks (2006); Bevington (2009).
85. Email to Listening to the City participants, December 17, 2002.
86. Polletta and Wood (2005).
87. Quoted in Sagalyn (2005: 51).
88. Pogrebin (2004).
89. Randolph and Klinkenborg (2006).
90. Wyatt (2003); Goldberger (2005).
91. Goldberg (2005) makes a similar point.
92. Weatherford and McDonnell (2007).
93. Barnett and Scott (2007).
94. Hendriks (2006).
95. Among others, see Baker (2010); Eskow (2010).
96. Fung (2010).

PART V

Conclusion

CHAPTER 13

Realizing the Promise of Public Participation in an Age of Inequality

CAROLINE W. LEE, MICHAEL MCQUARRIE,
AND EDWARD T. WALKER

The preceding chapters have, in our estimation, sparked a new critical and empirically grounded dialogue about the practice of participation, its pitfalls, and its promise. Inasmuch as we have selected contributions for the variety of perspectives they offer on participation over time, across particular contexts, at different scales, and with varying technologies, we conclude this volume not with a final verdict on the limitations of the new public participation in producing equality. Instead, we hope to provide readers with a more grounded sense of the opportunities and unintended consequences that participation might enable in a contemporary context of severe structural inequalities. In this respect, we end with more questions than we started with.

As such, in this conclusion, we briefly sketch four areas that we think provide fertile inspiration for new research on participation, based on common themes and surprising correspondences in the assembled contributions.

1. Investigating How Cultural Discourses around Participation Are Embedded in Historically Specific Political Environments

Much of the work in this volume documents contests over the valorization of participation. To be sure, this is not a new insight. James Morone points out that these contests intrigued Madison: "Consensus about (or 'unperplexed pursuit' of) the public good is 'more ardently to be wished for than seriously to be expected.'"[1] David Mathews argues that "democracy has many meanings, and debating its meaning is one of the characteristics of a democracy."[2] But far too often, scholars have failed to unpack the varied meanings of participation. In many ways, the apparent stability of the concept as a popular idea is part of its value to authorities. But as we see in the cases here, meanings and anxieties about power embedded in the concept shift over time in interesting ways. As Baiocchi and Ganuza argue, the concept entails "profound ambiguities," and scholars have too often gotten caught up in debates over what is or isn't "really" participation rather than investigating what the debates themselves tell us about the way "true" participation can be used to reframe or contest authority. Some readily dismiss corporate-sponsored participation as "astroturfing"—the kind of dismissal that would prevent the nuanced analysis that Walker undertakes in understanding, for example, the very real coalitions between major corporations and preexisting local community organizations that may result. Even as its promoters endeavor to ensure that the new public participation is "transparent" and "accountable," as Eliasoph notes, it remains slippery and multivalent. Attempts to construct "authentic participation" may make participation more marketable, as seen in Lee, McNulty, and Shaffer's chapter, even as they limit the range of concerns thought to entail the public good. This is a long way from the assumption (described in the introduction) that participation simply is a public good in and of itself.

2. Recontextualizing and Historicizing What Is Really "New" about the New Public Participation

The accounts offered by Kreiss, Baiocchi and Ganuza, and McQuarrie provide excellent examples of research that historicizes the development of particular modes of participation through the interactions of institutional actors and stakeholders. Baiocchi and Ganuza, McQuarrie, and Eliasoph draw attention to the roles of academics, politicians, advocacy professionals, and experts in promoting participatory forms like participatory budgeting and Asset-Based Community Development. It is important to realize that participation is often framed as "new" when in fact, as our introduction and these contributions show, many aspects of participation, and even many critiques of participation, have long-standing traditions in American life. How did William Jennings Bryan's database of millions of voters differ from technologies of managing voter participation today, as Kreiss asks and answers in his contribution? Posing such questions can put participation more squarely "in its place." But the study of the institutionalization of participation in particular contexts can also contribute to our understanding of participation as a set of practices and discourses that may be decoupled from their original settings and, in Baiocchi and Ganuza's case, travel around the world with "dizzying" speed. Investigating how the surface features of participatory tools or devices may remain constant, while their uses and meanings transform in translation, can provide a scholarly perspective on the ways in which participation moves and changes in dynamic and contingent fashion.

3. Tying the New Public Participation to Larger Trends in the Reinforcement of Inequality in the Present Moment

As chapters by Eliasoph, Lee and colleagues, Martin, and Walker demonstrate, case studies of participatory governance may neglect the forest for the trees. Empowerment practices may, counter to one's intentions, contribute to the demobilization of publics, the marginalization of the needy, or the reinforcement of the authority of existing elites. Participation enhances the legitimacy of institutions and their authority at moments when these are ripe for question—when failures of institutions to secure social rights at the most basic level are laid bare. Public recognition of the limits of participation in transforming the social order has produced widespread cynicism and skepticism. In order to leverage opportunities created by unfolding fiscal and political crises for challenging inequalities, we must understand the new public participation in broader macroeconomic and political terms. Participation under neoliberalism has taken a unique shape, but it is not enough simply to say that participation has been "neoliberalized," as Baiocchi and Ganuza warn us. The current participatory moment has been shaped by neoliberal authorities, progressive critiques of power, public resistance to managed participation, and authorities' attempts to respond to those critiques. With this understanding of how progressive impulses are deeply inscribed in contemporary forms of institutionalized participation, remedies for reclaiming the power of participation to effect social change seem much less straightforward.

4. Reevaluating the Continuing Promise of Participation Despite Mixed, Complex Results

Finally, many of the contributions to this volume offer hope for those interested in progressive social change to produce a just society. A more realistic, pragmatic sense of the limitations of participation can provide leverage in understanding the real opportunities it may afford—and especially in moving beyond facile dismissals of the ironies of the "top-down" grassroots efforts described in this book. As Vallas and colleagues, Meyer and Pullum, Schleifer and Panofsky, and Polletta show, there is indeed potential in participation, particularly in the ways that activists themselves have readily adapted tactics to account for the reshaping of participation and have made unusual alliances with elites and institutional sponsors. This finding challenges those critics who would catalogue a long line of participatory failures or frame participation as simply the latest or newest form of "tyranny." Even in the empowerment projects described by Eliasoph, the hopeful "prospectancy" entailed in institutionalized engagement can lead, in a roundabout way, to change. Polletta argues that advocacy for deliberation by institutional sponsors holds promise, while both Schleifer and Panofsky and Vallas and colleagues document creative convergences and pragmatic strategies to take advantage of new opportunities in a putatively democratized world. As Meyer and Pullum note, populism and establishment resources have been linked in many different ways over the course of the last two hundred years, and the alliances negotiated between the grassroots and elites are "inherently unstable": "Both successes and failures will strain these connections, and what emerges is likely to be more chaotic and unfocused than what has come before." In this still very much undetermined, often confusing welter of possible futures, we find rich and exciting potential. Assessing this promise in light of the critiques made in this volume should provide scholars with plenty of fodder for future research.

It should also provide us with a better understanding of the unique movement of contemporary society and politics. As Charles Postel notes in a catalogue of the changing perspectives of Americans on the legacy of the populists over the 20th century, ideas about the populists shifted in response to changing anxieties of the age about power and interests.[3] In the 21st century, it is useful to remember that future analysts may see the new public participation in a very different light than we have here. As such, the contributions in this volume are a first attempt to situate the relationship between our participatory strivings and deep ambivalence about power and the public interest in the present moment.

NOTES

1. Morone (1998: 8–9).
2. Quoted in McIvor, Barker, and McAfee (2012: vii).
3. Postel (2007: 9–10).

References

Abramowitz, Alan. 2010. *The Disappearing Center*. New Haven: Yale University Press.
Abramowitz, Alan, and Kyle Saunders. 2008. "Is Polarization a Myth?" *Journal of Politics* 70 (2): 542–555.
Agee, Bob, et al. 2009. "A New Era of Responsibility: Saving California Communities." Retrieved from http://www.savingca.org/doc/oped20090322/ on June 24, 2010.
Alexander, Jeffrey C. 2010. *The Performance of Politics: Obama's Victory and the Democratic Struggle for Power*. New York: Oxford University Press.
Alford, Robert R. 1969. "Bureaucracy and Participation in Four Wisconsin Cities." *Urban Affairs Review* 5: 5–30.
Ali, Ambreen. 2010, August 17. "Inviting Liberals to the Tea Party: Five Areas Where Liberals and Tea Party Members Could Find Agreement." Retrieved from http://www.congress.org/news/2010/08/17/inviting_liberals_to_the_tea_party?all=1.
Alinsky, Saul. 1989a. *Reveille for Radicals*. New York: Vintage.
———. 1989b. *Rules for Radicals*. New York: Vintage.
Allegretti, G. 2011. "Los presupuestos participativos en África y en Asia." In A. Falck and P. Paño, eds., *Democracia participativa y presupuestos participativos*. Málaga: Diputación Málaga y Unión Europea.
Almond, Gabriel A., and Sidney Verba. 1963. *The Civic Culture*. Princeton: Princeton University Press.
Amenta, Edwin. 1998. *Bold Relief*. Princeton: Princeton University Press.
Amenta, Edwin, Beth Gharrity Gardner, Amber Celina Tierney, Anaid Yerena, and Thomas Alan Elliott. 2012. "A Story-Centered Approach to the Newspaper Coverage of High-Profile SMOs." *Research in Social Movements, Conflict, and Change* 33: 83–107.
Americans for Prosperity. 2011a. "Chronicling Obamacare's Broken Promises." Retrieved from http://americansforprosperity.org/020411-chronicling-obamacares-broken-promises.
———. 2011b. "Issues." Retrieved from http://www.americansforprosperity.org/issues.
AmericaSpeaks. 2002. "The AmericaSpeaks Model: Taking Democracy to Scale." Retrieved from www.americaspeaks.org/history.html.
Anand, Geeta. 2006. *The Cure*. New York: Regan.
Anheier, Helmut. 2007. "Reflections on the Concept and Measurement of Global Civil Society." *Voluntas*, 18 (1): 1–15.
Anner, M., and P. Evans. 2004. "Building Bridges across a Double-Divide: Alliances between the US and Latin American Labor and NGOs." *Development in Practice* 14: 34–47.
Ansell, Chris, and Alison Gash. 2008. "Collaborative Governance in Theory and Practice." *Journal of Public Administration Research and Theory* 18 (4): 543–571.
Anstead, Nick, and Will Straw. 2009. *The Change We Need: What Britain Can Learn from Obama's Victory*. London: Fabian Society.

Appadurai, Arjun. 2004. "Culture and the Capacity to Aspire." In Vijayendra Rao and Michael Walton, eds., *Culture and Public Action*. New Delhi: Permanent Black.
Ardant, Gabriel. 1965. *Theorie sociologique de l'impôt*. Paris: SEVPEN.
Arendt, Hannah. 1990 [1963]. *On Revolution*. New York: Penguin.
———. 1998. *The Human Condition*. Chicago: University of Chicago Press.
Armbruster-Sandoval, R. 2005a. *Globalization and Cross Border Labor Solidarity in the Americas*. New York: Routledge.
———. 2005b. "Workers of the World Unite? The Contemporary Anti-sweatshop Movement and the Struggle for Social Justice in the Americas." *Work and Occupations* 32: 464–485.
Armstrong, Elizabeth A. 2002. *Forging Gay Identities*. Chicago: University of Chicago Press.
Aronowitz, Stanley. 1992. *False Promises*. Durham, N.C.: Duke University Press.
Austin, J. L. 1965. *How to Do Things with Words*. Oxford: Oxford University Press.
Avritzer, L. 2006. "New Public Spheres in Brazil: Local Democracy and Deliberative Politics." *International Journal of Urban and Regional Research* 30 (3): 623–637.
Babb, S. 2005. The Social Consequences of Structural Adjustment: Recent Evidence and Current Debates." *Annual Review of Sociology* 31: 199–222.
Bacque, Hélène, and Yves Sintomer. 2001. "Gestion de proximité et démocratie participative." *Annales de la recherche urbaine* 90: 148–155.
Bai, Matt. 2010. June 1. "Tea Party's Push on Senate Election Exposes Limits." *New York Times*. Retrieved from http://www.nytimes.com/2010/06/02/us/politics/02bai.html.
Baiocchi, Gianpaolo. 2003. "Emergent Public Spheres: Talking Politics in Participatory Governance." *American Sociological Review* 68: 52–74.
———. 2005. *Militants and Citizens*. Palo Alto, Calif.: Stanford University Press.
Baizerman, Michael, Ross Velure Roholt, and R. W. Hildreth. 2008. *Becoming Citizens: Deepening the Craft of Youth Civic Engagement*. New York: Routledge.
Baker, Dean. 2010, June 21. "America Speaks Back: Derailing the Drive to Cut Social Security and Medicare." *Huffington Post*.
Barber, Benjamin R. 1988. *Strong Democracy*. Berkeley: University of California Press.
Barker, Kristin K. 2011. "Listening to Lyrica: Contested Illnesses and Pharmaceutical Determinism." *Social Science and Medicine* 73 (6): 833–842.
Barley, Stephen R. 2010. "Building an Institutional Field to Corral a Government: A Case to Set an Agenda for Organization Studies." *Organization Studies* 31: 777–805.
Barnett, Clive, and Dianne Scott. 2007. "Space of Opposition: Activism and Deliberation in Post-apartheid Environmental Politics." *Environment and Planning A* 39 (11): 2612–2631.
Barry, Andrew, Thomas Osborne, and Nikolas Rose, eds. 1996. *Foucault and Political Reason*. Chicago: University of Chicago Press.
Bartley, Tim. 2003. "Certifying Forests and Factories: States, Social Movements and the Rise of Private Regulation in the Apparel and Forest Products Fields." *Politics and Society* 31 (3): 433–464.
———. 2007. "Institutional Emergence in an Era of Globalization: The Rise of Transnational Private Regulation of Labor and Environmental Conditions." *American Journal of Sociology* 113 (2): 297–351.
Bartley, Tim, and Curtis Child. 2011. "Movements, Markets, and Fields: The Effects of Anti-sweatshop Campaigns on U.S. Firms, 1993–2000." *Social Forces* 90: 425–451.
Bates, Robert H., and Da-Hsiang Donald Lien. 1985. "A Note on Taxation, Development, and Representative Government." *Politics and Society* 14 (1): 53–70.
Battilana, Julie, and Silvia Dorado. 2010. "Building Sustainable Hybrid Organizations: The

Case of Commercial Microfinance Organizations." *Academy of Management Journal* 53 (6): 1419–1440.
Baum, Joel A. C., and Walter W. Powell. 1995. "Cultivating an Institutional Ecology of Organizations: Comment on Hannan, Carroll, Dundon, and Torres." *American Sociological Review* 60: 529–538.
Bayer, Ronald. 1981. *Homosexuality and American Psychiatry*. New York: Basic Books.
Baysinger, Barry D., Gerald D. Keim, and Carl P. Zeithaml. 1985. "An Empirical Evaluation of the Potential for Including Shareholders in Corporate Constituency Programs." *Academy of Management Journal* 28: 180–200.
Bellah, Robert. 1970. "Between Religion and Social Science." In *Beyond Belief*. New York: Harper.
Benhabib, Seyla. 1996. "Toward a Deliberative Model of Democratic Legitimacy." In Seyla Benhabib, ed., *Democracy and Difference: Contesting the Boundaries of the Political*. Princeton: Princeton University Press.
Beniger, James R. 1986. *The Control Revolution: Technological and Economic Origins of the Information Society*. Cambridge: Harvard University Press.
Berger, Mathieu. 2008. "Bruxelles à l'épreuve de la participation: Les contrats de quartier en exercices." Brussels: Ministère de la Région de Bruxelles-Capitale/Kaligram.
Berger, Peter L., and Richard J. Neuhaus. 2000. "To Empower People: From State to Civil Society." In Don E. Eberly, ed., *The Essential Civil Society Reader*. New York: Rowman and Littlefield.
Berkrot, Bill. 2011. "Dendreon Plunges as Provenge Prospects Wither." *Reuters*.
Bernhardt, Annette, Heather Boushey, Laura Dresser, and Chris Tilly. 2008. *The Gloves-Off Economy: Workplace Standards at the Bottom of America's Labor Market*. Ithaca, N.Y.: ILR Press.
Best, Rachel Kahn. 2012. "Disease Politics and Medical Research Funding: Three Ways Advocacy Shapes Policy." *American Sociological Review* 77 (5): 780–803.
Bevington, Douglas. 2009. *The Rebirth of Environmentalism*. Washington, D.C.: Island Press.
Bhagwati, Jagdish N. 2004. *In Defense of Globalization*. New York: Oxford University Press.
Bimber, Bruce Allen, and Richard Davis. 2003. *Campaigning Online*. New York: Oxford University Press.
Bimber, Bruce, Andrew J. Flanagin, and Cynthia Stohl. 2005. "Reconceptualizing Collective Action in the Contemporary Media Environment." *Communication Theory* 15 (4): 365–388.
Binder, Amy. 2007. "For Love and Money: Organizations' Creative Responses to Multiple Environmental Logics." *Theory and Society* 36: 547–571.
Bingham, Lisa Blomgren, Tina Nabatchi, and Rosemary O'Leary. 2005. "The New Governance: Practices and Processes for Stakeholder and Citizen Participation in the Work of Government." *Public Administration Review* 65 (5): 547–558.
Block, Fred. 1977. "The Ruling Class Does Not Rule." *Socialist Review* 33: 6–28.
Bob, Clifford. 2001. "Marketing Rebellion: Insurgent Groups, International Media, and NGO Support." *International Politics* 38: 311–334.
Bohman, James. 1996. *Public Deliberation*. Cambridge: MIT Press.
Boltanski, Luc, and Eve Chiapello. 2005. *The New Spirit of Capitalism*. London: Verso.
Bonacich, Edna, and Richard P. Appelbaum. 2000. *Behind the Label: Inequality in the Los Angeles Apparel Industry*. Berkeley: University of California Press.
Bourdieu, Pierre. 1979. "Public Opinion Does Not Exist." In Armand Mattelart and Seth Siegelaub, eds., *Communication and Class Struggle*. New York: International General.

Bowler, Shaun, and Todd Donovan. 2006. "Direct Democracy and Political Parties in America." *Party Politics* 12 (5): 649–669.

Boyle, Mary-Ellen, and Ira Silver. 2005. "Poverty, Partnerships, and Privilege: Elite Institutions and Community Empowerment." *City and Community* 4: 233–253.

Boyte, H. C., and H. C. Boyte. 1980. *The Backyard Revolution*. Philadelphia: Temple University Press.

Brill, Steven. 2013, March. "Bitter Pill: Why Medical Bills Are Killing Us." *Time*. Retrieved from http://time.com/198/bitter-pill-why-medical-bills-are-killing-us/.

Briscoe, Forrest, and Sean Safford. 2008. "The Nixon-in-China Effect: Activism, Imitation, and the Institutionalization of Contentious Practices." *Administrative Science Quarterly* 53: 460–491.

Brock, Janet. 2012. "CMS Conflict of Interest Disclosures, Email Communication with David Schleifer." Baltimore, Md.: Centers for Medicare and Medicaid Services, Office of Clinical Standards and Quality.

Brody, David. 2001. "Labour Rights as Human Rights: A Reality Check." *British Journal of Industrial Relations* 39 (4): 601–605.

Bronfenbrenner, Kate. 1997. "We'll Close! Plant Closings, Plant-Closing Threats, Union Organizing and NAFTA." *Multinational Monitor* 18 (3): 8–14.

———. 2000. "Uneasy Terrain: The Impact of Capital Mobility on Workers, Wages, and Union Organizing." Washington, D.C./Ithaca, N.Y.: US Trade Deficit Review Commission/Cornell University.

Bronfenbrenner, Kate, and S. Luce. 2004. "The Changing Nature of Corporate Global Restructuring: The Impact of Production Shifts on Jobs in the US." Report submitted to the U.S.-China Economic and Security Review Commission, October 14. Ithaca, N.Y.: Cornell University.

Brooks, E. 2007. *Unraveling the Garment Industry*. Minneapolis: University of Minnesota Press.

Brown, Phil, Stephen Zavestoski, Sabrina McCormick, Brian Mayer, Rachel Morello-Frosch, and Rebecca Gasior Altman. 2004. "Embodied Health Movements: New Approaches to Social Movements in Health." *Sociology of Health and Illness* 26 (1): 50–80.

Buchanan, Wyatt, and Marisa Lagos. 2012, March 15. "Gov. Brown, Millionaire's-Tax Backers Join Forces." *San Francisco Chronicle*. Retrieved from http://www.sfgate.com/bayarea/article/Gov-Brown-millionaires-tax-backers-join-forces-3406794.php on June 28, 2013.

Buchanan, Wyatt. 2012, October 15. "Prop. 30's Big Donors Include Big Companies." *San Francisco Chronicle*. Retrieved from http://www.sfgate.com/news/article/Prop-30-s-big-donors-include-big-companies-3951475.php on June 28, 2013.

Burt, Ronald S. 1983. *Corporate Profits and Cooptation*. New York: Academic Press.

Button, Mark, and Kevin Mattson. 1999. "Deliberative Democracy in Practice: Challenges and Prospects for Civic Deliberation." *Polity* 31: 609–639.

Buycott Arizona. 2010. "Home Page." Retrieved from http://www.buycottarizona.com/Home_Page.php.

Cabannes, Y. 2006. "Les budgets participatifs en Amérique latine." *Mouvements* 5: 128–138.

Calhoun, Craig, ed. 1992. *Habermas and the Public Sphere*. Cambridge: MIT Press.

———. 1997. *Nationalism*. Minneapolis: University of Minnesota Press.

Calhoun, Craig, and Michael McQuarrie. 2007. "Public Discourse and Political Experience: T. J. Wooler and Transformations of the Public Sphere in Early Nineteenth-Century Britain." In Alex Benchimol and Willy Maley, eds., *Spheres of Influence*. Frankfurt: Peter Lang AG.

California Commission on Revenue and Taxation. 1906. "Report of the Commission on Revenue and Taxation of the State of California." Sacramento: California Commission on Revenue and Taxation.

California Forward. 2009. *Discussing Tax Reform*. Sacramento: California Forward.

Callon, Michel, Pierre Lascoumes, and Yannick Barthe. 2009. *Acting in an Uncertain World*. Cambridge: MIT Press.

Callon, Michel, Yuval Millo, and Fabian Muniesa. 2007. *Market Devices*. Hoboken, N.J.: Wiley-Blackwell.

Canovan, Margaret. 1999. "Trust the People! Populism and the Two Faces of Democracy." *Political Studies* 47 (1): 2–16.

Caren, Neil, Raj Andrew Ghoshal, and Vanesa Ribas. 2011. "A Social Movement Generation: Cohort and Period Trends in Protest Attendance and Petition Signing." *American Sociological Review* 76 (1): 125–151.

Carender, Keli. 2009a. "Blogger User Profile: Liberty Belle." Retrieved from http://www.blogger.com/profile/15903210730564785945.

———. 2009b. "Come and Take It." Retrieved from http://www.youtube.com/watch?v=_IYLqtYEYeI&feature=player_embedded.

———. 2009c. "Solution Revolution." Retrieved from http://redistributingknowledge.blogspot.com/2009_01_25_archive.html.

Carpenter, Daniel P. 2010. *Reputation and Power*. Princeton: Princeton University Press.

Carty, Victoria. 2004. "Transnational Labor Mobilizing in Two Mexican Maquiladoras: The Struggle for Democratic Globalization." *Mobilization* 9: 295–310.

———. 2010. *Wired and Mobilizing: Social Movements, New Technology, and Electoral Politics*. New York: Routledge.

Castellblanch, Ramon. 2003. "Challenging Pharmaceutical Industry Political Power in Maine and Vermont." *Journal of Health Politics Policy and Law* 28: 109–132.

Censky, Annalyn. 2011. "Stocks: Worst Day since 2008 Financial Crisis." *CNN Money*. Retrieved from http://money.cnn.com/2011/08/04/markets/markets_newyork/ on April 25, 2014.

Center for Advances in Public Engagement. 2008. "Public Engagement: A Primer from Public Agenda." New York: Public Agenda. Retrieved from http://www.publicagenda.org/files/pdf/public_engagement_primer_0.pdf.

Center for Deliberative Democracy. 2010. "By the People: Hard Times, Hard Choices: Michigan Residents Deliberate." Stanford University.

Centers for Medicare and Medicaid Services. 2010. "Data Compendium." In *Research, Statistics, Data and Systems*. Washington, D.C.: Centers for Medicare and Medicaid Services.

Cetina, Karin Knorr, and Alex Preda, eds. 2004. *The Sociology of Financial Markets*. New York: Oxford University Press.

Chadwick, Andrew. 2008. "Web 2.0: New Challenges for the Study of E-democracy in an Era of Informational Exuberance." *ISJLP* 5: 9.

Chambers, James D., and Peter J. Neumann. 2011. "Listening to Provenge—What a Costly Cancer Treatment Says about Future Medicare Policy." *New England Journal of Medicine*. 364: 1687–1689.

Chambers, Simone. 2003. "Deliberative Democratic Theory." *Annual Review of Political Science* 6: 307–326.

Charles, Julien. 2012. "Une participation éprouvante: Enquêtes sur l'autogestion, le management participatif, la participation citoyenne et l'empowerment." Doctoral dissertation, Department of Sociology, Université Catholique de Louvain, Louvain-la-Neuve, Belgium.

Charmaz, Kathy. 2006. *Constructing Grounded Theory: A Practical Guide through Qualitative Analysis*. London: Sage.

Chayko, Mary. 2008. *Portable Communities*. Albany: SUNY Press.

Chen, Katherine K. 2010. *Enabling Creative Chaos*. Chicago: University of Chicago Press.

Chimonas, Susan, Lisa Patterson, Victoria H. Raveis, and David J. Rothman. 2011. "Managing Conflicts of Interest in Clinical Care: A National Survey of Policies at US Medical Schools." *Academic Medicine* 86 (3): 293–299.

Clark, Anna. 1995. *The Struggle for the Breeches*. Berkeley: University of California Press.

Clavel, Pierre. 1986. *The Progressive City*. New Brunswick, N.J.: Rutgers University Press.

Cleaver, Frances. 1999. "Paradoxes of Participation: Questioning Participatory Approaches to Development." *Journal of International Development* 11: 597–612.

Clemens, Elisabeth S. 1997. *The People's Lobby*. Chicago: University of Chicago Press.

———. 2006. "The Constitution of Citizens: Political Theories of Nonprofit Organizations." In Walter Powell and Richard Steinberg, eds., *The Nonprofit Sector: A Research Handbook*. New Haven: Yale University Press.

Clemens, Elisabeth, and Doug Guthrie, eds. 2011. *Politics and Partnerships*. Chicago: University of Chicago Press.

Coetzee, Frans. 1990. *For Party or Country*. Oxford: Oxford University Press.

Coeytaux, Francine, and Barbara Pillsbury. 2001. "Bringing Emergency Contraception to American Women: The History and Remaining Challenges." *Women's Health Issues* 11 (2): 80–86.

Cohen, Jean L., and Andrew Arato. 1992. *Civil Society and Political Theory*. Cambridge: MIT Press.

Cohen, Jean L., and J. Rogers. 1995. *Associations and Democracy*. London: Verso.

Cohen, Joshua. 1989. "Deliberation and Democratic Legitimacy." In Alan Hamlin and Philip Pettit, eds., *The Good Polity*. London: Basil Blackwell.

Cohen, Lizabeth. 2003. *A Consumers' Republic*. New York: Knopf.

Coleman, Stephen. 2005. "The Lonely Citizen: Indirect Representation in an Age of Networks." *Political Communication* 22 (2): 197–214.

Collins, Randall. 2003. *Interaction Ritual Chains*. Princeton: Princeton University Press.

Compa, L. 2000. "Unfair Advantage: Workers' Freedom of Association in the United States under International Human Rights Standards." New York: Human Rights Watch.

———. 2008. "Labor's New Opening to International Human Rights Standards." *Journal of Labor and Society* 11 (March): 99–123.

Congressional Budget Office. 2008, December 23. "Factors Underlying the Decline in Manufacturing Employment since 2000." CBO Report. Washington, D.C.: U.S. Government Printing Office.

Connolly, S. 2004. "Unexpected Victories: Protecting Workers' Rights in Guatemala's Apparel-for-Export Sector." Master's thesis, Massachusetts Institute of Technology. Retrieved from http://dspace.mit.edu/bitstream/handle/1721.1/28801/60250058.pdf?sequence=1, on August 2, 2010.

Cooke, Bill, and Uma Kothari. 2001. *Participation: The New Tyranny?* London: Zed.

Cornes, Richard, and Todd Sandler. 1996. *The Theory of Externalities, Public Goods, and Club Goods*. Cambridge: Cambridge University Press.

Costain, Anne N. 1991. *Inviting Women's Rebellion*. Baltimore, Md.: Johns Hopkins University Press.

Crenson, Matthew A., and Benjamin Ginsberg. 2002. *Downsizing Democracy*. Baltimore, Md.: Johns Hopkins University Press.

Cruikshank, Barbara. 1999. *The Will to Empower*. Ithaca, N.Y.: Cornell University Press.

Cunningham, Randy. 2007. *Democratizing Cleveland*. Cleveland, Ohio: Arambala Press.

Dale, John G. 2010. *Free Burma*. Minneapolis: University of Minnesota Press.

Dalton, Russell. 2008. *The Good Citizen*. Washington, D.C.: CQ Press.

Davidson, Osha Gray. 2007. *The Best of Enemies*. Chapel Hill: University of North Carolina Press.

Davis, Gerald F., and Tracy A. Thompson. 1994. "A Social Movement Perspective on Corporate Control." *Administrative Science Quarterly* 39 (1): 141–173.

de Bakker, Frank G. A., Frank den Hond, Brayden King, and Klaus Weber. 2013. "Civil Society and Corporations: Taking Stock and Looking Ahead." *Organization Studies* 34: 573–593.

Delli Carpini, Michael X., Fay Lomax Cook, and Lawrence R. Jacobs. 2004. "Public Deliberation, Discursive Participation, and Citizen Engagement: A Review of the Empirical Literature." *Annual Review of Political Science* 7: 315–344.

Dembour, Marie-Benedicte. 2010. "What Are Human Rights? Four Schools of Thought." *Human Rights Quarterly* 32 (1): 1–20.

Dietz, Thomas, and Paul C. Stern, eds. 2008. *Public Participation in Environmental Assessment and Decision Making*. Washington, D.C.: National Research Council.

DiMaggio, Paul. 1988. "Interest and Agency in Institutional Theory." In L. G. Zucker, ed., *Institutional Patterns and Organizations*. New York: Ballinger.

DiMaggio, Paul J., and Walter W. Powell. 1983. "The Iron Cage Revisited: Institutional Isomorphism and Collective Rationality in Organizational Fields." *American Sociological Review* 48: 147–160.

Dixon, Marc. 2010. "Union Threat, Countermovement Organization, and Labor Policy in the States, 1944–1960." *Social Problems* 57: 157–174.

Donaldson, Thomas, and Lee E. Preston. 1995. "The Stakeholder Theory of the Corporation: Concepts, Evidence, and Implications." *Academy of Management Review* 20: 65–91.

Donovan, Todd, Shaun Bowler, and David McCuan. 2001. "Political Consultants and the Initiative Industrial Complex." In Larry J. Sabato, Howard R. Ernst, and Bruce A. Larson, eds., *Dangerous Democracy? The Battle over Ballot Initiatives in America*. Lanham, Md.: Rowman and Littlefield.

Dryzek, John S. 1990. *Discursive Democracy: Politics, Policy, and Political Science*. Cambridge, U.K.: Cambridge University Press.

———. 2000. *Deliberative Democracy and Beyond*. Oxford: Oxford University Press.

Duffy, Meghan M., Amy J. Binder, and John D. Skrentny. 2010. "Elite Status and Social Change: Using Field Analysis to Explain Policy Formation and Implementation." *Social Problems* 57: 49–73.

Dumont, Louis. 1986. *Essays on Individualism*. Chicago: University of Chicago Press.

DuPuis, E. Melanie. 2002. *Nature's Perfect Food*. New York: NYU Press.

Earl, Jennifer. 2003. "Tanks, Tear Gas and Taxes: Toward a Theory of Movement Repression." *Sociological Theory* 21: 44–68.

Earl, Jennifer, and Katrina Kimport. 2011. *Digitally Enabled Social Change: Activism in the Internet Age*. Cambridge: MIT Press.

Eesley, Charles, and Michael J. Lenox. 2006. "Firm Responses to Secondary Stakeholder Action." *Strategic Management Journal* 27: 765–781.

Eichler, Michael. 1998. "Organizing's Past, Present and Future." *Shelterforce*. Retrieved from http://www.nhi.org/online/issues/101/eichler.html on April 25, 2014.

Eksteins, Modris. 2000. *Rites of Spring*. New York: Mariner.

Eley, Geoff. 1980. *Reshaping the German Right*. New Haven: Yale University Press.

———. 1992. "Nations, Publics, and Political Cultures: Placing Habermas in the Nineteenth Century." In Craig Calhoun, ed., *Habermas and the Public Sphere*. Cambridge: MIT Press.

Eliasoph, Nina. 2009. "Top-Down Civic Projects Are Not Grassroots Associations: How the Differences Matter in Everyday Life." *Voluntas* 20: 291–308.

———. 2011. *Making Volunteers*. Princeton: Princeton University Press.

Elster, Jon. 1998. "Introduction." In Jon Elster, ed., *Deliberative Democracy*. New York: Cambridge University Press.

Epstein, James. 1994. *Radical Expression*. New York: Oxford University Press.

Epstein, Steven. 1996. *Impure Science*. Berkeley: University of California Press.

———. 2007. *Inclusion*. Chicago: University of Chicago Press.

———. 2008. "Patient Groups and Health Movements." In Edward J. Hackett, Olga Amsterdamska, Michael Lynch, and Judy Wajcman, eds., *The Handbook of Science and Technology Studies*. Cambridge: MIT Press.

Erikson, Erik. 1959. *Identity and the Life Cycle*. New York: International Universities Press.

Escobar, Arturo. 2010. "Latin America at a Crossroads: Alternative Modernizations, Post-liberalism, or Post-development?" *Cultural Studies* 24 (1): 1–65.

Eskow, Richard. 2010, June 23. "America 'Speaks' on Saturday, but There's an Anti-social Security Script." *Huffington Post*.

Espeland, Wendy Nelson, and Mitchell L. Stevens. 1998. "Commensuration as a Social Process." *Annual Review of Sociology* 24: 313–343.

Espenshade, J. 2004. *Monitoring Sweatshops*. Philadelphia: Temple University Press.

Evans, P. 2003. "Hybridity as an Administrative Strategy: Combining Bureaucratic Capacity with Market Signals and Deliberative Democracy." *Revista CLAD* 25: 1–15.

Evans, Sara. 1979. *Personal Politics*. New York: Vintage.

Evans, Sarah, and Harry Boyte. 1992. *Free Spaces*. Chicago: University of Chicago Press.

Exley, Zack. 2008. "The New Organizers, What's Really behind Obama's Ground Game." *Huffington Post*. Retrieved from http://www.huffingtonpost.com/zack-exley/the-new-organizers-part-1_b_132782.html on August 20, 2010.

Fagotto, Elena, and Archon Fung. 2006. "Embedded Deliberation: Entrepreneurs, Organizations, and Public Action." Report to the Hewlett Foundation.

Fainstein, Susan. 2005. "Ground Zero's Landlord: The Role of the Port Authority of New York and New Jersey in the Reconstruction of the World Trade Center Site." In John Mollenkopf, ed., *Contentious City: The Politics of Recovery in New York City*. New York: Russell Sage Foundation Press.

Ferguson, J. 2010. "The Uses of Neoliberalism." *Antipode* 41: 166–184.

Fernandez, Manny. 2003, November 16. "Sounding Off on City Problems; Housing, Schools, Crime Top Complaint List." *Washington Post*, C01.

Ferree, Myra Marx, William A. Gamson, Jurgen Gerhards, and Dieter Rucht. 2002. *Shaping Abortion Discourse*. Cambridge: Cambridge University Press.

Feuerstein, Adam. 2011. "Dendreon: Parsing Provenge's Problems." *The Street*. Retrieved from http://www.thestreet.com/story/11209599/1/dendreon-parsing-provenges-problems.html on April 25, 2014.

Field, Kelly. 2010, September 5. "For-Profits Spend Heavily to Fend Off New Rule." *Chronicle of*

Higher Education. Retrieved from http://chronicle.com/article/For-Profit-Colleges-Wage/124303/.
Fischer, Claude S. 2010. *Made in America: A Social History of American Culture and Character.* Chicago: University of Chicago Press.
Fischer, Frank. 2006. "Participatory Governance as Deliberative Empowerment: The Cultural Politics of Discursive Space." *American Review of Public Administration* 36: 19–40.
Fishkin, James S. 1991. *Democracy and Deliberation.* New Haven: Yale University Press.
———. 1995. *Voice of the People.* New Haven: Yale University Press.
Fleming, Peter. 2009. *Authenticity and the Cultural Politics of Work.* Oxford: Oxford University Press
Fligstein, Neil. 1996. "Markets as Politics: A Political-Cultural Approach to Market Institutions." *American Sociological Review* 61: 656–673.
Fligstein, Neil, and Taekjin Shin. 2007. "Shareholder Value and the Transformation of the U.S. Economy, 1984–2001." *Sociological Forum* 22 (4): 399–424.
Fombrun, Charles J., Naomi A. Gardberg, and Michael L. Barnett. 2000. "Opportunity Platforms and Safety Nets: Corporate Citizenship and Reputational Risk." *Business and Society Review* 105 (1):85–106.
Foner, Eric. 1970. *Free Soil, Free Labor, Free Men.* Oxford: Oxford University Press.
Foot, Kirsten A., and Steven M. Schneider. 2006. *Web Campaigning.* Cambridge: MIT Press.
Foote, Susan Bartlett. 2002. "Why Medicare Cannot Promulgate a National Coverage Rule: A Case of Regula Mortis." *Journal of Health Politics Policy and Law* 27 (5): 707–730.
Fourcade, Marion, and Kieran Healy. 2007. "Moral Views of Market Society." *Annual Review of Sociology* 33: 285–311.
Fraser, Nancy. 1992. "Rethinking the Public Sphere: A Contribution to the Critique of Actually Existing Democracy." In Craig Calhoun, ed., *Habermas and the Public Sphere.* Cambridge: MIT Press.
Freud, Sigmund. 2010. *Civilization and Its Discontents.* New York: Norton.
Frickel, Scott. 2004. *Chemical Consequences.* New Brunswick, N.J.: Rutgers University Press.
Frooman, Jeff. 1999. "Stakeholder Influence Strategies." *Academy of Management Review* 24: 191–205.
Frundt, H. 2000. "Models of Cross-Border Organizing in Maquila Industries." *Critical Sociology* 26 (1–2): 36–55.
———. 2002. "Central American Unions in the Era of Globalization." *Latin American Research Review* 37 (3): 7–53.
———. 2004. "Unions Wrestle with Corporate Codes of Conduct." *Working USA* 7 (4): 36–69.
Frye, Margaret. 2012. "Bright Futures in Malawi's New Dawn: Educational Aspirations as Assertions of Identity." *American Journal of Sociology* 117 (6): 1565–1624.
Fung, Archon. 2005. "Deliberation before the Revolution: Toward an Ethics of Deliberative Democracy in an Unjust World." *Political Theory* 33 (2): 397–419.
———. 2006. *Empowered Participation.* Princeton: Princeton University Press.
———. 2007. "Minipublics: Deliberative Designs and Their Consequences." In Shawn W. Rosenberg, ed., *Can the People Govern?* Hampshire, U.K.: Palgrave.
———. 2010, June 28. "Public Deliberation: The Left Should Learn to Trust Americans." *Huffington Post.*
Fung, Archon, and Erik Olin Wright. 2003a. *Deepening Democracy.* London: Verso.
———. 2003b. "Thinking about Empowered Participatory Governance." In Archon Fung and Erik Olin Wright, eds., *Deepening Democracy.* London: Verso.

Galaskiewicz, Joseph. 1985. *Social Organization of an Urban Grants Economy*. Orlando, Fla.: Academic Press.
———. 1991. "Making Corporate Actors Accountable: Institution-Building in Minneapolis–St. Paul." In Paul DiMaggio and Walter W. Powell, eds., *The New Institutionalism in Organizational Analysis*. Chicago: University of Chicago Press.
———. 1997. "An Urban Grants Economy Revisited: Corporate Charitable Contributions in the Twin Cities, 1979–81, 1987–89." *Administrative Science Quarterly* 42: 445–471.
Galaskiewicz, Joseph, and Ronald S. Burt. 1991. "Interorganization Contagion in Corporate Philanthropy." *Administrative Science Quarterly* 36: 88–105.
Garcia Bedolla, Lisa. 2010, December 8. "A Majority Minority State." Retrieved from http://www.nytimes.com/roomfordebate/2010/09/21/where-are-the-angry-california-voters/california-is-essentially-a-majority-minority-state.
Gastil, John. 2008. "A Comprehensive Approach to Evaluating Deliberative Public Engagement." Essay prepared for MASS-LBP and the Ontario Ministry of Health. Retrieved from http://ncdd.org/rc/item/4876.
Gastil, John, and Peter Levine, eds. 2005. *The Deliberative Democracy Handbook*. San Francisco: Jossey-Bass.
Gaventa, John. 2006. *Triumph, Deficit or Contestation?* Brighton, U.K.: Institute of Development Studies.
Genro, T. 1990. "Licoes da Intervencao." In J. A. d. Lima, ed., *A Intervencao Nos Transportes Coletivos*. São Paulo: CEDI.
———. 1999. "Um Debate Estratégico." In I. Magalhães, L. Barreto, and V. Trevas, eds., *Governo e Cidadania*. São Paulo: Editora Fundação Perseu Abramo.
Ginsberg, Benjamin, and Martin Shefter. 2002. *Politics by Other Means*. New York: Norton.
Giraudeau, Martin, and Jean-Pascal Gond. 2008. "Performativity as Politics: Unlocking Economic Sociology." Toulouse Workshop, October 23–24.
Gittell, Ross, and Avis Vidal. 1998. *Community Organizing*. Thousand Oaks, Calif.: Sage.
Givel, Michael. 2007. "Consent and Counter-Mobilization: The Case of the National Smokers Alliance." *Journal of Health Communication: International Perspectives* 12: 339–357.
Glaser, Barney, and Anselm Strauss. 1967. *The Discovery of Grounded Theory*. Chicago: Aldine.
Glickman, Lawrence B. 2009. *Buying Power*. Chicago: University of Chicago Press.
Goebel, Thomas. 2002. *A Government by the People*. Chapel Hill: University of North Carolina Press.
Goffman, Erving. 1959. *The Presentation of Self in Everyday Life*. Garden City, N.J.: Doubleday.
Goldberg, Arielle. 2005. "Civic Engagement in the Rebuilding of the World Trade Center." In John Mollenkopf, ed., *Contentious City*. New York: Russell Sage.
Goldberger, Paul. 2005. *Up From Zero: Politics, Architecture, and the Rebuilding of New York*. New York: Random House.
Goldscheid, Rudolf. 1917. *Staatssozialismus oder Staatskapitalismus*. Vienna: Duncker and Humblodt.
Goldstein, Kenneth M. 1999. *Interest Groups, Lobbying, and Participation in America*. New York: Cambridge University Press.
Goodin, Robert E. 2000. "Democratic Deliberation Within." *Philosophy and Public Affairs* 29 (1): 81–109.
Goodin, Robert E., and John S. Dryzek. 2006. "Deliberative Impacts: The Macro-political Uptake of Mini-publics." *Politics and Society* 34 (2): 219–244.
Goodin, Robert E., and Simon J. Niemeyer. 2003. "When Does Deliberation Begin? Internal

Reflection versus Public Discussion in Deliberative Democracy." *Political Studies* 51: 627–649.

Goodwyn, Lawrence. 1976. *Democratic Promise*. Oxford: Oxford University Press.

Goozner, Merrill. 2011. "Concerns about Provenge Simmer as CMS Ponders Coverage." *Journal of the National Cancer Institute* 103 (4): 288–289.

Gorney, Roderic. 1972. *The Human Agenda*. Los Angeles: Guild of Tutors Press.

Gorski, Eric. 2010. "Lobbyists Aid For-Profit College Student Group." *Huffington Post*. Retrieved from http://www.huffingtonpost.com/2010/06/14/lobbyists-aid-forprofit-c_n_610857.html.

Graeber, David. 2002. "The New Anarchists." *New Left Review* 13 (Jan.-Feb.): 61–73.

Grazia, G., and Ana Clara de Torres Ribeiro. 2002. *Orçamento participativo no Brasil*. Petrópolis: Editora Vozes.

Gregory, Steven. 1998. *Black Corona*. Princeton: Princeton University Press.

Greif, Karen F., and Jon F. Merz. 2007. *Current Controversies in the Biological Sciences*. Cambridge: MIT Press.

Gret, Marion, and Yves Sintomer. 2005. *The Porto Alegre Experiment: Learning Lessons for Better Democracy*. New York: Zed.

Griffin, Jennifer J., and Paul Dunn. 2004. "Corporate Public Affairs: Commitment, Resources, and Structure." *Business and Society* 43: 196–220.

Guins, Raiford. 2009. *Edited Clean Version: Technology and the Culture of Control*. Minneapolis: University of Minnesota Press.

Guthrie, Doug, Richard Arum, Josipa Roksa, and Sarah Damaske. 2008. "Giving to Local Schools: Corporate Philanthropy, Tax Incentives, and the Ecology of Need." *Social Science Research* 37: 856–873.

Guthrie, Doug, and Michael McQuarrie. 2008. "Providing for the Public Good: Corporate-Community Relations in the Era of the Receding Welfare State." *City and Community* 7: 113–139.

Gutmann, Amy. 1994. *Multiculturalism*. Princeton: Princeton University Press.

Gutmann, Amy, and Dennis Thompson. 2004. *Why Deliberative Democracy?* Princeton: Princeton University Press.

Habermas, Jürgen. 1984. *The Theory of Communicative Action*. Translated by Thomas McCarthy. Boston: Beacon.

———. 1985. "Civil Disobedience: Litmus Test for the Democratic State." Translated by John Torpey. *Berkeley Journal of Sociology* 30: 95–116.

———. 1989. *The Structural Transformation of the Public Sphere*. Cambridge: MIT Press.

———. 1996. *Between Facts and Norms*. Translated by William Rehg. Cambridge, U.K.: Polity Press.

Hacker, Jacob, and Paul Pierson. 2011. *Winner-Take-All Politics*. New York: Simon and Schuster.

Hajer, Maarten A. 2005. "Rebuilding Ground Zero: The Politics of Performance." *Planning Theory and Practice* 6: 445–464.

Hall, John. 2009. *Apocalypse from Antiquity to the Empire of Modernity*. New York: Polity Press.

Hallett, Tim, and Marc Ventresca. 2006a. "Inhabited Institutions: Social Interactions and Organizational Forms in Gouldner's Patterns of Industrial Bureaucracy." *Theory and Society* 35: 213–236.

Hallett, Tim, and Marc Ventresca. 2006b. "How Institutions Form: Loose Coupling as Mechanism in Gouldner's Patterns of Industrial Bureaucracy." *American Behavioral Scientist* 49: 908–924.

Hamill, Pete. 2002, July 22. "Thrilling Show of People Power." *New York Daily News*, 8.
Handler, Joel F. 1996. *Down from Bureaucracy*. Princeton: Princeton University Press.
Haney, Lynne. 2010. *Offending Women*. Berkeley: University of California Press.
Hannan, Michael T., and Glenn Carroll. 1992. *Dynamics of Organizational Populations*. New York: Oxford University Press.
Harnecker, M. 1993. *Brasil, la alcaldía de Porto alegre*. Cuba: Ediciones MEPLA.
Harrah's Entertainment. 2006. "You Have the Power." Retrieved from http://www.harrahs winningtogether.com/images/wtinsider/1170702115-wti_final_8_10_06%20(2).pdf on July 22, 2010.
Harris, John F. 2010, August 11. "Primary Night Yields Good News for President Obama and Democrats." *Politico*. Retrieved from http://www.politico.com/news/stories/0810/40941.html.
Harriss, John, Kristian Stokke, and Olle Törnquist, eds. 2004. *Politicising Democracy: The New Local Politics of Democratisation*. London: Palgrave.
Hawthorne, Fran. 2005. *Inside the FDA*. Hoboken, N.J.: John Wiley.
He, B. 2011. "Civic Engagement through Participatory Budgeting in China: Three Different Logics at Work." *Public Administration and Development* 31: 122–131.
Head, Brian W. 2007. "Community Engagement: Participation on Whose Terms?" *Australian Journal of Political Science* 42: 441–454.
Healy, Kieran. 2006. *Last Best Gifts*. Chicago: University of Chicago Press.
Heath, Robert L., William Douglas, and Michael Russell. 1995. "Constituency Building: Determining Employees' Willingness to Participate in Corporate Political Activities." *Journal of Public Relations Research* 7: 273–288.
Heimer, Carol, and Lisa Staffen. 1998. *For the Sake of the Children*. Chicago: University of Chicago Press.
Hendriks, Carolyn M. 2002. "Institutions of Deliberative Democratic Processes and Interest Groups: Roles, Tensions and Incentives." *Australian Journal of Public Administration* 61 (1): 64–75.
———. 2006. "When the Forum Meets Interest Politics: Strategic Uses of Public Deliberation." *Politics and Society* 34 (4): 571–602.
———. 2009. "Deliberative Governance in the Context of Power." *Policy and Society* 28: 173–184.
Hendriks, Carolyn M., and Lyn Carson. 2008. "Can the Market Help the Forum? Negotiating the Commercialization of Deliberative Democracy." *Policy Sciences* 41: 293–313.
Herdt, Timm. 2009, July 9. "CLU Hosting Town Hall on State Constitution Overhaul." *Ventura County Star*. Retrieved from http://www.vcstar.com/news/2009/jul/09/clu-hosting-town-hall-on-state-constitution/ on June 22, 2010.
Hess, David J. 2004. "Organic Food and Agriculture in the US: Object Conflicts in a Health-Environmental Social Movement." *Science as Culture* 13 (4): 493–513.
Hichborn, Franklin A. 1909. *The Story of the Session of the California Legislature of 1909*. San Francisco: J. H. Barry.
Hickey, Samuel, and Giles Mohan. 2006. "Participation—From Tyranny to Transformation? Exploring New Approaches to Participation in Development." *Progress in Development Studies* 6 (3): 292.
Higgens-Evenson, R. Rudy. 2003. *The Price of Progress*. Baltimore, Md.: Johns Hopkins University Press.

Hilgert, G. 2009. "Mapping the Boundaries of Human Rights at Work: Questioning How the ILO Defines Labor Rights and Social Justice." *Labor Studies Journal*, January 5.

Hillman, Amy J., and Michael A. Hitt. 1999. "Corporate Political Strategy Formulation: A Model of Approach, Participation, and Strategy Decisions." *Academy of Management Review* 24: 825–842.

Hillman, Amy J., Gerald D. Keim, and Douglas Schuler. 2004. "Corporate Political Activity: A Review and Research Agenda." *Journal of Management* 30: 837–857.

Hirschman, Albert O. 1970. *Exit, Voice, and Loyalty*. Cambridge: Harvard University Press.

———. 1982. "Rival Interpretations of Market Society: Civilizing, Destructive, or Feeble?" *Journal of Economic Literature* 20: 1463–1484.

Hoffman, Andrew J. 2001. *From Heresy to Dogma*. Stanford, Calif.: Stanford University Press.

Hoffman, Beatrix. 2010. "The Challenge of Universal Healthcare: Social Movements, Presidential Leadership and Private Power." In Jane Banaszak-Holl, Sandra Levitsky, and Mayer N. Zald, eds., *Social Movements and the Transformation of American Healthcare*. New York: Oxford University Press.

Horkheimer, Max, and Theodor Adorno. 2002. *Dialectic of Enlightenment*. Palo Alto, Calif.: Stanford University Press.

Howard, Philip N. 2006. *New Media Campaigns and the Managed Citizen*. Cambridge: Cambridge University Press.

Hughes, Virginia. 2010. "When Patients March In." *Nature Biotechnology* 28 (11): 1145–1148.

Ingram, Paul, Lori Qingyuan Yue, and Hayagreeva Rao. 2010. "Trouble in Store: Probes, Protests, and Store Openings by Wal-Mart, 1998–2007." *American Journal of Sociology* 116: 53–92.

Initiative and Referendum Institute. 2011. "California Statewide Initiatives." Retrieved from http://www.iandrinstitute.org/New%20IRI%20Website%20Info/I&R%20Research%20and%20History/I&R%20at%20the%20Statewide%20Level/Usage%20history/California.pdf.

Involve. 2005. *Full Report: The True Costs of Public Participation*. London: Involve. Retrieved from http://www.involve.org.uk/the_true_costs_of_public_participation/.

Jacobs, Lawrence R., Fay Lomax Cook, and Michael X. Delli Carpini. 2009. *Talking Together*. Chicago: University of Chicago Press.

Jacobs, Lawrence, Theodore Marmor, and Jonathan Oberlander. 1999. "The Oregon Health Plan and the Political Paradox of Rationing: What Advocates and Critics Have Claimed and What Oregon Did." *Journal of Health Politics, Policy and Law* 24 (1): 161–180.

Jalonick, Mary C. 2003. "Consultant Q&A: Grassroots Lobbying." *Campaigns and Elections* 24: 45–52.

Jasper, James. 1999. *The Art of Moral Protest*. Chicago: University of Chicago Press.

Jenkins, Henry. 2006. *Convergence Culture: Where Old and New Media Collide*. New York: NYU Press.

Johnson, Paul. 1978. *A Shopkeeper's Millennium: Society and Revivals in Rochester, New York, 1815–1837*. New York: Hill and Wang.

Kadlec, Alison, and Will Friedman. 2007. "Deliberative Democracy and the Problem of Power." *Journal of Public Deliberation* 3 (1): Article 8.

Kaminski, Margot. 2003. "PRISM's Legal Basis: How We Got Here, and What We Can Do to Get Back." *The Atlantic*. Retrieved from http://www.theatlantic.com/national/archive/2013/06/prisms-legal-basis-how-we-got-here-and-what-we-can-do-to-get-back/276667/ on June 10, 2013.

Kashefi, Elham, and Maggie Mort. 2004. "Grounded Citizens' Juries: A Tool for Health Activism?" *Health Expectations* 7: 290–302.
Katz, Jack. 2001. "From How to Why: On Luminous Description and Causal Inference in Ethnography." Part 1. *Ethnography* 2 (4): 443–473.
———. 2002. "From How to Why: On Luminous Description and Causal Inference in Ethnography." Part 2. *Ethnography* 3 (1): 63–90.
Kaufman, Leslie, and David Gonzalez. 2001, April 24. "Labor Standards Clash with Global Reality." *New York Times*, A10.
Kazin, Michael. *A Godly Hero*. New York: Anchor, 2007.
Keck, M., and K. Sikkink. 1998. *Activism beyond Borders*. Ithaca, N.Y.: Cornell University Press.
Kedrowski, Karen M., and Marilyn S. Sarow. 2007. *Cancer Activism*. Urbana: University of Illinois Press.
Kelty, Christopher. 2008. *Two Bits*. Durham, N.C.: Duke University Press.
Kennedy, David W. 2002. "The International Human Rights Movement: Part of the Problem?" *Harvard Human Rights Journal* 101 (15): 101–125.
Kennedy, Marie, and Chris Tilly. 2008. "Understanding Latin America's 'Third Left.'" *New Politics* 11: 4.
Keyssar, Alexander. 2000. *The Right to Vote*. New York: Basic Books.
Khimm, Suzy. 2011, April 22. "Dems Warn Constituents about the Evils of RyanCare." *Mother Jones*. Retrieved from http://motherjones.com/mojo/2011/04/democrats-attack-ryan-plan-medicare.
King, Samantha. 2006. *Pink Ribbons, Inc.* Minneapolis: University of Minnesota Press.
King, Brayden G. 2008. "A Political Mediation Model of Corporate Response to Social Movement Activism." *Administrative Science Quarterly* 53: 395–421.
King, Brayden G., and Sarah A. Soule. 2007. "Social Movements as Extra-institutional Entrepreneurs: The Effect of Protests on Stock Price Returns." *Administrative Science Quarterly* 52 (3): 413–442.
Kleinman, Daniel Lee. 2003. *Impure Cultures*. Madison: University of Wisconsin Press.
Kloppenburg, Jack Ralph. 1988. *First the Seed*. Cambridge, U.K.: Cambridge University Press.
Knight, G., and D. Wells. 2007. "Bringing the Local Back In: Trajectory of Contention and the Union Struggle at Kukdong/Mexmode." *Social Movement Studies* 6 (1): 83–103.
Knight, J., and J. Johnson. 1997. "What Sort of Political Equality Does Deliberative Democracy Require?" In James Bohman and William Rehg, eds., *Deliberative Democracy: Essays on Reason and Politics*. Cambridge: MIT Press.
Kolben, K. 2010. "Labor Rights as Human Rights." *Virginia Journal of International Law* 50: 449–484.
Koopmans, Ruud. 2004. "Movements and Media: Selection Processes and Evolutionary Dynamics in the Public Sphere." *Theory and Society* 33: 367–391.
Kornhauser, William. 2008. *The Politics of Mass Society*. Piscataway, N.J.: Transaction.
Kreiss, Daniel. 2009. "Developing the 'Good Citizen': Digital Artifacts, Peer Networks, and Formal Organization during the 2003–2004 Howard Dean Campaign." *Journal of Information Technology and Politics* 6 (3/4): 281–297.
———. 2012. *Taking Our Country Back*. New York: Oxford University Press.
Kretzman, John, and John McKnight. 1993. "Building Communities from the Inside Out: A Path toward Finding and Mobilizing a Community's Assets." Evanston, Ill.: Institute for Policy Research.
———. 2005. "Discovering Community Power: A Guide to Mobilizing Local Assets and Your

Organization's Capacity." Evanston, Ill.: Assets-Based Community Development Institute, Northwestern University/Kellogg Foundation.

Krumholz, Norman, W. Dennis Keating, Philip D. Star, and Mark C. Chupp. 2006. "The Long-Term Impact of CDCs on Urban Neighborhoods: Case Studies of Cleveland's Broadway-Slavic Village and Tremont Neighborhoods." *Community Development* 37 (4): 33–52.

Kuttner, Robert. 1980. *The Revolt of the Haves: Tax Rebellions and Hard Times.* New York: Simon and Schuster.

Kweit, Mary Grisez, and Robert W. Kweit. 1981. *Implementing Citizen Participation in a Bureaucratic Society.* New York: Praeger.

Lampland, Martha, and Susan Leigh Star. 2009. *Standards and Their Stories.* Ithaca, N.Y.: Cornell University Press.

Lascoumes, P., and P. Le Gales. 2007. "Introduction: Understanding Public Policy through Its Instruments? From the Nature of Instruments to the Sociology of Public Policy Instrumentation." *Governance* 20 (1): 1–21.

Latour, Bruno. 1987. *Science in Action.* Cambridge: Harvard University Press.

———. 2005. *Reassembling the Social, an Introduction to Actor-Network-Theory.* Oxford: Oxford University Press.

Law, J. 2002. "Objects and Spaces." *Theory, Culture and Society* 19: 91–105.

Law, J., and A. Mol. 2001. "Situating Technoscience: An Inquiry into Spatialities." *Environment and Planning D* 19: 609–621.

Leahy, Michael, Hans Löfgren, and Evelyne de Leeuw. 2011. "Consumer Groups and the Democratization of Health Policy." In Hans Löfgren, Evelyne de Leeuw, and Michael Leahy, eds., *Democratizing Health.* Cheltenham, U.K.: Elgar.

Leal, Pablo Alejandro. 2007. "Participation: The Ascendancy of a Buzzword in the Neo-liberal Era." *Development in Practice* 17 (4): 539–548.

Lee, Caroline W. 2007. "Is There a Place for Private Conversation in Public Dialogue? Comparing Stakeholder Assessments of Informal Communication in Collaborative Regional Planning." *American Journal of Sociology* 113 (1): 41–96.

———. 2011. "Five Assumptions Academics Make about Public Deliberation, and Why They Deserve Rethinking." *Journal of Public Deliberation* 7: 1–48.

Lee, Caroline W., Kelly McNulty, and Sarah Shaffer. 2013. "'Hard Times, Hard Choices': Marketing Retrenchment as Civic Empowerment in an Era of Neoliberal Crisis." *Socio-Economic Review* 11: 81–106.

Lee, Caroline W., and Francesca Polletta. 2009. "The 2009 Dialogue and Deliberation Practitioners Survey." Retrieved from http://sites.lafayette.edu/ddps/.

Lee, Caroline W., and Zachary Romano. 2013. "Democracy's New Discipline: Public Deliberation as Organizational Strategy." *Organization Studies* 34 (5–6): 733–753.

Leibovich, Mark. 2010, September 29. "Being Glenn Beck." *New York Times Sunday Magazine.* Retrieved from http://www.nytimes.com/2010/10/03/magazine/03beck-t.html.

Leighninger, Matt. 2006. *The Next Form of Democracy.* Nashville, Tenn.: Vanderbilt University Press.

———. 2009a. "Creating Spaces for Change." W. K. Kellogg Foundation.

———. 2009b. "Funding and Fostering Local Democracy: What Philanthropy Should Know about the Emerging Field of Deliberation and Democratic Governance." Denver, Colo.: Philanthropy for Active Civic Engagement.

Lerbinger, Otto. 2006. *Corporate Public Affairs.* London: Routledge.

Lerner, Barron H. 2001. *The Breast Cancer Wars.* New York: Oxford University Press.

Levi, Margaret. 1989. *Of Rule and Revenue*. Berkeley: University of California Press.
Levine, Peter, and Rose Marie Nierras. 2007. "Activists' Views of Deliberation." *Journal of Public Deliberation* 3 (1): Article 4.
Levitsky, Sandra, and Jane Banaszak-Holl. 2010. "Social Movements and the Transformation of U.S. Healthcare: Introduction." In Jane Banaszak-Holl, Sandra Levitsky, and Mayer N. Zald, eds., *Social Movements and the Transformation of American Healthcare*. New York: Oxford University Press.
Li, Tania Murray. 2005. *The Will to Improve: Governmentality, Development, and the Practice of Politics*. Durham, N.C.: Duke University Press.
Lichtblau, Eric. 2011, December 9. "With Lobbying Blitz, For-Profit Colleges Diluted New Rules." *New York Times*.
Lichtenstein, Nelson. 2003. "The Rights Revolution." *New Labor Forum* 12 (1): 61–73.
Lichterman, Paul. 2002. "Seeing Structure Happen." In Bert Klandermans and Suzanne Staggenborg, eds. *Methods of Social Movement Research*. Minneapolis: University of Minnesota Press.
Lippmann, Walter. 1925. *The Phantom Public*. New York: Harcourt Brace.
———. 1997. *Public Opinion*. New York: Free Press.
Lipset, Seymour Martin, and George Trow. 1956. *Union Democracy*. New York: Free Press.
Lipsky, Michael. 1968. "Protest as a Political Resource." *American Political Science Review* 62: 1144–1158.
———. 1970. *Protest in City Politics*. Chicago: Rand-McNally.
Liptak, Adam. 2013, June 13. "Justices, 9–0, Bar Patenting Human Genes." *New York Times*, A1.
Listening to the City. 2002. "Listening to the City, Final Report." Retrieved from www.listeningtothecity.org/background/final_report_9_20.pdf.
Lo, Clarence. 1990. *Small Property versus Big Government: The Social Origins of the Property Tax Revolt*. Berkeley: University of California Press.
Logan, John, and Harvey Molotch. 1987. *Urban Fortunes*. Berkeley: University of California Press.
Loncar, Bradley. 2011. "Shareholder Proposal Presented to Richard Brewer, Chairman of the Board, Dendreon Corporation." Lenexa, Kan.: Office of Brad Loncar.
Lopatto, Elizabeth. 2012. "Dendreon Surges after Fourth-Quarter Product Revenue Triples." *San Francisco Chronicle*.
Lord, Michael D. 2000a. "Constituency-Based Lobbying as Corporate Political Strategy: Testing an Agency Theory Perspective." *Business and Politics* 2: 289–308.
———. 2000b. "Corporate Political Strategy and Legislative Decision Making." *Business and Society* 39: 76–93.
———. 2003. "Constituency Building as the Foundation for Corporate Political Strategy." *Academy of Management Executive* 17: 112–124.
Lounsbury, Michael, Marc Ventresca, and Paul M. Hirsch. 2003. "Social Movements, Field Frames and Industry Emergence: A Cultural-Political Perspective on US Recycling." *Socio-Economic Review* 1: 71–104.
Lovan, W. Robert, Michael Murray, and Ron Shaffer, eds. 2004. *Participatory Governance*. Burlington, Vt.: Ashgate.
Lower Manhattan Development Corporation (LMDC). 2002. *Principles and Preliminary Blueprint for the Future of Lower Manhattan*. New York: LMDC.
Lucas, J. Anthony 1986. *Common Ground*. New York: Vintage.

Luders, Joseph. 2006. "The Economics of Movement Success: Business Responses to Civil Rights Mobilization." *American Journal of Sociology* 111 (4): 963–998.

Lukensmeyer, Carolyn J. 2007. "Large-Scale Citizen Engagement and the Rebuilding of New Orleans: A Case Study." *National Civic Review* 182: 3–15.

Lukensmeyer, Carolyn J., and Steve Brigham. 2002. "Taking Democracy to Scale: Creating a Town Hall Meeting for the Twenty-First Century." *National Civic Review* 91 (4): 351–366.

Lukes, Steven. 1982. "Can a Marxist Believe in Human Rights?" *Praxis* 1 (4): 334–345.

Lyon, Thomas P., and John W. Maxwell. 2008. "Corporate Social Responsibility and the Environment: A Theoretical Perspective." *Review of Environmental Economics and Policy* 2: 240–260.

MacIntyre, Alasdair. 1981. *After Virtue*. South Bend, Ind.: University of Notre Dame Press.

Macklem, Patrick. 2004, July. "The Right to Bargain Collectively in International Law: Workers' Right, Human Right, International Right?" University of Toronto Public Law Research Paper No. 04-14.

Maginn, Paul J. 2007. "Deliberative Democracy or Discursively Biased? Perth's Dialogue with the City Initiative." *Space and Polity* 11: 331–352.

Magliari, Michael. 1989. "Populism, Steamboats, and the Octopus: Transportation Rates and Monopoly in California's Wheat Regions, 1890–1896." *Pacific Historical Review* 58 (4): 449–469.

Magzamen, Sheryl, Annemarie Charlesworth, and Stanton A Glantz. 2001. "Print Media Coverage of California's Smokefree Bar Law." *Tobacco Control* 10: 154–160.

Mann, Michael. 1980. "State and Society, 1130–1815: An Analysis of English State Finances." *Political Power and Social Theory* 1: 165–208.

Mansbridge, Jane. 1980. *Beyond Adversary Democracy*. Chicago: University of Chicago Press.

———. 1987. *Why We Lost the ERA*. Chicago: University of Chicago Press.

———. 2007. "Deliberative Democracy or Democratic Deliberation." In Shawn Rosenberg, ed., *Deliberation, Participation and Democracy: Can the People Govern?* New York: Palgrave Macmillan.

Marcus, Alfred A., and Mark S. Irion. 1987. "The Continued Growth of the Corporate Public Affairs Function." *Academy of Management Executive* 1: 247–250.

Marcus, George. 1998. "Ethnography in/of the World System: The Emergence of Multi-sited Ethnography." In George Marcus, ed., *Ethnography through Thick and Thin*. Princeton: Princeton University Press.

Marcuse, Herbert. 1964. *One-Dimensional Man*. Boston: Beacon.

Marquis, Christopher, Mary Ann Glynn, and Gerald F. Davis. 2007. "Community Isomorphism and Corporate Social Action." *Academy of Management Review* 32: 925–945.

Marshall, T. H. 1950. *Class, Citizenship, and Social Development*. New York: Anchor.

Martin, Andrew W. 2008. "The Institutional Logic of Union Organizing and the Effectiveness of Social Movement Repertoires." *American Journal of Sociology* 113: 1067–1103.

Martin, Jonathan, and James Hohmann. 2010, September 18. "'Values Voters' Tell Republicans: You Still Need Us." *Politico*. Retrieved from http://www.politico.com/news/stories/0910/42370.html.

Marwell, Nicole. 2004. "Privatizing the Welfare State: Nonprofit Community-Based Organizations as Political Actors." *American Sociological Review* 69: 265–291.

———. 2007. *Bargaining for Brooklyn*. Chicago: University of Chicago Press.

Mayer, Jane. 2010, August 21. "Covert Operations: The Billionaire Brothers Who Are Waging a War against Obama." *The New Yorker*. Retrieved from http://www.newyorker.com/reporting/2010/08/30/100830fa_fact_mayer.

McAdam, Doug. 1982. *Political Process and the Development of Black Insurgency, 1930–1970*. Chicago: University of Chicago Press.

———. 1983. "Tactical Innovation and the Pace of Insurgency." *American Sociological Review* 48: 735–754.

McCormick, Sabrina, Phil Brown, and Stephen Zavestocki. 2003. "The Personal Is Scientific, the Scientific Is Political: The Public Paradigm of the Environmental Breast Cancer Movement." *Sociological Forum* 18 (4): 545–576.

McCoy, Martha L., and Patrick L. Scully. 2002. "Deliberative Dialogue to Expand Civic Engagement: What Kind of Talk Does Democracy Need?" *National Civic Review* 91 (2): 117–135.

McCuan, David, Shaun Bowler, Todd Donovan, and Ken Fernandez. 1998. "California's Political Warriors: Campaign Professionals and the Initiative Process." In Shaun Bowler, Todd Donovan, and Caroline J. Tolbert, eds., *Citizens as Legislators: Direct Democracy in the United States*. Columbus: Ohio State University Press.

McCubbins, Colin H., and Matthew McCubbins. 2010. "Proposition 13 and the Fiscal Shell Game." *California Journal of Politics and Policy* 2 (2): Article 6.

McFall, Liz. 2009. "Devices and Desires: How Useful Is the 'New' New Economic Sociology for Understanding Market Attachment?" *Sociology Compass* 3: 267–282.

McGerr, Michael E. 1988. *The Decline of Popular Politics*. New York: Oxford University Press.

McGrath, Mike. 2009. "The New Laboratories of Democracy: How Local Government Is Reinventing Civic Engagement." National Civic League.

McIvor, David W., Derek W. M. Barker, and Noëlle McAfee, eds. 2012. *Democratizing Deliberation*. Dayton, Ohio: Kettering Foundation Press.

McQuarrie, Michael 2013a. "Community Organizations in the Foreclosure Crisis: The Failure of Neoliberal Civil Society." *Politics and Society* 41 (1): 73–101.

———. 2013b. "No Contest: Technologies of Participation and the Transformation of Urban Authority." *Public Culture* 25 (1): 143–175.

McVeigh, Rory. 2009. *The Rise of the Ku Klux Klan*. Minneapolis: University of Minnesota Press.

McWilliams, Abagail, and Donald Siegel. 2001. "Corporate Social Responsibility: A Theory of the Firm Perspective." *Academy of Management Review* 26: 117–127.

McWilliams, Abagail, Donald S. Siegel, and Patrick M. Wright. 2006. "Corporate Social Responsibility: Strategic Implications." *Journal of Management Studies* 43 (1): 1–18.

MEDCAC. 2010a. "Draft Questions: Autologous Cellular Immunotherapy Treatment of Metastatic Prostate Cancer." Baltimore, Md.: Centers for Medicare and Medicaid Services.

———. 2010b. "Provenge Hearing Transcript." Baltimore, Md.: Centers for Medicare and Medicaid Services.

Mendelberg, Tali. 2002. "The Deliberative Citizen: Theory and Evidence." In Michael X. Delli Carpini, Leonie Huddy, and Robert Y. Shapiro, eds., *Political Decision Making, Deliberation and Participation*. Amsterdam: JAI.

Merry, Sally E. 2000. "Crossing Boundaries: Ethnography in the Twenty-First Century." *PoLAR: The Political and Legal Anthropology Review* 23: 127–133.

Meyer, David S. 1990. *A Winter of Discontent*. New York: Praeger.

———. 2004. "Protest and Political Opportunities." *Annual Review of Sociology* 30: 125–145.

Meyer, David S., and Catherine Corrigall-Brown. 2005. "Coalitions and Political Context: U.S. Movements against Wars in Iraq." *Mobilization* 10: 327–344.

Meyer, David S., and Debra Minkoff. 2004. "Conceptualizing Political Opportunity." *Social Forces* 82 (4): 1457–1492.

Meyer, David S., and Amanda Pullum. 2014. "The Tea Party and the Dilemmas of Conservative Populism." In Nella van Dyke and David S. Meyer, eds., *Understanding the Tea Party Movement*. Surrey, U.K.: Ashgate.

Meyer, David S., and Sidney Tarrow. 1998. "Introduction." In David S. Meyer and Sidney Tarrow, eds., *The Social Movement Society*. Lanham, Md.: Rowman and Littlefield.

Meyer, David S., and Suzanne Staggenborg. 1996. "Movements, Countermovements, and the Structure of Political Opportunity." *American Journal of Sociology* 101: 1628–1660.

Meyer, John W., and Brian Rowan. 1977. "Institutionalized Organizations: Formal Structure as Myth and Ceremony." *American Journal of Sociology* 83: 340–363.

Meznar, Martin B., and Douglas Nigh. 1995. "Buffer or Bridge? Environmental and Organizational Determinants of Public Affairs Activities in American Firms." *Academy of Management Journal* 38: 975–996.

Michels, Robert. 1959. *Political Parties*. Translated by Eden and Cedar Paul. New York: Dover.

Midthun, Karen. 2011. "Letter to Michael Labson and Carla Cartwright, Re: Docket FDA 2010-N-0621; Avastin." Rockville, Md.: Food and Drug Administration.

Miller, James. 1987. *Democracy Is in the Streets*. Cambridge: Harvard University Press.

Miller, Warren E., and National Election Studies/Center for Political Studies. 2000. "American National Election Study, 1978." Computer file. Conducted by University of Michigan, Center for Political Studies. 3rd ICPSR ed. Ann Arbor, MI: Inter-university Consortium for Political and Social Research.

Mills, C. Wright. 2000. *The Power Elite*. New York: Oxford University Press.

Mills, Joel. 2007. "Designer Democracy and the Future of National Renewal." Paper presented at Global Democracy Conference, Longwood University.

Minkoff, Debra, Silke Aisenbrey, and Jon Agnone. 2008. "Organizational Diversity in the US Advocacy Sector." *Social Problems* 55 (4): 525–548.

Minkoff, Debra C., and Walter W. Powell. 2006. "Nonprofit Mission: Constancy, Responsiveness, or Deflection?" In Walter W. Powell and Richard Steinberg, eds., *The Non-profit Sector: A Research Handbook*, 2nd ed. New Haven: Yale University Press.

Mische, Ann. 2009. *Partisan Publics*. Princeton: Princeton University Press.

Molinier, Pascale. 2005. "Le care á l'épreuve du travail: Vulnérabilités croisées et savoirs-faires discrets." In Patricia Paperman and Sandra Laugier, eds., *Le Souci des Autres*, Vol. 16. Paris: Éditions de l'École des Hautes Études en Sciences Sociales.

Molotch, Harvey. 1976. "The City as a Growth Machine: Toward a Political Economy of Place." *American Journal of Sociology* 82: 309–332.

Morone, James A. 1998. *The Democratic Wish*. New Haven: Yale University Press.

Mosley, L., and S. Uno. 2007. "Racing to the Bottom or Climbing to the Top? Economic Globalization and Collective Labor Rights." *Comparative Political Studies* 40: 923–948.

Mosse, David. 2003. "The Making and Marketing of Participatory Development." In Philip Quarles van Ufford and Ananta Kumar Giri, eds., *A Moral Critique of Development: In Search of Global Responsibilities*. London: Routledge.

Mouffe, Chantal. 1996. "Democracy, Power and 'The Political.'" In Seyla Benhabib, ed., *Democracy and Difference*. Princeton: Princeton University Press.

Mudge, Stephanie Lee. 2008. "What Is Neo-liberalism?" *Socio-Economic Review* 6 (4): 703–731.

Murphy, Michelle. 2006. *Sick Building Syndrome and the Problem of Uncertainty*. Durham, N.C.: Duke University Press.

Mutz, Diana. 2008. "Is Deliberative Democracy a Falsifiable Theory?" *Annual Review of Political Science* 11: 521–538.
Nathanson, Constance A. 2010. "The Limitations of Social Movements as Catalysts for Change." In Jane Banaszak-Holl, Sandra Levitsky, and Mayer N. Zald, eds., *Social Movements and the Transformation of American Healthcare*. New York: Oxford University Press.
National Conference on Citizenship. 2007. "America's Civic Health Index." Retrieved from http://www.ncoc.net/index.php?tray=content&tid=top5&cid=99.
Navarro, Z. 1996. "'Participatory Budgeting'—the Case of Porto Alegre (Brazil)." In *Regional Workshop: Decentralization in Latin America—Innovations and Policy Implications*. Caracas, Venezuela.
Nelson, Alondra. 2011. *Body and Soul*. Minneapolis: University of Minnesota Press.
Nestle, Marion. 2001. "Food Company Sponsorship of Nutrition Research and Professional Activities: A Conflict of Interest?" *Public Health Nutrition* 4 (5): 1015–1022.
———. 2002. *Food Politics*. Berkeley: University of California Press.
Neuman, Tricia. 2010. "Medicare 101: The Basics." Kaiser Family Foundation.
New York Times/CBS News. 2010. "National Survey of Tea Party Supporters." Retrieved from http://documents.nytimes.com/new-york-timescbs-news-poll-national-survey-of-tea-party-supporters?ref=politics--document/p38.
Newcomer, Mabel. 1917. "Separation of State and Local Revenues in the United States." PhD dissertation, Columbia University Department of Political Science.
Nielsen, Rasmus Kleis. 2012. *Ground Wars*. Princeton: Princeton University Press.
9-12 Project, The. 2009. "9 Principles, 12 Values." Retrieved from http://www.the912project.com/the-912-2/.
Norman, Donald A., and Bryan Collyer. 2011. *The Design of Everyday Things*. Old Saybrook, Conn.: Tantor Media, 2011.
Norris, Pippa. 2002. *Democratic Phoenix*. New York: Cambridge University Press.
Novas, Carlos. 2006. "The Political Economy of Hope: Patients' Organizations, Science and Biovalue." *BioSocieties* 1 (3): 289–305.
O'Donovan, Orla. 2007. "Corporate Colonization of Health Activism? Irish Health Advocacy Organizations' Modes of Engagement with Pharmaceutical Corporations." *International Journal of Health Services* 37 (4): 711–733.
Olin, Spencer C., Jr. 1966. "Hiram Johnson, the Lincoln-Roosevelt League, and the Election of 1910." *California Historical Society Quarterly* 45 (3): 225–240.
Oliver, Christine, and Ingo Holzinger. 2008. "The Effectiveness of Strategic Political Management: A Dynamic Capabilities Framework." *Academy of Management Review* 33: 496–520.
Oliver, Christine. 1991. "Strategic Responses to Institutional Processes." *Academy of Management Review* 16: 145–179.
Ong, S. 2006. *Neoliberalism as Exception: Mutations in Citizenship and Sovereignty*. Durham, N.C.: Duke University Press.
Orsi, Fabienne, and Cristina d'Almeida. 2010. "Soaring Antiretroviral Prices, TRIPS and TRIPS Flexibilities: A Burning Issue for Antiretroviral Treatment Scale-Up in Developing Countries." *Current Opinion in HIV and AIDS* 5 (3): 237–241.
Ostrom, Elinor. 1990. *Governing the Commons*. Cambridge, U.K.: Cambridge University Press.
Panofsky, Aaron. 2011. "Generating Sociability to Drive Science: Patient Advocacy Organizations and Genetics Research." *Social Studies of Science* 41: 31–57.
Patel, Kavita. 2010. "Health Reform's Tortuous Route to the Patient-Centered Outcomes Research Institute." *Health Affairs* 29 (10): 1777–1782.

Pateman, Carole. 1970. *Participation and Democratic Theory*. Cambridge, U.K.: Cambridge University Press.

Payne, Charles M. 1995. *I've Got the Light of Freedom*. Berkeley: University of California Press.

Peck, J. 2011. "Geographies of Policy: From Transfer-Diffusion to Mobility-Mutation." *Progress in Human Geography* 34: 773–797.

Peck, J., and N. Theodore. 2010. "Mobilizing Policy: Models, Methods, and Mutations." *Geoforum* 41: 169–174.

Pedersen, Martin C. 2002. "Missing Persons: Who Will—and Won't—Be Deciding What Gets Built at the World Trade Center Site." *Metropolis* 21 (6): 20–30.

Perrow, Charles. 1961. "Organizational Prestige: Some Functions and Dysfunctions." *American Journal of Sociology* 66: 335–341.

Perrucci, Carolyn C., Robert Perrucci, Dena B. Targ, and Harry R. Targ. 1988. *Plant Closings*. Hawthorne, N.Y.: Aldine De Gruyter.

Pharr, Susan J., and Robert D. Putnam. 2000. *Disaffected Democracies*. Princeton: Princeton University Press.

Pincock, Heather. 2012. "Does Deliberation Make Better Citizens?" In Tina Nabatchi and John Gastil, eds., *Democracy in Motion: Evaluating the Practice and Impact of Deliberative Civic Engagement*. New York: Oxford University Press.

Pipkin, S. 2004. "Written in Invisible Ink: A Case Study on the Politics of Free Trade Reform and Labor Regulation in Guatemala." Master's thesis, Massachusetts Institute of Technology. Retrieved from http://dspace.mit.edu/bitstream/handle/1721.1/37666/124064353.pdf?sequence=1 on August 2, 2010.

Plankey Videla. Nancy. 2012. *We Are in This Dance Together*. New Brunswick, N.J.: Rutgers University Press.

Plehn, Carl C. 1907. "Revenue Systems of State and Local Governments: A Digest of Constitutional and Statutory Provisions Relating to Taxation in the Different States and Territories in 1902." Washington, D.C.: Government Printing Office.

———. 1911. "Tax Reform in California." *American Review of Reviews* 43: 85–87.

———. 1912. "Tax Reform in California." *Proceedings of the Fifth Annual Conference on State and Local Taxation under the Auspices of the National Tax Association*: 114–136.

Pocock, J. G. A. 1975. *The Machiavellian Moment*. Princeton: Princeton University Press.

Podolny, Joel M., and Karen L. Page. 1998. "Network Forms of Organization." *Annual Review of Sociology* 24: 57–76.

Pogrebin, Robin. 2004, June 20. "The Incredible Shrinking Daniel Libeskind." *New York Times*, 1.

Polletta, Francesca. 2002. *Freedom Is an Endless Meeting*. Chicago: University of Chicago Press.

———. 2007. "Just Talk: Public Deliberation after 9/11." *Journal of Public Deliberation* 4 (1): Article 2.

Polletta, Francesca, and Pang Ching Bobby Chen. 2013. "Gender and Public Talk: Accounting for Women's Variable Participation in the Public Sphere." *Sociological Theory* 31 (4): 291–317.

Polletta, Francesca, Pang Ching Bobby Chen, and Christopher Anderson. 2008. "Is Information Good for Democracy? Link-Posting in an Online Forum." *Journal of Public Deliberation* 5 (1): Article 2.

Polletta, Francesca, and John Lee. 2006. "Is Telling Stories Good for Democracy? Rhetoric in Public Deliberation after 9/11." *American Sociological Review* 71 (5): 699-721.

Polletta, Francesca, and Lesley Wood. 2005. "Public Deliberation after 9/11." In Nancy Foner,

ed., *Wounded City: The Social Effects of the World Trade Center Attack on New York City.* New York: Russell Sage Foundation Press.
Polsby, Nelson W. 1983. *Consequences of Party Reform.* New York: Oxford University Press.
Poole, Keith T., and Howard Rosenthal. 2001. "D-Nominate after 10 Years: A Comparative Update to Congress: A Political-Economic History of Roll-Call Voting." *Legislative Studies Quarterly* 26: 5–29.
Porter, Michael E., and Mark R. Kramer. 2002. "The Competitive Advantage of Corporate Philanthropy." *Harvard Business Review* 80: 56–68.
Postel, Charles. 2007. *The Populist Vision.* New York: Oxford University Press.
Potoski, Matthew, and Aseem Prakash, eds. 2009. *Voluntary Programs: A Club Theory Perspective.* Cambridge: MIT Press.
Prostate Cancer Roundtable. 2010. "Prostate Cancer Roundtable Issues a 'Red Alert'—MEDCAC Meeting Tomorrow." PR Newswire.
Public Affairs Council. 1998. "Public Affairs: Its Origin, Its Present, and Its Trends." Retrieved from http://web.archive.org/web/19980111071443/pac.org/whatis/index.htm on July 22, 2010.
———. 2008. *Grassroots Benchmarking Report.* Washington, D.C.: Public Affairs Council.
———. 2010. "Frequently Asked Questions." Retrieved from http://pac.org/faq on July 22, 2010.
Putnam, Robert D. 2001. *Bowling Alone.* New York: Simon and Schuster.
Quinn, Sarah. 2008. "The Transformation of Morals in Markets: Death, Benefits, and the Exchange of Life Insurance Policies." *American Journal of Sociology* 114: 738–780.
Raban, Jonathan. 2010, March 25. "At the Tea Party." *New York Review of Books.* Retrieved from http://www.nybooks.com/articles/archives/2010/mar/25/at-the-tea-party/.
Radkau, Joachim. 2009. *Max Weber.* Cambridge, U.K.: Polity.
Raeburn, Nicole Christine. 2004. *Changing Corporate America from Inside Out.* Minneapolis: University of Minnesota Press.
Ragin, Charles, and Howard Becker. 1992. *What Is a Case?* Cambridge, U.K.: Cambridge University Press.
Randolph, Eleanor, and Verlyn Klinkenborg. 2006, October 18. "At Ground Zero, a Grand Vision in Retreat." *New York Times.*
Rao, Hayagreeva. 2008. *Market Rebels.* Princeton: Princeton University Press.
Rao, Hayagreeva, Calvin Morrill, and Mayer N. Zald. 2000. "Power Plays: How Social Movements and Collective Action Create New Organizational Forms." *Research in Organizational Behavior* 22: 237–282.
Raphaelidis, Leia. 1997. "Sewing Discontent in Nicaragua: The Harsh Regime of Asian Garment Companies in Nicaragua." *Multinational Monitor* 18 (9). Retrieved from http://multinationalmonitor.org/hyper/mm0997.08.html on August 2, 2010.
Rauch, Jonathan. 2010, September 11. "How Tea Party Organizes without Leaders." *National Journal.* Retrieved from http://www.nationaljournal.com/njmagazine/cs_20100911_8855.php.
Rawls, John. 1971. *Theory of Justice.* Oxford: Oxford University Press.
RetireSafe. 2011. "Baseline Issues: Where We Stand." RetireSafe.
Richmond Tea Party. 2010. "Cuccinelli Gives Report on Health Care Lawsuit." Retrieved from http://www.richmondteaparty.com/2010/08/cuccinelli-gives-report-on-health-care-lawsuit/.
Ricker, T., and D. Wimberley. 2003. "Transnational Advocacy Networking: Labor Rights Movements and Nicaragua's Maquilas, 2000–2001." In W. Dunaway, ed., *Emerging Issues in the 21st Century World-System.* Westport, Conn.: Praeger.

Riesman, David, Nathan Glazer, and Reuel Denney. 1963. *The Lonely Crowd*. New Haven: Yale University Press.
Roberts, Matthew. 2007. "Popular Conservatism in Britain, 1832–1914." *Parliamentary History* 26 (3): 387–410.
Roberts, Nancy. 2004. "Public Deliberation in an Age of Direct Citizen Participation." *American Review of Public Administration* 34 (4): 315–353.
Robinson, Ian. 2008. "Politics, Markets, or Both?" Contribution to Symposium on Gay Seidman's Beyond the Boycott." *Labour History* 49 (3): 358–364.
Rodgers, Daniel T. 1998. *Atlantic Crossings*. Cambridge: Harvard University Press.
Rodriguez-Garavito, C. 2005. "Global Governance and Labor Rights: Codes of Conduct and Anti-sweatshop Struggles in Global Apparel Factories in Mexico and Guatemala." *Politics and Society* 33 (2): 203–233.
Rogin, Michael. 1968. "Progressivism and the California Electorate." *Journal of American History* 55 (2): 297–314.
Rosell, Steven A., Isabella Furth, and Heidi Gantwerk. 2008. *Beyond Wishful Thinking*. San Diego: California Forward and Viewpoint Learning.
Rosenberg, Shawn, ed. 2007. *Can the People Govern?* Hampshire, U.K.: Palgrave.
Rosenstone, Steven, and John M. Hansen. 1993. *Mobilization, Participation and Democracy in America*. New York: Macmillan.
Ross, Michael L. 2004. "Does Taxation Lead to Representation?" *British Journal of Political Science* 34 (2): 229–249.
Ross, R. J. S. 2006. "A Tale of Two Factories: Successful Resistance to Sweatshops and the Limits of Firefighting." *Labor Studies Journal* 30 (4): 65–85.
Ross, R. J. S., & C. Kernaghan. 2000, September. "Countdown in Managua." *Nation*, 25–27.
Rothman, Sheila M., Victoria H. Raveis, Anne Friedman, and David J. Rothman. 2011. "Health Advocacy Organizations and the Pharmaceutical Industry: An Analysis of Disclosure Practices." *American Journal of Public Health* 101 (4): 602–609.
Rowe, Sylvia, Nick Alexander, Fergus M. Clydesdale, Rhona S. Applebaum, Stephanie Atkinson, Richard M. Black, Johanna T. Dwyer, Eric Hentges, Nancy A. Higley, Michael Lefevre, Joanne R. Lupton, Sanford A. Miller, Doris L. Tancredi, Connie M. Weaver, Catherine E. Woteki, and Elaine Wedral. 2009. "Funding Food Science and Nutrition Research: Financial Conflicts and Scientific Integrity." *American Journal of Clinical Nutrition* 89 (5): 1285–1291.
Rowell, Andrew. 1996. *Green Backlash: Global Subversion of the Environmental Movement*. London: Routledge.
Rowley, Timothy J., and Mihnea Moldoveanu. 2003. "When Will Stakeholder Groups Act? An Interest- and Identity-Based Model of Stakeholder Group Mobilization." *Academy of Management Review* 28: 204–219.
Roy, Arundhati. 2004. *Public Power in the Age of Empire*. New York: Seven Stories Press.
Rubin, Herbert. 2000. *Renewing Hope within Neighborhoods of Despair*. Albany: SUNY Press.
Rudra, N. 2005. "Are Workers in the Developing World 'Winners' or 'Losers' in the Current Era of Globalization?" *Studies in Comparative International Development* 40 (3): 29–64.
Rueben, Kim, and Pedro Cerdán. 2003. *Fiscal Effects of Voter Approval Requirements on Local Government*. San Francisco: Public Policy Institute of California.
Ryan, Mary P. 1992. "Gender and Public Access: Women's Politics in Nineteenth-Century America." In Craig Calhoun, ed., *Habermas and the Public Sphere*. Cambridge: MIT Press.
Ryfe, David Michael. 2002. "The Practice of Deliberative Democracy: A Study of 16 Deliberative Organizations." *Political Communication* 19: 359–377.

Ryfe, David Michael. 2007. "The Next Form of Democracy." *Journal of Public Deliberation* 3: Article 2. Retrieved from http://services.bepress.com/jpd/vol3/iss1/art2.
Sabato, Larry J. 1981. *The Rise of Political Consultants*. New York: Basic Books.
SAC. 2011. "Students for Academic Choice: Let's Join Our Voices and Make Ourselves Heard!" Retrieved from http://www.studentsforacademicchoices.org.
Sagalyn, Lynne B. 2005. "The Politics of Planning the World's Most Visible Urban Redevelopment Project." In John Mollenkopf, ed., *Contentious City: The Politics of Recovery in New York City*. New York: Russell Sage.
sallijane. 2013. "Well, it has been a long time . . ." Get FISA Right blog. Retrieved from http://getfisaright.wordpress.com/2013/06/06/well-it-has-been-a-long-time/ on June 10, 2013.
Sampson, Steven. 1996. "The Social Life of Projects: Importing Civil Society to Albania." In Chris Hann and Elizabeth Dunn, eds., *Civil Society*. New York: Routledge.
Sanders, Lynn M. 1997. "Against Deliberation." *Political Theory* 25: 347–364.
Santos, Bonaventura de Souza. 1998. "Participatory Budgeting in Porto Alegre: Toward a Redistributive Democracy." *Politics and Society* 4: 461–510.
Savage, Larry. 2009. "Workers' Rights as Human Rights: Organized Labor and Rights Discourse in Canada." *Labor Studies Journal* 34 (1): 8–20.
Schappert, Stefanie. 2010, April 27. "Arizona Immigration Bill Backed by Tea Party." Retrieved from http://www.examiner.com/tea-party-in-new-york/arizona-immigration-bill-backed-by-tea-party.
Schepers, Donald H. 2006. "The Impact of NGO Network Conflict on the Corporate Social Responsibility Strategies of Multinational Corporations." *Business and Society* 45: 282–299.
Scheppele, Kim L. 2004. "Constitutional Ethnography." *Law and Society Review* 38: 389–406.
Schleifer, David. 2012. "The Perfect Solution: How Trans Fats Became the Healthy Replacement for Saturated Fats." *Technology and Culture* 53 (1): 94–119.
Schlozman, Kay Lehman, Benjamin I. Page, Sidney Verba, and Morris P. Fiorina. 2005. "Inequalities of Political Voice." In Lawrence R. Jacobs and Theda Skocpol, eds., *Inequality and American Democracy*. New York: Russell Sage Foundation.
Schmidt, David D. 1989. *Citizen Lawmakers*. Philadelphia: Temple University Press.
Schrag, Peter. 1998. *Paradise Lost: California's Experience, America's Future*. Berkeley: University of California Press.
Schudson, Michael. 1998. *The Good Citizen*. New York: Martin Kessler.
Schumpeter, Joseph. 1991. "The Crisis of the Tax State." In Richard Swedberg, ed., *The Economics and Sociology of Capitalism*. Princeton: Princeton University Press.
Schurman, Rachel, and William A. Munro. 2010. *Fighting for the Future of Food*. Minneapolis: University of Minnesota Press.
Segall, Shlomi. 2005. "Political Participation as an Engine of Social Solidarity: A Sceptical View." *Political Studies* 53: 362–378.
Seidman, Gay. 2007. *Beyond the Boycott: Labor Rights, Human Rights and Transnational Activism*. New York: Sage.
———. 2008. "Citizenship at Work. In Symposium on Beyond the Boycott." *Labour History* 49: 364–368.
Selznick, Philip. 1949. *TVA and the Grass Roots*. Berkeley: University of California Press.
Sennett, Richard. 1980. *Authority*. New York: Norton.
Shefter, Martin. 1983. "Regional Receptivity to Reform: The Legacy of the Progressive Era." *Political Science Quarterly* 98 (3): 459–483.
Shirky, Clay. 2008. *Here Comes Everybody*. New York: Penguin.

Sills, David L. 1957. *The Volunteers*. Glencoe, Ill.: Free Press.
Silverman, Ed. 2011, January 6. "Yet Another Group Sues Medicare over Provenge." Pharmalot blog, *Wall Street Journal*.
Sintomer, Y., C. Herzberg, and A. Röcke. 2008. *Démocratie participative et modernisation des services publics*. Paris: La Découverte.
Sintomer, Y., Carsten Herzberg, and Giovanni Allegretti. 2010. *Learning from the South*. Bonn, Germany: InWEnt gGmbH.
Sirianni, Carmen. 2009. *Investing in Democracy*. Washington, D.C.: Brookings Institution Press.
Sirianni, Carmen, and Lewis Friedland. 2001. *Civic Innovation in America*. Berkeley: University of California Press.
Skocpol, Theda. 2003. *Diminished Democracy*. Norman: University of Oklahoma Press.
Skocpol, Theda, and Vanessa Williamson. 2012. *The Tea Party and the Remaking of Republican Conservatism*. New York: Oxford University Press.
Small, Bryan, and Bita Neyestani. 2008. *Citizen Engagement Projects in California*. Common Sense California.
Smith, Aaron, Kay Lehman Schlozman, Sidney Verba, and Henry Brady. 2009. *The Internet and Civic Engagement*. Washington, D.C.: Pew Internet and American Life Project, a Project of the Pew Research Center. Retrieved from http://pewinternet.com/~/media/Files/Reports/2009/The%20Internet%20and%20Civic%20Engagement.pdf.
Smith, David Horton. 1997. "The Rest of the Nonprofit Sector: Grassroots Associations as the Dark Matter Ignored in Prevailing 'Flat Earth' Maps of the Sector." *Nonprofit and Voluntary Sector Quarterly* 26 (2): 114–131.
Smith, William. 2004. "Democracy, Deliberation and Disobedience." *Res Publica* 10: 353–377.
Snider, J. H. 2010. "Deterring Fake Public Participation." *International Journal of Public Participation* 4: 90–102.
Snow, David A. 2004. "Framing Processes, Ideology, and Discursive Fields." In David A. Snow, Sarah A. Soule, and Hanspeter Kriesi, eds., *The Blackwell Companion to Social Movements*. New York: Blackwell.
Snow, David, Louis A. Zurcher Jr., and Sheldon Ekland-Olsen. 1980. "Social Networks and Social Movements: A Microstructural Approach to Differential Recruitment." *American Sociological Review* 45 (5): 787–801.
Somers, Margaret R. 2005. "Let Them Eat Social Capital: Socializing the Market versus Marketizing the Social." *Thesis Eleven* 81: 5–19.
Soule, Sarah. 2009. *Contention and Corporate Social Responsibility*. New York: Cambridge University Press.
Source Watch. 2011. "Council for Government Reform." Retrieved from http://www.sourcewatch.org/index.php?title=Council_for_Government_Reform.
Sparks, Holloway. 1997. "Dissident Citizenship: Democratic Theory, Political Courage, and Activist Women." *Hypatia* 12 (4): 74–110.
Stamatakis, Emmanuel, Richard Weiler, and John P. A. Ioannidis. 2013. "Undue Industry Influences That Distort Healthcare Research, Strategy, Expenditure and Practice: A Review." *European Journal of Clinical Investigation* 43 (5): 469–475.
Starr, Amory, and Jason Adams. 2003. "Anti-globalization: The Global Fight for Local Autonomy." *New Political Science* 25 (1): 19–42.
Stinchcombe, Arthur L. 1965. "Social Structure and Organizations." In J. G. March, ed., *Handbook of Organizations*. New York: Rand McNally.

Stockdale, Alan. 1999. "Waiting for the Cure: Mapping the Social Relations of Human Gene Therapy Research." *Sociology of Health and Illness* 21 (5): 579–596.

Stoecker, Randy. 1997. "The Community Development Corporation Model of Community Development: A Critique and an Alternative." *Journal of Urban Affairs* 19: 1–23.

Stone, Peter. 1993, May 30. "Fertilizing the Grass Roots: Latest in Lobbying." *Baltimore Sun*, 1C.

Strange, Susan. 1996. *The Retreat of the State: The Diffusion of Power in the World Economy*. Cambridge, U.K.: Cambridge University Press.

Suchman, Mark C. 1995. "Managing Legitimacy: Strategic and Institutional Approaches." *Academy of Management Review* 20: 571–610.

Sulik, Gayle A. 2011. *Pink Ribbon Blues*. New York: Oxford University Press.

Supreme Court of California. 1990. "John Moore v. the Regents of the University of California."

Swanstrom, Todd. 1985. *The Crisis of Growth Politics*. Philadelphia: Temple University Press.

Swidler, Ann, and Susan Cott Watkins. 2008. "'Teach a Man to Fish': The Sustainability Doctrine and Its Social Consequences." *World Development* 37 (7): 1182–1196.

Swyngedouw, Erik. 2005. "Governance Innovation and the Citizen: The Janus Face of Governance-beyond-the-State." *Urban Studies* 42: 1991–2006.

Talisse, Robert B. 2005. "Deliberativist Responses to Activist Challenges: A Continuation of Young's Dialectic." *Philosophy and Social Criticism* 31 (4): 423–444.

Talpin, Julien. 2011. "How Ordinary Citizens (Sometimes) Become Competent in Participatory Budgeting Institutions." Colchester, U.K.: European Consortium for Political Research Press.

Tavory, Iddo, and Nina Eliasoph. 2013. "Coordinating Futures: Towards a Theory of Anticipation." *American Journal of Sociology* 18: 908–942.

Teaford, Jon. 2002. *The Rise of the States: The Evolution of State Government*. Baltimore, Md.: Johns Hopkins University Press.

Teixeira, Ana Claudia. 2002. "O OP em pequenos municípios rurais: Contextos, condições, e formatos de experiência." In Zander Navarro, ed., *A inovação democrática no Brasil*. São Paulo: Cortez.

Teles, Steven M. 2010. *The Rise of the Conservative Legal Movement*. Princeton: Princeton University Press.

Tepper, Steven J. 2009. "Stop the Beat: Quiet Regulation and Cultural Conflict." *Sociological Forum* 24: 276–306.

Thompson, Dennis F. 2008. "Deliberative Democratic Theory and Empirical Political Science." *Annual Review of Political Science* 11: 497–520.

Thompson, E. P. 1968. *The Making of the English Working Class*. New York: Vintage.

Thompson, G. 2001, September 8. "Mexico Labor Protest Gets Results." *New York Times*, A3.

Thornton, Patricia, and William Ocasio. 1999. 'Institutional Logics and the Historical Contingency of Power in Organizations: Executive Succession in the Higher Education Publishing Industry, 1958–1990." *American Journal of Sociology* 105 (3): 801–843.

Thrift, Nigel. 2005. *Knowing Capitalism*. London: Sage.

Tilly, Charles. 1978. *From Mobilization to Revolution*. Reading, Mass.: Addison-Wesley.

——. 1992. *Coercion, Capital, and European States, AD 990–1992*. Malden, Mass.: Blackwell.

——. 1995. *Popular Contention in Great Britain, 1758–1834*. Cambridge: Harvard University Press.

——. 1999. "From Interactions to Outcomes in Social Movement." In Marco Giugni, Doug McAdam, and Charles Tilly, eds., *How Social Movements Matter*. Minneapolis: University of Minnesota Press.

———. 2004. *Social Movements, 1768–2004*. Boulder, Colo.: Paradigm.

———. 2007. *Democracy*. Cambridge, U.K.: Cambridge University Press.

———. 2009. "Extraction and Democracy." In Isaac William Martin, Ajay K. Mehrotra, and Monica Prasad, eds., *The New Fiscal Sociology*. Cambridge, U.K.: Cambridge University Press.

Timmerman, Luke. 2011, April 1. "Dendreon Faces Internet-Fueled Shareholder Uprising, Led by a Little Guy in Kansas." Retrieved from http://www.xconomy.com/seattle/2011/04/01/dendreon-faces-internet-fueled-shareholder-uprising-led-by-a-little-guy-in-kansas/.

Timmermans, Stefan, and Mara Buchbinder. 2010. "Patients-in-Waiting." *Journal of Health and Social Behavior* 51 (4): 408–423.

Todorov, Tzvetan. 1993. *On Human Diversity*. Cambridge: Harvard University Press.

TransDerm. 2012. "About Us." Santa Cruz, Calif.: TransDerm Incorporated.

Traub-Werner, M., and A. Cravey. 2002. "Spatiality, Sweatshops and Solidarity in Guatemala." *Social and Cultural Geography* 3: 383–401.

Trumpy, Alexa J. 2008. "Subject to Negotiation: The Mechanisms behind Co-optation and Corporate Reform." *Social Problems* 55 (4): 480–500.

Tunis, Sean R. 2004. "Why Medicare Has Not Established Criteria for Coverage Decisions." *New England Journal of Medicine* 350 (21): 2196–2198.

Turner, Fred. 2006. *From Counterculture to Cyberculture*. Chicago: University of Chicago Press.

U.S. Census Bureau. 2010a. "Number of Governmental Units, by Type." Table 416 in Statistical Abstract of the United States. Retrieved from www.census.gov/compendia/statab/2010/tables/10s0416.pdf on September 15, 2010.

U.S. Census Bureau. 2010b. "Employer Firms, Employment, and Annual Payroll by Employment Size of Firm and Industry: 2006." Table 746 in Statistical Abstract of the United States. Retrieved from www.census.gov/compendia/statab/2010/tables/10s0746.pdf on September 15, 2010.

United States Congress. 2008. "Physician Payments Sunshine Act, 42 U.S.C. 1301."

United States Court of Appeals for the Sixth Circuit. 2011. "Care to Live v. FDA, Case Number 09-4084."

United States District Court for the Southern District of Ohio (Eastern Division). 2010. "Care to Live v. CMS, Complaint for Violation of Freedom of Information Act."

United States Supreme Court. 2013. "The Association for Molecular Pathology et al v. Myriad Genetics, Inc. et al."

Urban Institute. National Center for Charitable Statistics. 2009. "Number of Nonprofit Organizations in the United States, 1998–2008." Database. Retrieved from http://nccsdataweb.urban.org/PubApps/profile1.php on September 15, 2010.

Us TOO. 2005–2011. "Us TOO Corporate Sponsors." Downers Grove, Ill.: Us TOO International.

———. 2010. "Return of Organization Exempt from Income Tax, IRS Form 990." Downers Grove, Ill.: Us TOO International.

Useem, Bert, and Mayer N. Zald. 1982. "From Pressure Group to Social Movement: Organizational Dilemmas of the Effort to Promote Nuclear Power." *Social Problems* 30: 144–156.

Verba, Sidney. 2003. "Would the Dream of Political Equality Turn Out to Be a Nightmare?" *Perspectives on Politics* 1: 663–679.

Vernon, James. 1993. *Politics and the People*. Cambridge, U.K.: Cambridge University Press.

Vliegenthart, Rens, Dirk Oegema, and Bert Klandermans. 2005. "Media Coverage and Organizational Support in the Dutch Environmental Movement." *Mobilization* 10: 365–381.

Vogel, David. 1989. *Fluctuating Fortunes*. New York: Basic Books.
———. 2005. *The Market for Virtue*. Washington, D.C.: Brookings Institution Press.
———. 2008. "Private Global Business Regulation." *Annual Review of Political Science* 11: 261–282.
Vogel, Kenneth P. 2010, March 25. "Tea Partiers Air Doubts about Armey." *Politico*. Retrieved from http://www.politico.com/news/stories/0310/34990.html.
Vogus, Timothy J., and Gerald F. Davis. 2005. "Elite Mobilizations for Antitakeover Legislation, 1982–1990." In Gerald F. Davis, Doug McAdam, W. Richard Scott, and Mayer N. Zald, eds., *Social Movements and Organization Theory*. Cambridge, U.K.: Cambridge University Press.
Von Hoffman, Alexander. 2004. *House by House, Block by Block*. Oxford: Oxford University Press.
Wahlström, Mattias, and Abby Peterson. 2006. "Between the State and the Market: Expanding the Concept of 'Political Opportunity Structure.'" *Acta Sociologica* 49 (4): 363–377.
Walker, Edward T. 2009. "Privatizing Participation: Civic Change and the Organizational Dynamics of Grassroots Lobbying Firms." *American Sociological Review* 74: 83–105.
———. 2010. "Industry-Driven Activism." *Contexts* 9 (2): 44–49.
———. 2014. *Grassroots for Hire: Public Affairs Consultants in American Democracy*. Cambridge, U.K.: Cambridge University Press.
Walker, Edward T., and John D. McCarthy. 2010. "Legitimacy, Strategy, and Resources in the Survival of Community-Based Organizations." *Social Problems* 57: 315–340.
Walker, Edward T., John D. McCarthy, and Frank R. Baumgartner. 2011. "Replacing Members with Managers? Mutualism among Membership and Non-Membership Advocacy Organizations in the U.S." *American Journal of Sociology* 116 (4): 1284–1337.
Wampler, B. 2007. "A Guide to Participatory Budgeting." In Anwar Shan, ed., *Participatory Budgeting*. Washington D.C.: World Bank.
Wampler, B., and L. Avritzer. 2005. "The Spread of Participatory Budgeting in Brazil: From Radical Democracy to Participatory Good Government." *Journal of Latin American Urban Studies* 7: 37–52.
Ward, Doug. 2010, October 9. "American Revolution, Part 2." *Vancouver Sun*. Retrieved from http://www2.canada.com/vancouversun/news/westcoastnews/story.html?id=c9c9297c-283d-49f0-b5be-ed35bf2bed17.
Warner, Michael. 2002. *Publics and Counterpublics*. New York: Zone.
Weatherford, M. Stephen, and Lorraine M. McDonnell. 2007. "Deliberation with a Purpose: Reconnecting Communities and Schools." In Shawn W. Rosenberg, ed., *Can the People Govern?* Hampshire, U.K.: Palgrave.
Weber, Max. 1978. *Economy and Society*. Vols. 1, 2. Berkeley: University of California Press.
Weiner, Jonathan. 2004. *His Brother's Keeper*. New York: Ecco.
Whelan, James, and Peter Oliver. 2005. "Regional Community-Based Planning: The Challenge of Participatory Environmental Governance." *Australasian Journal of Environmental Management* 12 (3): 126–135.
Williamson, Abigail. 2007, March 21. "Citizen Participation in the Unified New Orleans Plan." Cambridge, Mass.: Kennedy School of Government.
Wolfe, Alan. 1989. *Whose Keeper?* Berkeley: University of California Press.
Wolfowitz, P. 2006. "Good Governance and Development—A Time for Action." Jakarta, Indonesia: World Bank.
Wolfson, Mark, and Maria Parries. 2010. "The Institutionalization of Community Action in Public Health." In Jane Banaszak-Holl, Sandra R. Levitsky, and Mayer N. Zald, eds., *Social

Movements and the Transformation of American Health Care, vol. 1. New York: Oxford University Press.

Wolin, Sheldon S. 2004. *Politics and Vision*. Princeton: Princeton University Press.

———. 2010. *Democracy, Inc.* Princeton: Princeton University Press.

Wright, Erik Olin. 1994. "The Class Analysis of Poverty." In *Interrogating Inequality*. London: Verso.

———. 2010. "Real Utopias: Emancipatory Projects, Institutional Designs, Possible Futures: 2012 Annual Meeting Theme: 107th ASA Annual Meeting, August 17–20, Denver, CO." Washington, D.C.: American Sociological Association. Retrieved from http://www.asanet.org/AM2012/meeting_theme.cfm.

Wyatt, Edward. 2003, September 13. "Ground Zero Plan Seems to Circle Back." *New York Times*, B1.

Yin, Jordan. 1998. "The Community Development Industry System: A Case Study of Politics and Institutions in Cleveland, 1967–1997." *Journal of Urban Affairs* 20: 137–157.

Young, Iris Marion. 2000. *Inclusion and Democracy*. New York: Oxford University Press.

———. 2001. "Activist Challenges to Deliberative Democracy." *Political Theory* 29 (5): 670–690.

Zacharzewski, Anthony. 2010. "Democracy Pays: How Democratic Engagement Can Cut the Cost of Government." Brighton, U.K.: The Democratic Society and Public-i.

Zavestoski, Stephen, Phil Brown, Meadow Linder, Sabrina McCormick, and Brian Mayer. 2002. "Science, Policy, Activism and War: Defining the Health of Gulf War Veterans." *Science, Technology, and Human Values* 27 (2): 171–205.

Zelizer, Viviana A. 1979. *Morals and Markets*. New York: Columbia University Press.

Zernike, Kate. 2010, March 12. "Tea Party Avoids Divisive Social Issues." *New York Times*. Retrieved from http://www.nytimes.com/2010/03/13/us/politics/13tea.html.

Zucker, Lynne G. 1987. "Institutional Theories of Organization." *Annual Review of Sociology* 13: 443–464.

About the Contributors

Gianpaolo Baiocchi is Associate Professor of Individualized Studies and Sociology at NYU and Director of the Urban Democracy Lab and Civic Engagement at the Gallatin School at NYU. His most recent book, *The Civic Imagination* (2014), coauthored with Elizabeth Bennett, Alissa Cordner, Peter Taylor Klein, and Stephanie Savell, examines the contours and limits of the democratic conversation in the United States today.

Craig Calhoun is Director of the London School of Economics and Political Science. He formerly served as University Professor of the Social Sciences at New York University and Director of NYU's Institute for Public Knowledge, as well as the president of the Social Science Research Council. He is the author of several books, including *Nations Matter* (2007), *Critical Social Theory* (1995), *Neither Gods nor Emperors* (1994), and, most recently, *The Roots of Radicalism* (2012).

Emily R. Cummins is a PhD candidate in sociology at Northeastern University. She studies gender, race, and class inequalities. Her dissertation centers on struggles between poor and minority residents and utility companies in Detroit.

Nina Eliasoph is Professor of Sociology at the University of Southern California. She is the author of *Avoiding Politics: How Americans Produce Apathy in Everyday Life* (1998), *Making Volunteers: Civic Life after Welfare's End* (2011), and *The Politics of Volunteering* (2013).

Ernesto Ganuza is Research Scientist at the Spanish National Research Council (Consejo Superior de Investigaciones Cientificas). He studied in Madrid, Spain, and has been a visiting researcher in Berlin (Centre Marc Bloch), Paris (CNRS), and Providence (Brown University). He works on issues of democracy, participatory budgeting, and civil society, and he has published articles and books on these topics.

J. Matthew Judge is a PhD candidate in sociology at Northeastern University, focusing in particular on environmental sociology. His dissertation explores community responses to toxic exposures and the rise of environmental movements in the American Midwest.

Daniel Kreiss is Assistant Professor in the School of Journalism and Mass Communication at the University of North Carolina at Chapel Hill. He is the author of *Taking

Our Country Back: The Crafting of Networked Politics from Howard Dean to Barack Obama (2012).

Caroline W. Lee is Associate Professor of Sociology at Lafayette College. Her research explores the intersection of social movements, business, and democracy in American politics. Her book *Do-It-Yourself Democracy: The Rise of the Public Engagement Industry* is forthcoming from Oxford University Press.

Isaac William Martin is Professor of Sociology at the University of California, San Diego. He is the author of *Rich People's Movements* (2013) and *The Permanent Tax Revolt* (2008), and he is a coeditor of *The New Fiscal Sociology* (2009) and *After the Tax Revolt: California's Proposition 13 Turns 30* (2009).

Michael McQuarrie is Associate Professor of Sociology at the London School of Economics and Political Science and a Poiesis Fellow at NYU's Institute for Public Knowledge. His work on urban politics has been published in venues such as *Politics and Society, Public Culture, City and Community, Annals*, and *Research in Political Sociology*. He recently coedited *Remaking Urban Citizenship* with Michael Peter Smith.

Kelly McNulty is a graduate of Lafayette College and a Fulbright Scholar.

David S. Meyer is Professor of Sociology and Political Science at the University of California, Irvine. He has written numerous scholarly articles on social movements and is the author or editor of eight books. The most recent is *The Politics of Protest: Social Movements in America*, 2nd edition (2014).

Aaron Panofsky is Associate Professor in the Department of Public Policy and the Institute for Society and Genetics at the University of California, Los Angeles. His research focuses on public participation in science and scientists' inquiries into the genetics of behavior and race. He is the author of *Misbehaving Science: Controversy and the Development of Behavior Genetics* (2014).

Francesca Polletta is Professor of Sociology at the University of California, Irvine. She is the author of *It Was Like a Fever: Storytelling in Protest and Politics* (2006) and *Freedom Is an Endless Meeting: Democracy in American Social Movements* (2002), and she is a coeditor, with Jeff Goodwin and James M. Jasper, of *Passionate Politics: Emotions and Social Movements* (2001).

Amanda Pullum is a PhD candidate in sociology at the University of California, Irvine. Her dissertation investigates the influence of political and economic contexts on strategic decision-making processes employed by teachers' unions to oppose legislative threats to collective bargaining and tenure.

David Schleifer researches and writes about health care, technology, food, and education. He is a Senior Research Associate at Public Agenda, where he conducts research on policy and public opinion in areas including health care costs and prices, K–12, and higher education. Schleifer received his PhD in sociology from New York University. The views expressed here are not necessarily those of Public Agenda or its funders.

Sarah Shaffer is a graduate of Lafayette College and the recipient of the Outstanding Achievement Award from the LVAIC Undergraduate Conference in Women's Studies Research.

Steven Vallas is Professor and Chair of the Department of Sociology and Anthropology at Northeastern University. He is the author of many articles and books in the sociology of work; his most recent book is *Work: A Critique* (2012).

Edward T. Walker is Associate Professor and Vice Chair in the Department of Sociology at the University of California, Los Angeles. His research examines how organizations and institutional contexts shape public participation. His research has appeared in the *American Sociological Review, American Journal of Sociology, Public Opinion Quarterly*, and *Social Problems*. His broader study of the role of consultants in mobilizing the public, *Grassroots for Hire: Public Affairs Consultants in American Democracy*, was published in 2014 by Cambridge University Press.

Index

accountability, 36, 38–39, 140, 168
"accountability politics," 61, 63
activism: deliberation and (*see* deliberation–activism relationship); as direct action, 224–225; grassroots (*see* grassroots activism/lobbying); health (*see* health activism); transnational, 51, 57, 62, 65n35
AFL-CIO, 60
Africa, 46, 197, 200
Age of Revolution, 9–10
Agnone, Jon, 127
Aisenbrey, Silke, 127
Alinsky, Saul, 11, 95, 96
ALS Therapy Development Institute, 151
Alta Gracia, 48, 54, 56, 59–62
Amenta, Edwin, 225
American Civil Liberties Union (ACLU), 147
American Majority, 211
Americans for Prosperity, 211, 213–216
AmericaSpeaks, 236, 239
Anand, Geeta, 149–150
Anderson, Barbara, 6–7
Angle, Sharron, 213, 217
anti-sweatshop movements, 47–52, 65n45, 235–236. *See also* conjoining workers' and human rights movements
anticipatory consultation, 108, 109
anticorporate protest, 67–70, 72–73, 88, 91
Argus Group, 57
Arizona, 215
Armey, Dick, 211, 214
arts, deliberative processes and, 35–36
Asia, participatory budgeting in, 197
Asian-European Congress on participatory budgeting, 197

Asset-Based Community Development (ABCD), 179
The Association for Molecular Pathology et al v. Myriad Genetics, Inc. et al, 147
Association of Private Sector Colleges and Universities, 4
astroturfing, 28, 155
AT Children's Project, 148
AT&T, 74
authenticity: in citizenship, 30; of civic transformations, 40; in digital campaigning, 126; of entrepreneurial health activists, 144; and framing of deliberation, 37–38; process design for, 34–35; and technologies of management, 41; transformational nature of, 39
authority, 85; of Cleveland's community organizations, 89–91, 93–94; of elites, and online electoral participation, 127, 140; of experts, 15; new modes of, 96; participation as creation tool for, 8; participation component of, 84; relationship between participation, political subjectivity, justice, and, 17–18; reproduction of, 17; in 19th-century American politics, 10; urban, 58, 96, 100. *See also* technologies of participation

Baiocchi, Gianpaolo, 168, 228, 247–249
Bangladesh, anti-sweatshop campaign in, 51
Bartley, Tim, 62–63
Bates, Robert H., 106
Baumgartner, Frank R., 127
Beck, Glenn, 210, 211, 213
Bellah, Robert, 183
Berkeley, student movement at, 11–12

Best, Rachel Kahn, 145
Best Buy, 69
Between Facts and Norms (Jürgen Habermas), 66
Bevington, Douglas, 238
Bhagwati, Jagdish N., 51
biomedical research grants, 16
Biotechnology Industry Organization, 153
Blue Grassroots Network (Best Buy), 69
Blue State Digital (BSD), 132, 141n36
Brazil, participatory budgeting in, 189–196
Bringing Back the Seventies (street club), 6
Britain, in Age of Revolution, 9–10
Brooks, E., 51
Brown, Phil, 144
Brown Scott, 217
Bryan, William Jennings, 130, 248
Buck, Ken, 217
bureaucracies, 10–13
Burson-Marsteller, 73
Button, Mark, 231

California, new deliberative assemblies in, 102–104, 109–119, 122n36
California Forward, 102
Calypso, 48, 54, 56, 57, 59
Cameroon, participatory budgeting in, 197
Canovan, Margaret, 133
Career College Association (CCA), 4, 5
Carender, Keli ("Liberty Belle"), 204–205, 210, 219
Caribbean, workers' rights in, 46. *See also* conjoining workers' and human rights movements
Carson, Lyn, 29, 38
Carty, Victoria, 138
Center for Deliberative Democracy, 3
Centers for Disease Control (CDC), 16
Centers for Medicare and Medicaid Services (CMS), 145, 146, 152–155
Central America, workers' rights in, 53. *See also* conjoining workers' and human rights movements
Central General de Trabajadores (CGT), 56
changes of mind, by deliberativists and activists, 225–226, 230–232
Chen, Katherine K., 135

Chentex, 48, 53, 55, 56, 59
Child, Curtis, 62–63
Childs, David, 238
China, participatory budgeting in, 197
Choice-Dialogues™, 27
Choishin, 48, 53, 54, 56, 59–61
Cintas, 57
Citizen Choicework, 27
citizen(s), 106; conflict between states and, 107; consultation between states and (*see* new deliberative assemblies); entrepreneurial, 187; escalating demands of, 107–109
citizenship: "authentic" and "responsible," 30; in 19th-century United States, 10
Civic Alliance, 226, 229, 234, 236–238
civic engagement: authenticity for, 39; as programmatic goal, 9; scholars' and reformers' vision of, 27. *See also* public engagement
civic engagement projects, 168
civic goals, participatory budgeting and, 194
civic-ized market, 30, 41–42. *See also* deliberation consulting industry
civic participation, 121n11; decline of, in the United States, 103–104; by disadvantaged people (*see* empowerment projects); new forms of (*see* new deliberative assemblies); in Obama's 2008 campaign, 125 (*see also* online electoral participation); paradox of, 105; rise in opportunities for, 103–104. *See also* public participation
civic participation programs: Cleveland's CBOs, 83–85 (*see also* technologies of participation); as programmatic goal, 9
civic spaces: and authenticity of processes, 35; created by markets, 41–42; privately-sponsored, 41–42; production and promotion of, 28
civic transformation: as business imperative, 36–40; deliberation as means of invoking, 34–36
civility, norms of, 97
civilizing markets, 28–30
Clean Clothes Campaign, 56
Cleveland, Ohio, 83–84; civic participation in, 5–8; community-based organizations

in, 83–85; community development ideas in, 92–95; consensus organizing in, 95–98; crisis of authority in, 83–100; growth politics in, 83, 86–89; participation and contention in, 89–92; politics in 1960s and 1970s, 86
clientelist CDCs, 85, 93–94, 96
Club for Growth, 211
cognitive legitimacy, 71
Coleman, Mary Sue, 3
collaboration, between deliberativists and activists, 228
collaborative spirit, 33–34
collective actors, recognition of (in PB), 192
Comcast, 74
communicative ethics, 23n58
communitarianism, 10
community: as organizational territory, 94; of professional deliberation consultants, 33–34; sense of, 35–36, 38
Community Action Network (Wal-Mart), 68–69
Community Action Programs, 16
community-based organizations (CBOs): in Cleveland, 83–85, 87, 88 (*see also* technologies of participation); legitimacy versus effectiveness of, 84; stages of, 85
community-based participatory research (CBPR), 16
community congresses (Cleveland), 87–91, 93–96
community development corporations (CDCs), 85, 87, 88, 91–97
community development industry system, 91
community organizing, 84, 85, 87–93, 95–96, 227–228
Compa, L., 49
conflict, solidarity versus, 14–15
conflict of interest, 149–151
conflict organizing, 95
conjoining workers' and human rights movements, 46–63; advocates of, 49–52; analysis of, 52–61; consequences of, 61–62; critical view of, 51–52; distinctions between movements, 48–49; wariness of, 49–52
Connor, Dawn, 4–5
consensus, conflict as prerequisite to, 15

Consensus Conferences, 27
consensus organizing, 95–98
conservatism, participation in government and, 10
conservative legal movement, 16–17
conservative populism, 214–215
conservative social movements, 208. *See also* Tea Party movement
conservatives, activism influenced by, 211–212
Constitutional amendments, Tea Party views on, 216
constitutional democracy, as byproduct of need for taxation, 106
consultant (term), 31. *See also* deliberation consulting industry; professional deliberation consultants
consultation, 43n30; anticipatory, 108, 109; explaining innovative forms of, 103; fiscal theory of, 105–110, 119; rise in opportunities for, 104, 105; between states and citizens (*see* new deliberative assemblies)
consumerism, in health care, 145
contentious politics approach (health activism research), 145
Cook, Fay Lomax, 104, 110
Core Values Awards (IAP$_2$), 39, 45n88
corporate legitimacy, 66–78; data sources and measures for study, 74–76; grassroots mobilization programs for, 67–70; linking reputation to grassroots activities, 70; management of, 72; responses to anticorporate protest, 72–73; stakeholder relations and, 71–72
corporate political activity (CPA), 70
corporate power, 8
corporate social responsibility (CSR), 39, 63, 72
corporations: expanding power of, 67; lessons from solidarity movements, 63; Mills on, 11; and New Participatory practices, 12; relationships between health activists and, 144; selective grassroots mobilization by, 17; usefulness of deliberation for, 37
Costain, Anne N., 209

Council for Government Reform, 155
COVERCO, 60
creativity, 35–36, 38
Crist, Charlie, 215
crowdsourcing, 7
Crowley, John, 149–150
cultural circuit of capitalism, 41
culture war (1960s), 12
customer satisfaction, 38
cybernetics, 11
Cystic Fibrosis Foundation, 149

Dean, Howard, 126, 129–132, 137, 139
decision making: environmental, 35; health care, 151; impact of deliberation/activism on, 226, 232–236; stakeholder voices in, 8
deliberation. *See* public deliberation
deliberation consulting industry, 27–42; and citizen "accountability," 38–39; as community of practice, 33–34; consequences of constructed civic-ized market for, 41–42; and corporate accountability, 36; defining, 30–32; interest in civic outcomes of deliberation, 36–37, 40; moralization of market for deliberation, 28–30; motivation for practitioners, 41; process design in, 34–36; research methods, 32–33; software used in, 39–40. *See also* new deliberative assemblies; professional deliberation consultants
deliberation–activism relationship, 222–240; decision makers and impact of movements, 226, 232–236; and difficulty of deliberative activism, 236–240; and inequality, 223–227; roles of deliberativists and activists, 227–230; and willingness to change one's mind, 225–226, 230–232
deliberative democracy, 7; activism and, 227–230; evolution from contentious to collaborative, 227–228; and market forces, 29 (*see also* deliberation consulting industry); and Tea Party shutdowns, 218
Deliberative Polling®, 27
deliberative practice: presumed equality among participants in, 3; professional process production in, 29

deliberative processes, 31, 44n59; branding of, 35; and changes of mind, 225–226, 230–232; corporate change management models for, 39; cost of, 27; deliberation professionals' views of, 33–34; design of, 34–36; value to clients, 40. *See also* deliberation–activism relationship; new public participation
deliberative reforms: marketing of, 28; scholar's assumption about, 27
Delli Carpini, Michael X., 104, 110
democracy: in American political system, 217; associational versus direct, 202n8; constitutional, as byproduct of need for taxation, 106; deliberative, 7, 29, 218, 227–230; designer, 17, 34, 35; as institutionalized form of consultation, 106; redemptive and pragmatic faces of, 133; Tea Party's varying definitions of, 205; theory of, new deliberative assemblies and, 120
democracy, inc., 28
democratic deficits, 13, 29
democratic governance reforms, 29
Democratic Party, 125, 126, 131–133, 210, 214, 217, 218
democratization: participation and, 18–19, 85; participatory budgeting as form of, 192; and social movement society, 207; and structural problems of modern societies, 8; in 19th century, 10; tyranny versus, 14. *See also* fiscal theory of democratization
Dendreon, 151, 153–155
Denney, Reuel, 11
designer democracy, 17, 34, 35
destructive markets, 28–30, 43n25
devices (term), 199
Dickies, 57
Dicks, Norman, 204–205
digital media, 125–126. *See also* online electoral participation
disadvantaged people: helping (*see* empowerment projects); social protests by, 207
disclosure of interests, 152–153, 157–158
Dominican Republic, participatory budgeting in, 196

drug prices, 146, 152
drug reimbursement, 151–156
Dutra, Olívio, 189

Eastern Europe, participatory budgeting in, 197
economic development programs, 15–16
economic dimensions of deliberative processes, 29
Economic Opportunity Act (1964), 16
economic value of "intangible" civic outcomes, 36
economics: export-oriented strategies, 46; incompatibility of participation and, 33
education, for-profit, 4–5
Edwards, John, 131
Eichler, Michael, 95–96
El Salvador, anti-sweatshop campaign in, 51
electoral participation: online (*see* online electoral participation); Tea Party stance on, 216
Eliasoph, Nina, 16, 248, 249
elite organizations, participation mandate for grantees of, 16
elites: CBOs and authority of, 84; civic innovations facilitated by, 7 (*see also* new public participation); in Cleveland, 88; control over political life, 128; efforts to mobilize public by, 16–17, 66–67; online electoral participation and authority of, 127, 140; participation as resource for, 99; and participatory inequality, 105; participatory practices underpinning power of, 14; social movement techniques appropriated by, 6; social movements mobilized by, 73; tools of authority for (*see* technologies of participation)
empowered participatory governance, 9
empowerment: and accountability, 38; through creative processes, 36
empowerment practices, 248–249
empowerment projects, 165–185; decoupling goals in everyday interaction, 166–168; and development of participants beyond "being needy," 179–181; economic development programs, 15–16; enabled by professional consultants, 17; future potential participation versus helping the needy, 171–179; inequality presupposition in, 170–179; meshing tangled missions of, 181–185; method and field of study, 168–170; missions of, 165; participants as volunteers in, 170–171; plug-in volunteering in, 177–178; temporal leapfrog in, 165–167, 171–179, 181–185; top-down, 42
empowerment talk, 165
enabling rights, protective rights versus, 50, 59
engagement. *See* civic engagement; public engagement
Enlightenment thought, 9, 10
entrepreneurial citizens, 187, 233
entrepreneurial health activism, 143–159; disclosure of interests, 152–153, 157–158; drug reimbursement, 151–152; and history of health activism, 144–145; managing conflict of interest, 149–151; property rights, 146–149; and state roles in health care, 153–156
environmental decision making, 35
equal participation, new deliberative assemblies and, 103
equality: and control of deliberative forums, 224; fiction of, 184–185. *See also* inequality
equity, participation and, 18
Erundina, Luiza, 194
escalation of citizens' demands, 107–109
Espenshade, J., 50
ethnographic research, 32
Europe: consultation institutions in, 109; participatory budgeting in, 196, 197
European Union (EU), participatory budgeting in, 195, 196
experts: authority of, 15; in bureaucracies, 10–12; contemporary views of, 12
extraction (resource acquisition), 106–119; and anticipatory consultation, 108; in California, 110–119; conflict over, 106–107, 109–110; and escalation of citizen's demands, 107–108; and information arbitrage, 108–109; intensive, 108, 110; in New York, 110–112, 114–116

facilitator (term), 31. *See also* professional deliberation consultants
Fair Labor Association, 59, 60
"false needs," in industrial societies, 11
Farmer's Alliance, 10
Fast Forum Opinionnaires®, 27
federal aid to colleges, 5
Federal University, Porto Alegre, Brazil, 196
feeble markets, 28–30
fiscal bargains, 107–108, 119. *See also* extraction (resource acquisition)
fiscal sociology, 105, 106. *See also* new deliberative assemblies
fiscal theory of consultation: anticipatory consultation, 108, 109; and consultation explosion in California, 109–110; on content of fiscal bargains, 119; escalation of citizens' demands, 107–109; evolution of consultation institutions, 109; and fiscal theory of democratization, 105–107; information arbitrage, 108–109
fiscal theory of democratization, 105–107; and generalization from NGOs to states, 119–120; Great Consultation in California, 118–119; and invention of new public consultation institutions/procedures, 107–111 (*see also* fiscal theory of consultation); purpose of, 107
Fishkin, James, 3–4
Fleming, Peter, 38
Food and Drug Administration (FDA), 152–154
for-profit education, 4–5
Ford Foundation, 92, 96
Ford Motor Company, 74
foreign policy, 216
Forum Nacional de Participação Popular (FNPP), 195
Foucauldians, 12
FreedomWorks, 211, 213–216, 219
Freud, Sigmund, 10
Friedland, Lewis, 104, 110, 172, 227–228
Fruit of the Loom, 56
Fung, Archon, 225, 236

gainful employment rule, 5
Ganuza, Ernesto, 247–249
the Gap, 53, 57, 60. *See also* NLC-Gap
Garvin, Alex, 234, 235
Gastil, John, 36
Generalized System of Preferences (GSP), 58
Genetic Alliance, 147
Genzyme, 147
Get FISA Right protest, 137–139, 140
Gildan, 48, 55, 56, 58–59
Gincotta, Gail, 89
Glazer, Nathan, 11
globalization, 46, 47, 50, 187
Globe University, 4
Goldscheid, Rudolf, 106, 120
Goodman, Clifford, 154
Gore, Al, 129
governance: California structure for, 102; in Cleveland, 83, 86–88; of conflicts of interest, 149; empowered participatory governance, 9; and loss of expert authority, 15; and participatory budgeting, 194, 198
government-sponsored deliberative forums, 17
government(s): adoption of participation by, 13; authenticity of public administrators, 39; mandates for public consultation, 110; Mills on, 11; neoliberal, 187; and New Participatory practices, 12; public consultation to agencies, 104
Granholm, Jennifer, 3
grassroots activism/lobbying, 249; and corporate legitimacy, 67–70; of corporations, 74–78; corporations' selective mobilization for, 17; deliberation used in tandem with, 42; linking corporate reputation and, 70; mobilization of, 211–212 (*see also* mobilization of public participation); by RetireSafe, 155; by Tea Party, 210, 212, 216
grassroots campaign industry, 77–78
growth politics, 83, 86–89, 99
Gutmann, Amy, 224

Habermas, Jürgen, 12, 22–23n58, 66, 224
Hamill, Pete, 234
Hansen, John M., 139
"Hard Time, Hard Choices" (Michigan event), 3–4

Harrah's Entertainment, 69
health activism, 143–145, 156. *See also* entrepreneurial health activism
health care reform, 214, 216–218, 235, 240
health sciences research, 16
Heierbacher, Sandy, 31
Hendriks, Carolyn M., 29, 38, 229, 238
Heywood, Jamie, 151
Holman, Kwame, 3
hopeful speech, 184–185
housing development, as CDC tool, 92–93
Howard, Philip N., 136
Hughes, Virginia, 149
human rights movements: distinctions between workers' movement and, 47–49; globalization and, 46, 47. *See also* conjoining workers' and human rights movements

IBM, 74
image consulting, 128
Imagine New York, 227, 234–235, 237, 238
immigration issue, 215
Independent Monitoring Group of El Salvador (GMIES), 60
India, participatory budgeting in, 197
Indonesia, participatory budgeting in, 197
inequality: in health care, 144, 158 (*see also* entrepreneurial health activism); participatory, 103, 105 (*see also* new deliberative assemblies); political, and escalating demands, 108–109; presupposed in empowerment projects, 170–179; public deliberation/participation and, 7–9, 17–19, 223–227, 247–250; socioeconomic, 8; temporal leapfrogging of, 165–166, 181–185 (*see also* empowerment projects)
inevitable relation to hoped-for future, 184–185
information arbitrage, 108–109
infrastructural intermediaries, 126–132
intellectual property (IP), 33, 143, 146–149
intellectual research, informed by mid-20th century movements, 12
interest politics, in health, 145
intermediaries: in digital electoral campaigns, 126–132; political consultancies, 131–132; between states and citizens, 108–109
International Association of Public Participation (IAP$_2$), 31, 35, 39
International Association of Public Participation Practitioners (IAP$_3$), 31
international development agencies, 187
International Labor Rights Forum, 53
Internet, political campaign use of, 129. *See also* online electoral participation
inverted totalitarianism, 12, 14
Issues Forums, 27

Jacobs, Lawrence R., 36, 104, 110
Jaksic, Kathy, 90–91
Japan, participatory budgeting in, 197
J.C. Penney, 53, 58, 60
John Moore v. the Regents of the University of California, 146
Johnson, Hiram, 113–114
justice: relationship between participation, political subjectivity, authority, and, 17–18; social solidarity and, 15

Kallick, David, 235, 238
Kashefi, Elham, 29
Kazin, Michael, 130
Keck, M., 61, 63
Kennedy, David W., 50
Kerry, John, 131
Kiefert, James, 154
Kimi, 53, 55, 56, 58, 60–61
Koch brothers, 205, 211, 213–214
Kolben, K., 50
Kriess, Daniel, 248
Kucinich, Dennis, 86–88, 98
Kukdong, 53, 54, 56, 58–61

Labor Community Action Network (LCAN), 229, 235
Labor Education in the Americas Project, 60
Lan Dau, 57
Latin America, 65–66n32; *autonomista* movements in, 52; participatory budgeting in, 195, 197; workers' rights in, 46 (*see also* conjoining workers' and human rights movements)

Law, J., 188, 200
Leal, Pablo Alejandro, 187
Lee, Caroline W., 17, 37, 104, 227, 248
legitimacy, 71; built by deliberation consultants, 17; of CDCs, 97; of Cleveland's CBOs, 84; constitutive and sociopolitical, 79n36; of corporations (*see* corporate legitimacy); of deliberative forums, 224; enhanced by participation, 249; of health activism, 143, 144; moral, 71; in political campaigns, 138, 140
Leicht, Holly, 236, 239
Leighninger, Matt, 228
Levi, Margaret, 106
Lewis, Fannie, 6
LGBT community, 12
Liebeskind Daniel, 238
Lien, Da-Hsiang Donald, 106
Limbaugh, Rush, 211
Lippmann, Walter, 11
LISC, 96
Listening to the City, 227, 229–231, 233–239
Liz Claiborne, 53, 58, 60
lobbying: by for-profit colleges, 5; mobilizing public as force for, 8. *See also* grassroots activism/lobbying
localized democratic vernacular, 34
Loncar, Bradley, 153–156
The Lonely Crowd (Riesman, Glazer, and Denney), 11
Los Angeles Chamber of Commerce, 102
Lower Manhattan Development Corporation (LMDC), 226, 229, 233–239

Macy's, 60
Malawi education project, 167
management software, 40
management tool, participation as, 13, 14
Maquila Solidarity Network (MSN), 53, 56, 58–59
Marcuse, Herbert, 11
Margus, Brad, 148, 150
market for facilitated deliberation: "civicized," 30 (*see also* deliberation consulting industry); consequences of, 41–42; moralization of, 28–30; protection of civic spaces from, 28; views of, 28–30

Martin, Isaac William, 36–37, 248
Mathews, David, 247
Mattson, Kevin, 231
maximum feasible participation, 16
Mayer, Jane, 211
McAdam, Doug, 209
McCain, John, 129
McCarthy, John D., 127
McCoy, Martha L., 227
McDonnell, Lorraine M., 239
McGerr, Michael, 128
McIntyre, Alistair, 51
McNulty, Kelly, 248
McQuarrie, Michael, 127, 140, 167, 248
media: digital, 125–126 (*see also* online electoral participation); movements' use of, 225, 233; sensationalism in worker's rights/human rights campaigns, 57, 61; Tea Party coverage by, 208
Medicaid, 151, 235
Medicare, 151–154, 214, 216
Merck, 69, 70
Merck Action Network, 69, 70
Meyer, David S., 207, 227, 249
Miami Children's Hospital, 147
Michigan, public economic debate in, 3–4, 7
middle class, 11, 206
military, 11, 12
Miller, Joe, 213
Mills, C. Wright, 11
Minkoff, Debra, 127
mobilization of public participation: in electoral campaigns (*see* online electoral participation); elite-driven efforts for, 16–17, 66–67; as force for lobbying, 8; interests underlying, 211–212; linking populist anger and establishment resources for, 219; in political opportunity theory, 210; post–World War II, 206; by Tea Party, 212–214. *See also* grassroots activism/lobbying; social movements
Mol, Annemarie, 188
Molotch, Harvey, 36, 71
moral discourse/issues: and framing of deliberative performances, 38; moralization of market for deliberation, 28–30, 41, 42; in

practitioners' construction of activities, 41; stakes involved in producing pure civic spaces, 28
moral legitimacy, 71
morally-ambivalent products, 30
Morone, James, 247
Mort, Maggie, 29
Mosse, David, 29
multinational companies, 71, 72
Municipal Art Society, 226, 234, 236, 237
mutable mobile, 188, 200
Myriad Genetics, 147
"name and shame" campaigns, 47, 54, 58, 235–236
National Coalition for Dialogue and Deliberation (NCDD), 31
National Institutes of Health (NIH), 16
National Labor Committee (NLC), 57, 60. *See also* NLC-Gap
National People's Action (NPA), 89, 90
National Research Council, 35
National Smokers' Alliance (NSA), 73
nationalism, 10
nativism, 215
neoliberalism, 13–14, 16, 187, 249
Network-9, 196
network forms of business organization, 8
new deliberative assemblies, 102–120; in California, 102, 103, 110–119, 122n36; explained, 103–104; fiscal theory of consultation, 105–111; fiscal theory of democratization, 105–107, 118–120; in New York, 110–112, 114–116; and paradox of participation, 103–105
New Left, 11
new media, 139. *See also* online electoral participation
new public participation, 7; implications for authority and governance, 8; opportunities and unintended consequences of, 247–250. *See also* new deliberative assemblies
New York, new deliberative assemblies in, 110–112, 114–116
New York City: anti-sweatshop campaign in, 51; rebuilding of Ground Zero in, 226–227, 229–231, 233–239

New York Times, 225
Nielsen 2012, 128
Nike, 53, 60
9-12 Project, 213
NLC-Gap, 53, 54, 56–61
nongovernmental organizations (NGOs): as buffer between state and public, 15–16; generalization of conditions to states from, 119–120; and participatory budgeting, 197; in workers' rights/human rights cases, 57, 58, 61
nonprofit organizations, usefulness of deliberation for, 37
North America, participatory budgeting in, 197
Novazyme Pharmaceuticals, 149–150
Nuclear Freeze movement, 212

Obama, Barack, 125, 131, 133, 137; "birthers'" beliefs about, 206; health care stance of, 218; presidential campaign of 2008, 125–128, 131–140, 210; and Take Back America campaign, 205; Tea Party opposition to, 212, 214, 218
Obama administration: conservatives' opposition to, 211; Tea Party's attacks on, 208, 217
O'Donnell, Christine, 217
One-Dimensional Man (Marcuse), 11
online deliberation software, 39–40
online electoral participation, 125–140; crafting digital campaigns, 128–132; in Dean's 2004 campaign, 126, 129–131, 137; limits of, 137–138; in Obama's 2008 campaign, 125–128, 131–140; and political consultancies, 131–132; transactional, 127, 133, 135–137; transformative, 133–135
Open Space process, 35–36, 38
Oregon, health care in, 235, 240
organizing (in electoral politics), 135–138

Pagliarulo, Philip, 116
Palin, Sarah, 213
Panofsky, Aaron, 145, 150, 249
paradox of participation, 103–105
participation. *See* public participation

participatory budgeting (PB), 187–201; and administrative reform, 191; as a best practice, 188, 198; individual-association pendulum in, 190; international spread of, 195–198; opposition of neighborhood associations, 192; original versus best-practice version of, 188; in Porto Alegre, 189–193, 228; software for, 39; spread through Brazil of, 193–195
participatory inequality, 103, 105. See also new deliberative assemblies
participatory practices: in digital campaigning (see online electoral participation); heroic claims for, 187; institutionalization of, 8. See also technologies of participation
PartyBuilder, 132
patient advocates. See health activism
PatientsLikeMe.com, 151
Paul, Ron, 210
performing arts, deliberative processes and, 35–36
personality cults, 6
personalized political communication, 128–129
Peru, participatory budgeting in, 196
Pfizer, 69, 74
PG&E, 74
Philip Morris (Altria), 73
Phillips, Thair, 155
Phillips Van Heusen, 53, 55, 56, 58, 59
PhRMA, 69–70
Plehn, Carl, 113
plug-in volunteering, 177–178
policy instruments, 199–200
political consultancies, 131–132
political opportunity theory, 209–216
political parties, 133, 207; in election of 2008, 210; Tea Party's relationships to, 209. See also Democratic Party; Republican Party
political polarization, expansion of, 8
political processes: electoral campaigns (see online electoral participation); impact of economic logics on, 29
political subjectivity, relationship between participation, authority, justice, and, 17–18

political theory, 12, 13, 43n47
politics: "accountability politics," 61, 63; in Age of Revolution, 9–10; aggregative, 224; appearing to be free of, 239–240; in Cleveland, 86–89; interest politics in health care, 145; moral values associated with, 30; parties versus candidate-centric, 133; social movement tactics in, 207; in 19th-century United States, 10–11; of urban growth, 83, 86–89, 99
Polletta, Francesca, 249
populism, 10, 249, 250; conservative, 214–215; and large money interests, 212; and Tea Party movement, 205, 208
Populist Party, 10
Port Authority (NYC), 226, 234, 237
Porto Alegre, Brazil, municipal budgeting, 189–196, 228
Postel, Charles, 250
power elite, 11–12
The Power Elite (Mills), 11
practitioner (term), 31. See also professional deliberation consultants
pragmatic legitimacy, 71
private clients, 33–34
private property rights, 106, 146–149
private-sector organizations, adoption of participation by, 13
proactive deliberative processes, 37
process design, 34–36
Procter & Gamble, 74
productivity, 37, 46
professional (term), 31
professional deliberation consultants, 17, 31; client lists of, 27; management of commercial dimensions of work, 28; motivations of, 41; as "portable community," 32
professional facilitation of public deliberation, 17; development of field, 30–31; infrastructural intermediaries in electoral campaigns, 126–127. See also deliberation consulting industry
professional public engagement facilitation: birth of field, 104. See also deliberation consulting industry
Progama de Gestion Urbana (PGU), 196
Progressive movement, 10

property rights, in entrepreneurial health activism, 146–149
prospectancy, 182–183
protective rights, enabling rights versus, 50, 59
protests: as alternative to aggregative politics, 224; anticorporate, 67–70, 72–73, 88, 91; and deliberation (*see* deliberation–activism relationship); in social movement society, 206–208 (*see also* social movements); as strategy, 211
Provenge, 151–156, 158
Public Affairs Council (PAC), 68–70, 80n62
public affairs function, 68, 72
public deliberation, 31; and activism (*see* deliberation–activism relationship); development of, 227; government-sponsored forums, 17; and inequality, 223–227; "organizational infrastructure for," 27; pitfalls and promise of, 247–250; processes of, 31; professional facilitation of, 17; purposes of, 6; "reasonableness" in, 224; scholars' and reformers' vision of, 27; in theory versus "real," 43–44n47; and welfare of citizenry as a whole, 8. *See also* public engagement; public participation
public deliberation consultants. *See* professional deliberation consultants
public deliberation consulting firms: responsibilities of, 32; select mobilization by, 17. *See also* deliberation consulting industry
public dialogue, 27, 31. *See also* public deliberation
public engagement, 31; corporate forms of, 67 (*see also* corporate legitimacy); in political campaigns, 127; software used for, 39–40. *See also* civic engagement; public deliberation; public participation
public interest, 159
Public Opinion (Lippmann), 11
public participation, 3–21, 31; authority and, 84; as buzzword, 187; current views of, 7; democratization and, 18–19, 85; economic dimensions of, 27 (*see also* deliberation consulting industry); evolution of, 15–18; in historical context, 9–10; incompatibility of economics and, 33; inequality and, 17–19; marketing and commodification of, 29; "new," 7, 8, 247–250 (*see also* new deliberative assemblies); new context for, 3–9; paradox of, 103–105; pitfalls and promise of, 247–250; positive outcomes of, 8–9; primary tensions in, 14–15; purposes of, 6; for realizing particularistic interests, 8; relationship between political subjectivity, authority, justice, and, 17–18; renaissance in, 13–14; Tea Party-supported voter legislation, 205; as tool for creation of authority, 8; "true" or "real," 247–248; in unequal context, 7–9, 247–250. *See also* civic participation; public deliberation; public engagement
public-private partnerships, 92
public sector, contesting of bureaucratic expertise in, 8
public sphere, 23n58; for participatory budgeting, 191; as social space, 66
Pullum, Amanda, 249
PXE International, 147, 148

recruitment, for deliberative forums, 229
Reebok, 53
Regional Youth Empowerment Project (Regional YEP), 168. *See also* empowerment projects
religious revivalism, 10
Republican Party, 113, 114, 204, 206, 209–211, 213–215, 217–218
reputation: linking corporate grassroots activities and, 70; moderating effects of, 72. *See also* corporate legitimacy
reputation capital, 36
resource acquisition by states. *See* extraction
RetireSafe, 155
Richardson, Bill, 131
Riesman, David, 11
Rodriguez-Garavito, C., 50
Romano, Zachary, 37, 104
Roosevelt, Franklin Delano, 10
Rosenstone, Steven, 139
Rospars, Joe, 132
Roy, Arundhati, 15–16

Russell Athletic, 53, 54, 56, 58, 59, 61, 62
Russo, Sal, 213
Ryan, Paul, 216
Ryfe, David Michael, 29, 228

Santelli, Rick, 210
Schleifer, David, 145, 249
Schumpeter, Joseph, 106
Scully, Patrick L., 227
secret-ballot elections, 110
Seidman, Gay, 50–52
Selznick, Philip, 14
Shaffer, Sarah, 248
Shah, Anwar, 198
Sikkink, K., 61, 63
Silverstein, Larry, 238
Sirianni, Carmen, 104, 110, 172, 227–228
Smith, William, 224, 225
smoking, 73
Snowy Prairie, 169. *See also* empowerment projects
social alienation, 11
social aspects of deliberation, 35–36
social capital, 15, 30
social justice, participatory budgeting and, 194
social legitimacy, 72
social liberals, in 1960s culture war, 12
social movement society, 206–209, 219
social movement theory, 205–206, 208–209
social movements: disagreement and tension in, 212; elites' appropriation of techniques from, 6; history of, 206–208; mobilized by elites, 73; policy impact of, 232–233; as province of disadvantaged groups, 206; as source of democratic renewal, 205; in the United States, 206–207
social solidarity, conflict versus, 14–15
social space, public sphere as, 66
socialization tool, participation as, 14
socioeconomic inequality, 7–8, 13–14
software, 39–40
SOHIO Corporation, 88, 91
solidarity, conflict versus, 14–15
solidarity movements/campaigns, 48; goals of, 62; "learning" effect in, 61; mimicking consumer capitalism, 52; transnational, 51. *See also* conjoining workers' and human rights movements
Somers, Margaret R., 30
South Africa, environmental assessment in, 229, 235, 239
South Korea, participatory budgeting in, 197
Southern Pacific Railroad Company, 112–113
Sparks, Holloway, 224
special interest groups, 207
Specter, Arlen, 210, 215
sponsors, 31–32; of campaigns/social movements, 211–212; usefulness of deliberation for, 37; value of civic outcomes to, 36
stakeholder dialogue sessions, 7
stakeholder engagement processes, 27
stakeholder engagement software, 39–40
stakeholder management software, 40
stakeholder relations, corporate legitimacy and, 71–72
stakeholders: authentic engagement experiences for, 39; demands for rights and services by, 38; empowered, 12; in organizational decision making, 8
state-mandated participation, 16
state(s), 106; conflict between citizens and, 107; consultation between citizens and, 106 (*see also* new deliberative assemblies); health care roles of, 153–156; resource acquisition by (*see* extraction)
Stockdale, Alan, 149
street clubs, 89, 95–97
The Structural Transformation of the Pubic Sphere (Jürgen Habermas), 66
student loans, 5
student movement, 11
Student Non-violent Coordinating Committee, 11
Students for Academic Choice (SAC), 4–5, 7
Sunstein, Cass, 5
SweatFree Communities (SFC), 53, 57, 60
sweatshops, 46. *See also* anti-sweatshop movements
Swyngedouw, Erik, 29
symbolic realism, 183–184

Talisse, Robert B., 224, 225
Tarrow, Sidney, 207, 227

taxation, 214, 216. *See also* extraction (resource acquisition)
Tea Party Express, 213–215
Tea Party movement, 204–220; coalitions, 212–214; history of social movements, 206; inconsistencies/disagreements within, 205, 209, 212, 214; and interests underlying resource mobilization, 211–212; policy debates and political coalitions, 214–216; and political opportunity theory, 209–216; and reality of American political system, 217–218; and social movement theory, 208–209
Tea Party Nation, 213
Tea Party Patriots, 212–213, 215, 219
technocratic CDCs, 85, 93–96
technocratic movements, 10–11
technologies of participation, 83–100; broad-based organizing, 89–92; and community-based organization practices, 83–85; community development and professional closure, 92–95; consensus organizing, 95–98; and growth politics, 86–89
technology, in electoral campaigns. *See* online electoral participation
Teles, Steven, 16
temporal leapfrog, 165–167, 171–179, 181–185. *See also* empowerment projects
Tennessee Valley Authority, 14
tensions in participation, 14–15
Terry, Sharon, 147–148, 150–151
Thailand, participatory budgeting in, 197
theory of democracy, new deliberative assemblies and, 120
Thomas, Scott, 134, 135
Thompson, Dennis, 224
Thrift, Nigel, 41
Tilly, Charles, 106, 107, 210
Todd, Laurel, 153
total quality management, 13
totalitarianism, inverted, 12, 14
town hall meetings, 7
traditionalists, in 1960s culture war, 12
transactional electioneering, 127, 133, 135–137
TransDerm Incorporated, 149
transformative electioneering, 133–135
transnational activism, 51, 57, 62, 65n35
Trapp, Shel, 89
traveling best practices, 188. *See also* participatory budgeting (PB)
triadic exchange, 93
Trippi, Joe, 130
21st Century Town Meetings®, 27
tyranny, democratization versus, 14

Union of Neighborhood Associations (UAMPA), 189, 190, 192
unions and unionism, 12; and human rights movement, 47, 49, 51; and outsourcing/offshoring, 46; in workers' rights/human rights cases, 61
UNITE, 57, 58, 60
United States: access to political influence in, 207; in Age of Revolution, 9–10; decline in mass civic activity in, 103–104; education costs in, 181; empowerment projects in, 168, 172; health activism in, 143; health care decision making in, 151; history of social movements in, 206–208; inequalities in, 8; participatory budgeting in, 196; political system of, 217–218; resurgence of sweatshops in, 46; state-mandated participation in, 16; 19th century politics in, 10
United Students Against Sweatshops (USAS), 53, 56
United Way, 178–179
universal participation, 189, 193. *See also* participatory budgeting (PB)
urban authority, 85; challenging, 100; changed nature of, 96. *See also* technologies of participation

Vallas, Steven, 249
value(s): of civic outcomes of deliberation, 36, 40; in rationalized markets, 30
Venezuela, participatory budgeting in, 196
Verizon, 74
Vilsack, Tom, 131
visual arts, deliberative processes and, 35–36
Voinovich, George, 86, 87, 91
voluntarism, 135–137. *See also* empowerment projects
voter participation, 128. *See also* online electoral participation

W. K. Kellogg Foundation, 3
Wachovia, 69
Wal-Mart, 53, 68–70, 74
Walker, Edward T., 17, 127, 248
ward politics (Cleveland), 93–94
Washington, D.C., citizen summit, 222, 225
Waste Management, 74
Weatherford, M. Stephen, 239
web-based open government initiatives, 7
Weber, Max, 10
Wells Fargo, 69
Weslian, Marlene, 90
Winning Together program (Harrah's), 69
Wolin, Sheldon, 12, 14
Women's Capital Corporation, 146
women's movement, 12
workers' movements: distinctions between human rights movement and, 47–49; globalization and, 46, 47. *See also* conjoining workers' and human rights movements
Workers' Party (PT, Brazil), 189, 190, 193–196
Worker Rights Consortium (WRC), 53, 56, 57, 60
World Bank, 15, 197
World Social Forum, 195, 196
World Trade Center site, 226–227, 229–231, 233–239
World War I, 10
World War II, 11

Yaro, Robert, 236–237
Young, Iris Marion, 224, 225